LYNCHBURG COLLEGE
SYMPOSIUM READINGS

CLASSICAL SELECTIONS ON
GREAT ISSUES

SERIES ONE
VOLUME II

EDUCATION:
ENDS AND MEANS

Plato
Aristotle
Rousseau
Montaigne
Milton
Whitehead
Newman
Jefferson
Locke
Dewey
Ruskin

UNIVERSITY
PRESS OF
AMERICA

LANHAM • NEW YORK • LONDON

SERIES ONE

SYMPOSIUM READINGS

Lynchburg College in Virginia

Compiled and Edited by the
following faculty members of Lynchburg College:

Kenneth E. Alrutz, A.M., University of Pennsylvania; Assistant
Professor of English

Virginia B. Berger, M.A., Harvard University; Associate Professor
of Music

Anne Marshall Bippus, Ed.D., University of Virginia; Associate
Professor of Education

James L. Campbell, Ph.D., University of Virginia; Associate Professor of English

Robert L. Frey, Ph.D., University of Minnesota; Professor of
History

James A. Huston, Ph.D., New York University; Dean of the College,
Professor of History and International Relations

Shannon McIntyre Jordan, Ph.D., University of Georgia; Instructor
in Philosophy

Jan G. Linn, D.Min., Christian Theological Seminary; Assistant
Professor, College Chaplain

Peggy S. Pittas, M.A., Dalhousie University; Associate Professor
of Psychology

Clifton W. Potter, Jr., Ph.D., University of Virginia; Professor
of History

Julius A. Sigler, Ph.D., University of Virginia; Professor of
Physics

Phillip H. Stump, Ph.D., University of California at Los Angeles;
Assistant Professor of History

Thomas C. Tiller, Ph.D., Florida State University; Dean of Student
Affairs, Professor of Education

Library of Congress Cataloging in Publication Data
Main entry under title:

Education : ends and means.

(Classical selections on great issues; series 1, v. 2)
Compiled and edited by the faculty members of
Lynchburg College.
1. Education–Aims and objectives–Addresses,
essays, lectures. I. Plato. II. Lynchburg College. III.
Series.
LB41.E3346   1982   370.11   82–45157
ISBN 0–8191–2464–8
ISBN 0–8191–2465–6 (pbk.)

ACKNOWLEDGEMENTS

The authors express appreciation for use of the
following:

From *Experience and Education* by John Dewey. c.1938,
Kappa Delta Pi.

From *The Aims of Education and Other Essays,* "The Aims
of Education" by Alfred North Whitehead. c.1929, The
New American Library.

INTRODUCTION

In American society, the ends and means of education have been debated vigorously throughout its history. Most Americans enthusiastically and eagerly supported the development of public education in the mid-19th century. They perceived it to be a positive force for mobility and democracy. While some complained that too much "book learning" was a waste of time, most Americans were delighted with the developments of the American educational system which appeared to be a foundation for our political system.

Today, we face a different situation. Our efforts to achieve differing goals have placed added strains on educational institutions. Since World War II, the American educational system has been viewed increasingly as a means to social mobility. Efforts to create equality through the public education system have been frequent, particularly in the 1960s. On the other hand, the traditional emphasis on quality has remained a cherished goal of American education. Thus the real question, whether it is possible for the educational system to meet both goals - equality and quality - faces us today. This has resulted in a conflict which is likely to be with us for years to come.

The readings for this theme present some of the most clearly identified statements on the ends and means of education found in our Western tradition.

Is it possible to achieve excellence in education while at the same time promoting equality?

How does society define the role of public education? Who should control our schools?

How do you know when you are educated?

CONTENTS

Plato,   THE REPUBLIC   (Trans. by Benjamin Jowett)

1. How does Plato justify censorship? Does his posi-
    tion make sense to you? Do people today make simi-
    lar arguments to support censorship? Give examples.

2. What should be the goals of education according to
    Plato? Does Plato prefer an educational system
    that emphasizes equality or one that emphasizes ex-
    cellence? Explain.

3. What role does Plato see for the state in educa-
    tion?

4. Why does Plato cite dialectics as the highest branch
    of study? What characteristics must a superior dia-
    lectician possess? Are these seen as valuable
    traits today? What might be the dangers of training
    dialecticians?

5. What should the nature of early education be accord-
    ing to Plato? How does this relate to his view of
    human nature?

        Plato's (427?-347? B.C.) writings on an ideal
state devote substantial space to the ends and means of
education. It is important to remember that as a young
man Plato lived through the defeat of his city-state
by the Spartans. To make matters worse, his teacher,
Socrates, was sentenced to death by his fellow citizens
in Athens. Plato's ideal state is constructed to avoid
a similar disaster.

THE REPUBLIC

And what shall be their education? Can we find a better than the traditional sort? — and this has two divisions, gymnastic for the body, and music for the soul.

True.

Shall we begin education with music, and go on to gymnastic afterwards?

By all means.

And when you speak of music, do you include literature or not?

I do.

And literature may be either true or false?

Yes.

And the young should be trained in both kinds, and we begin with the false?

I do not understand your meaning, he said.

You know, I said, that we begin by telling children stories which, though not wholly destitute of truth, are in the main fictitious; and these stories are told them when they are not of an age to learn gymnastics.

Very true.

That was my meaning when I said that we must teach music before gymnastics.

Quite right, he said.

You know also that the beginning is the most important part of any work, especially in the case of a young and tender thing; for that is the time at which the character is being formed and the desired impression is more readily taken.

Quite true.

And shall we just carelessly allow children to hear any casual tales which may be devised by casual persons, and to receive into their minds ideas for the most part the very opposite of those which we should wish them to have when they are grown up?

We can not.

Then the first thing will be to establish a censorship of the writers of fiction, and let the censors receive any tale of fiction which is good, and reject the bad; and we will desire mothers and nurses to tell their children the authorized ones only. Let them fashion the mind with such tales, even more fondly than they mould the body with their hands; but most of those which are now in use must be discarded.

Of what tales are you speaking? he said.

You may find a model of the lesser in the greater, I said; for they are necessarily of the same type, and there is the same spirit in both of them.

Very likely, he replied; but I do not as yet know what you would term the greater.

Those, I said, which are narrated by Homer and

Hesiod, and the rest of the poets, who have ever been the great story-tellers of mankind.

But which stories do you mean, he said; and what fault do you find with them?

A fault which is most serious, I said; the fault of telling a lie, and, what is more, a bad lie.

But when is this fault committed?

Whenever an erroneous representation is made of the nature of gods and heroes, — as when a painter paints a portrait not having the shadow of a likeness to the original.

Yes, he said, that sort of thing is certainly very blamable; but what are the stories which you mean?

First of all, I said, there was that greatest of all lies in high places, which the poet told about Uranus, and which was a bad lie too, — I mean what Hesiod says that Uranus did, and how Cronus retaliated on him. The doings of Cronus, and the sufferings which in turn his son inflicted upon him, even if they were true, ought certainly not to be lightly told to young and thoughtless persons; if possible, they had better be buried in silence. But if there is an absolute necessity for their mention, a chosen few might hear them in a mystery, and they should sacrifice not a common [Eleusinian] pig, but some huge and unprocurable victim; and then the number of the hearers will be very few indeed.

Why, yes, said he, those stories are extremely objectionable.

Yes, Adeimantus, they are stories not to be repeated in our State; the young man should not be told that in committing the worst of crimes he is far from doing anything outrageous; and that even if he chastises his father when he does wrong, in whatever manner, he will only be following the example of the first and greatest among the gods.

I entirely agee with you, he said; in my opinion those stories are quite unfit to be repeated.

Neither, if we mean our future guardians to regard the habit of quarrelling among themselves as of all things the basest, should any word be said to them of the wars in heaven, and of the plots and fightings of the gods against one another, for they are not true. No, we shall never mention the battles of the giants, or let them be embroidered on garments; and we shall be silent about the innumerable other quarrels of gods and heroes with their friends and relatives. If they would only believe us we would tell them that quarrelling is unholy, and that never up to this time has there been any quarrel between citizens; this is what old men and old women should begin by telling children; and when they grow up, the poets also should be told to compose for them in a similar spirit.[1] But the narrative of Hephaestus binding Here his mother, or how on another occasion Zeus sent him flying for taking her part when she was being beaten, and all the battles of the gods in Homer — these tales must not be admitted into our State, whether they are supposed to have an allegorical meaning or not. For a young person can not judge what is allegorical and what is literal; anything that he receives into his mind at that age is likely to become indelible and unalterable; and therefore it is most important that the tales which the young first hear should be models of virtuous thoughts.

There you are right, he replied; but if any one asks where are such models to be found and of what tales are you speaking — how shall we answer him?

I said to him, You and I, Adeimantus, at this moment are not poets, but founders of a State: now the founders of a State ought to know the general forms

[1] Placing the comma after γραυσί and not after γιγνομένοις

in which poets should cast their tales, and the limits which must be observed by them, but to make the tales is not their business.

Very true, he said; but what are these forms of theology which you mean?

Something of this kind, I replied: — God is always to be represented as he truly is, whatever be the sort of poetry, epic, lyric or tragic, in which the representation is given.

Right.

And is he not truly good? and must he not be represented as such?

Certainly.

And no good thing is hurtful?

No, indeed.

And that which is not hurtful hurts not?

Certainly not.

And that which hurts not does no evil?

No.

And can that which does no evil be a cause of evil?

Impossible.

And the good is advantageous?

Yes.

And therefore the cause of well-being?

Yes.

It follows therefore that the good is not the cause of all things, but of the good only?

Assuredly.

Then God, if he be good, is not the author of all things, as the many assert, but he is the cause of a few things only, and not of most things that occur to men. For few are the goods of human life, and many are the evils, and the good is to be attributed to God alone; of the evils the causes are to be sought elsewhere, and not in him.

That appears to me to be most true, he said.

Then we must not listen to' Homer or to any other poet who is guilty of the folly of saying that two casks

" Lie at the threshold of Zeus, full of lots, one of good, the other of evil lots," [1]

and that he to whom Zeus gives a mixture of the two

" Sometimes meets with evil fortune, at other times with good; "

but that he to whom is given the cup of unmingled ill,

" Him wild hunger drives o'er the beauteous earth."

And again —

" Zeus, who is the dispenser of good and evil to us."

And if any one asserts that the violation of oaths and treaties, which was really the work of Pandarus,[2] was brought about by Athene and Zeus, or that the strife and contention of the gods was instigated by Themis and Zeus,[3] he shall not have our approval; neither will we allow our young men to hear the words of Æschylus, that

" God plants guilt among men when he desires utterly to destroy a house."

And if a poet writes of the sufferings of Niobe — the subject of the tragedy in which these iambic verses occur — or of the house of Pelops, or of the Trojan war or on any similar theme, either we must not permit him to say that these are the works of God, or if they are of God, he must devise some explanation of them such as we are seeking; he must say that God did what was just and right, and they were the better for being punished; but that those who are punished are miserable, and that God is the author of their misery — the poet is not to be permitted to say;

1 Iliad xxiv. 527.   2 Iliad ii. 69.   3 Ib. xx.

though he may say that the wicked are miserable because they require to be punished, and are benefited by receiving punishment from God; but that God being good is the author of evil to any one is to be strenuously denied, and not to be said or sung or heard in verse or prose by any one whether old or young in any well-ordered commonwealth. Such a fiction is suicidal, ruinous, impious.

I agree with you, he replied, and am ready to give my assent to the law.

Let this then be one of our rules and principles concerning the gods, to which our poets and reciters will be expected to conform, — that God is not the author of all things, but of good only.

That will do, he said.

And what do you think of a second principle? Shall I ask you whether God is a magician, and of a nature to appear insidiously now in one shape, and now in another — sometimes himself changing and passing into many forms, sometimes deceiving us with the semblance of such transformations; or is he one and the same immutably fixed in his own proper image?

I can not answer you, he said, without more thought.

Well, I said; but if we suppose a change in anything, that change must be effected either by the thing itself, or by some other thing?

Most certainly.

And things which are at their best are also least liable to be altered or discomposed; for example, when healthiest and strongest, the human frame is least liable to be affected by meats and drinks, and the plant which is in the fullest vigor also suffers least from winds or the heat of the sun or any similar causes.

Of course.

And will not the bravest and wisest soul be least confused or deranged by any external influence?

True.

And the same principle, as I should suppose, applies to all composite things — furniture, houses, garments: when good and well made, they are least altered by time and circumstances.

Very true.

Then everything which is good, whether made by art or nature, or both, is least liable to suffer change from without?

True.

But surely God and the things of God are in every way perfect?

Of course they are.

Then he can hardly be compelled by external influence to take many shapes?

He can not.

But may he not change and transform himself?

Clearly, he said, that must be the case if he is changed at all.

And will he then change himself for the better and fairer, or for the worse and more unsightly?

If he change at all he can only change for the worse, for we can not suppose him to be deficient either in virtue or beauty.

Very true, Adeimantus; but then, would any one, whether God or man, desire to make himself worse?

Impossible.

Then it is impossible that God should ever be willing to change; being, as is supposed, the fairest and best that is conceivable, every God remains absolutely and forever in his own form.

That necessarily follows, he said, in my judgment.

Then, I said, my dear friend, let none of the poets tell us that

THE REPUBLIC

" The gods, taking the disguise of strangers from other lands, walk up and down cities in all sorts of forms; "[1]

and let no one slander Proteus and Thetis, neither let any one, either in tragedy or in any other kind of poetry, introduce Here disguised in the likeness of a priestess asking an alms

" For the life-giving daughters of Inachus the river of Argos; "

— let us have no more lies of that sort. Neither must we have mothers under the influence of the poets scaring their children with a bad version of these myths — telling how certain gods, as they say, " Go about by night in the likeness of so many strangers and in divers forms; " but let them take heed lest they make cowards of their children, and at the same time speak blasphemy against the gods.

Heaven forbid, he said.

But although the gods are themselves unchangeable, still by witchcraft and deception they may make us think that they appear in various forms?

Perhaps, he replied.

Well, but can you imagine that God will be willing to lie, whether in word or deed, or to put forth a phantom of himself?

I can not say, he replied.

Do you not know, I said, that the true lie, if such an expression may be allowed, is hated of gods and men?

What do you mean? he said.

I mean that no one is willingly deceived in that which is the truest and highest part of himself, or about the truest and highest matters; there, above all, he is most afraid of a lie having possession of him.

Still, he said, I do not comprehend you.

[1] Hom. Od. xvii 485

10

The reason is, I replied, that you attribute some profound meaning to my words; but I am only saying that deception, or being deceived or uninformed about the highest realities in the highest part of them selves, which is the soul, and in that part of them to have and to hold the lie, is what mankind least like; — that, I say, is what they utterly detest.

There is nothing more hateful to them.

And, as I was just now remarking, this ignorance in the soul of him who is deceived may be called the true lie; for the lie in words is only a kind of imitation and shadowy image of a previous affection of the soul, not pure unadulterated falsehood. Am I not right?

Perfectly right.

The true lie is hated not only by the gods, but also by men?

Yes.

Whereas the lie in words is in certain cases useful and not hateful; in dealing with enemies — that would be an instance; or again, when those whom we call our friends in a fit of madness or illusion are going to do some harm, then it is useful and is a sort of medicine or preventive; also in the tales of mythology, of which we were just now speaking — because we do not know the truth about ancient times, we make falsehood as much like truth as we can, and so turn it to account.

Very true, he said.

But can any of these reasons apply to God? Can we suppose that he is ignorant of antiquity, and therefore has recourse to invention?

That would be ridiculous, he said.

Then the lying poet has no place in our idea of God?

I should say not.

Or perhaps he may tell a lie because he is afraid of enemies?

That is inconceivable.

But he may have friends who are senseless or mad?

But no mad or senseless person can be a friend of God.

Then no motive can be imagined why God should lie?

None whatever.

Then the superhuman and divine is absolutely incapable of falsehood?

Yes.

Then is God perfectly simple and true both in word and deed;[1] he changes not; he deceives not, either by sign or word, by dream or waking vision.

Your thoughts, he said, are the reflection of my own.

You agree with me then, I said, that this is the second type or form in which we should write and speak about divine things. The gods are not magicians who transform themselves, neither do they deceive mankind in any way.

I grant that.

Then, although we are admirers of Homer, we do not admire the lying dream which Zeus sends to Agamemnon; neither will we praise the verses of Æschylus in which Thetis says that Apollo at her nuptials

"Was celebrating in song her fair progeny whose days were to be long, and to know no sickness. And when he had spoken of my lot as in all things blessed of heaven he raised a note of triumph and cheered my soul. And I thought that the word of Phoebus, being divine and full of prophecy, would not fail. And now he himself who uttered the strain, he who was present at the banquet, and who said this — he it is who has slain my son."[2]

[1] Omitting κατὰ φαντασίας   [2] From a lost play.

These are the kind of sentiments about the gods which will arouse our anger; and he who utters them shall be refused a chorus; neither shall we allow teachers to make use of them in the instruction of the young, meaning, as we do, that our guardians, as far as men can be, should be true worshippers of the gods and like them.

I entirely agree, he said, in these principles, and promise to make them my laws.

Then shall we proceed to show that the corruption of the majority is also unavoidable, and that this is not to be laid to the charge of philosophy any more than the other?

By all means.

And let us ask and answer in turn, first going back to the description of the gentle and noble nature. Truth, as you will remember, was his leader, whom he followed always and in all things; failing in this, he was an impostor, and had no part or lot in true philosophy.

Yes, that was said.

Well, and is not this one quality, to mention no others, greatly at variance with present notions of him?

Certainly, he said.

And have we not a right to say in his defence, that the true lover of knowledge is always striving after being — that is his nature; he will not rest in the multiplicity of individuals which is an appearance only, but will go on — the keen edge will not be blunted, nor the force of his desire abate until he have attained the knowledge of the true nature of every essence by a sympathetic and kindred power in the soul, and by that power drawing near and mingling and becoming incorporate with very being, having begotten mind and truth, he will have knowledge and will live and grow truly, and then, and not till then, will he cease from his travail.

Nothing, he said, can be more just than such a description of him.

And will the love of a lie be any part of a philosopher's nature? Will he not utterly hate a lie?

He will.

And when truth is the captain, we can not suspect any evil of the band which he leads?

Impossible.

Justice and health of mind will be of the company, and temperance will follow after?

True, he replied.

Neither is there any reason why I should again set in array the philosopher's virtues, as you will doubtless remember that courage, magnificence, apprehension, memory, were his natural gifts. And you objected that, although no one could deny what I then said, still, if you leave words and look at facts, the persons who are thus described are some of them manifestly useless, and the greater number utterly depraved; we were then led to inquire into the grounds of these accusations, and have now arrived at the point of asking why are the majority bad, which question of necessity brought us back to the examination and definition of the true philosopher.

Exactly.

And we have next to consider the corruptions of the philosophic nature, why so many are spoiled and so few escape spoiling — I am speaking of those who were said to be useless but not wicked — and, when we have done with them, we will speak of the imitators of philosophy, what manner of men are they who aspire after a profession which is above them and of which they are unworthy, and then, by their manifold inconsistencies, bring upon philosophy, and upon all philosophers, that universal reprobation of which we speak.

What are these corruptions? he said.

I will see if I can explain them to you. Every one will admit that a nature having in perfection all the qualities which we required in a philosopher, is a rare plant which is seldom seen among men.

Rare indeed.

And what numberless and powerful causes tend to destroy these rare natures!

What causes?

In the first place there are their own virtues, their courage, temperance, and the rest of them, every one of which praiseworthy qualities (and this is a most singular circumstance) destroys and distracts from philosophy the soul which is the possessor of them.

That is very singular, he replied.

Then there are all the ordinary goods of life — beauty, wealth, strength, rank, and great connections in the State — you understand the sort of things

— these also have a corrupting and distracting effect.

I understand; but I should like to know more precisely what you mean about them.

Grasp the truth as a whole, I said, and in the right
way; you will then have no difficulty in apprehending
the preceding remarks, and they will no longer appear strange to you.

And how am I to do so? he asked.

Why, I said, we know that all germs or seeds,
whether vegetable or animal, when they fail to meet
with proper nutriment or climate or soil, in proportion to their vigor, are all the more sensitive to the
want of a suitable environment, for evil is a greater
enemy to what is good than to what is not.

Very true.

There is reason in supposing that the finest natures,
when under alien conditions, receive more injury than
the inferior, because the contrast is greater.

Certainly.

And may we not say, Adeimantus, that the most
gifted minds, when they are ill-educated, become pre-
eminently bad? Do not great crimes and the spirit
of pure evil spring out of a fulness of nature ruined
by education rather than from any inferiority, whereas
weak natures are scarcely capable of any very great
good or very great evil?

There I think that you are right.

And our philosopher follows the same analogy —
he is like a plant which, having proper nurture, must
necessarily grow and mature into all virtue, but, if
sown and planted in an alien soil, becomes the most
noxious of all weeds, unless he be preserved by some
divine power. Do you really think, as people so often
say, that our youth are corrupted by Sophists, or that
private teachers of the art corrupt them in any de-

gree worth speaking of? Are not the public who say these things the greatest of all Sophists? And do they not educate to perfection young and old, men and women alike, and fashion them after their own hearts?

When is this accomplished? he said.

When they meet together, and the world sits down at an assembly, or in a court of law, or a theatre, or a camp, or in any other popular resort, and there is a great uproar, and they praise some things which are being said or done, and blame other things, equally exaggerating both, shouting and clapping their hands, and the echo of the rocks and the place in which they are assembled redoubles the sound of the praise or blame — at such a time will not a young man's heart, as they say, leap within him? Will any private training enable him to stand firm against the overwhelming flood of popular opinion? or will he be carried away by the stream? Will he not have the notions of good and evil which the public in general have — he will do as they do, and as they are, such will he be?

Yes, Socrates; necessity will compel him.

And yet, I said, there is a still greater necessity, which has not been mentioned.

What is that?

The gentle force of attainder or confiscation or death, which, as you are aware, these new Sophists and educators, who are the public, apply when their words are powerless.

Indeed they do; and in right good earnest.

Now what opinion of any other Sophist, or of any private person, can be expected to overcome in such an unequal contest?

None, he replied.

No, indeed, I said, even to make the attempt is a great piece of folly; there neither is, nor has been, nor is ever likely to be, any different type of character [1] which has had no other training in virtue but that which is supplied by public opinion [1] — I speak, my friend, of human virtue only; what is more than human, as the proverb says, is not included: for I would not have you ignorant that, in the present evil state of governments, whatever is saved and comes to good is saved by the power of God, as we may truly say.

I quite assent, he replied.

Then let me crave your assent also to a further observation.

What are you going to say?

Why, that all those mercenary individuals, whom the many call Sophists and whom they deem to be their adversaries, do, in fact, teach nothing but the opinion of the many, that is to say, the opinions of their assemblies; and this is their wisdom. I might compare them to a man who should study the tempers and desires of a mighty strong beast who is fed by him — he would learn how to approach and handle him, also at what times and from what causes he is dangerous or the reverse, and what is the meaning of his several cries, and by what sounds, when another utters them, he is soothed or infuriated; and you may suppose further, that when, by continually attending upon him, he has become perfect in all this, he calls his knowledge wisdom, and makes of it a system or art, which he proceeds to teach, although he has no real notion of what he means by the principles or passions of which he is speaking, but calls this honorable and that dishonorable, or good or evil, or just or unjust, all in accordance with the tastes and tempers of the great brute. Good he pronounces to be that in which the beast delights and evil to be that

[1] Or, taking παρά in another sense, "trained to virtue on their principles."

which he dislikes; and he can give no other account of them except that the just and noble are the necessary, having never himself seen, and having no power of explaining to others the nature of either, or the difference between them, which is immense. By heaven, would not such an one be a rare educator?

Indeed he would.

And in what way does he who thinks that wisdom is the discernment of the tempers and tastes of the motley multitude, whether in painting or music, or, finally, in politics, differ from him whom I have been describing? For when a man consorts with the many, and exhibits to them his poem or other work of art or the service which he has done the State, making them his judges [1] when he is not obliged, the so-called necessity of Diomede will oblige him to produce whatever they praise. And yet the reasons are utterly ludicrous which they give in confirmation of their own notions about the honorable and good. Did you ever hear any of them which were not?

No, nor am I likely to hear.

You recognize the truth of what I have been saying? Then let me ask you to consider further whether the world will ever be induced to believe in the existence of absolute beauty rather than of the many beautiful, or of the absolute in each kind rather than of the many in each kind?

Certainly not.

Then the world can not possibly be a philosopher?

Impossible.

And therefore philosophers must inevitably fall under the censure of the world?

They must.

And of individuals who consort with the mob and seek to please them?

[1] Putting a comma after τῶν ἀναγκαίων.

That is evident.

Then, do you see any way in which the philosopher can be preserved in his calling to the end? and remember what we were saying of him, that he was to have quickness and memory and courage and magnificence — these were admitted by us to be the true philosopher's gifts.

Yes.

Will not such an one from his early childhood be in all things first among all, especially if his bodily endowments are like his mental ones?

Certainly, he said.

And his friends and fellow-citizens will want to use him as he gets older for their own purposes?

No question.

Falling at his feet, they will make requests to him and do him honor and flatter him, because they want to get into their hands now, the power which he will one day possess.

That often happens, he said.

And what will a man such as he is be likely to do under such circumstances, especially if he be a citizen of a great city, rich and noble, and a tall proper youth? Will he not be full of boundless aspirations, and fancy himself able to manage the affairs of Hellenes and of barbarians, and having got such notions into his head will he not dilate and elevate himself in the fulness of vain pomp and senseless pride?

To be sure he will.

Now, when he is in this state of mind, if some one gently comes to him and tells him that he is a fool and must get understanding, which can only be got by slaving for it, do you think that, under such adverse circumstances, he will be easily induced to listen?

Far otherwise.

And even if there be some one who through inherent goodness or natural reasonableness has had his eyes opened a little and is humbled and taken captive by philosophy, how will his friends behave when they think that they are likely to lose the advantage which they were hoping to reap from his companionship? Will they not do and say anything to prevent him from yielding to his better nature and to render his teacher powerless, using to this end private intrigues as well as public prosecutions?

There can be no doubt of it.

And how can one who is thus circumstanced ever become a philosopher?

Impossible.

Then were we not right in saying that even the very qualities which make a man a philosopher may, if he be ill-educated, divert him from philosophy, no less than riches and their accompaniments and the other so-called goods of life?

We were quite right.

Thus, my excellent friend, is brought about all that ruin and failure which I have been describing of the natures best adapted to the best of all pursuits; they are natures which we maintain to be rare at any time; this being the class out of which come the men who are the authors of the greatest evil to States and individuals; and also of the greatest good when the tide carries them in that direction; but a small man never was the doer of any great thing either to individuals or to States.

That is most true, he said.

And so philosophy is left desolate, with her marriage rite incomplete: for her own have fallen away and forsaken her, and while they are leading a false and unbecoming life, other unworthy persons, seeing that she has no kinsmen to be her protectors, enter in and dishonor her; and fasten upon her the reproaches which, as you say, her reprovers utter, who affirm of her votaries that some are good for nothing, and that the greater number deserve the severest punishment.

That is certainly what people say.

Yes; and what else would you expect, I said, when you think of the puny creatures who, seeing this land open to them — a land well stocked with fair names and showy titles — like prisoners running out of prison into a sanctuary, take a leap out of their trades into philosophy; those who do so being probably the cleverest hands at their own miserable crafts? For, although philosophy be in this evil case, still there remains a dignity about her which is not to be found in the arts. And many are thus attracted by her whose natures are imperfect and whose souls are maimed and disfigured by their meannesses, as their bodies are by their trades and crafts. Is not this unavoidable?

Yes.

Are they not exactly like a bald little tinker who has just got out of durance and come into a fortune; he takes a bath and puts on a new coat, and is decked out as a bridegroom going to marry his master's daughter, who is left poor and desolate?

A most exact parallel.

What will be the issue of such marriages? Will they not be vile and bastard?

There can be no question of it.

And when persons who are unworthy of education approach philosophy and make an alliance with her who is in a rank above them, what sort of ideas and opinions are likely to be generated? [1] Will they not be sophisms captivating to the ear,[1] having nothing in them genuine, or worthy of or akin to true wisdom?

[1] Or, "will they not deserve to be called sophisms," . . .

No doubt, he said.

Then, Adeimantus, I said, the worthy disciples of philosophy will be but a small remnant: perchance some noble and well-educated person, detained by exile in her service, who in the absence of corrupting influences remains devoted to her; or some lofty soul born in a mean city, the politics of which he contemns and neglects; and there may be a gifted few who leave the arts, which they justly despise, and come to her; — or peradventure there are some who are restrained by our friend Theages' bridle; for everything in the life of Theages conspired to divert him from philosophy; but ill-health kept him away from politics. My own case of the internal sign is hardly worth mentioning, for rarely, if ever, has such a monitor been given to any other man. Those who belong to this small class have tasted how sweet and blessed a possession philosophy is, and have also seen enough of the madness of the multitude; and they know that no politician is honest, nor is there any champion of justice at whose side they may fight and be saved. Such an one may be compared to a man who has fallen among wild beasts — he will not join in the wickedness of his fellows, but neither is he able singly to resist all their fierce natures, and therefore seeing that he would be of no use to the State or to his friends, and reflecting that he would have to throw away his life without doing any good either to himself or others, he holds his peace, and goes his own way. He is like one who, in the storm of dust and sleet which the driving wind hurries along, retires under the shelter of a wall; and seeing the rest of mankind full of wickedness, he is content, if only he can live his own life and be pure from evil or unrighteousness, and depart in peace and good-will, with bright hopes.

Yes, he said, and he will have done a great work before he departs.

A great work — yes; but not the greatest, unless he find a State suitable to him; for in a State which is suitable to him, he will have a larger growth and be the savior of his country, as well as of himself.

The causes why philosophy is in such an evil name have now been sufficiently explained: the injustice of the charges against her has been shown — is there anything more which you wish to say?

Nothing more on that subject, he replied; but I should like to know which of the governments now existing is in your opinion the one adapted to her.

Not any of them, I said; and that is precisely the accusation which I bring against them — not one of them is worthy of the philosophic nature, and hence that nature is warped and estranged; — as the exotic seed which is sown in a foreign land becomes denaturalized, and is wont to be overpowered and to lose itself in the new soil, even so this growth of philosophy, instead of persisting, degenerates and receives another character. But if philosophy ever finds in the State that perfection which she herself is, then will be seen that she is in truth divine, and that all other things, whether natures of men or institutions, are but human; — and now, I know, that you are going to ask, What that State is:

No, he said; there you are wrong, for I was going to ask another question — whether it is the State of which we are the founders and inventors, or some other?

Yes, I replied, ours in most respects; but you may remember my saying before, that some living authority would always be required in the State having the same idea of the constitution which guided you when as legislator you were laying down the laws.

That was said, he replied.

Yes, but not in a satisfactory manner; you frightened us by interposing objections, which certainly showed that the discussion would be long and difficult; and what still remains is the reverse of easy.

What is there remaining?

The question how the study of philosophy may be so ordered as not to be the ruin of the State: All great attempts are attended with risk; "hard is the good," as men say.

Still, he said, let the point be cleared up, and the inquiry will then be complete.

I shall not be hindered, I said, by any want of will, but, if at all, by a want of power: my zeal you may see for yourselves; and please to remark in what I am about to say how boldly and unhesitatingly I declare that States should pursue philosophy, not as they do now, but in a different spirit.

In what manner?

At present, I said, the students of philosophy are quite young; beginning when they are hardly past childhood, they devote only the time saved from moneymaking and housekeeping to such pursuits; and even those of them who are reputed to have most of the philosophic spirit, when they come within sight of the great difficulty of the subject, I mean dialectic, take themselves off. In after life when invited by some one else, they may, perhaps, go and hear a lecture, and about this they make much ado, for philosophy is not considered by them to be their proper business: at last, when they grow old, in most cases they are extinguished more truly than Heracleitus' sun, inasmuch as they never light up again.[1]

But what ought to be their course?

---

[1] Heracleitus said that the sun was extinguished every evening and relighted every morning.

Just the opposite. In childhood and youth their study, and what philosophy they learn, should be suited to their tender years: during this period while they are growing up towards manhood, the chief and special care should be given to their bodies that they may have them to use in the service of philosophy; as life advances and the intellect begins to mature, let them increase the gymnastics of the soul; but when the strength of our citizens fails and is past civil and military duties, then let them range at will and engage in no serious labor, as we intend them to live happily here, and to crown this life with a similar happiness in another.

How truly in earnest you are, Socrates! he said; I am sure of that; and yet most of your hearers, if I am not mistaken, are likely to be still more earnest in their opposition to you, and will never be convinced; Thrasymachus least of all.

Do not make a quarrel, I said, between Thrasymachus and me, who have recently become friends, although, indeed, we were never enemies; for I shall go on striving to the utmost until I either convert him and other men, or do something which may profit them against the day when they live again, and hold the like discourse in another state of existence.

You are speaking of a time which is not very near.

Rather, I replied, of a time which is as nothing in comparison with eternity. Nevertheless, I do not wonder that the many refuse to believe; for they have never seen that of which we are now speaking realized; they have seen only a conventional imitation of philosophy, consisting of words artificially brought together, not like these of ours having a natural unity. But a human being who in word and work is perfectly moulded, as far as can be, into the proportion and likeness of virtue — such a man ruling in a city which bears the same image, they have never yet seen, neither one nor many of them — do you think that they ever did?

No indeed.

No, my friend, and they have seldom, if ever, heard free and noble sentiments; such as men utter when they are earnestly and by every means in their power seeking after truth for the sake of knowledge, while they look coldly on the subtleties of controversy, of which the end is opinion and strife, whether they meet with them in the courts of law or in society.

They are strangers, he said, to the words of which you speak.

And this was what we foresaw, and this was the reason why truth forced us to admit, not without fear and hesitation, that neither cities nor States nor individuals will ever attain perfection until the small class of philosophers whom we termed useless but not corrupt are providentially compelled, whether they will or not, to take care of the State, and until a like necessity be laid on the State to obey them;[1] or until kings, or if not kings, the sons of kings or princes, are divinely inspired with a true love of true philosophy. That either or both of these alternatives are impossible, I see no reason to affirm: if they were so, we might indeed be justly ridiculed as dreamers and visionaries. Am I not right?

Quite right.

If then, in the countless ages of the past, or at the present hour in some foreign clime which is far away and beyond our ken, the perfected philosopher is or has been or hereafter shall be compelled by a superior power to have the charge of the State, we are ready to assert to the death, that this our constitution has been, and is — yea, and will be whenever the Muse of Phi-

---

[1] Reading κατηκόῳ or κατηκόοις.

losophy is queen. There is no impossibility in all this; that there is a difficulty, we acknowledge ourselves.

My opinion agrees with yours, he said.

But do you mean to say that this is not the opinion of the multitude?

I should imagine not, he replied.

O my friend, I said, do not attack the multitude: they will change their minds, if, not in an aggressive spirit, but gently and with the view of soothing them and removing their dislike of over-education, you show them your philosophers as they really are and describe as you were just now doing their character and profession, and then mankind will see that he of whom you are speaking is not such as they supposed — if they view him in this new light, they will surely change their notion of him, and answer in another strain.[1] Who can be at enmity with one who loves them, who that is himself gentle and free from envy will be jealous of one in whom there is no jealousy? Nay, let me answer for you, that in a few this harsh temper may be found but not in the majority of mankind.

I quite agree with you, he said.

And do you not also think, as I do, that the harsh feeling which the many entertain towards philosophy originates in the pretenders, who rush in uninvited, and are always abusing them, and finding fault with them, who make persons instead of things the theme of their conversation? and nothing can be more unbecoming in philosophers than this.

It is most unbecoming.

For he, Adeimantus, whose mind is fixed upon true being, has surely no time to look down upon the

---

[1] Reading ἢ καὶ ἐὰν οὕτω θεῶνται without a question, and ἀλλοίαν τοι : or, retaining the question and taking ἀλλοίαν δόξαν in a new sense: " Do you mean to say really that, viewing him in this light, they will be of another mind from yours, and answer in another strain? "

affairs of earth, or to be filled with malice and envy, contending against men; his eye is ever directed towards things fixed and immutable, which he sees neither injuring nor injured by one another, but all in order moving according to reason; these he imitates, and to these he will, as far as he can, conform himself. Can a man help imitating that with which he holds reverential converse?

Impossible.

And the philosopher holding converse with the divine order, becomes orderly and divine, as far as the nature of man allows; but like every one else, he will suffer from detraction.

Of course.

And if a necessity be laid upon him of fashioning, not only himself, but human nature generally, whether in States or individuals, into that which he beholds elsewhere, will he, think you, be an unskilful artificer of justice, temperance, and every civil virtue?

Anything but unskilful.

And if the world perceives that what we are saying about him is the truth, will they be angry with philosophy? Will they disbelieve us, when we tell them that no State can be happy which is not designed by artists who imitate the heavenly pattern?

They will not be angry if they understand, he said. But how will they draw out the plan of which you are speaking?

They will begin by taking the State and the manners of men, from which, as from a tablet, they will rub out the picture, and leave a clean surface. This is no easy task. But whether easy or not, herein will lie the difference between them and every other legislator, — they will have nothing to do either with individual or State, and will inscribe no laws, until they have either found, or themselves made, a clean surface.

They will be very right, he said.

Having effected this, they will proceed to trace an outline of the constitution?

No doubt.

And when they are filling in the work, as I conceive, they will often turn their eyes upwards and downwards: I mean that they will first look at absolute justice and beauty and temperance, and again at the human copy; and will mingle and temper the various elements of life into the image of a man; and this they will conceive according to that other image, which, when existing among men, Homer calls the form and likeness of God.

Very true, he said.

And one feature they will erase, and another they will put in, until they have made the ways of men, as far as possible, agreeable to the ways of God?

Indeed, he said, in no way could they make a fairer picture.

And now, I said, are we beginning to persuade those whom you described as rushing at us with might and main, that the painter of constitutions is such an one as we were praising; at whom they were so very indignant because to his hands we committed the State; and are they growing a little calmer at what they have just heard?

Much calmer, if there is any sense in them.

Why, where can they still find any ground for objection? Will they doubt that the philosopher is a lover of truth and being?

They would not be so unreasonable.

Or that his nature, being such as we have delineated, is akin to the highest good?

Neither can they doubt this.

But again, will they tell us that such a nature,

placed under favorable circumstances, will not be perfectly good and wise if any ever was? Or will they prefer those whom we have rejected?

Surely not.

Then will they still be angry at our saying, that, until philosophers bear rule, States and individuals will have no rest from evil, nor will this our imaginary State ever be realized?

I think that they will be less angry.

Shall we assume that they are not only less angry but quite gentle, and that they have been converted and for very shame, if for no other reason, can not refuse to come to terms?

By all means, he said.

Then let us suppose that the reconciliation has been effected. Will any one deny the other point, that there may be sons of kings or princes who are by nature philosophers?

Surely no man, he said.

And when they have come into being will any one say that they must of necessity be destroyed: that they can hardly be saved is not denied even by us; but that in the whole course of ages no single one of them can escape — who will venture to affirm this?

Who indeed!

But, said I, one is enough; let there be one man who has a city obedient to his will, and he might bring into existence the ideal polity about which the world is so incredulous.

Yes, one is enough.

The ruler may impose the laws and institutions which we have been describing, and the citizens may possibly be willing to obey them?

Certainly.

And that others should approve, of what we approve, is no miracle or impossibility?

I think not.

But we have sufficiently shown, in what has preceded, that all this, if only possible, is assuredly for the best.

We have.

And now we say not only that our laws, if they could be enacted, would be for the best, but also that the enactment of them, though difficult, is not impossible.

Very good.

And so with pain and toil we have reached the end of one subject, but more remains to be discussed; — how and by what studies and pursuits will the saviors of the constitution be created, and at what ages are they to apply themselves to their several studies?

Certainly.

I omitted the troublesome business of the possession of women, and the procreation of children, and the appointment of the rulers, because I knew that the perfect State would be eyed with jealousy and was difficult of attainment; but that piece of cleverness was not of much service to me, for I had to discuss them all the same. The women and children are now disposed of, but the other question of the rulers must be investigated from the very beginning. We were saying, as you will remember, that they were to be lovers of their country, tried by the test of pleasures and pains, and neither in hardships, nor in dangers, nor at any other critical moment were to lose their patriotism — he was to be rejected who failed, but he who always came forth pure, like gold tried in the refiner's fire, was to be made a ruler, and to receive honors and rewards in life and after death. This was the sort of thing which was being said, and then the argument turned aside and veiled her face: not liking to stir the question which has now arisen.

I perfectly remember, he said.

Yes, my friend, I said, and I then shrank from hazarding the bold word; but now let me dare to say — that the perfect guardian must be a philosopher.

Yes, he said, let that be affirmed.

And do not suppose that there will be many of them; for the gifts which were deemed by us to be essential rarely grow together; they are mostly found in shreds and patches.

What do you mean? he said.

You are aware, I replied, that quick intelligence, memory, sagacity, cleverness, and similar qualities, do not often grow together, and that persons who possess them and are at the same time high-spirited and magnanimous are not so constituted by nature as to live orderly and in a peaceful and settled manner; they are driven any way by their impulses, and all solid principle goes out of them.

Very true, he said.

On the other hand, those steadfast natures which can better be depended upon, which in a battle are impregnable to fear and immovable, are equally immovable when there is anything to be learned; they are always in a torpid state, and are apt to yawn and go to sleep over any intellectual toil.

Quite true.

And yet we were saying that both qualities were necessary in those to whom the higher education is to be imparted, and who are to share in any office or command.

Certainly, he said.

And will they be a class which is rarely found?

Yes, indeed.

Then the aspirant must not only be tested in those labors and dangers and pleasures which we mentioned before, but there is another kind of probation which we did not mention — he must be exercised also in many kinds of knowledge, to see whether the soul will be able to endure the highest of all, or will faint under them, as in any other studies and exercises.

Yes, he said, you are quite right in testing him. But what do you mean by the highest of all knowledge?

You may remember, I said, that we divided the soul into three parts; and distinguished the several natures of justice, temperance, courage, and wisdom?

Indeed, he said, if I had forgotten, I should not deserve to hear more.

And do you remember the word of caution which preceded the discussion of them?[1]

To what do you refer?

We were saying, if I am not mistaken, that he who wanted to see them in their perfect beauty must take a longer and more circuitous way, at the end of which they would appear; but that we could add on a popular exposition of them on a level with the discussion which had preceded. And you replied that such an exposition would be enough for you, and so the inquiry was continued in what to me seemed to be a very inaccurate manner; whether you were satisfied or not, it is for you to say.

Yes, he said, I thought and the others thought that you gave us a fair measure of truth.

But, my friend, I said, a measure of such things which in any degree falls short of the whole truth is not fair measure; for nothing imperfect is the measure of anything, although persons are too apt to be contented and think that they need search no further.

Not an uncommon case when people are indolent.

Yes, I said; and there can not be any worse fault in a guardian of the State and of the laws.

´ Cp. IV 435 D.

The process, I said, is not the turning over of an oyster-shell,[1] but the turning round of a soul passing from a day which is little better than night to the true day of being, that is, the ascent from below,[2] which we affirm to be true philosophy?

Quite so.

And should we not inquire what sort of knowledge has the power of effecting such a change?

Certainly.

What sort of knowledge is there which would draw the soul from becoming to being? And another consideration has just occurred to me: You will remember that our young men are to be warrior athletes?

Yes, that was said.

Then this new kind of knowledge must have an additional quality?

What quality?

Usefulness in war.

Yes, if possible.

There were two parts in our former scheme of education, were there not?

Just so.

There was gymnastic which presided over the growth and decay of the body, and may therefore be regarded as having to do with generation and corruption?

True.

Then that is not the knowledge which we are seeking to discover?

No.

But what do you say of music, what also entered to a certain extent into our former scheme?

Music, he said, as you will remember, was the

[1] In allusion to a game in which two parties fled or pursued according as an oyster-shell which was thrown into the air fell with the dark or light side uppermost.   [2] Reading οὖσαν ἐπάνοδον.

counterpart of gymnastic, and trained the guardians by the influences of habit, by harmony making them harmonious, by rhythm rhythmical, but not giving them science; and the words, whether fabulous or possibly true, had kindred elements of rhythm and harmony in them. But in music there was nothing which tended to that good which you are now seeking.

You are most accurate, I said, in your recollection; in music there certainly was nothing of the kind. But what branch of knowledge is there, my dear Glaucon, which is of the desired nature; since all the useful arts were reckoned mean by us?

Undoubtedly; and yet if music and gymnastic are excluded, and the arts are also excluded, what remains?

Well, I said, there may be nothing left of our special subjects; and then we shall have to take something which is not special, but of universal application.

What may that be?

A something which all arts and sciences and intelligences use in common, and which every one first has to learn among the elements of education.

What is that?

The little matter of distinguishing one, two, and three — in a word, number and calculation: — do not all arts and sciences necessarily partake of them?

Yes.

Then the art of war partakes of them?

To be sure.

Then Palamedes, whenever he appears in tragedy, proves Agamemnon ridiculously unfit to be a general. Did you never remark how he declares that he had invented number, and had numbered the ships and set in array the ranks of the army at Troy; which implies that they had never been numbered before, and

Agamemnon must be supposed literally to have been incapable of counting his own feet — how could he if he was ignorant of number? And if that is true, what sort of general must he have been?

I should say a very strange one, if this was as you say.

Can we deny that a warrior should have a knowledge of arithmetic?

Certainly he should, if he is to have the smallest understanding of military tactics, or indeed, I should rather say, if he is to be a man at all.

I should like to know whether you have the same notion which I have of this study?

What is your notion?

It appears to me to be a study of the kind which we are seeking, and which leads naturally to reflection, but never to have been rightly used; for the true use of it is simply to draw the soul towards being.

Will you explain your meaning? he said.

I will try, I said; and I wish you would share the inquiry with me, and say "yes" or "no" when I attempt to distinguish in my own mind what branches of knowledge have this attracting power, in order that we may have clearer proof that arithmetic is, as I suspect, one of them.

Explain, he said.

I mean to say that objects of sense are of two kinds; some of them do not invite thought because the sense is an adequate judge of them; while in the case of other objects sense is so untrustworthy that further inquiry is imperatively demanded.

You are clearly referring, he said, to the manner in which the senses are imposed upon by distance, and by painting in light and shade.

No, I said, that is not at all my meaning.

Then what is your meaning?

When speaking of uninviting objects, I mean those which do not pass from one sensation to the opposite; inviting objects are those which do; in this latter case the sense coming upon the object, whether at a distance or near, gives no more vivid idea of anything in particular than of its opposite. An illustration will make my meaning clearer: — here are three fingers — a little finger, a second finger, and a middle finger.

Very good.

You may suppose that they are seen quite close: And here comes the point.

What is it?

Each of them equally appears a finger, whether seen in the middle or at the extremity, whether white or black, or thick or thin — it makes no difference; a finger is a finger all the same. In these cases a man is not compelled to ask of thought the question what is a finger? for the sight never intimates to the mind that a finger is other than a finger.

True.

And therefore, I said, as we might expect, there is nothing here which invites or excites intelligence.

There is not, he said.

But is this equally true of the greatness and smallness of the fingers? Can sight adequately perceive them? and is no difference made by the circumstance that one of the fingers is in the middle and another at the extremity? And in like manner does the touch adequately perceive the qualities of thickness or thinness, of softness or hardness? And so of the other senses; do they give perfect intimations of such matters? Is not their mode of operation on this wise — the sense which is concerned with the quality of hardness is necessarily concerned also with the quality of softness, and only intimates to the soul that the same thing is felt to be both hard and soft?

You are quite right, he said.

And must not the soul be perplexed at this intimation which the sense gives of a hard which is also soft? What, again, is the meaning of light and heavy, if that which is light is also heavy, and that which is heavy, light?

Yes, he said, these intimations which the soul receives are very curious and require to be explained.

Yes, I said, and in these perplexities the soul naturally summons to her aid calculation and intelligence, that she may see whether the several objects announced to her are one or two.

True.

And if they turn out to be two, is not each of them one and different?

Certainly.

And if each is one, and both are two, she will conceive the two as in a state of division, for if they were undivided they could only be conceived of as one?

True.

The eye certainly did see both small and great, but only in a confused manner; they were not distinguished.

Yes.

Whereas the thinking mind, intending to light up the chaos, was compelled to reverse the process, and look at small and great as separate and not confused.

Very true.

Was not this the beginning of the inquiry " What is great? " and " What is small? "

Exactly so.

And thus arose the distinction of the visible and the intelligible.

Most true.

This was what I meant when I spoke of impressions which invited the intellect, or the reverse — those which are simultaneous with opposite impressions, invite thought; those which are simultaneous do not.

I understand, he said, and agree with you.

And to which class do unity and number belong?

I do not know, he replied.

Think a little and you will see that what has preceded will supply the answer; for if simple unity could be adequately perceived by the sight or by any other sense, then, as we were saying in the case of the finger, there would be nothing to attract towards being; but when there is some contradiction always present, and one is the reverse of one and involves the conception of plurality, then thought begins to be aroused within us, and the soul perplexed and wanting to arrive at a decision asks "What is absolute unity?" This is the way in which the study of the one has a power of drawing and converting the mind to the contemplation of true being.

And surely, he said, this occurs notably in the case of one; for we see the same thing to be both one and infinite in multitude?

Yes, I said; and this being true of one must be equally true of all number?

Certainly.

And all arithmetic and calculation have to do with number?

Yes.

And they appear to lead the mind towards truth?

Yes, in a very remarkable manner.

Then this is knowledge of the kind for which we are seeking, having a double use, military and philosophical; for the man of war must learn the art of number or he will not know how to array his troops, and the philosopher also, because he has to rise out of the sea of change and lay hold of true being, and therefore he must be an arithmetician.

That is true.

And our guardian is both warrior and philosopher?

Certainly.

Then this is a kind of knowledge which legislation may fitly prescribe; and we must endeavor to persuade those who are to be the principal men of our State to go and learn arithmetic, not as amateurs, but they must carry on the study until they see the nature of numbers with the mind only; nor again, like merchants or retail-traders, with a view to buying or selling, but for the sake of their military use, and of the soul herself; and because this will be the easiest way for her to pass from becoming to truth and being.

That is excellent, he said.

Yes, I said, and now having spoken of it, I must add how charming the science is! and in how many ways it conduces to our desired end, if pursued in the spirit of a philosopher, and not of a shopkeeper!

How do you mean?

I mean, as I was saying, that arithmetic has a very great and elevating effect, compelling the soul to reason about abstract number, and rebelling against the introduction of visible or tangible objects into the argument. You know how steadily the masters of the art repel and ridicule any one who attempts to divide absolute unity when he is calculating, and if you divide, they multiply,[1] taking care that one shall continue one and not become lost in fractions.

That is very true.

Now, suppose a person were to say to them: O my

---

[1] Meaning either (1) that they integrate the number because they deny the possibility of fractions ; or (2) that division is regarded by them as a process of multiplication, for the fractions of one continue to be units.

friends, what are these wonderful numbers about which you are reasoning, in which, as you say, there is a unity such as you demand, and each unit is equal, invariable, indivisible, — what would they answer?

They would answer, as I should conceive, that they were speaking of those numbers which can only be realized in thought.

Then you see that this knowledge may be truly called necessary, necessitating as it clearly does the use of the pure intelligence in the attainment of pure truth?

Yes; that is a marked characteristic of it.

And have you further observed, that those who have a natural talent for calculation are generally quick at every other kind of knowledge; and even the dull, if they have had an arithmetical training, although they may derive no other advantage from it, always become much quicker than they would otherwise have been.

Very true, he said.

And indeed, you will not easily find a more difficult study, and not many as difficult.

You will not.

And, for all these reasons, arithmetic is a kind of knowledge in which the best natures should be trained, and which must not be given up.

I agree.

Let this then be made one of our subjects of education. And next, shall we inquire whether the kindred science also concerns us?

You mean geometry?

Exactly so.

Clearly, he said, we are concerned with that part of geometry which relates to war; for in pitching a camp, or taking up a position, or closing or extending the lines of an army, or any other military manœuvre, whether in actual battle or on a march, it will make all the difference whether a general is or is not a geometrician.

Yes, I said, but for that purpose a very little of either geometry or calculation will be enough; the question relates rather to the greater and more advanced part of geometry — whether that tends in any degree to make more easy the vision of the idea of good; and thither, as I was saying, all things tend which compel the soul to turn her gaze towards that place, where is the full perfection of being, which she ought, by all means, to behold.

True, he said.

Then if geometry compels us to view being, it concerns us; if becoming only, it does not concern us?

Yes, that is what we assert.

Yet anybody who has the least acquaintance with geometry will not deny that such a conception of the science is in flat contradiction to the ordinary language of geometricians.

How so?

They have in view practice only, and are always speaking, in a narrow and ridiculous manner, of squaring and extending and applying and the like — they confuse the necessities of geometry with those of daily life; whereas knowledge is the real object of the whole science.

Certainly, he said.

Then must not a further admission be made?

What admission?

That the knowledge at which geometry aims is knowledge of the eternal, and not of aught perishing and transient.

That, he replied, may be readily allowed, and is true.

Then, my noble friend, geometry will draw the soul

towards truth, and create the spirit of philosophy,
and raise up that which is now unhappily allowed to
fall down.

Nothing will be more likely to have such an effect.

Then nothing should be more sternly laid down
than that the inhabitants of your fair city should by
all means learn geometry. Moreover the science has
indirect effects, which are not small.

Of what kind? he said.

There are the military advantages of which you
spoke, I said; and in all departments of knowledge,
as experience proves, any one who has studied geometry is infinitely quicker of apprehension than one
who has not.

Yes indeed, he said, there is an infinite difference
between them.

Then shall we propose this as a second branch of
knowledge which our youth will study?

Let us do so, he replied.

And suppose we make astronomy the third — what
do you say?

I am strongly inclined to it, he said; the observation of the seasons and of months and years is as essential to the general as it is to the farmer or sailor.

I am amused, I said, at your fear of the world,
which makes you guard against the appearance of
insisting upon useless studies; and I quite admit the
difficulty of believing that in every man there is an
eye of the soul which, when by other pursuits lost and
dimmed, is by these purified and re-illumined; and
is more precious far than ten thousand bodily eyes,
for by it alone is truth seen. Now there are two
classes of persons: one class of those who will agree
with you and will take your words as a revelation;
another class to whom they will be utterly unmeaning, and who will naturally deem them to be idle tales,

for they see no sort of profit which is to be obtained from them. And therefore you had better decide at once with which of the two you are proposing to argue. You will very likely say with neither, and that your chief aim in carrying on the argument is your own improvement; at the same time you do not grudge to others any benefit which they may receive.

I think that I should prefer to carry on the argument mainly on my own behalf.

Then take a step backward, for we have gone wrong in the order of the sciences.

What was the mistake? he said.

After plane geometry, I said, we proceeded at once to solids in revolution, instead of taking solids in themselves; whereas after the second dimension the third, which is concerned with cubes and dimensions of depth, ought to have followed.

That is true, Socrates; but so little seems to be known as yet about these subjects.

Why, yes, I said, and for two reasons: — in the first place, no government patronizes them; this leads to a want of energy in the pursuit of them, and they are difficult; in the second place, students can not learn them unless they have a director. But then a director can hardly be found, and even if he could, as matters now stand, the students, who are very conceited, would not attend to him. That, however, would be otherwise if the whole State became the director of these studies and gave honor to them; then disciples would want to come, and there would be continuous and earnest search, and discoveries would be made; since even now, disregarded as they are by the world, and maimed of their fair proportions, and although none of their votaries can tell the use of them, still these studies force their way by their natural charm.

and very likely, if they had the help of the State, they would some day emerge into light.

Yes, he said, there is a remarkable charm in them. But I do not clearly understand the change in the order. First you began with a geometry of plane surfaces?

Yes, I said.

And you placed astronomy next, and then you made a step backward?

Yes, and I have delayed you by my hurry; the ludicrous state of solid geometry, which in natural order, should have followed, made me pass over this branch and go on to astronomy, or motion of solids.

True, he said.

Then assuming that the science now omitted would come into existence if encouraged by the State, let us go on to astronomy, which will be fourth.

The right order, he replied. And now, Socrates, as you rebuked the vulgar manner in which I praised astronomy before, my praise shall be given in your own spirit. For every one, as I think, must see that astronomy compels the soul to look upwards and leads us from this world to another.

Every one but myself, I said; to every one else this may be clear, but not to me.

And what then would you say?

I should rather say that those who elevate astronomy into philosophy appear to me to make us look downwards and not upwards.

What do you mean? he asked.

You, I replied, have in your mind a truly sublime conception of our knowledge of the things above. And I dare say that if a person were to throw his head back and study the fretted ceiling, you would still think that his mind was the percipient, and not his eyes. And you are very likely right, and I may be

᱐ simpleton: but, in my opinion, that knowledge only which is of being and of the unseen can make the soul look upwards, and whether a man gapes at the heavens or blinks on the ground, seeking to learn some particular of sense, I would deny that he can learn, for nothing of that sort is matter of science; his soul is looking downwards, not upwards, whether his way to knowledge is by water or by land, whether he floats, or only lies on his back.

I acknowledge, he said, the justice of your rebuke. Still, I should like to ascertain how astronomy can be learned in any manner more conducive to that knowledge of which we are speaking?

I will tell you, I said: The starry heaven which we behold is wrought upon a visible ground, and therefore, although the fairest and most perfect of visible things, must necessarily be deemed inferior far to the true motions of absolute swiftness and absolute slowness, which are relative to each other, and carry with them that which is contained in them, in the true number and in every true figure. Now, these are to be apprehended by reason and intelligence, but not by sight.

True, he replied.

The spangled heavens should be used as a pattern and with a view to that higher knowledge; their beauty is like the beauty of figures or pictures excellently wrought by the hand of Daedalus, or some other great artist, which we may chance to behold; any geometrician who saw them would appreciate the exquisiteness of their workmanship, but he would never dream of thinking that in them he could find the true equal or the true double, or the truth of any other proportion.

No, he replied, such an idea would be ridiculous.

And will not a true astronomer have the same feeling when he looks at the movements of the stars?

Will he not think that heaven and the things in heaven are framed by the Creator of them in the most perfect manner? But he will never imagine that the proportions of night and day, or of both to the month, or of the month to the year, or of the stars to these and to one another, and any other things that are material and visible can also be eternal and subject to no deviation — that would be absurd; and it is equally absurd to take so much pains in investigating their exact truth.

I quite agree, though I never thought of this before.

Then, I said, in astronomy, as in geometry, we should employ problems, and let the heavens alone if we would approach the subject in the right way and so make the natural gift of reason to be any of real use.

That, he said, is a work infinitely beyond our present astronomers.

Yes, I said; and there are many other things which must also have a similar extension given to them, if our legislation is to be of any value. But can you tell me of any other suitable study?

No, he said, not without thinking.

Motion, I said, has many forms, and not one only; two of them are obvious enough even to wits no better than ours; and there are others, as I imagine, which may be left to wiser persons.

But where are the two?

There is a second, I said, which is the counterpart of the one already named.

And what may that be?

The second, I said, would seem relatively to the ears to be what the first is to the eyes; for I conceive that as the eyes are designed to look up at the stars, so are the ears to hear harmonious motions; and these are sister sciences — as the Pythagoreans say, and we, Glaucon, agree with them?

Yes, he replied.

But this, I said, is a laborious study, and therefore we had better go and learn of them; and they will tell us whether there are any other applications of these sciences. At the same time, we must not lose sight of our own higher object.

What is that?

There is a perfection which all knowledge ought to reach, and which our pupils ought also to attain, and not to fall short of, as I was saying that they did in astronomy. For in the science of harmony, as you probably know, the same thing happens. The teachers of harmony compare the sounds and consonances which are heard only, and their labor, like that of the astronomers, is in vain.

Yes, by heaven! he said; and 'tis as good as a play to hear them talking about their condensed notes, as they call them; they put their ears close alongside of the strings like persons catching a sound from their neighbor's wall [1] — one set of them declaring that they distinguish an intermediate note and have found the least interval which should be the unit of measurement; the others insisting that the two sounds have passed into the same — either party setting their ears before their understanding.

You mean, I said, those gentlemen who tease and torture the strings and rack them on the pegs of the instrument: I might carry on the metaphor and speak after their manner of the blows which the plectrum gives, and make accusations against the strings, both of backwardness and forwardness to sound; but this would be tedious, and therefore I will only say that

[1] Or, "close alongside of their neighbor's instruments, as if to catch a sound from them."

these are not the men, and that I am referring to the Pythagoreans, of whom I was just now proposing to inquire about harmony. For they too are in error, like the astronomers; they investigate the numbers of the harmonies which are heard, but they never attain to problems — · that is to say, they never reach the natural harmonies of number, or reflect why some numbers are harmonious and others not.

That, he said, is a thing of more than mortal knowledge.

A thing, I replied, which I would rather call useful; that is, if sought after with a view to the beautiful and good; but if pursued in any other spirit, useless.

Very true, he said.

Now, when all these studies reach the point of inter-communion and connection with one another, and come to be considered in their mutual affinities, then, I think, but not till then, will the pursuit of them have a value for our objects; otherwise there is no profit in them.

I suspect so; but you are speaking, Socrates, of a vast work.

What do you mean? I said; the prelude or what? Do you not know that all this is but the prelude to the actual strain which we have to learn? For you surely would not regard the skilled mathematician as a dialectician?

Assuredly not, he said; I have hardly ever known a mathematician who was capable of reasoning.

But do you imagine that men who are unable to give and take a reason will have the knowledge which we require of them?

Neither can this be supposed.

And so, Glaucon, I said, we have at last arrived at the hymn of dialectic. This is that strain which is of the intellect only, but which the faculty of sight will nevertheless be found to imitate; for sight, as you may remember, was imagined by us after a while to behold the real animals and stars, and last of all the sun himself. And so with dialectic; when a person starts on the discovery of the absolute by the light of reason only, and without any assistance of sense, and perseveres until by pure intelligence he arrives at the perception of the absolute good, he at last finds himself at the end of the intellectual world, as in the case of sight at the end of the visible.

Exactly, he said.

Then this is the progress which you call dialectic?

True.

But the release of the prisoners from chains, and their translation from the shadows to the images and to the light, and the ascent from the underground den to the sun, while in his presence they are vainly trying to look on animals and plants and the light of the sun, but are able to perceive even with their weak eyes the images[1] in the water [which are divine], and are the shadows of true existence (not shadows of images cast by a light of fire, which compared with the sun is only an image) — this power of elevating the highest principle in the soul to the contemplation of that which is best in existence, with which we may compare the raising of that faculty which is the very light of the body to the sight of that which is brightest in the material and visible world — this power is given, as I was saying, by all that study and pursuit of the arts which has been described.

I agree in what you are saying, he replied, which may be hard to believe, yet, from another point of view, is harder still to deny. This however is not a theme to be treated of in passing only, but will have

---

[1] Omitting ἐνταῦθα δὲ πρὸς φαντάσματα. The word θεῖα is bracketed by Stallbaum.

to be discussed again and again. And so, whether our conclusion be true or false, let us assume all this, and proceed at once from the prelude or preamble to the chief strain,[1] and describe that in like manner. Say, then, what is the nature and what are the divisions of dialectic, and what are the paths which lead thither; for these paths will also lead to our final rest.

Dear Glaucon, I said, you will not be able to follow me here, though I would do my best, and you should behold not an image only but the absolute truth, according to my notion. Whether what I told you would or would not have been a reality I can not venture to say; but you would have seen something like reality; of that I am confident.

Doubtless, he replied.

But I must also remind you, that the power of dialectic alone can reveal this, and only to one who is a disciple of the previous sciences.

Of that assertion you may be as confident as of the last.

And assuredly no one will argue that there is any other method of comprehending by any regular process all true existence or of ascertaining what each thing is in its own nature; for the arts in general are concerned with the desires or opinions of men, or are cultivated with a view to production and construction, or for the preservation of such productions and constructions; and as to the mathematical sciences which, as we were saying, have some apprehension of true being — geometry and the like — they only dream about being, but never can they behold the waking reality so long as they leave the hypotheses which they use unexamined, and are unable to give an account of them. For when a man knows not his own first prin-

[1] A play upon the word νόμος, which means both " law " and " strain "

ciple, and when the conclusion and intermediate steps are also constructed out of he knows not what, how can he imagine that such a fabric of convention can ever become science?

Impossible, he said.

Then dialectic, and dialectic alone, goes directly to the first principle and is the only science which does away with hypotheses in order to make her ground secure; the eye of the soul, which is literally buried in an outlandish slough, is by her gentle aid lifted upwards; and she uses as handmaids and helpers in the work of conversion, the sciences which we have been discussing. Custom terms them sciences, but they ought to have some other name, implying greater clearness than opinion and less clearness than science: and this, in our previous sketch, was called understanding. But why should we dispute about names when we have realities of such importance to consider?

Why indeed, he said, when any name will do which expresses the thought of the mind with clearness?

At any rate, we are satisfied, as before, to have four divisions; two for intellect and two for opinion, and to call the first division science, the second understanding, the third belief, and the fourth perception of shadows, opinion being concerned with becoming, and intellect with being; and so to make a proportion:

As being is to becoming, so is pure intellect to opinion.
And as intellect is to opinion, so is science to belief, and understanding to the perception of shadows.

But let us defer the further correlation and subdivision of the subjects of opinion and of intellect, for it will be a long inquiry, many times longer than this has been.

As far as I understand, he said, I agree.

And do you also agree, I said, in describing the

dialectician as one who attains a conception of the essence of each thing? And he who does not possess and is therefore unable to impart this conception, in whatever degree he fails, may in that degree also be said to fail in intelligence? Will you admit so much?

Yes, he said; how can I deny it?

And you would say the same of the conception of the good? Until the person is able to abstract and define rationally the idea of good, and unless he can run the gauntlet of all objections, and is ready to disprove them, not by appeals to opinion, but to absolute truth, never faltering at any step of the argument — unless he can do all this, you would say that he knows neither the idea of good nor any other good; he apprehends only a shadow, if anything at all, which is given by opinion and not by science; — dreaming and slumbering in this life, before he is well awake here, he arrives at the world below, and has his final quietus.

In all that I should most certainly agree with you.

And surely you would not have the children of your ideal State, whom you are nurturing and educating — if the ideal ever becomes a reality — you would not allow the future rulers to be like posts,[1] having no reason in them, and yet to be set in authority over the highest matters?

Certainly not.

Then you will make a law that they shall have such an education as will enable them to attain the greatest skill in asking and answering questions?

Yes, he said, you and I together will make it.

Dialectic, then, as you will agree, is the coping-stone of the sciences, and is set over them; no other science can be placed higher — the nature of knowledge can no further go?

γραμμάς, literally "lines," probably the starting-point of a race-course.

I agree, he said.

But to whom we are to assign these studies, and in what way they are to be assigned, are questions which remain to be considered.

Yes, clearly.

You remember, I said, how the rulers were chosen before?

Certainly, he said.

The same natures must still be chosen, and the preference again given to the surest and the bravest, and, if possible, to the fairest; and, having noble and generous tempers, they should also have the natural gifts which will facilitate their education.

And what are these?

Such gifts as keenness and ready powers of acquisition; for the mind more often faints from the severity of study than from the severity of gymnastics: the toil is more entirely the mind's own, and is not shared with the body.

Very true, he replied.

Further, he of whom we are in search should have a good memory, and be an unwearied solid man who is a lover of labor in any line; or he will never be able to endure the great amount of bodily exercise and to go through all the intellectual discipline and study which we require of him.

Certainly, he said; he must have natural gifts.

The mistake at present is, that those who study philosophy have no vocation, and this, as I was before saying, is the reason why she has fallen into disrepute: her true sons should take her by the hand and not bastards.

What do you mean?

In the first place, her votary should not have a lame or halting industry — I mean, that he should not be half industrious and half idle: as, for example, when a man is a lover of gymnastic and hunting, and all other bodily exercises, but a hater rather than a lover of the labor of learning or listening or inquiring. Or the occupation to which he devotes himself may be of an opposite kind, and he may have the other sort of lameness.

Certainly, he said.

And as to truth, I said, is not a soul equally to be deemed halt and lame which hates voluntary falsehood and is extremely indignant at herself and others when they tell lies, but is patient of involuntary falsehood, and does not mind wallowing like a swinish beast in the mire of ignorance, and has no shame at being detected?

To be sure.

And, again, in respect of temperance, courage, magnificence, and every other virtue, should we not carefully distinguish between the true son and the bastard? for where there is no discernment of such qualities states and individuals unconsciously err; and the state makes a ruler, and the individual a friend, of one who, being defective in some part of virtue, is in a figure lame or a bastard.

That is very true, he said.

All these things, then, will have to be carefully considered by us; and if only those whom we introduce to this vast system of education and training are sound in body and mind, justice herself will have nothing to say against us, and we shall be the saviors of the constitution and of the State; but, if our pupils are men of another stamp, the reverse will happen, and we shall pour a still greater flood of ridicule on philosophy than she has to endure at present.

That would not be creditable.

Certainly not, I said; and yet perhaps, in thus turning jest into earnest I am equally ridiculous.

In what respect?

I had forgotten, I said, that we were not serious and spoke with too much excitement. For when I saw philosophy so undeservedly trampled under foot of men I could not help feeling a sort of indignation at the authors of her disgrace: and my anger made me too vehement.

Indeed! I was listening, and did not think so.

But I, who am the speaker, felt that I was. And now let me remind you that, although in our former selection we chose old men, we must not do so in this. Solon was under a delusion when he said that a man when he grows old may learn many things — for he can no more learn much than he can run much; youth is the time for any extraordinary toil.

Of course.

And, therefore, calculation and geometry and all the other elements of instruction, which are a preparation for dialectic, should be presented to the mind in childhood; not, however, under any notion of forcing our system of education.

Why not?

Because a freeman ought not to be a slave in the acquisition of knowledge of any kind. Bodily exercise, when compulsory, does no harm to the body; but knowledge which is acquired under compulsion obtains no hold on the mind.

Very true.

Then, my good friend, I said, do not use compulsion, but let early education be a sort of amusement; you will then be better able to find out the natural bent.

That is a very rational notion, he said.

Do you remember that the children, too, were to be taken to see the battle on horseback; and that if there were no danger they were to be brought close up and, like young hounds, have a taste of blood given them?

Yes, I remember.

The same practice may be followed, I said, in all these things — labors, lessons, dangers — and he who is most at home in all of them ought to be enrolled in a select number.

At what age?

At the age when the necessary gymnastics are over: the period whether of two or three years which passes in this sort of training is useless for any other purpose; for sleep and exercise are unpropitious to learning; and the trial of who is first in gymnastic exercises is one of the most important tests to which our youth are subjected.

Certainly, he replied.

After that time those who are selected from the class of twenty years old will be promoted to higher honor, and the sciences which they learned without any order in their early education will now be brought together, and they will be able to see the natural relationship of them to one another and to true being.

Yes, he said, that is the only kind of knowledge which takes lasting root.

Yes, I said; and the capacity for such knowledge is the great criterion of dialectical talent; the comprehensive mind is always the dialectical.

I agree with you, he said.

These, I said, are the points which you must consider; and those who have most of this comprehension, and who are most steadfast in their learning, and in their military and other appointed duties, when they have arrived at the age of thirty will have to be chosen by you out of the select class, and elevated to higher honor; and you will have to prove them by the help of dialectic, in order to learn which of them is able to give up the use of sight and the other senses, and in company with truth to attain absolute being: And here, my friend, great caution is required.

Why great caution?

Do you not remark, I said, how great is the evil which dialectic has introduced?

What evil? he said.

The students of the art are filled with lawlessness.

Quite true, he said.

Do you think that there is anything so very unnatural or inexcusable in their case? or will you make allowance for them?

In what way make allowance?

I want you, I said, by way of parallel, to imagine a supposititious son who is brought up in great wealth; he is one of a great and numerous family, and has many flatterers. When he grows up to manhood, he learns that his alleged are not his real parents; but who the real are he is unable to discover. Can you guess how he will be likely to behave towards his flatterers and his supposed parents, first of all during the period when he is ignorant of the false relation, and then again when he knows? Or shall I guess for you?

If you please.

Then I should say, that while he is ignorant of the truth he will be likely to honor his father and his mother and his supposed relations more than the flatterers; he will be less inclined to neglect them when in need, or to do or say anything against them; and he will be less willing to disobey them in any important matter.

He will.

But when he has made the discovery, I should imagine that he would diminish his honor and regard for them, and would become more devoted to the flat-terers; their influence over him would greatly increase; he would now live after their ways, and openly associate with them, and, unless he were of an unusually good disposition, he would trouble himself no more about his supposed parents or other relations.

Well, all that is very probable. But how is the image applicable to the disciples of philosophy?

In this way: you know that there are certain principles about justice and honor, which were taught us in childhood, and under their parental authority we have been brought up, obeying and honoring them.

That is true.

There are also opposite maxims and habits of pleasure which flatter and attract the soul, but do not influence those of us who have any sense of right, and they continue to obey and honor the maxims of their fathers.

True.

Now, when a man is in this state, and the questioning spirit asks what is fair or honorable, and he answers as the legislator has taught him, and then arguments many and diverse refute his words, until he is driven into believing that nothing is honorable any more than dishonorable, or just and good any more than the reverse, and so of all the notions which he most valued, do you think that he will still honor and obey them as before?

Impossible.

And when he ceases to think them honorable and natural as heretofore, and he fails to discover the true, can he be expected to pursue any life other than that which flatters his desires?

He can not.

And from being a keeper of the law he is converted into a breaker of it?

Unquestionably.

Now all this is very natural in students of philosophy such as I have described, and also, as I was just now saying, most excusable.

Yes, he said; and, I may add, pitiable.

Therefore, that your feelings may not be moved to pity about our citizens who are now thirty years of age, every care must be taken in introducing them to dialectic.

Certainly.

There is a danger lest they should taste the dear delight too early; for youngsters, as you may have observed, when they first get the taste in their mouths, argue for amusement, and are always contradicting and refuting others in imitation of those who refute them; like puppy-dogs, they rejoice in pulling and tearing at all who come near them.

Yes, he said, there is nothing which they like better.

And when they have made many conquests and received defeats at the hands of many, they violently and speedily get into a way of not believing anything which they believed before, and hence, not only they, but philosophy and all that relates to it is apt to have a bad name with the rest of the world.

Too true, he said.

But when a man begins to get older, he will no longer be guilty of such insanity; he will imitate the dialectician who is seeking for truth, and not the eristic, who is contradicting for the sake of amusement; and the greater moderation of his character will increase instead of diminishing the honor of the pursuit.

Very true, he said.

And did we not make special provision for this, when we said that the disciples of philosophy were to be orderly and steadfast, not, as now, any chance aspirant or intruder?

Very true.

Suppose, I said, the study of philosophy to take the place of gymnastics and to be continued diligently and earnestly and exclusively for twice the number of years which were passed in bodily exercise — will that be enough?

Would you say six or four years? he asked.

Say five years, I replied; at the end of the time they must be sent down again into the den and compelled to hold any military or other office which young men are qualified to hold: in this way they will get their experience of life, and there will be an opportunity of trying whether, when they are drawn all manner of ways by temptation, they will stand firm or flinch.

And how long is this stage of their lives to last?

Fifteen years, I answered; and when they have reached fifty years of age, then let those who still survive and have distinguished themselves in every action of their lives and in every branch of knowledge come at last to their consummation: the time has now arrived at which they must raise the eye of the soul to the universal light which lightens all things, and behold the absolute good; for that is the pattern according to which they are to order the State and the lives of individuals, and the remainder of their own lives also; making philosophy their chief pursuit, but, when their turn comes, toiling also at politics and ruling for the public good, not as though they were performing some heroic action, but simply as a matter of duty; and when they have brought up in each generation others like themselves and left them in their place to be governors of the State, then they will depart to the Islands of the Blest and dwell there; and the city will give them public memorials and sacrifices and honor them, if the Pythian oracle consent, as demigods, but if not, as in any case blessed and divine.

You are a sculptor, Socrates, and have made statues of our governors faultless in beauty.

Yes, I said, Glaucon, and of our governesses too; for you must not suppose that what I have been saying applies to men only and not to women as far as their natures can go.

There you are right, he said, since we have made them to share in all things like the men.

Well, I said, and you would agree (would you not?) that what has been said about the State and the government is not a mere dream, and although difficult not impossible, but only possible in the way which has been supposed; that is to say, when the true philosopher kings are born in a State, one or more of them, despising the honors of this present world which they deem mean and worthless, esteeming above all things right and the honor that springs from right, and regarding justice as the greatest and most necessary of all things, whose ministers they are, and whose principles will be exalted by them when they set in order their own city?

How will they proceed?

They will begin by sending out into the country all the inhabitants of the city who are more than ten years old, and will take possession of their children, who will be unaffected by the habits of their parents; these they will train in their own habits and laws, I mean in the laws which we have given them: and in this way the State and constitution of which we were speaking will soonest and most easily attain happiness, and the nation which has such a constitution will gain most.

Yes, that will be the best way. And I think

Socrates, that you have very well described how, if ever, such a constitution might come into being.

Enough then of the perfect State, and of the man who bears its image — there is no difficulty in seeing how we shall describe him.

There is no difficulty, he replied; and I agree with you in thinking that nothing more need be said.

Aristotle,   NICOMACHEAN ETHICS   (Trans. & Ed. by John Burnet)
              POLITICS

1. What are the goals of education from Aristotle's
    point of view?

2. What is the relationship between education and
    politics?

3. In what ways does Aristotle's writing on education
    support the concept of the liberal arts? In what
    ways does it support the idea of vocational educa-
    tion?

4. How does Aristotle define quality - in education
    or in any aspect of life?

5. What is the role of education in molding goodness
    of intellect? What is the role of education in
    molding goodness of character?

6. What is Aristotle's distinction between liberal and
    illiberal studies? How might you describe this
    difference in today's society? Why do you think he
    seems to have a "hang-up" with this distinction? Do
    you think your college has a similar "hang-up"?
    Explain.

7. At one point, Aristotle says that education "re-
    quire(s) us to be trained from our earliest youth,
    as Plato has it, to feel pleasure and pain at the
    right things. True education is just that." What
    does Aristotle mean here? What application might
    this have to modern education?

Only a small part of what must have been a more
complete work on education by Aristotle (384-322 B.C.),
is known today. Furthermore, Aristotle's view is presented in a lecture format and is not as carefully composed as Plato's view on education. Nonetheless, many
Western thinkers are influenced by Aristotle's view of
the ends and means of education.

ETHICS.

V. GOODNESS. HOW IS IT PRODUCED? *Goodness of character does not come by nature, but is produced by habituation.* (II. 1—2, § 5.)

Goodness, then, being of two kinds, goodness of intellect and goodness of character, intellectual goodness is both produced and increased mainly by teaching, and therefore experience and time are required for it. Goodness of character, on the other hand, is the outcome of habit, and accordingly the word " *ēthos*," character, is derived from " *ĕthos*," habit, by a slight modification in the quantity of the vowel.

From this it is evident that no form of goodness of character is produced in us by nature; nothing which is by nature can be habituated to be other than it is. For example, a stone, which naturally tends to fall downwards, cannot be habituated to rise upwards, not even if we try to train it by throwing it up an indefinite number of times, nor can anything else that acts in one way by nature be habituated to act in another way. Goodness, then, is not produced in us either by nature or in opposition to nature; we are naturally capable of receiving it, and we attain our full development by habituation[1].

Secondly, in the case of everything that comes to us by nature, we first acquire the capacities and then produce the activities. This is clear if we test it by the senses. It is not

"good" and "goodness." To a Greek all efficiency was goodness, and nothing else was.

[1] This really depends upon a distinction which Aristotle makes elsewhere between natural and rational capacities. A natural capacity can only give rise to one kind of activity, while a rational capacity is essentially a capacity of opposites. That is why training and habituation are necessary for the production of goodness of character. The capacity of being bad is the same thing as the capacity for being good, and it all depends on the training and habituation in which of the two ways the capacity will become active. This is the fundamental fact upon which all education must be based.

by seeing often or hearing often that we got the senses of sight and hearing. On the contrary, we had the senses first and then used them ; we did not get them by using them. The various forms of goodness, on the other hand, we get by the previous exercise of activities, just as we do the arts. The things which we are to do when we have learnt them, we learn by doing them ; we become, for instance, good builders by building and good lyre-players by playing the lyre. In the same way it is by doing just acts that we become just, by doing temperate acts that we become temperate, and by doing brave deeds that we become brave. What actually happens in states is evidence of this. It is by habituation that lawgivers make citizens good, and this is the aim of every lawgiver. Those who do not do it well, fail in their aim, and this is just the difference between a good constitution and a bad one.

Again, the material from which and the means by which any form of goodness is produced and those by which it is destroyed are the same[1]. This is so too with any form of art ; for it is by playing the lyre that both good and bad lyre-players are produced, and it is the same with builders and the rest. It is by building well that they will become good builders and by building badly that they will become bad builders. If it were otherwise, we should have no need of anyone to teach us ; all would become good or bad as the case might be. So too in the case of goodness. It is by acting in business

[1] This is a further application of the same principle. Not only are the capacities for goodness and badness one and the same, but their material is also the same. The matter of which goodness is the form consists in feelings and actions, and these very same feelings and actions are also the materials of badness. This also is a fundamental fact in education. It is not by suppressing the feelings or by removing all opportunities for wrong action that you can make people good. It is by letting them have the feelings and do the actions, and by directing them so that these feelings and actions shall form a training in right feeling and action, not in wrong.

transactions between man and man that we become just or unjust as the case may be, and it is by acting in the moment of danger and habituating ourselves to fear and not to fear that we become cowards or brave men. So too it is with our desires and feelings of anger. Some people become moral and good-tempered, while others become immoral and bad-tempered, according as they behave themselves in one way or another in these matters. In one word, conditions of soul arise from activities of like character to the conditions[1]. What we have to do, then, is to *qualify our activities*, since the differences between the conditions of soul correspond to the differences of the activities which give rise to them. It is of no little importance, then, that we should be habituated this way or that from the earliest youth; it is of great importance, or rather all-important.

Now our present study is not, like others, a theoretical one. The object of our inquiry is not to know what goodness is, but to become good ourselves. Otherwise it would be of no use whatever. We must therefore consider actions, and how they ought to be performed; for, as we have said, it depends entirely upon our actions what the character of our conditions of soul will be.

That we should act according to the right rule[2] is common ground and we may assume it. But we must come to an understanding at the outset that every description of how we should act must be a mere sketch; it cannot be exact. At the very start we laid down that the kind of discussion

[1] This is the formula which lies at the root of Aristotle's whole theory of education. We must give the activities a certain quality and then the conditions of soul which these activities produce will have that quality too.

[2] This is a Platonic formula. There is always a right rule and a wrong one in every class of feelings and actions. This rule Aristotle tells us later on exists in the soul of the man of practical wisdom, the lawgiver or educator. He must be conscious of the rule or principle upon which habituation proceeds.

required in any case must be such as the subject-matter admits of, and that our statements about action and what is good for us can have no fixity, any more than statements about health. And, if this is true of the subject generally, it will be still more true that the discussion of particular points admits of no exactitude. They do not fall under any art or professional tradition, but the agents themselves must in every case consider what the occasion demands, just as in the case of navigation and medicine[1]. Still, though this is the nature of the present subject, we must do what we can to come to the rescue.

Analogy shows that the sort of activities which will produce goodness are activities in a mean. The mean is in feelings and actions, mainly in pleasure and pain, which are the true materials of goodness. (II. 3, §§ 6—11.)

The first point to be observed, then, is that in things of this character excess and defect are both destructive. We must use as evidence of what is obscure such things as are clear, and we see that this is so in the case of health and strength. Both excess and defect of gymnastic exercises destroy strength, and in the same way excess and defect of food and drink destroy health, while the right proportion produces, increases, and preserves it. It is the same with temperance, courage, and the other forms of goodness. The man that shuns and fears everything and faces nothing becomes a coward; the man that fears nothing and goes to meet every danger becomes rash. In the same way, the man who indulges in every pleasure and never refrains from any becomes intemperate, and the man who shuns all pleasures, like the

[1] You cannot give hard and fast rules as to how actions are to be performed. The reason is that every action is particular, it is this particular act in certain particular circumstances, and the rule is universal. The rule is of no use at all without the power of seeing how it applies in a given case, which is a matter of perception. No science and no rule can reach the particular.

boors[1], becomes insensible. So temperance and courage are destroyed both by excess and defect, and preserved by the mean[2].

Not only, however, do we find that the material and the means of the production, development and destruction of these conditions are the same, but also that the activities which arise from the conditions when formed have the same objects[3]. This is so in the less obscure cases, for instance in the case of strength. Strength is produced by taking a great deal of nourishment and undergoing a great deal of exertion, and it is just the strong man that can do these things best. So it is in the case of goodness. It is by abstaining from pleasures that we become temperate, and it is when we have become temperate that we are best able to abstain from them. So again with courage; it is by habituating ourselves to despise objects of fear and by facing them that we become courageous, and it is when we have become courageous that we shall best be able to face them.

We must take the pleasures and pains that supervene upon our actions as symptoms of our condition. The man who abstains from bodily pleasures and actually enjoys doing so

---

[1] The reference is to a stock character in contemporary Greek comedy.

[2] It is characteristic of Aristotle's method that the doctrine of the Mean appeared in the first place simply as a practical rule for "qualifying our activities" based on the analogy of medicine. All this prepares the way for the more scientific account of it a little later. The doctrine of the Mean has been more misunderstood than any other part of Aristotle's ethical teaching. It is important to bear in mind that here we are only looking for a practical rule to guide us in habituation, and we must be careful not to go beyond what Aristotle actually says. The way in which we have been looking at goodness, namely as a "condition," suggests at once the analogy of the arts of medicine and gymnastics.

[3] This prepares us for the view which we shall come to later on, that goodness is itself, in the sense to be then explained, a Mean. We note for the present as a practical point that the activities which go to form the condition known as goodness are of the very same quality as the activities which proceed from that condition once it is formed.

is temperate, while the man who does so but dislikes it is intemperate. The man who faces danger and enjoys it, or at any rate is not pained by it, is brave ; but the man who faces it with pain is a coward. For goodness of character has to do with pleasures and pains. It is pleasure that makes us do what is bad, and pain that makes us abstain from what is right. That is why we require to be trained from our earliest youth, as Plato has it, to feel pleasure and pain at the right things. True education is just that[1].

Again, the sphere of goodness is acts and feelings, and every feeling and act is accompanied by pleasure or pain. That too shows that goodness has to do with pleasure and pain. Another indication is afforded by their use as a means of punishment ; for punishments act as it were medicinally, and the natural medicines are those which are opposite to the diseases. Again, as was stated on a previous occasion, the very things which naturally make a given condition of soul better or worse are also the things in relation to which it shows its nature, the proper sphere of its activity. Now it is pleasure and pain that make men bad, when they pursue and avoid the wrong ones, or at the wrong time, or in the wrong manner, or in any other of the ways in which we may violate the rule. That is just why some people define all forms of goodness as absences of feeling or "quiescences[2]"; but they are wrong in so far as they speak of absence of feeling without reservation, and do not add the qualifications of the right way or the wrong way, the right time and the wrong time, and the rest of them.

We assume, then, that goodness is that condition of soul or attitude towards pleasures and pains that produces the best

[1] This is the best account of the training of character that has ever been given and should be engraved in the heart of every educator.

[2] The reference is to Speusippos, Plato's nephew and successor. The same view has, of course, reappeared in different forms over and over again in the history of thought. The chief value of Aristotle's educational theory lies just in its opposition to all views of the kind.

B. 4

actions and badness the opposite, and we may also make this clear to ourselves in another way. There are three things that are the objects of choice, the beautiful, the useful and the pleasant, and there are three things that we shun, the ugly, the harmful, and the painful. Now with regard to all of these the good man tends to go right and the bad man to go wrong, but above all with regard to pleasure. For pleasure is a thing we share with all animals and it accompanies everything that is an object of choice; for even the beautiful and the useful present themselves to us as pleasant. Further, this feeling has grown up with us from our earliest infancy, so it is hard to remove it, engrained as it is like a stain in our life. Again we all, though in varying degrees, take pleasure and pain as the standard of our actions. For these reasons our present study must necessarily be concerned throughout with pleasure and pain; for right and wrong feelings of pleasure and pain have a great deal to do with our actions. Again, it is harder, as Herakleitos says, to fight with pleasure than with anger[1], and in all cases it is the more difficult thing that is the sphere of any form of art or goodness; for their excellence comes out best in it. That is another reason why goodness and the art of Politics have to busy themselves all through with pleasures and pains; for the man who uses these aright is a good man, and the man who uses them wrongly is a bad man.

We may take it, then, that the sphere of goodness is pleasures and pains, that the causes of its production are also the means of its developement, or of its destruction, if their character be reversed, and that the sphere of its activity is to be found in the very things by which it was produced.

The account which we have given of the way in which good-ness is produced raises a difficulty. It appears that it is by doing

---

[1] The quotation is not quite accurate nor was the meaning of Hera-kleitos quite what Aristotle takes it to have been. See my *Early Greek Philosophy,* p. 140. But this does not, of course, affect the argument.

good acts that we become good, which seems to be a vicious circle.
We must therefore explain how the activities which proceed from
a formed condition differ from those which have gone to form it.
(II. 4.)

A difficulty may, however, be raised as to what we mean by
saying that the right way to become just is to perform just acts,
and the right way to become temperate is to act temperately.
If, it may be said, men do what is just and temperate, they are
just and temperate already, just as, if they spell correctly or
play the right notes, they are already scholars and musicians.

Surely, however, this does not hold even of the arts ; for it
is quite possible to spell correctly by chance or at the suggestion
of another. We cannot call a man a scholar till he not only
spells correctly, but does it as a scholar, that is, in virtue of the
scholarship in his own soul. In the second place there is
a distinction between the case of the arts and that of goodness.
The products of the arts have their goodness in themselves, so
it is quite sufficient in their case that they should have a certain
character when produced. Actions in conformity with goodness, on the other hand, are not, for instance, justly or temperately performed if they are merely of a certain character
looked at in themselves, but only if the agent is in a certain
condition when he performs them, in the first place if he acts
with knowledge, in the second, if he wills them and wills them
for their own sake, and thirdly, if they proceed from a fixed
and unalterable condition of soul. In the case of the arts, we
do not take these requirements into account, except indeed
that of knowledge, whereas in the case of goodness, mere
knowledge is of little or no importance; what is not of little
importance, but all-important, is the other requirements, since
those only can be good who have acted repeatedly in a just
and temperate way. We say, then, that deeds are just and
temperate when they are such as a just or temperate man
would perform, but that a just or temperate man is not merely

4—2

the man who does these deeds, but the man who does them as just and temperate people do them[1].

It is quite right, then, to say that it is by doing just deeds that a just man is made, and that a temperate man is made by acting temperately. There is not the slightest prospect of anyone being made good by any other process. Most men, indeed, shirk it and take refuge in the theory of goodness. They fancy that they are philosophers, and that this will make them good. But they are really just like people who listen attentively to what their doctor has to say and do not obey one of his prescriptions. There is about as much chance of those who study philosophy in this way gaining health of soul as of such people getting well and strong in body[2].

VI. GOODNESS. WHAT IS IT? *It is (a) a Condition, (b) a Mean.*

(a) *The genus of Goodness. It is a condition of the soul with regard to feeling.* (II. 5.)

The next question we have to consider is what goodness is[3].

[1] This amounts to saying that, though the activities which go to form a condition are outwardly the same as those which proceed from it when it is formed, their inner nature is quite different. Good conduct is not merely the doing of certain things, but the doing of them from certain motives and in a certain spirit.

[2] It is well worth while to note carefully all that Aristotle says as to the relation between theory and practice in education. He does not disparage theory, indeed he holds that it is absolutely impossible for us to do anything without it. What he does object to is the tendency to put theory in the place of practice. It is the same point that we had above p. 17.

[3] We might be inclined to say that this was the first question to be settled, but Aristotle has his own reasons for taking the subjects up in this order, and it is to be observed that we have hitherto been discussing, not the nature of good acts as such, but of the acts which produce goodness. By this preliminary discussion we have been prepared to understand the scientific definition of goodness when we come to it. Most of the points are already familiar, and we have now only to put them into the shape of a formal definition.

Book II.

Now, there are three things by which the soul may be qualified, feelings, capacities and conditions. Goodness, therefore, will be one of these three[1]. By feelings I mean desire, anger, fear and boldness, envy and joy, love and hate, regret, emulation and pity, and in general, everything that is accompanied by pleasure and pain. By capacities I mean those qualities in respect of which we are said to be capable of such feelings, for instance, the capacity of getting angry or of feeling pain or pity. By conditions I mean those qualities of soul in respect of which we are spoken of as having a good or a bad attitude towards these feelings. For example, our attitude towards anger will be bad if it is one of too great tension or relaxation[2]; if it is in the mean between these, it is good, and the same applies to the other feelings.

Now the different forms of goodness or badness are none of them feelings; for it is not the feelings that get us the name of good or bad, while our goodness and badness do. Again, we are not praised or blamed for our feelings—the man who is afraid or angry is not praised for it, nor is a man blamed simply for being angry, but only for being angry in a certain way—but we are praised and blamed for our goodness and badness.·

[1] Aristotle here takes for granted a good deal of his own teaching which is to be found elsewhere, and which he probably regarded as a part of "general culture" (cf. p. 17 n. 1). In the first place he assumes that goodness is a quality, and a quality of the appetitive part of the soul, the part in which the feelings arise. In the second place he assumes that his hearers know the classification of qualities, which he gives elsewhere, into capacities, affections, conditions, and forms. Form or shape is left out of account as having no application to the soul, and the other three are understood as having the meaning which they would naturally have as applied to the appetitive soul.

[2] It is well to note in passing this metaphor from the tuning of musical instruments. It had passed at an early date from music to medicine and is of great use in helping us to understand the doctrine of the Mean. Here we see that our condition in relation to the feeling of anger is good if it resembles that of a well-tuned instrument, tuned to a pitch that is neither too high nor too low.

Further, we are angry or afraid without an act of will, while goodness is a form of will, or at any rate necessarily implies will. Lastly, we are said to be "moved" in respect of our feelings, but in respect of goodness and badness we are not said to be moved, but to be "disposed" in a certain way.

The same reasons may be adduced to show that the different forms of goodness are not capacities. We are not called good or bad, nor are we praised or blamed, simply for having a capacity of feeling. Again, our capacities come by nature; but we do not become good or bad by nature. That point has been settled already[1]. If, then, goodness in all its forms is neither a feeling nor a capacity, it remains that it must be a condition of the soul.

(*b*) *The specific difference of Goodness. It is a Mean between excess and defect.* (II. 6.)

We have now stated the genus to which goodness belongs. It is not, however, enough merely to describe it as a condition; we must also explain what sort of condition it is.

We must lay down, then, that every form of goodness produces a good state in that of which it is the goodness, and enables it to perform its function well. For example, the goodness of an eye makes the eye good and also its function, since it is by reason of the eye's goodness that we see well. In the same way, the goodness of a horse makes a horse good, good at running, and good at carrying its rider and facing the enemy. Now, if this applies in all cases, the goodness of man will be the condition that makes a good man and enables him to perform his proper function well. We have already explained how this will be[2]; but we can also make it plain by considering the true nature of goodness.

In everything that is continuous and divisible, it is possible to take a quantity which is greater, smaller, or equal to a given

[1] See above p. 44.
[2] See above p. 47.

quantity[1], and that either in relation to the object or to us. The equal is the mean between excess and defect. By the mean *in relation to the object*, I understand the point which is equally distant from both extremes, and this is one and the same for everybody. By the mean *in relation to ourselves* I understand that which is neither too much nor too little, and that is not one and the same point for everybody. For instance, if 10 is much and 2 little, we take 6 as the mean in relation to the object; for 6 exceeds and is exceeded by an equal number, and is therefore the arithmetical mean. But we cannot arrive at the mean in relation to ourselves by this method. It does not follow, if ten pounds of meat are much and two are little for a man to eat, that the trainer will prescribe six pounds; that would be little for Milo, but much for a beginner in gymnastics, and the same will hold good in racing and wrestling[2]. Thus it is that everyone who proceeds

[1] The best way to understand this is to think of a graduated scale like that of a thermometer, which admits of an infinite number of degrees between zero and boiling-point. Zero will be the total absence of anger —to take the example given above—and the boiling-point will be the greatest amount of anger that a human being can endure. The right amount of anger will necessarily correspond to some intermediate point in the scale. Or, to take the other illustration which is much in Aristotle's mind, that from the tuning of instruments, we may say the one extreme is the lowest note in the scale and the other the highest, and from this it follows that the right pitch will be something intermediate between the two. Both these are instances of continuous quantity, which is infinitely divisible, and Aristotle speaks of continuous rather than of discrete quantity just because he wishes to bring out that there is an infinite number of possible degrees of feeling.

[2] It is not enough to speak of the mean without adding "relatively to us." We cannot say that the right degree of anger will be exactly half-way between zero and boiling-point, or that all instruments must be tuned to a pitch exactly midway between the lowest and the highest note of the scale. This is the common misunderstanding of the doctrine, but Aristotle himself is perfectly clear on the subject. The mean is not to be found by the simple arithmetical process of dividing by two; it is at first an unknown x, which must be ascertained by some application of the rule of three.

scientifically avoids both excess and defect; he pursues the mean and adopts it, not, however, the mean in relation to the object, but that in relation to ourselves.

Every science, then, discharges its function well if it fixes its attention on the mean and brings up all its products to that standard. That is just the meaning of the praise commonly bestowed on successful works, that it is impossible to take anything from them or add anything to them, a way of speaking which implies that excess and defect alike destroy excellence while the mean preserves it. So too, good artists, as we say, keep the mean in view as they work. But goodness is more exact and higher than any art, just as nature is, and therefore aims at the mean. I speak, of course, of goodness of character; for it is that which has to do with feelings and actions, and it is in them that we find excess and defect and the mean. For instance, it is possible to fear or feel bold, to desire, to get angry, to feel pity, and in general, to feel pleasure or pain, in a greater or less degree, and in both cases wrongly; but to have these feelings at the right times and on the right occasions and towards the right persons and with the right motive and in the right way is the mean and therefore right in the highest degree, and that is what shows goodness. In the same way, we may have excess and defect and the mean in actions as well as feelings[1]. Now the sphere of goodness is just feelings and actions, and it is in them that excess and defect are alike wrong, whereas the mean is praised and is right. Goodness, then, is a mean, in so far as it aims at the mean.

Further, it is possible to go wrong in many ways—for evil belongs to the infinite, as the Pythagoreans said in a

---

[1] Take for instance the virtue of liberality, which is a mean in action and not in feeling. We may either give away all we have or nothing at all; but the precisely right sum for us, being who we are, to give to certain persons in given circumstances will be found somewhere between these points. To give more will then be prodigality and to give less will be meanness.

figure[1], and good to the finite—but there is only one way of being right. That is just why the one is easy and the other difficult; it is easy to miss a mark and hard to hit it. This, then, also goes to show that excess and defect are a sign of badness and the mean of goodness. As the poet says:

> The good are simply good, the bad are manifold.

We may therefore define goodness as *A condition of the soul which wills the mean relatively to ourselves*, the mean which is determined by rule or by whatever the wise man would determine it by[2].

It is a mean, in the first place, as lying between two forms of badness, one in excess and the other in defect, and secondly because, whereas badness either falls short of or goes beyond the right point in feelings and actions, goodness discovers the mean and adopts it. If, then, we look at goodness in its true nature and in the light of its definition, it is a mean, though, if we look at it from the point of view of worth or excellence, it is an extreme[3].

---

[1] See my *Early Greek Philosophy*, p. 312. To the Pythagoreans everything was to be explained by the combination of the limit with the unlimited, and it is the limit that gives definite form to what is otherwise formless. The point here is that there is an infinite number of degrees in the scale that are wrong either by excess or defect, while there is only one point that is precisely right for us in the given circumstances.

[2] The wise man here is the lawgiver or educator who has the rule in his soul. It is he that in the last resort determines the degree of feeling which is precisely right in given circumstances for particular people. In a later part of the *Ethics* Aristotle comes back to this, and we find that what the wise man determines it by is his knowledge of the means that tend to produce human good. But this cannot be fully worked out till we come to discuss goodness of intellect.

[3] This shows how absurd it is to say that Aristotle "makes a merely quantitative distinction between vice and virtue." It is true that he brings out the quantitative element in the distinction, and he was perfectly right to do so. It depends upon his great doctrine that the material of goodness is the same as that of badness. If that is so, it is clear that the difference between them can only be quantitative *so far as their material is concerned*,

But it is not every action or every feeling that admits of a mean; the very names of some at once imply badness; for example, malice, shamelessness, envy, and, among actions, adultery, theft, murder. All these and others of a like kind hàve been named as in themselves bad, and not merely bad in excess or defect. It is impossible, then, ever to perform them aright; they are always wrong. Right is not distinguished from wrong in the case of adultery by its being committed with the right person or at the right time or in the right way; but to do anything of that kind is always wrong. And it would be just as great a mistake to insist that there must be a mean and an excess and a defect in unjust, cowardly or immoral actions; for, if that were so, we should have a mean within an excess or defect, and an excess of an excess and a defect of a defect. But, just as in the case of temperance and courage there can be no excess or defect, because the mean is, in one sense, an extreme, so neither can there be a mean or an excess or a defect in these cases, but however they are done they are wrong. For, in general, there is no mean in an excess or defect, nor can there be excess or defect in the mean.

Application of the definition to particular forms of goodness. The Table of the Virtues. (II. 7.)

It is not, however, sufficient to make a general statement of this kind; it must be shown to fit the particulars. In all discussions of actions, general statements cover a larger number of cases, but particular ones come nearer to the truth of the matter. The sphere of action is particulars, so our statements

but the material is not everything. Some of the criticisms that have been made upon Aristotle's doctrine would only have any point if he had said that the rash man was twice as brave as the brave man, and the coward half as brave. What he does say is that the rash man habitually fears less than the brave man, and the coward habitually fears more, which is obviously true. The next paragraph seems to have been written in anticipation of some such possible misunderstanding.

must be shown to be in harmony with the particular application of them. We must take our particulars, then, from the
Table of Virtues[1].

With regard to feelings of fear and boldness, the mean state
is Courage. Of those who exceed, he who exceeds in fearlessness is nameless—there are many nameless states—while he
who exceeds in boldness is called rash. On the other hand,
he who exceeds in fearing and is deficient in boldness is called
a coward.

With regard to pleasures and pains,—though not all pleasures
and pains[2], and to a less extent with regard to pains than
pleasures,—the mean is Temperance, and the excess is Intemperance. People who are defective with regard to pleasures
are not very common, so that they again have not received
a name. We may call them insensible.

With regard to the giving and getting of money, the mean
state is Liberality, the excess and defect are Prodigality and
Meanness. Here we find that they exceed and fall short of the
mean in opposite ways; the prodigal exceeds in throwing away
and is deficient in getting, the mean man exceeds in taking
and is deficient in giving. Of course we are only giving a
summary sketch, and that is sufficient for the present purpose;
later on we shall have to define all these types more exactly.

There are other states besides that have to do with money.
Munificence is a mean, and the munificent man is different
from the liberal man; the former has to do with large sums
and the latter with small ones. The excess corresponding to
munificence is bad taste or Vulgarity, the defect Shabbiness.
These differ from the excess and defect that correspond to
liberality; in what respect they differ, we shall explain
later on.

[1] At this point the lecture appears to have been illustrated by a dia-
gram.

[2] Later on we find that it is confined to pleasures of touch, including
those of taste so far as taste may be reduced to touch.

With regard to honour and dishonour the mean is Pride; the excess is Vanity and the defect is Want of spirit. And there is a state which is related to pride just as we said that liberality was related to munificence, that is, differing from it as having to do with smaller objects. This state has to do with small honours just as pride has to do with great honour; for it is possible to strive for such honour in the right way, or to a greater or less degree than is right. Now the man that exceeds in this is called ambitious, and the man that falls short unambitious, but the man who hits the mean is nameless. The conditions of soul are nameless too except that that of the ambitious man is called Ambition. This explains why it is that each of the extremes claims the intervening space as its own property, why we sometimes call the man who hits the mean ambitious and sometimes unambitious, and why we sometimes praise the ambitious and sometimes the unambitious man[1]. The explanation of this will be given later on; we must now discuss the other conditions in accordance with the method hitherto followed.

Anger, too, admits of excess, defect and the mean. They are mostly nameless, but we may call the man who hits the mean gentle and the mean condition Gentleness. Of the extremes, if a man goes wrong in the direction of excess, we may call him irascible and the bad condition Irascibility; if he errs by defect, impassive, and the defect itself Impassivity.

And there are three other means which have a certain resemblance to one another, and yet differ from one another. They all have to do with intercourse in words and deeds, but they differ in that one has to do with truthfulness in such intercourse and the other two with agreeableness, one with agreeableness in amusement and the other with agreeableness in all the relations of life. These states, too, must be discussed, in order that we may see more distinctly that in all cases the

---

[1] It is interesting to note that the usage of the English language corresponds exactly to that of the Greek in these respects.

mean condition is an object of praise, while the extremes are neither praiseworthy nor right, but blameable. No doubt most of these are also nameless, but, just as in the case of the rest, we must try to invent names, so that the argument may be clear and easy to follow.

With regard to truth, then, the man that hits the mean may be called truthful, and the mean itself Truthfulness. Pretence, if it takes the form of exaggeration, is called Boastfulness, and the man who is in this state is called a braggart; but, if it takes the form of depreciation, it is called Irony, and the man who possesses it is called ironical[1].

With regard to agreeableness in amusement, the man who hits the mean is called witty, and the disposition Wittiness; the excess is Buffoonery and the man who has it is called a buffoon, while he who is deficient may be called a churl and his state Churlishness.

With regard to the remaining kind of agreeableness, that which has to do with the business of life, the man who is agreeable in the right way is called friendly, and the mean condition is Friendliness. The man who goes to excess, if he has no further object in view, is called obsequious, if his object is his own advantage, a flatterer, while the man who falls short and is disagreeable on every occasion may be called quarrelsome and morose.

There are also mean conditions with regard to the feelings. Shame, for instance, is not a form of goodness, and yet the man who feels shame is praised. In this respect, too, we find that one man is said to hit the mean and another to exceed it, for instance the bashful man who is ashamed at everything.

---

[1] Not, of course, in the modern sense. The Greek word originally meant "sly," and was applied especially to foxes. It generally implies evasiveness, the tendency to get out of doing what is expected of you by pretending to depreciate your own abilities. It is a pity we have no current word for this very common defect. It is something rather more definite than "mock modesty."

He who errs by defect or who is never ashamed at any thing is called shameless, while the man who observes the mean is called modest.

Righteous indignation, again, is a mean state between envy and malicious joy at the misfortunes of others. The sphere of all these feelings is the pain or pleasure which we feel at the fortunes of others. The man who is righteously indignant is pained by undeserved success, but the envious man exceeds this and is pained at all success whatsoever, while the malicious man falls so far short of being pained at the misfortunes of others that he actually rejoices in them.

We shall, however, have occasion to discuss all these points in another place. In regard to justice, as the word is used in more senses than one, we shall have to distinguish these senses, and show how in each of them it is a mean[1].

The relation between the mean and the extremes. (II. 8.)

We see, then, that there are three states or conditions of soul, two of them being forms of badness, one in excess and one in defect, and one condition, the mean, which is the corresponding form of goodness. These are all opposed to each other in some way or other. The extremes are opposed both to the mean and to each other, and the mean is opposed to the extremes. Just as the equal is greater if compared with the less, but less if compared with the greater, so mean conditions, whether in feelings or actions, exceed if compared with the defect and fall short if compared with the excess. Thus the brave man appears rash in contrast to the coward, and cowardly as compared with the rash man, and similarly the temperate man appears intemperate in contrast to the in-

---

[1] Courage and Temperance are discussed in the second part of the Third Book (omitted in these selections), Liberality and the rest in the Fourth Book, while the Fifth Book is entirely devoted to Justice. The main object in every case is to show how the doctrine of the mean applies to them all.

sensible man, and insensible in contrast to the intemperate. So too the liberal man strikes us as a prodigal when compared with the mean man, and as mean when compared with the prodigal. That explains the fact that the extremes drive the mean from one to the other; the coward calls the brave man rash, and the rash man calls him a coward, and so in the other cases.

But, while there is this opposition between the extremes and the mean, there is more opposition between the two extremes than between either of them and the mean; for they are separated by a wider interval from each other than from the mean, just as the great is further apart from the small, and the small from the great, than either of them is from the equal. Again, some extremes have a certain resemblance to the mean, as for instance rashness has to courage, and liberality to prodigality, but there is always the greatest possible dissimilarity between the extremes. Now, we define opposites as the things that are furthest apart from one another[1], so that the further things are apart from another, the more opposite they will be.

Now it is sometimes the defect and sometimes the excess that is more opposite to the mean. For instance, it is not the excess, rashness, but the defect, cowardice, which is the more opposed to courage, and it is not the defect, insensibility, but the excess, intemperance, which is the more opposed to temperance. This arises from two causes. One of these is in the nature of the thing itself; where one of the extremes is nearer and more similar to the mean, it is not that extreme but its opposite which we chiefly oppose to the mean. For instance, rashness is believed to be nearer and more similar to courage than cowardice, so it is cowardice that we chiefly oppose to courage; for the things which are furthest removed from the mean strike us as more opposite to it. This is the first cause, then, that which arises from the very nature of the thing; the

[1] The full definition is "the things that are furthest apart *in the same genus.*"

other cause arises from ourselves.   It is the things to which we
are ourselves naturally more prone that appear to be more
opposed to the mean.   Thus we are all naturally more prone
to pleasure than pain, and therefore we have a greater tendency
to intemperance than to temperance.   Now those things which
lie most in the line of our natural developement, we speak of
as being more opposed to the mean, and this is another reason
for the excess, intemperance, being more opposed to temperance than insensibility is.

Practical rules for attaining the Mean.   (II. 9.)

It has now been shown sufficiently that goodness of
character is a mean, and in what sense it is a mean, and
further that it is a mean condition lying between two forms of
badness, one in excess and the other in defect, and lastly that
it is so because it aims at the mean alike in feelings and
actions.

That is why it is so hard a task to be good.   It is always
a hard task to find a mean in anything ; even the centre of
a circle cannot be found by anybody, but only by the man who
knows how.   In the same way anyone can get angry,—that is
quite easy,—and anyone can give or spend money ; but to give
it to the right people and the right amount at the right time,
with the right motive and in the right way, is no longer a thing
that anyone can do nor is it easy.   That is why excellence is
rare, laudable and fair.

A man who aims at the mean must, in the first place, keep
away from the extreme which is the more contrary to the mean.
This is the advice given by Kalypso[1] when she says :

> Far from this smoke and swell hold thou thy course.

Of the extremes there is always one that is more wrong and one

[1] *Od.* XII. 219.   It is not, however, Kalypso, but Odysseus who speaks.
The slip is due to a confused recollection on Aristotle's part that some
goddess had something to do with the words.   Really they refer to the
warning with regard to Scylla and Charybdis given by Circe to Odysseus.

that is less so, and since it is hard to hit the mean precisely, we must take the next best course and choose the least of the evils. We shall succeed best in doing this if we follow the rule just given.

Secondly, we must watch the direction in which we are most easily carried by our own natural tendencies. Some people have one tendency and others have others, but we may find out what ours are by observing our feelings of pleasure and pain. Then we must drag ourselves in the opposite direction; for if we remove ourselves as far as we can from what is wrong, we shall reach the mean. That is just how people straighten pieces of wood that are warped.

Thirdly, we must in every case be specially on our guard against pleasure and the pleasant. Where it is concerned, we are a bribed jury. We ought to feel towards pleasure as the Trojan elders felt towards Helen, and we should always apply to it the words they use[1]. If we send it away as they were for sending away Helen, we shall be less liable to go wrong. To sum the matter up, it is by behaving in this way that we shall enable ourselves to hit the mean.

Of course, this is no easy task, especially when we come to particular cases. It is not easy to determine, for instance, what is the right way to be angry or the right objects, occasions and duration of anger. Sometimes we even praise people who are deficient in anger and call them gentle, and sometimes we call angry men manly and brave. Of course it is not a slight deviation from what is right, but only a great one, whether in excess or defect, that is blamed; for such a deviation is felt at once. It is not, indeed, at all easy to determine by rule how far and up to what point a man may go wrong before he is

---

[1] *Il.* III. 156, thus translated by Mr Leaf: " Small blame is it that Trojans and well-greaved Achaians should for such a woman long time suffer hardships; marvellously like is she to the immortal goddesses to look upon. Yet even so, though she be so goodly, let her go upon their ships, and not stay to vex us and our children after us."

B.   5

blamed, but that is a difficulty which applies equally to every-thing which is an object of perception. Such things are all particulars, and can be judged by perception alone[1]. We can see plainly as much as this, that in all cases the mean condition is the object of praise, but that we must sometimes incline towards the excess and sometimes towards the defect; for that is the easiest way to hit the mean, to attain to excellence.

POLITICS.

II. THE EDUCATION OF YOUTH.

(1) *Preliminary Questions.* (VIII. 1—3.)

In the first place we have to consider (1) whether we are to establish any system of supervision for our children, next (2) whether this supervision should be public or of a private character, as in the majority of states at the present day, and lastly (3) what the character of this supervision should be.

(1) That the education of the young has a special claim on the lawgiver's attention is beyond question. In the first place, any neglect of this by a state is injurious to its constitution. A given constitution demands an education in

---

[1] This promise is not fulfilled.

conformity with it; for the maintenance of any constitution, like its first establishment, is due, as a rule, to the presence of the spirit or character proper to that constitution. The establishment and maintenance of democracy is due to the presence of a democratic spirit, and that of oligarchy to the presence of an oligarchic spirit. The better the spirit, the better the constitution it gives rise to[1].

In the second place, in all arts and crafts we require a preliminary education and habituation to enable us to exercise them, and the same will hold of the production of activities according to goodness.

(2) Again, since the state as a whole has a single end, it is plain that the education of all must be one and the same, and that the supervision of this education must be public and not private, as it is on the present system, under which everyone looks after his own children privately and gives them any private instruction he thinks proper. Public training is wanted in all things that are of public interest. Besides, it is wrong for any citizen to think that he belongs to himself. All must be regarded as belonging to the state: for each man is a part of the state, and the treatment of the part is naturally determined by that of the whole. This is a thing for which the Lacedaemonians deserve all praise; they are thoroughly in earnest about their children, and that as a community[2].

---

[1] Cf. Introd. p. 5.

[2] Nothing is said now about the possibility of fathers of families acquiring the legislative art for domestic use. Cf. p. 97, n. 2. The sort of question that Aristotle raises here is really the same as that which divides France at the present moment. The objection of the French Government to the teaching of the religious orders is just that it does not produce a "Republican spirit" in the pupils, that it is not, in Aristotelian phrase, an education in conformity with the constitution. It is not likely that Aristotle would have found much to admire in the constitution of the French Republic; but he would have said that French statesmen were bound to defend and preserve it, and that therefore they were so far justified

Book VIII.

(3) We now see that we shall have to legislate on the subject of education, and that education must be public; but we must not overlook the question of the character and method of this education. As it is, there is a dispute about subjects[1]. There is no agreement as to what the young should learn, either with a view to the production of goodness or the best life, nor is it settled whether we ought to keep the intellect or the character chiefly in view. If we start from the education we see around us, the inquiry is perplexing, and there is no certainty as to whether education should be a training in what is useful for life or in what tends to promote goodness or in more out-of-the-way subjects[2]. Each of these views finds some supporters; but there is not even any agreement as to what tends to promote goodness. To begin with, all people do not appreciate the same kind of goodness, so it is only to be expected that they should differ about the required training.

It is, of course, obvious that we shall have to teach our

in the measures they have taken. In any case, he would refuse altogether to admit the claim that fathers of families have a right to determine the character of their children's education. That would seem to him a return to the stage of civilisation represented by the Cyclops. Cf. p. 97. It may be a question whether the size of modern states does not require some modification of Aristotle's view; but it is still as true as ever it was that education should make young people feel that they are parts of a larger whole.

[1] It is rather disheartening to reflect that these words were written a good deal more than two thousand years ago, and that they might just as well be written to-day. We see that Aristotle has exactly our own problems to deal with, and it is worth while to consider whether his doctrine that the highest aim of education is to fit us for the right enjoyment of leisure may not still have something in it that may bring us nearer to a solution of them.

[2] The word literally means "extras," and was used by the Greeks from quite early times of all studies that went beyond the practical necessities of life. The Greek would think chiefly of geometry and astronomy; "classics and mathematics" at once suggest themselves to us.

children such useful knowledge as is indispensable for them; but it is equally plain that all useful knowledge is not suitable for education. There is a distinction between liberal and illiberal subjects, and it is clear that only such knowledge as does not make the learner mechanical[1] should enter into education. By mechanical subjects we must understand all arts and studies that make the body, soul, or intellect of freemen unserviceable for the use and exercise of goodness. That is why we call such pursuits as produce an inferior condition of body mechanical, and all wage-earning occupations. They allow the mind no leisure, and they drag it down to a lower level. There are even some liberal arts, the acquisition of which up to a certain point is not unworthy of freemen, but which, if studied with excessive devotion or minuteness are open to the charge of being injurious in the manner described. The object with which we engage in or study them also makes a great difference; if it is for our own sakes or that of our friends, or to produce goodness, they are not illiberal, while a man engaging in the very same pursuits

---

[1] The Greek word has almost become naturalised in the form "banausic." Apparently it was originally used of all occupations that involved much contact with fire, but Aristotle uses it in a wider sense. It is sometimes said that the Greeks were unduly sensitive to the dangers of mechanical occupations, and that they despised honest work. This is partly true, but there is another side to the question. It is just as well to be reminded that the conditions of life in a factory are not exactly favourable to the attainment of the good for man, though a recognition of this fact need not lead us to despise those who have to lead such a life. To the Greeks slavery afforded an easy way out of the difficulty. That way has become impossible for us, but the price we have to pay for our superior moral sentiment is the degradation of free labour to the servile point. A little consideration of this will perhaps make us more tolerant of Aristotle's defence of slavery, and it will do us no harm to reflect that we have not yet found anything to take its place. Time will show whether the further developement of labour-saving appliances will ever improve the life of the workman to the same extent as they have already enriched his employer.

to please strangers would in many cases be regarded as following the occupation of a slave or a serf[1].

Now the subjects most widely disseminated at present show a double face, as was remarked above. There are, speaking broadly, four which usually enter into education, (1) Reading and writing, (2) Gymnastics and (3) Music, to which some add (4) Drawing[2]. Reading and writing is taught on the ground that it is of the highest utility for practical life, and gymnastics as tending to promote courage; but, when, we come to music, we may feel at a loss. At the present day, most people take it up with the idea that its object is pleasure; but the ancients gave it its place in education because Nature herself, as we have often observed, seeks not only to be rightly busy, but also the power of using leisure aright. That is the root of the whole matter, if we may recur to the point once more. Both are wanted, but leisure is more worth having and more of an end than business, so we must find out how we are to employ our leisure. Not, surely, in playing games; for that would imply that amusement is the end of life. That it cannot be, and it is rather in our busy times that we should have recourse to games. It is the hardworked man that needs rest, and the object of play is rest, and we find that it is business that involves hard work and strain. So, when we introduce games, we should do so with a due regard to times and seasons, applying them medicinally; for motion of this character is a relaxation of the soul, and from its pleasantness gives it rest. Leisure, on the other hand, we regard as containing pleasure— nay, happiness and the blessed life—in itself. That is not a thing that we find in busy people, but only in people at leisure.

[1] We shall understand the point of view here if we think of "professionalism" in football. The Greeks felt the same about music and many other things, as we shall see.

[2] On the apparently narrow range of subjects included in Greek education see Bosanquet, *Education of the Young, &c.*, pp. 2 ff. It is unnecessary to repeat here what has been so well said there.

The busy man is busy for some end,—which implies that he has not got it,—while happiness is itself the end and by universal consent involves not pain but pleasure. To be sure, when we come to the question " What pleasure?" we no longer find a universal agreement. Each man determines it in his own way, the best man choosing the best and that which has the fairest source.

It is clear, then, that there are subjects which ought to form part of education solely with a view to the right employment of leisure, and that this education and those studies exist for their own sake, while those that have business in view are studied as being necessary and for the sake of something else. That is why our predecessors gave music a place in education, not as a necessary thing,—there is nothing necessary about it,—nor yet as a useful thing, as reading and writing are useful for making money and the management of property and many political occupations. Even drawing is supposed to be useful in enabling us to judge the work of craftsmen better. Nor again is music useful like gymnastics for health and the production of military prowess ; we see no such result accruing from it. There is no object left for it, then, but the right employment of our time in leisure, and, as a matter of fact, it is just in this way that the ancients do introduce it ; for it is in what they regard as the right way for free men to enjoy leisure that they give it a place. That is why Homer made the verses beginning " 'Tis meet alone to bid to the bounteous feast," and, after mentioning some others, adds "who bid the minstrel to delight them all." And in another place Odysseus says that the best way of spending time is when men are merry and "the banqueters throughout the hall give ear to the minstrel, all seated in a row[1]."

We conclude, then, that there is such a thing as a subject in which we must educate our sons, not because it is necessary,

[1] *Od.* XVII. 382 ff., IX. 7 ff. The text is, as usual, rather inaccurately quoted. On the subject of "leisure" cf. Introd. p. 9.

but because it is fine and worthy of free men. Whether there is only one such or a larger number we shall have to discuss later on. At present, from our consideration of the received subjects, we have gained this point, that we can quote the evidence of the ancients in favour of our view. The case of music shows that. Further we have found that our children must be educated even in some of the "useful" subjects, as for instance in reading and writing, not merely for their utility, but because they enable us to acquire many other subjects. Drawing is to be taught, not merely to save us from making blunders in our private purchases, to secure us against being cheated in the buying and selling of furniture, but still more because it enables us to see bodily beauty. To seek utility everywhere is by no means the way of free men with a sense of their own dignity.

(2) *Gymnastics.* (VIII. 4.)

Education must clearly use habit as its instrument before theory, and the education of the body must precede that of the mind[1]. We see, then, that we must entrust our children to the arts of gymnastic training and drill; the former gives a

---

[1] The reason why the education of the body must precede that of the soul is thus given in an earlier passage: " In human beings reasoning and thought form the end or completion of their nature, so that their birth and training in habits ought to be ordered with a view to these. Secondly, as the soul and body are two, we see also that there are two parts of the soul, the rational and the irrational (cf. p. 41), and two states corresponding to these, appetition and thought. Now, as the body is prior in order of generation to the soul, so is the irrational prior to the rational. This is evident from the fact that temper, wish, and desire too (the three forms of appetition, cf. p. 42, n. 4) are found in children from their very birth, while reasoning and thought only arise as they grow older. That is why the care of the body must precede that of the soul, and why that of appetition should come next. Yet the training of appetition should be for the sake of reason, and that of the body for the sake of the soul."

proper character to the condition of the body, the latter to its exercises[1].

Some of the states which are most celebrated at the present day for their care of their children produce in them an athletic condition of body, but ruin their appearance and stunt their growth. The Lacedaemonians have not fallen into this error, but they brutalize their children by excessive exercises, with the idea that this is the best way to produce courage. Courage, however, as has been more than once observed, is neither the only thing nor the chief thing to keep in view in the supervision of children; and besides, even if we confine our attention to courage, they do not go to work in the right way. Neither in the case of the lower animals nor in that of barbarous nations do we find courage associated with the most savage natures, but rather with the more gentle and lion-like. There are many tribes that have no scruples about killing and eating human beings,—for instance, the Achaioi and the Heniochoi among the tribes of the Black Sea, and other continental races in an equal or even in a higher degree,—and which are given to brigandage but destitute of courage. Further, we know that the Lacedaemonians themselves excelled everyone else so long as they were the only people that devoted themselves to gymnastic pursuits, but that now they are distanced by others both in gymnastic and military trials of strength. Their superiority was not due to

---

[1] The gymnastic trainer looked after the bodily condition generally, the drill-master taught particular accomplishments, such as shooting with bows and javelins, and easy military exercises. In the best days of Greece these two arts were carefully distinguished; in later days, when displays and performances were everything, the science of physical culture was lost in the art of the drill instructor and the teacher of what was then called "gymnastics." It is very important to notice that, when Plato and Aristotle speak of gymnastics, they do not mean the art of performing feats of strength and agility, but the scientific training of the bodily constitution. In later days Greece "became a land in which athletes were everywhere to be found and soldiers nowhere."

the way in which they trained their youth, but to their having
as competitors only people who did not train at all while they
did. So it is beauty and not brutality that should play the
leading *rôle* ; for it is not the wolf or any other of the lower
animals that can engage in any fine and dangerous contest, but
rather the good man. Those who give their boys too free
a rein in such pursuits and leave them without training in
the necessary elements of education, make them mechanical,
if we take the true view of the thing, by making them useful
for one political function only, and useful for that,—so says
the argument,—in an inferior degree to others. We must not
judge the Lacedaemonians by their record in the past, but by
their present achievement ; now-a-days they have competitors
in education and in the past they had none[1].

We find, then, that there is a general agreement as to the
need of employing gymnastics, and also as to the method of
its employment. Up to the age of puberty we must prescribe
the lighter gymnastic exercises, excluding all forced diet and
compulsory exercise, so as not to interfere with the growth
in any way. As to the possibility of their producing this
effect, it is very significant that in the list of Olympic victors
you can find two or three cases at most of the same person
being victorious both in the competitions of boys and in those
of men[2]. The reason is that the young are robbed of their
strength in the course of training by compulsory gymnastic
exercises. When, on the other hand, they have devoted themselves for three years after puberty to other studies, then
it is fitting to occupy the succeeding age with exercises and

[1] Plato in his *Laws* had already pointed out the one-sided character
of the Spartan training. No Spartan knew how to enjoy leisure, says
Aristotle.

[2] Aristotle himself compiled lists of this kind, which some have thought
a strange occupation for so great a man. We see, however, from this
remark, that he knew how to use his lists. He was really the first
statistician.

compulsory diet. It is wrong to work the mind and body hard at the same time. The natural effect of these two kinds of exercise is just the opposite ; bodily exercise impedes the mind and mental exercise the body.

(3) *Music.* (VIII. 5—7.)

We have raised some of the difficulties with regard to music in our previous discussion, but this is the right place to take them up again and develop them ; they will serve to strike the key-note of the views we shall have to express about it. It is not an easy matter to settle either what is the real effect of music nor with what object we ought to take it up. Is it for the sake of amusement and rest like sleep and drink? These are not in themselves good but pleasant, and at the same time they "chase away care," as Euripides says[1]. That is why people put music on a level with them, and employ them all,—sleep, drink, and music,—in the same way, some adding dancing to the list. Or are we rather to hold that music tends in some way to promote goodness, that music is able to produce a certain quality of character by habituating us to enjoy rightly, just as gymnastics produces in us a certain quality of body? Or does it contribute in some way to the right employment of leisure? for we must set that down as the third among the aims enumerated. Well, there can be no question that it is not our business to educate the young for the sake of amusement. They are not at play when they are learning ; for learning is accompanied by pain. Nor again can the right employment of leisure be appropriately assigned as an object to children and the early stages of life ; for what is not full-grown has nothing to do with the end[2]. It may,

[1] In the great chorus of the *Bacchae*, for which see Professor Murray's *Euripides*, pp. 95—98.
[2] They do not fulfil the requirement "in a complete life." See p. 28, n. 1.

indeed, be supposed that children have to study it seriously for the sake of the amusement it will give them when they are grown up; but, if that is how the matter stands, what is the good of their learning it themselves instead of getting the pleasure and instruction of it, like the kings of the Medes and Persians, through the performances of others? People who have made this very thing the business of their lives must necessarily execute it better than those who have only attended to it long enough to learn it; and, if they are to work hard at this sort of thing themselves, they will also have to get up the subject of cookery for themselves, which is absurd. The very same difficulty arises even if we assume that music is able to improve the character. What is the good of learning it themselves instead of listening to others and so enjoying it rightly and being able to judge of it like the Lacedaemonians? They do not learn music, but they are quite able, they say, to tell good tunes from bad ones for all that. And the same thing may be said even if music is to be employed with a view to a sunny and refined use of leisure. Why learn it ourselves instead of getting the benefit of other people's performances? Look at the way we picture the gods. The Zeus of the poets does not sing and play the lyre himself; we even call people who do so mechanical, and we think the occupation unfit for a gentleman unless he is in drink or amusing himself.

These points, I dare say, will have to be considered later; the first question we have to settle is whether we ought or ought not to give music a place in education, and which of the three effects mentioned in our enumeration of difficulties it is capable of producing,—education or amusement or the right use of leisure. Now it is easy to see how it comes in under each of these heads and how each of these elements enters into it. Amusement exists for the sake of rest, and rest must of necessity be pleasant; for it is a remedy for the pain produced by hard work. Secondly, the right use of leisure

8—2

must admittedly involve not only beauty but pleasure; for happiness is made up of both. Now we all say that music is one of the pleasantest of things, whether it be simple instrumental music or with a vocal accompaniment. At any rate Musaeus[1] says "Sweetest to mortals is song," and so it is easy to explain why people introduce it into social gatherings and seasons of leisure, for its power of giving pleasure. On this ground alone we may assume that it should form part of the education of youth. All innocent pleasures are adapted not only to the full enjoyment of the end of life, but also for rest. Now since, as a matter of fact, men are but seldom in a position to enjoy the end of life fully, but often rest and make use of amusement, not so much with a further end in view as for their pleasure, it may be well to let them find rest from time to time in the pleasure of music.

It happens, indeed, that men make their amusements their end; for the end no doubt involves a certain pleasure, though not any and every pleasure. They are seeking for right pleasure, but they let themselves be put off with the wrong one, seeing that it has a certain resemblance to the end of all their action. The end of life is not a thing that we choose for the sake of anything else that is to come of it, and in the same way the pleasures we are describing do not exist for the sake of anything to come, but solely for that of what is past, namely, painful exertion[2]. That, we may fairly assume, is the reason why they seek to get happiness by means of such pleasures; but, if we consider their devotion to music, that is not the only reason. It is also because it is useful in giving rest, it seems. But, for all that, we have to consider whether this is not after all only an incidental use of it, while its true

---

[1] A mythical personage to whom many early hymns were attributed.

[2] This is rather differently put from the statement in the *Ethics* as to rest and relaxation. See p. 86. There we were told that relaxation was required in view of the subsequent activity. But the difference is mainly verbal, the point here being that if the soul had not been overstrained previously, it would not require relaxation.

nature is something that stands higher in the scale of value than the use just mentioned. In that case we must do more than appreciate the universally felt pleasure of it,—everybody is conscious of that; for the pleasantness of music is natural, and the use of it is therefore attractive to all ages and characters,—we have also to see whether it has any bearing upon character and the soul, and it will be clear that it has if our character is in any way altered by it. Now there are many things which show that music affects our character; but there is no better proof than the airs of Olympos[1]. These admittedly make our souls enthusiastic, and enthusiasm is a modification of the soul's character. Further, when we listen to imitations of feelings, we all share these feelings, quite apart from the actual rhythms and melodies.

It appears, then, that music belongs to the class of things pleasant, and the sphere of goodness is just right enjoyment and hatred and love. Obviously there is nothing we want to learn and habituate ourselves to so much as judging aright and enjoying aright good characters and fine actions. Further, it is in rhythms and melodies that we find likenesses of anger and gentleness that approach most closely to the real things[2],

[1] Another mythical personage to whom were attributed certain wild compositions on the flute which were used in orgiastic forms of worship, such as those of Sabazios, which were mostly imported from Phrygia. We shall return to these presently. It is enough to point out here that Aristotle is referring to what was an admitted fact, namely that this wild music did affect the state of the soul in some way.

[2] We come now to what sounds strangest of all to a modern reader. The Greeks regarded music as the most imitative of all arts, not because it could imitate the sounds of nature—that sort of imitation they agree with us in thinking inartistic—but because music could give a closer imitation of a state of soul than sculpture or painting could of the form of a body. To understand this (so far as it is possible for us to understand it at all) we must remember that Greek music differed from ours in several very important particulars. In the first place, what we call harmony was altogether unknown to the Greeks except in the most rudimentary form. In the second place, Greek melodies were, so far as we have any means of judging,

and so with courage and temperance and qualities of character generally. Facts prove it ; for we are altered in soul as we listen to them. Now to acquire the habit of feeling pain and joy at the likenesses is next-door to acquiring the same habit with regard to the originals. For example, if a man feels joy at beholding some one's portrait for no other reason than the mere look of it, the actual view of the person whose portrait he contemplates must necessarily be pleasant to him too. Further, we find that, in the objects of the other senses, such as touch and taste, there is no resemblance to characters, though in those of sight there is a faint one. There are forms which possess this character, but only to a slight degree, and all share in this sort of perception. Besides, the forms are not

of a more rudimentary and primitive type than the simplest of ours. On the other hand, there were certain respects in which Greek music was more complicated and elaborate than the most elaborate modern music. In the first place, Greek rhythms were far more varied and complex. Such times as ⅝ are quite common in Greek lyrics, and the possibilities of passing from one rhythm to another were very much greater than we have any idea of now. In the second place, the Greek ear was far more sensitive to pitch and modulation than ours is. They were able to appreciate quarter-tones without difficulty, and we shall see presently that this power was not confined to experts. It is not surprising, then, that whereas our music recognises only two "modes," the major and the minor, the Greeks had a large number of scales, each with its own peculiar character. We may see, then, that it is quite possible Greek theory on this subject was less extravagant than it sometimes appears to us, if we bear in mind the following three points. (1) Greek music surpassed ours in the number and variety of its rhythms and modes. (2) It is always of the rhythms and modes that Greek writers speak when they are discussing the imitative character of music. (3) It is precisely in such things that even we are conscious of a certain affinity between music and the state of the soul. We too speak of rhythms as martial or languid, as stately or playful, and so forth, and everyone is conscious of the ethical difference between the major and the minor. We have only to imagine these feelings intensified so as to come within measurable distance of Greek feeling on the subject. For a brief and easily intelligible account of the modes, see Bosanquet, *The Education of the Young in the Republic of Plato,* p. 92, n. 2.

really *likenesses* of character ; it is truer to say that the forms and colours which occur are *signs* of character, and these arise only in the body under the influence of the feelings [1]. For all that, so far as there is a difference in the contemplation of forms, it is not Pauson's works that young people should look at but those of Polygnotos [2], and such other painters and sculptors as express character. But it is in the actual melodies themselves that the imitations of characters are to be found.

That this is so is evident. There is a fundamental distinction between the nature of the scales, so that, when we hear them, we are put into a different frame of mind by each of them and into a different condition. Some make us feel more mournful and oppressed, like the so-called Mixolydian [3], others gentler in mind, like the "relaxed" scales. Another scale again puts us into an intermediate, calm mood, and this is held to be the peculiar property of the Dorian scale, while the Phrygian makes us enthusiastic. Those who have made a philosophical study of this branch of education are quite right in these points ; for they derive the evidence of their theories from the actual facts. The same thing too holds good of rhythms ; some have a stately character, while others have more motion, and the motions of the latter are in some cases more vulgar, in others more refined. All this proves that music has the power of modifying the character of the soul; and if it has this power we must of course make use of it and educate the young by it. And the teaching of music is very well adapted to a young nature. Their age prevents the young tolerating anything unsweetened if they can help it, and music is essentially a sweetened thing. Besides there seems to be a certain affinity between the soul and rhythms and

---

[1] Aristotle is thinking of the blush of shame and the pallor of fear.

[2] Cf. *Poetics*, II. 2. " Polygnotos painted men as better than they are, Pauson as inferior, Dionysios drew them true to life." Polygnotos, then, stands for the ideal school of painting. Pauson made caricatures.

[3] This is said to have been invented by Sappho.

scales, which accounts for the fact that many wise men say either that the soul is or has a musical pitch[1].

We come now to the discussion of the difficulty previously raised, whether they are to learn by singing themselves and by actual manipulation of musical instruments or not. There can be no doubt that it makes a great difference to the production of a certain condition of character if one takes part personally in playing. It is a thing impossible, or at least extremely difficult, to become a good judge of music without taking actual part in playing it. Besides, children must have something to do with their time, and the "rattle of Archytas[2]" which is given to children so that they may use it instead of breaking the things in the house, is an invention to be commended ; for nothing young is able to keep quiet. This applies of course to children when they are quite small, but all

---

[1] This refers to the Pythagorean view, which is generally, though quite wrongly, referred to as the doctrine that the soul is a harmony. As already stated, the Greeks knew practically nothing of harmony, and the Greek word *harmonia*, which is used here, does not mean this. It meant originally *tuning*, then *pitch*, and then by a natural extension *octave*. It was used of the various scales or octaves, otherwise called *modes*. The meaning of the Pythagorean doctrine was this. According to the earliest view, the human body was supposed to be made up of a combination of certain opposites, the cold and the warm, the moist and the dry. Life and health were regarded as consisting in the due proportion of these, as standing to them in fact as the true pitch or tuning of a string stands to the highest and the lowest note of a scale. This passed afterwards into medical theory, and so had a great deal to do with Aristotle's formulation of the doctrine of the mean.

[2] Archytas of Taras (*Tarentum, Taranto*) in Southern Italy was one of the later generation of Pythagoreans. He was a distinguished general and statesman, besides being one of the first mathematicians of his time. The science of mechanics owes its origin to him, and it would be pleasing to think that he also invented some form of baby's rattle. The remark that follows is not intended to depreciate education. Aristotle only means that education does not produce its full effect till the child grows up, but that even in childhood it has the secondary purpose of keeping him out of mischief.

education is just a rattle for children of an older growth. Such considerations show that they ought to learn actual playing ; and it is no hard task to determine what is fitting or not fitting for certain ages, and so to find the answer to those who urge that the study is mechanical. In the first place, since they are to acquire the art of playing in order to be able to judge, they must practise it when they are young and be let off from playing when they get older, but so as still to retain from the teaching of their youth the power of distinguishing fine things and enjoying them rightly. And, as for the criticism sometimes made that music makes people mechanical, it is not hard to find the answer if we consider up to what point those who are being brought up to be good citizens should actually learn to play, and what sort of melodies and rhythms they should be taught. A further point is what instruments they should get their teaching on ; for we may expect that to make a difference too. It is on such points that our answer to this criticism must turn ; for it cannot be denied that some forms of music may possibly produce the alleged bad effects.

It is obvious, then, that their study of music must not be such as to impede their subsequent activities nor to make their bodies mechanical and unserviceable for military and civil exercises, that is, useless for bodily exercises now and for other studies later on. The right rule for the study is not to burden them with anything that is only wanted for professional performances, nor with those out-of-the-way marvels of execution that have entered into such performances at the present day and have passed from them into education[1]. And even what they do study they should study only so far as to be capable of feeling delight, not merely in that part of music that everybody can appreciate, even some of the lower animals or a crowd of servants and children, but in fine melodies and rhythms.

[1] Another touch which makes us feel how near Aristotle is to our own problems.

This shows us what sort of instruments we ought to use. We must not admit into education flutes[1] or any other instrument requiring professional skill, such as the harp or any other instrument of that kind. We only want such as will make them good recipients of musical or any other form of education. Besides, the flute does not express character; it is rather an orgiastic instrument, and is therefore to be employed when the effect intended to be produced by the performance is the purgation[2] of the feelings rather than instruction. We must add too another objection to the use of the flute in education, namely that flute-playing stands in the way of using the voice for singing the words. The ancients were therefore quite right in rejecting the flute as an instrument for boys and freemen, though at an earlier period they had adopted it. When their material resources were increased and when they had more leisure, when their aspirations after excellence became higher, and when they were flushed with the pride of their achievements, not only after the Persian wars but even earlier, they clutched at every form of learning indiscriminately in an experimental way. So it was that they introduced flute-playing into education. At Lacedaemon there was a choregos who led the chorus in person with the flute, and at Athens the instrument became so much at home that the majority of freemen were able to play it. This is proved by the votive tablet set up by Thrasippos when he furnished the chorus to Ekphantides[3]. Later on, however, experience led to its

---

[1] Plato also rejected the flute (or, more accurately, the clarinette). Cf. Bosanquet, *The Education of the Young in the Republic of Plato*, p. 96, n. 1.

[2] On "purgation" see below p. 124, n. 2.

[3] Properly speaking, the duty of the *choregos* was to provide the accessories of the play. See p. 32, n. 1. Aristotle's researches brought out the fact that in that wonderful period, the beginning of the fifth century B.C., there were cases of the *choregos* playing the flute in person. Cf. what Professor Murray says in his *Euripides*, p. xxi: "There has been, perhaps, no period in the world's history, not even the openings of the French Revolution, when the prospects of the human race can have

rejection, when men were better able to judge what tended to promote goodness and what did not, and in the same way they came to reject many of the ancient instruments, such as the *pektis* and the *barbitos* and all that tend only to produce pleasure in the hearers, such as the *heptagon*, the *triangle*, and the *sambuca*[1], and all that require scientific manipulation. There is a moral too in the ancient fable about the flute, which tells how Athena invented it and then threw it away. It is not amiss to say that what made the goddess dislike it was the way it distorted the face, but it is perhaps even better to say it was because learning to play the flute does no good to the mind; for we ascribe science and art to Athena.

Accordingly we reject professional instruments and professional execution,—and by professional we mean that which has public performances in view; for in this case the performer practises the art, not with a view to his own advancement in goodness, but with the view of giving pleasure to the audience, and that a vulgar pleasure. That is why we do not regard the execution of such music as fit for freemen, but as servile, and we find that the performers become mechanical; for the aim which they adopt as their end is a bad one. The audience is vulgar and tends to lower the music. It even gives its own character to the performers themselves, and actually affects

appeared so brilliant as they did to the highest minds of Eastern Greece about the years 470—445 B.C. To us, looking critically back upon that time, it is as though the tree of human life had burst suddenly into flower, into that exquisite and short-lived bloom which seems so disturbing among the ordinary processes of historical growth. One wonders how it must have felt to the men who lived in it. We have but little direct testimony.... In the main the men of that day were too busy, one would fain think too happy, to write books." Aristotle is far removed from the spirit of those "spacious times," but there is a touch of restrained enthusiasm in the way he speaks of them all the same.

[1] These were all complicated instruments, mostly of Asiatic origin.

their bodies through the motions which it expects from them.

That being so, we have still to consider scales and rhythms. Are we to make use of all scales and rhythms in education or are we to make a classification? And are we to make the same classification for those who are engaged in educational work or a different one? We see that music is produced by melody and rhythm, and we must be clear as to the educational influence of each of these, and whether we ought to prefer melodious music or rhythmical for this purpose. Now we believe that some of the musicians of the present day treat this subject very well, and also such philosophers as have had experience in musical education[1]; we shall therefore refer those who wish a full and minute discussion to them. We shall only speak of it for form's sake, giving the outlines only.

We accept the classification of melodies given by some philosophers into melodies of character, melodies of action, and orgiastic melodies. They say further that each of these has a scale which naturally corresponds to it. We say, however, that music is to be studied for the sake of many benefits and not of one only. It is to be studied with a view to education, with a view to purgation,—we use this term without explanation for the present; when we come to speak of poetry, we shall give a clearer account of it[2],—and thirdly

---

[1] As Plato says, "Let us refer these matters to Damon."

[2] Unfortunately the part of the *Poetics* where the doctrine of "purgation" was fully explained has not come down to us. Owing to the great authority which this work has enjoyed the subject has been discussed in many writers. Lessing was practically the first to see that it meant something more than a mere "purification of the feelings by pity and terror," but even he did not succeed in coming anywhere near to the real meaning. There is still much controversy as to the details of the theory, but its main outlines may be regarded as firmly established, and they must be given here as they are of fundamental importance in the theory of education.

Aristoxenos, who was personally acquainted with the last survivors of

with a view to the right use of leisure and for relaxation and rest after exertion. It is clear, then, that we must use all the scales, but not all in the same way. For educational purposes

the school, tells us that the Pythagoreans used medicine to purge their bodies and music to purge their souls. There is no doubt that the word *katharsis* is a medical term, and that it means a "purge." Aristotle is always strongly influenced by the medical associations of the terms he uses, and it is clear that this was what the word meant to him first and foremost. It was also used, however, in a religious sense of all ritual purifications intended to produce ceremonial "cleanness." The reference here to the Corybàntic orgies, with which the flute music of Olympos was associated (cf. p. 117, n. 1), seems to show that this idea was not absent from Aristotle's mind either. It was a fact of experience that persons who suffered from an excess of wild religious emotion could be cured, as it were, homoeopathically. If they were systematically roused up to frenzy by the wild strains of the flute, the result was that they worked off their surplus emotion and were restored to a calm and normal condition. Here Aristotle tells us that this is only an extreme case of what we find everywhere else. We are all, in a greater or less degree, susceptible to feelings like pity and fear, and these may easily accumulate in us and lead to a morbid sentimentalism which is inconsistent with the requirements of the good life. If, however, by means of music or any other art, these emotions can be systematically stirred up, they find a natural outlet in that way, and we are at once alleviated. When we see a great tragedy, our accumulations of emotion are all discharged upon a great and worthy object instead of forming a constant source of weakness in our own lives. So far, I think, we may safely go in the interpretation of Aristotle's theory. It is his answer to Plato's Puritanism, and is obviously a conception of the highest paedagogic value. It is worthy of note that Milton, in the Preface to *Samson Agonistes*, comes very near to the modern interpretation. He says: "Tragedy, as it was anciently composed, hath been ever held the gravest, moralest, and most profitable of all other poems; therefore said by Aristotle to be of power, by raising pity and fear, or terrour, to purge the mind of these and suchlike passions; that is to temper or reduce them to just measure with a kind of delight stirred up by reading or seeing those passages well imitated. Nor is Nature herself wanting in her own efforts to make good his assertion, for so, in physick, things of melancholick hue and quality are used against melancholy, sour against sour, salt to remove salt humours." On the whole subject see Butcher, *Aristotle's Theory of Poetry and Fine Art*, Chapter VI.

we must use those that best express character, but we may use melodies of action and enthusiastic melodies for concerts where other people perform. For every feeling that affects some souls violently affects all souls more or less; the difference is only one of degree. Take pity and fear, for example, or again enthusiasm. Some people are liable to become possessed by the latter emotion, but we see that, when they have made use of the melodies which fill the soul with orgiastic feeling, they are brought back by these sacred melodies to a normal condition as if they had been medically treated and taken a purge. Those who are subject to the emotions of pity and fear and the feelings generally will necessarily be affected in the same way; and so will other men in exact proportion to their susceptibility to such emotions. All experience a certain purgation and pleasant relief. In the same manner purgative melodies give innocent joy to men. Such, then, are the scales and melodies we must prescribe for professional performers in the theatre to employ in their performances. As, however, there are two kinds of audiences, one of free and educated men, the other a vulgar crowd of mechanics, day-labourers and the like, we must appoint competitions and spectacles for the latter class too with a view to relaxation and rest. In these the melodies and scales will correspond to the audience. Just as their souls are distorted from their natural condition, so there are some scales which are unnatural and melodies which are high-pitched and unnaturally coloured. Now that which is appropriate to his own nature is what produces pleasure in every man, and so we must allow public performers to employ this kind of music with audiences of a lower type[1]. For educational purposes, however, as has been

---

[1] This is not, as might be supposed, an apology for the Music Hall. Aristotle would doubtless have held that the sort of music that prevails there did represent character, only that the character was bad. It would correspond to the painting of Pauson. The curious point is this. The

said, we must only use melodies and scales that express character. Such a scale is the Dorian, as was remarked above; and we must also admit any others that are approved by those who have been initiated both into philosophy and the study of music. The Socrates of the *Republic* is wrong in leaving only the Phrygian scale along with the Dorian, and that too after rejecting the flute; for the Phrygian scale has exactly the same effect among scales as the flute among instruments. Both are orgiastic and express emotion. This is proved by actual compositions. All Bacchic frenzy and emotions of a similar character are adapted to the flute above all other instruments, and find their appropriate expression in the Phrygian above all other scales. For instance the dithyramb[1] is admittedly in the Phrygian scale, a fact of which musical connoisseurs give many proofs, among others that Philoxenos, when he tried to compose his dithyramb, "The Mysians," in the Dorian mode, found it impossible, and was driven back by nature herself into the appropriate scale, the Phrygian. But all men agree that the Dorian scale is the most stately and most manly. And again, we say that the mean between two extremes is to be praised and sought after, and that is just the natural relation of the Dorian to the other scales, so it is evident that the Dorian is the most appropriate scale for the education of the young[2].

sort of compositions which he recommends for the relaxation of "a crowd of day-labourers" is precisely the most artificial, that which deals in quarter-tones, diminished sevenths, and eccentric varieties of the chromatic and diatonic scales. If we want a modern parallel, it would almost be fair to say that Aristotle suggests that such music as Wagner's may be tolerated as affording relaxation to the overstrained, but that, for the right enjoyment of leisure by the truly cultured, we require something of a more classical type.

[1] Originally a hymn in honour of Dionysos, but the name was used at a later date for any elaborate lyrical composition of what we should call an operatic character.

[2] Milton has expressed the Greek feeling about the Dorian mode, the

The Politics *of Aristotle.*

Aristotle's discussion of Education ends here. The ending is abrupt, and it is clear that much has been lost. A later writer has added another short section, which I omit[1].

old national minor scale of the Greeks, in *Paradise Lost*, Book I. 250 ff. It is interesting to find the doctrine of the mean applied to it. The Phrygian and Lydian scales were rudimentary major modes, pitched higher and lower than the Dorian, which alone seemed natural.

[1] Even the account of music is not complete; for nothing has been said yet of rhythm. What is still more unfortunate, we have nothing from Aristotle as to the training of the mind directly and not through the feelings. As Mr Newman points out, "Our latest glimpse of the youthful object of Aristotle's care is obtained at the moment when at the age of 19 or there-abouts he is committed for the first time to the tender mercies of the sterner form of gymnastics, and left, we do not exactly know for what period, but probably till the age of 21, in the hands of the gymnastic trainer."

Jean Jacques Rousseau, EMILE (Trans. by Barbara Foxley)

1. According to Rousseau, what is the meaning of education?

2. Define communal education and domestic education. Which does Rousseau consider the most desirable? Do you agree or disagree? Why?

3. Do Rousseau and Dewey agree on the subject of discipline of the child? Explain.

4. Define what Rousseau means by:
   a. the law of necessity
   b. negative education
   c. the principle of utility

5. What would be the curriculum for Emile up to age eighteen? How would the various subjects be taught?

6. Which book would be the first to be read by Emile? Why do you think Rousseau selected this particular book for Emile?

7. Which trade would Rousseau choose for Emile? Why? Does he consider this the main apprecticeship for Emile? Explain.

8. How does Emile's education change at age twenty?

9. What is Rousseau's remedy for vanity? How would he prevent Emile from acquiring this undesirable trait? What do you think about this type of cure?

10. Is religion a part of Emile's education? If so, when would it begin and how would it be acquired? If not, how does Rousseau explain this?

11. What does Rousseau say about the value of the classics? How would Emile acquire his taste in literature and arts?

Jean Jacques Rousseau (1712-1778) believed in the natural goodness of men and that education (and political institutions) often made men evil and thus needed to be reformed. In *Emile* (1762), Rousseau described in detail the kind of education which he thought would be desirable. All kinds of people began educating Emiles after this pattern. As a consequence, education was given a completely different direction.

Since its first appearance, *Emile* has been highly controversial among parents and educators. It was burned in Paris and Geneva, but Kant noted that no other book had moved him more deeply, and Goethe said that it should be "the teacher's gospel".

Professor William Boyd, while disagreeing at a number of points, wrote, "I believe...that the *Emile* with all its faults is the most profound modern discussion of the fundamentals of education, the only modern work of the kind worthy to be put alongside *The Republic* of Plato."

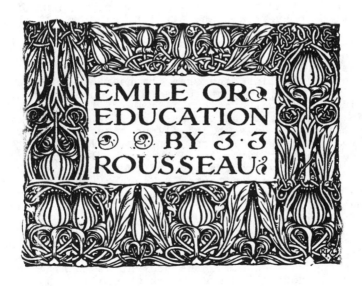

With our foolish and pedantic methods we are always preventing children from learning what they could
learn much better by themselves, while we neglect what
we alone can teach them. Can anything be sillier than
the pains taken to teach them to walk, as if there were
anyone who was unable to walk when he grows up through
his nurse's neglect? How many we see walking badly all
their life because they were ill taught?

. . . . .

As their strength increases, children have also
less need for tears. They can do more for themselves,
they need the help of others less frequently. With
strength comes the sense to use it. It is with this
second phase that the real personal life has its beginning; it is then that the child becomes conscious of
himself. During every moment of his life memory calls
up the feeling of self; he becomes really one person,
always the same, and therefore capable of joy or sorrow.
Hence we must begin to consider him as a moral being.

. . . . .

Men, be kind to your fellow-men; this is your first
duty, kind to every age and station, kind to all that
is not foreign to humanity. What wisdom can you find
that is greater than kindness? Love childhood, indulge
its sports, its pleasures, its delightful instincts.
Who has not sometimes regretted that age when laughter
was ever on the lips, and when the heart was ever at
peace? Why rob these innocents of the joys which pass
so quickly, of that precious gift which they cannot a-
buse? Why fill with bitterness the fleeting days of
early childhood, days which will no more return for
them than for you? Fathers, can you tell when death
will call your children to him? Do not lay up sorrow
for yourselves by robbing them of the short span which
nature has allotted to them. As soon as they are aware
of the joy of life, let them rejoice in it, so that
whenever God calls them they may not die without having
tasted the joy of life.

How people will cry out against you! I hear from
afar the shouts of that false wisdom which is ever drag-
ging us onwards, counting the present as nothing, and
pursuing without a pause a future which flies as we
pursue, that false wisdom which removes us from our
place and never brings us to any other.

Now is the time, you say, to correct his evil tendencies; we must increase suffering in childhood, when
it is less keenly felt, to lessen it in manhood. But
how do you know that you can carry out all these fine
schemes; how do you know that all this fine teaching
with which you overwhelm the feeble mind of the child
will not do him more harm than good in the future? How
do you know that you can spare him anything by the vex-
ations you heap upon him now? Why inflict on him more
ills than befit his present condition unless you are
quite sure that these present ills will save him future
ill? And what proof can you give me that those evil
tendencies you profess to cure are not the result of
your foolish precautions rather than of nature? What a
poor sort of foresight, to make a child wretched in the
present with the more or less doubtful hope of making
him happy at some future day. If such blundering thinkers fail to distinguish between liberty and licence,
between a merry child and a spoilt darling, let them
learn to discriminate.

Let us not forget what befits our present state in
the pursuit of vain fancies. Mankind has its place in
the sequence of things; childhood has its place in the
sequence of human life; the man must be treated as a
man and the child as a child. Give each his place, and
keep him there. Control human passions according to
man's nature; that is all we can do for his welfare.
The rest depends on external forces, which are beyond
our control.

Absolute good and evil are unknown to us. In this
life they are blended together; we never enjoy any perfectly pure feeling, nor do we remain for more than a
moment in the same state. The feelings of our minds,
like the changes in our bodies, are in a continual flux.
Good and ill are common to all, but in varying proportions. The happiest is he who suffers least; the most
miserable is he who enjoys least. Ever more sorrow
than joy - this is the lot of all of us. Man's happiness in this world is but a negative state; it must be
reckoned by the fewness of his ills.

Every feeling of hardship is inseparable from the
desire to escape from it; every idea of pleasure from
the desire to enjoy it. All desire implies a want, and
all wants are painful; hence our wretchedness consists
in the disproportion between our desires and our powers.

A conscious being whose powers were equal to his desires would be perfectly happy.

What then is human wisdom? Where is the path of true happiness? The mere limitation of our desires is not enough, for if they were less than our powers, part of our faculties would be idle, and we should not enjoy our whole being; neither is the mere extension of our powers enough, for if our desires were also increased we should only be more miserable. True happiness consists in decreasing the difference between our desires and our powers, in establishing perfect equilibrium between the power and the will. Then only, when all its forces are employed, will the soul be at rest and man will find himself in his true position.

. . . . . .

There is only one man who gets his own way - he who can get it single-handed; therefore freedom, not power, is the greatest good. That man is truly free who desires what he is able to perform, and does what he desires. This is my fundamental maxim. Apply it to childhood, and all the rules of education spring from it.

. . . . . .

There are two kinds of dependence: dependence on things, which is the work of nature; and dependence on men, which is the work of society. Dependence on things, being non-moral, does no injury to liberty and begets no vices; dependence on men, being out of order, gives rise to every kind of vice, and through this master and slave become mutually depraved. If there is any cure for this social evil, it is to be found in the substitution of law for the individual; in arming the general will with a real strength beyond the power of any individual will. If the laws of nations, like the laws of nature, could never be broken by any human power, dependence on men would become dependence on things; all the advantages of a state of nature would be combined with all the advantages of social life in the commonwealth. The liberty which preserves a man from vice would be united with the morality which raises him to virtue.

Keep the child dependent on things only. By this course of education you will have followed the order of nature. Let his unreasonable wishes meet with physical obstacles only, or the punishment which results from his own actions, lessons which will be recalled when the same circumstances occur again. It is enough to prevent him from wrong doing without forbidding him to do wrong. Experience or lack of power should take the place of law. Give him, not what he wants, but what he needs. Let there be no question of obedience for him or tyranny for you. Supply the strength he lacks just so far as is required for freedom, not for power, so that he may receive your services with a sort of shame, and look forward to the time when he may dispense with them and may achieve the honour of self-help.

Nature provides for the child's growth in her own fashion, and this should never be thwarted. Do not make him sit still when he wants to run about, nor run when he wants to be quiet. If we did not spoil our children's wills by our blunders their desires would be free from caprice. Let them run, jump, and shout to their heart's content. All their own activities are instincts of the body for its growth in strength; but you should regard with suspicion those wishes which they cannot carry out for themselves, those which others must carry out for them. Then you must distinguish carefully between natural and artificial needs, between the needs of budding caprice and the needs which spring from the overflowing life just described.

. . . . . .

There is such a thing as excessive severity as well as excessive indulgence, and both alike should be avoided. If you let children suffer you risk their health and life; you make them miserable now; if you take too much pains to spare them every kind of uneasiness you are laying up much misery for them in the future; you are making them delicate and over-sensitive; you are taking them out of their place among men, a place to which they must sooner or later return, in spite of all your pains. You will say I am falling into the same mistake as those bad fathers whom I blamed for sacrificing the present happiness of their children to a future which may never be theirs.

Not so; for the liberty I give my pupil makes up for the slight hardships to which he is exposed. I see

little fellows playing in the snow, stiff and blue with
cold, scarcely able to stir a finger. They could go
and warm themselves if they chose, but they do not choose;
if you forced them to come in they would feel the harshness of constraint a hundredfold more than the sharpness of the cold. Then what becomes of your grievance?
Shall I make your child miserable by exposing him to
hardships which he is perfectly ready to endure? I
secure his present good by leaving him his freedom, and
his future good by arming him against the evils he will
have to bear. If he had his choice, would he hesitate
for a moment between you and me?

Do you think any man can find true happiness elsewhere than in his natural state; and when you try to
spare him all suffering, are you not taking him out of
his natural state? Indeed I maintain that to enjoy
great happiness he must experience slight ills; such is
his nature. Too much bodily prosperity corrupts the
morals. A man who knew nothing of suffering would be
incapable of tenderness towards his fellow-creatures
and ignorant of the joys of pity; he would be hard-
hearted, unsocial, a very monster among men.

Do you know the surest way to make your child
miserable? Let him have everything he wants; for as
his wants increase in proportion to the ease with which
they are satisfied, you will be compelled, sooner or
later, to refuse his demands, and this unlooked-for refusal will hurt him more than the lack of what he wants.
He will want your stick first, then your watch, the
bird that flies, or the star that shines above him. He
will want all he sets eyes on, and unless you were God
himself, how could you satisfy him?

Man naturally considers all that he can get as his
own. In this sense Hobbes' theory is true to a certain
extent: Multiply both our wishes and the means of satisfying them, and each will be master of all. Thus the
child, who has only to ask and have, thinks himself the
master of the universe; he considers all men as his
slaves; and when you are at last compelled to refuse,
he takes your refusal as an act of rebellion, for he
thinks he has only to command. All the reasons you
give him, while he is still too young to reason, are
so many pretences in his eyes; they seem to him only
unkindness; the sense of injustice embitters his dis-

position; he hates every one. Though he has never felt grateful for kindness, he resents all opposition.

How should I suppose that such a child can ever be happy? He is the slave of anger, a prey to the fiercest passions. Happy! He is a tyrant, at once the basest of slaves and the most wretched of creatures. I have known children brought up like this who expected you to knock the house down, to give them the weather cock on the steeple, to stop a regiment on the march so that they might listen to the band; when they could not get their way they screamed and cried and would pay no attention to any one. In vain everybody strove to please them; as their desires were stimulated by the ease with which they got their own way, they set their hearts on impossibilities, and found themselves face to face with opposition and difficulty, pain and grief. Scolding, sulking, or in a rage, they wept and cried all day. Were they really so greatly favoured? Weakness, combined with love of power, produces nothing but folly and suffering. One spoilt child beats the table; another whips the sea. They may beat and whip long enough before they find contentment.

. . . . . .

Let us come back to the primitive law. Nature has made children helpless and in need of affection; did she make them to be obeyed and feared? Has she given them an imposing manner, a stern eye, a loud and threatening voice with which to make themselves feared? I understand how the roaring of the lion strikes terror into the other beasts, so that they tremble when they behold his terrible mane, but of all unseemly, hateful, and ridiculous sights, was there ever anything like a body of statesmen in their robes of office with their chief at their head bowing down before a swaddled babe, addressing him in pompous phrases, while he cries and slavers in reply?

. . . . . .

On the other hand, do you not see how children are fettered by the weakness of infancy? Do you not see how cruel it is to increase this servitude by obedience to our caprices, by depriving them of such liberty as they have, a liberty which they can scarcely abuse, a liberty the loss of which will do so little good to them

or us. If there is nothing more ridiculous than a
haughty child, there is nothing that claims our pity
like a timid child. With the age of reason the child
becomes the slave of the community; then why forestall
this by slavery in the home? Let this brief hour of
life be free from a yoke which nature has not laid upon
it; leave the child the use of his natural liberty,
which for a time at least, secures him from the vices
of the slave. Bring me those harsh masters, and those
fathers who are the slaves of their children, bring
them both with their frivolous objections, and before
they boast of their own methods let them for once learn
the method of nature.

I return to practical matters. I have already said
your child must not get what he asks, but what he needs;
he must never act from obedience, but from necessity.

The very words *obey* and *command* will be excluded
from his vocabulary, still more those of *duty* and *obligation;* but the words strength, necessity, weakness,
and constraint must have a large place in it. Before
the age of reason it is impossible to form any idea of
moral beings or social relations; so avoid, as far as
may be, the use of words which express these ideas,
lest the child at an early age should attach wrong ideas
to them, ideas which you cannot or will not destroy
when he is older. The first mistaken idea he gets into
his head is the germ of error and vice; it is the first
step that needs watching. Act in such a way that while
he only notices external objects his ideas are confined
to sensations; let him only see the physical world
around him. If not, you may be sure that either he
will pay no heed to you at all, or he will form fantastic ideas of the moral world of which you prate, ideas
which you will never efface as long as he lives.

"Reason with children" was Locke's chief maxim; it
is in the height of fashion at present, and I hardly
think it is justified by its results; those children
who have been constantly reasoned with strike me as exceedingly silly. Of all man's faculties, reason, which
is, so to speak, compounded of all the rest, is the last
and choicest growth, and it is this you would use for
the child's early training. To make a man reasonable
is the coping stone of a good education, and yet you
profess to train a child through his reason! You begin
at the wrong end, you make the end the means. If chil-

dren understood reason they would not need education,
but by talking to them from their earliest age in a
language they do not understand you accustom them to
be satisfied with words, to question all that is said
to them, to think themselves as wise as their teachers;
you train them to be argumentative and rebellious; and
whatever you think you gain from motives of reason, you
really gain from greediness, fear, or vanity with which
you are obliged to reinforce your reasoning.

Most of the moral lessons which are and can be
given to children may be reduced to this formula:
Master. You must not do that.
Child. Why not?
Master. Because it is wrong.
Child. Wrong! What is wrong?
Master. What is forbidden you.
Child. Why is it wrong to do what is forbidden?
Master. You will be punished for disobedience.
Child. I will do it when no one is looking.
Master. We shall watch you.
Child. I will hide.
Master. We shall ask you what you were doing.
Child. I shall tell a lie.
Master. You must not tell lies.
Child. Why must not I tell lies?
Master. Because it is wrong, etc.

That is the inevitable circle. Go beyond it, and
the child will not understand you. What sort of use is
there in such teaching? I should greatly like to know
what you would substitute for this dialogue. It would
have puzzled Locke himself. It is no part of a child's
business to know right and wrong, to perceive the reason for a man's duties.

Nature would have them children before they are
men. If we try to invert this order we shall produce
a forced fruit immature and flavorless, fruit which
will be rotten before it is ripe; we shall have young
doctors and old children. Childhood has its own ways of
seeing, thinking, and feeling; nothing is more foolish
than to try and substitute our ways; and I should no
more expect judgment in a ten-year-old child than I
should expect him to be five feet high. Indeed, what
use would reason be to him at that age? It is the curb
of strength, and the child does not need the curb.

. . . . . .

Treat your scholar according to his age. Put him in his place from the first, and keep him in it, so that he no longer tries to leave it. Then before he knows what goodness is, he will be practicing its chief lesson. Give him no orders at all, absolutely none. Do not even let him think that you claim any authority over him. Let him only know that he is weak and you are strong, that his condition and yours puts him at your mercy; let this be perceived, learned and felt. Let him early find upon his proud neck, the heavy yoke which nature has imposed upon us, the heavy yoke of necessity, under which every finite being must bow. Let him find this necessity in things, not in the caprices of man; let the curb be force, not authority. If there is something he should not do, do not forbid him, but prevent him without explanation or reasoning; what you give him, give it at his first word without prayers or entreatries, above all without conditions. Give willingly, refuse unwillingly, but let your refusal be irrevocable; let no entreaties move you; let your "No," once uttered, be a wall of brass, against which the child may exhaust his strength some five or six times, but in the end he will try no more to overthrow it.

. . . . . .

It is very strange that ever since people began to think about education they should have hit upon no other way of guiding children than emulation, jealousy, envy, vanity, greediness, base cowardice, all the most dangerous passions, passions ever ready to ferment, ever prepared to corrupt the soul even before the body is full-grown. With every piece of precocious instruction which you try to force into their minds you plant a vice in the depths of their hearts; foolish teachers think they are doing wonders when they are making their scholars wicked in order to teach them what goodness is, and then they tell us seriously, "Such is man." Yes, such is man, as you have made him. Every means has been tried except one, the very one which might succeed - well-regulated liberty.

. . . . . .

Give your scholar no verbal lessons; he should be taught by experience alone; never punish him, for he does not know what it is to do wrong; never make him say, "Forgive me," for he does not know how to do you wrong. Wholly unmoral in his actions, he can do nothing morally wrong, and he deserves neither punishment nor reproof.

.   .   .   .   .   .

Let us lay it down as an incontrovertible rule that the first impulses of nature are always right; there is no original sin in the human heart, the how and why of the entrance of every vice can be traced. The only natural passion is self-love or selfishness taken in a wider sense. This selfishness is good in itself and in relation to ourselves; and as the child has no necessary relations to other people he is naturally indifferent to them; his self-love only becomes good or bad by the use made of it and the relations established by its means. Until the time is ripe for the appearance of reason, that guide of selfishness, the main thing is that the child shall do nothing because you are watching him or listening to him; in a word, nothing because of other people, but only what nature asks of him; then he will never do wrong.

I do not mean to say that he will never do any mischief, never hurt himself, never break a costly ornament if you leave it within his reach. He might do much damage without doing wrong, since wrong-doing depends on the harmful intention which will never be his. If once he meant to do harm, his whole education would be ruined; he would be almost hopelessly bad.

.   .   .   .   .   .

But if, in spite of your precautions, the child contrives to do some damage, if he breaks some useful article, do not punish him for your carelessness, do not even scold him; let him hear no word of reproval, do not even let him see that he has vexed you; behave just as if the thing had come to pieces of itself; you may consider you have done great things if you have managed to hold your tongue.

May I venture at this point to state the greatest, the most important, the most useful rule of education? It is: Do not save time, but lose it. I hope that every day readers will excuse my paradoxes; you cannot avoid paradox if you think for yourself, and whatever you may say I would rather fall into paradox than into prejudice. The most dangerous period in human life

lies between birth and the age of twelve. It is the
time when errors and vices spring up, while as yet there
is no means to destroy them; when the means of destruction are ready, the roots have gone too deep to be
pulled up. If the infant sprang at one bound from its
mother's breast to the age of reason, the present type
of education would be quite suitable, but its natural
growth calls for quite a different training. The mind
should be left undisturbed till its faculties have developed; for while it is blind it cannot see the torch
you offer it, nor can it follow through the vast ex-
panse of ideas a path so faintly traced by reason that
the best eyes can scarcely follow it.

Therefore the education of the earliest years
should be merely negative. It consists, not in teaching virtue or truth, but in preserving the heart from
vice and from the spirit of error. If only you could
let well alone, and get others to follow your example;
if you could bring your scholar to the age of twelve
strong and healthy, but unable to tell his right hand
from his left, the eyes of his understanding would be
open to reason as soon as you began to teach him. Free
from prejudices and free from habits, there would be
nothing in him to counteract the effects of your labours. In your hands he would soon become the wisest of
men; by doing nothing to begin with, you would end with
a prodigy of education.

Reverse the usual practice and you will almost always do right. Fathers and teachers who want to make
the child, not a child but a man of learning, think it
never too soon to scold, correct, reprove, threaten,
bribe, teach, and reason. Do better than they; be
reasonable, and do not reason with your pupil, more
especially do not try to make him approve what he dislikes; for if reason is always connected with disagreeable matters, you make it distasteful to him, you dis-
credit it at an early age in a mind not yet ready to
understand it. Exercise his body, his limbs, his senses,
his strength, but keep his mind idle as long as you can.
Distrust all opinions which appear before the judgment
to discriminate between them. Restrain and ward off
strange impressions; and to prevent the birth of evil
do not hasten to do well for goodness is only possible
when enlightened by reason. Regard all delays as so
much time gained; you have achieved much, you approach
the boundary without loss. Leave childhood to ripen

in your children. In a word, beware of giving anything they need today if it can be deferred without danger to tomorrow.

There is another point to be considered which confirms tho suitability of this method. it is the child's individual bent, which must be thoroughly known before we can choose the fittest moral training. Every mind has its own form, in accordance with which it must be controlled; and the success of the pains taken depends largely on the fact that he is controlled in this way and no other. Oh, wise men, take time to observe nature; watch your scholar well before you say a word to him; first leave the germ of his character free to show itself, do not constrain him in anything, the better to see him as he really is. Do you think this time of liberty is wasted? On the contrary, your scholar will be the better employed, for this is the way you yourself will learn not to lose a single moment when time is of more value. If, however, you begin to act before you know what to do, you act at random; you may make mistakes, and must retrace your steps; your haste to reach your goal will only take you further from it. Do not imitate the miser who loses much lest he should lose a little. Sacrifice a little time in early childhood, and it will be repaid you with usury when your scholar is older.

. . . . . .

Remember you must be a man yourself before you try to train a man; you yourself must set the pattern he shall copy. While the child is still unconscious there is time to prepare his surroundings, so that nothing shall strike his eye but what is fit for his sight. Gain the respect of every one, begin to win their hearts, so that they may try to please you. You will not be master of the child if you cannot control everyone about him; and this authority will never suffice unless it rests upon respect for your goodness. There is no question of squandering one's means and giving money right and left; I never knew money to win love. You must neither be harsh nor niggardly, nor must you merely pity misery when you can relieve it; but in vain will you open your purse if you do not open your heart along with it, the hearts of others will always be closed to you. You must give your own time, attention, affection,

your very self; for whatever you do, people always perceive that your money is not you.

. . . . .

In the village a tutor will have much more control
over the things he wishes to show the child; his reputation, his words, his example, will have a weight they
would never have in the town; he is of use to everyone,
so everyone is eager to oblige him, to win his esteem,
to appear before the disciple what the master would
have him be; if vice is not corrected, public scandal
is at least avoided, which is all that our present purpose requires.

. . . . . .

Zealous teachers, be simple, sensible, and reti-
cent; be in no hurry to act unless to prevent the actions
of others. Again and again I say, reject, if it may be, a
good lesson for fear of giving a bad one.   Beware of
playing the tempter in this world, which nature intended
as an earthly paradise for men, and do not attempt to
give the innocent child the knowledge of good and evil;
since you cannot prevent the child learning by what he
sees outside himself, restrict your own efforts to im-
pressing those examples on his mind in the form best
suited for him.

The explosive passions produce a great effect upon
the child when he sees them; their outward expression
is very marked; he is struck by this and his attention
is arrested.   Anger especially is so noisy in its rage
that it is impossible not to perceive it if you are
within reach.   You need not ask yourself whether this
is an opportunity for a pedagogue to frame a fine disquisition.   What! No fine disquisition, nothing, not a
word!   Let the child come to you; impressed by what he
has seen, he will not fail to ask you questions.   The
answer is easy; it is drawn from the very things which
have appealed to his senses.   He sees a flushed face,
flashing eyes, threatening gestures, he hears cries;
everything shows that the body is ill at ease. Tell him
plainly, without affectation or mystery, "This poor man
is ill, he is in a fever."   You may take the opportunity
of giving him in a few words some idea of disease and
its effects; for that too belongs to nature, and is one
of the bonds of necessity which he must recognize.   By

means of this idea, which is not false in itself, may he not early acquire a certain aversion to giving way to excessive passions, which he regards as diseases; and do you not think that such a notion, given at the right moment, will produce a more wholesome effect than the most tedious sermon? But consider the aftereffects of this idea; you have authority, if ever you find it necessary to treat the rebellious child as a sick child; to keep him in his room, in bed if need be, to diet him, to make him afraid of his growing vices, to make him hate and dread them without ever regarding as a punishment the strict measures you will perhaps have to use for his recovery. If it happens that you yourself in a moment's heat depart from the calm and self-control which you should aim at, do not try to conceal your fault, but tell him frankly, with a gentle reproach, "My dear, you have hurt me."

. . . . . .

I do not propose to enter into every detail, but only to explain general rules and to give illustrations in cases of difficulty. I think it is impossible to train a child up to the age of twelve in the midst of society, without giving him some idea of the relations between one man and another, and of the morality of human actions. It is enough to delay the development of these ideas as long as possible, and when they can no longer be avoided to limit them to present needs, so that he may neither think himself master of everything nor do harm to others without knowing or caring. There are calm and gentle characters which can be led a long way in their first innocence without any danger; but there are also stormy dispositions whose passions develop early; you must hasten to make men of them lest you should have to keep them in chains.

Our first duties are to ourselves; our first feelings are centered on self; all our instincts are at first directed to our own preservation and our own welfare. Thus the first notion of justice springs not from what we owe to others, but from what is due to us. Here is another error in popular methods of education. If you talk to children of their duties, and not of their rights, you are beginning at the wrong end, and telling them what they cannot understand, what cannot be of any interest to them.

. . . . . .

Your ill-tempered child destroys everything he touches. Do not vex yourself; put anything he can spoil out of his reach. He breaks the things he is using; do not be in a hurry to give him more; let him feel the want of them. He breaks the windows of his room; let the wind blow upon him night and day, and do not be afraid of his catching cold; it is better to catch cold than to be reckless.

. . . . . .

I have already said enough to show that children should never receive punishment merely as such; it should always come as the natural consequence of their fault. Thus you will not exclaim against their false-hood, you will not exactly punish them for lying, but you will arrange that all the ill effects of lying, such as not being believed when we speak the truth, or being accused of what we have not done in spite of our pro-tests, shall fall on their heads when they have told a lie. But let us explain what lying means to the child.

There are two kinds of lies: one concerns an ac-complished fact, the other concerns a future duty. The first occurs when we falsely deny or assert that we did or did not do something, or to put it in general terms, when we knowingly say what is contrary to facts. The other occurs when we promise what we do not mean to perform, or in general terms, when we profess an inten-tion which we do not really mean to carry out. These two kinds of lie are sometimes found in combination, but their differences are my present business.

He who feels the need of help from others, he who is constantly experiencing their kindness, has nothing to gain by deceiving them; it is plainly to his advan-tage that they should see things as they are, lest they should mistake his interests. It is therefore plain that lying with regard to actual facts is not natural to children, but lying is made necessary by the law of obedience; since obedience is disagreeable, children disobey as far as they can in secret, and the present good of avoiding punishment or reproof outweighs the remoter good of speaking the truth. Under a free and natural education why should your child lie? What has he to conceal from you? You do not thrwart him, you do not punish him, you demand nothing from him. Why should he not tell everything to you as simply as to his playmate? He cannot see anything more risky in the one course than in the other.

The lie concerning duty is even less natural, since promises to do or refrain from doing are conventional agreements which are outside the state of nature and detract from our liberty. Moreover, all promises made by children are in themselves void; when they pledge themselves they do not know what they are doing, for their narrow vision cannot look beyond the present. A child can hardly lie when he makes a promise; for he is only thinking how he can get out of the present diffi- culty, any means which has not an immediate result is the same to him; when he promises for the future he promises nothing, and his imagination is as yet incapa- ble of projecting him into the future while he lives in the present. If he could escape a whipping or get a packet of sweets by promising to throw himself out of the window tomorrow, he would promise on the spot. This is why the law disregards all promises made by minors, and when fathers and teachers are stricter and demand that promises shall be kept, it is only when the prom- ise refers to something the child ought to do even if he had made no promise.

The child cannot lie when he makes a promise, for he does not know what he is doing when he makes his promise. The case is different when he breaks his prom- ise, which is a sort of retrospective falsehood; for he clearly remembers making the promise, but he fails to see the importance of keeping it. Unable to look into the future, he cannot forsee the results of things, and when he breaks his promises he does nothing con- trary to his stage of reasoning.

Children's lies are therefore entirely the work of their teachers, and to teach them to speak the truth is nothing less than to teach them the art of lying. In your zeal to rule, control, and teach them, you never find sufficient means at your disposal. You wish to gain fresh influence over their minds by baseless max- ims, by unreasonable precepts; and you would rather they knew their lessons and told lies, than leave them ignorant and truthful.

We, who only give our scholars lessons in practice, who prefer to have them good rather than clever, never demand the truth lest they should conceal it, and never

claim any promise lest they should be tempted to break
it. If some mischief has been done in my absence and I
do not know who did it, I shall take care not to accuse
Emile, nor to say, "Did you do it?" For in so doing
what should I do but teach him to deny it? If his difficult temperament compels me to make some agreement
with him, I will take good care that the suggestion always comes from him, never from me; that when he undertakes anything he has always a present and effective
interest in fulfilling his promise, and if he ever fails
this lie will bring down on him all the unpleasant consequences which he sees arising from the natural order
of things, and not from his tutor's vengeance.

· · · · · ·

The detailed treatment I have just given to lying
may be applied in many respects to all the other duties
imposed upon children, whereby these duties are made
not only hateful but impracticable. For the sake of a
show of preaching virtue you make them love every vice;
you instill these vices by forbidding them. Would you
have them pious, you take them to church till they are
sick of it; you teach them to gabble prayers until they
long for the happy time when they will not have to pray
to God. To teach them charity you make them give alms
as if you scorned to give yourself. It is not the child,
but the master, who should give; however much he loves
his pupil he should vie with him for this honour; he
should make him think that he is too young to deserve
it. Alms giving is the deed of a man who can measure
the worth of his gift and the needs of his fellow men.
The child, who knows nothing of these, can have no
merit in giving; he gives without charity, without
kindness; he is amost ashamed to give, for, to judge
by your practice and his own, he thinks it is only
children who give, and that there is no need for charity when we are grown up.

· · · · · ·

Silly children grow into ordinary men. I know no
generalization more certain than this. It is the most
difficult thing in the world to distinguish between
genuine stupidity, and that apparent and deceitful
stupidity which is the sign of a strong character. At
first sight it seems strange that the two extremes
should have the same outward signs; and yet it may

well be so, for at an age when man has as yet no true
ideas, the whole difference between the genius and the
rest consists in this: the latter only take in false
ideas, while the former, finding nothing but false
ideas, receives no ideas at all. In this he resembles
the fool, the one is fit for nothing, the other finds
nothing fit for him. The only way of distinguishing
between them depends upon chance, which may offer the
genius some idea which he can understand, while the
fool is always the same.

. . . . . .

Hold childhood in reverence, and do not be in any
hurry to judge it for good or ill. Leave exceptional
cases to show themselves, let their qualities be tested
and confirmed, before special methods are adopted. Give
nature time to work before you take over her business,
lest you interfere with her dealings. You assert that
you know the value of time and are afraid to waste it.
You fail to perceive that it is a greater waste of time
to use it ill than to do nothing, and that a child ill
taught is further from virtue than a child who has
learnt nothing at all. You are afraid to see him spending his early years doing nothing. What! Is it nothing
to be happy, nothing to run and jump all day? He will
never be so busy again all his life long. Plato, in
his *Republic*, which is considered so stern, teaches the
children only through festivals, games, songs, and
amusements. It seems as if he had accomplished his purpose when he had taught them to be happy; and Seneca,
speaking of the Roman lads in olden days, says, "They
were always on their feet, they were never taught anything which kept them sitting." Were they any the
worse for it in manhood? Do not be afraid, therefore,
of this so-called idleness. What would you think of a
man who refused to sleep lest he should waste part of
his life? You would say, "He is mad; he is not enjoying his life, he is robbing himself of part of it; to
avoid sleep he is hastening his death." Remember that
these two cases are alike, and that childhood is the
sleep of reason.

The apparent ease with which children learn is
their ruin. You fail to see that this very facility
proves that they are not learning. Their shining, pol-
ished brain reflects, as in a mirror, the things you
show them, but nothing sinks in. The child remembers

the words and the ideas are reflected back; his hearers understand them, but to him they are meaningless.

Although memory and reason are wholly different faculties, the one does not really develop apart from the other. Before the age of reason the child receives images, not ideas; and there is this difference between them: images are merely the pictures of external objects, while ideas are notions about those objects determined by their relations. An image when it is recalled may exist by itself in the mind, but every idea implies other ideas. When we image we merely perceive, when we reason we compare. Our sensations are merely passive, our notions or ideas spring from an active principle which judges. The proof of this will be given later.

I maintain, therefore, that as children are incapable of judging, they have no true memory. They retain sounds, form, sensation, but rarely ideas, and still more rarely relations. You tell me they acquire some rudiments of geometry, and you think you prove your case; not so, it is mine you prove; you show that far from being able to reason themselves, children are unable to retain the reasoning of others; for if you follow the method of these little geometricians you will see they only retain the exact impression of the figure and the terms of the demonstration. They cannot meet the slightest new objection; if the figure is reversed they can do nothing. All their knowledge is on the sensation level, nothing has penetrated to their understanding. Their memory is little better than their other powers, for they always have to learn over again, when they are grown up, what they learnt as children.

I am far from thinking, however, that children have no sort of reason. On the contrary, I think they reason very well with regard to things that affect their actual and sensible well-being. But people are mistaken as to the extent of their information, and they attribute to them knowledge they do not possess, and make them reason about things they cannot understand. Another mistake is to try to turn their attention to matters which do not concern them in the least, such as their future interest, their happiness when they are grown up, the opinion people will have of them when they are men - terms which are absolutely meaningless when addressed to creatures who are entirely without

foresight. But all the forced studies of these poor
little wretches are directed towards matters utterly
remote from their minds. You may judge how much attention they can give to them.

The pedagogues, who make a great display of the
teaching they give their pupils, are paid to say just
the opposite; yet their actions show that they think
just as I do. For what do they teach? Words! words!
words! Among the various sciences they boast of teaching their scholars, they take good care never to choose
those which might be really useful to them, for then
they would be compelled to deal with things and would
fail utterly; the sciences they choose are those we
seem to know when we know their technical terms - heraldry,
geography, chronology, languages, etc., studies so remote from man, and even more remote from the child,
that it is a wonder if he can ever make any use of any
part of them.

You will be surprised to find that I reckon the
study of languages among the useless lumber of education; but you must remember that I am speaking of the
studies of the earliest years, and whatever you may say,
I do not believe any child under twelve or fifteen ever
really acquired two languages.

If the study of languages were merely the study of
words, that is, of the symbols by which language expresses itself, then this might be a suitable study for
children; but languages, as they change the symbols,
also modify the ideas which the symbols express. Minds
are formed by language, thoughts take their colour from
its ideas. Reason alone is common to all. Every language has its own form, a difference which may be partly
cause and partly effect of differences in national
character; this conjecture appears to be confirmed by
the fact that in every nation under the sun speech follows the changes of manners, and is preserved or altered
along with them.

By use the child acquires one of these different
forms, and it is the only language he retains till the
age of reason. To acquire two languages he must be
able to compare their ideas, and how can he compare
ideas he can barely understand? Everything may have
a thousand meanings to him, but each idea can only have
one form, so he can only learn one language. You assure

me he learns several languages; I deny it. I have seen
those little prodigies who are supposed to speak half a
dozen languages. I have heard them speak first in German, then in Latin, French, or Italian; true, they used
half a dozen different vocabularies, but they always
spoke German. In a word, you may give children as many
synonyms as you like; it is not their language but their
words that you change; they will never have but one
language.

. . . . . .

In any study whatsoever the symbols are of no
value without the idea of the things symbolised. Yet
the education of the child is confined to those symbols, while no one ever succeeds in making him understand the thing signified. You think you are teaching
him what the world is like; he is only learning the
map; he is taught the names of towns, countries, rivers, which have no existence for him except on the paper
before him. I remember seeing a geography somewhere
which began with: "What is the world?" - "A sphere of
cardboard." That is the child's geography. I maintain
that after two years' work with the globe and cosmo-
graphy, there is not a single ten-year-old child who
could find his way from Paris to Saint Denis by the
help of the rules he has learnt. I maintain that not
one of these children could find his way by the map
about the paths on his father's estate without getting
lost. These are the young doctors who can tell us the
position of Pekin, Ispahan, Mexico, and every country
in the world.

You tell me the child must be employed on studies
which only need eyes. That may be; but if there are
any such studies, they are unknown to me.

It is a still more ridiculous error to set them to
study history, which is considered within their grasp
because it is merely a collection of facts. But what
is meant by this word "fact"? Do you think the relations which determine the facts of history are so easy
to grasp that the corresponding ideas are easily developed in the child's mind? Do you think that a real
knowledge of events can exist apart from the knowledge
of their causes and effects, and that history has so
little relation to words that the one can be learnt
without the other? If you perceive nothing in a man's

actions beyond merely physical and external movements,
what do you learn from history? Absolutely nothing;
while this study, robbed of all that makes it interesting, gives you neither pleasure nor information. If
you want to judge actions by their moral bearings, try
to make these moral bearings intelligible to your scholars. You will soon find out if they are old enough to
learn history.

. . . . . .

Such words as king, emperor, war, conquest, law,
and revolution are easily put into their mouths; but
when it is a question of attaching clear ideas to these
words the explanations are very different from our talk
with Robert the gardener.

. . . . . .

Without the study of books, such a memory as the
child may possess is not left idle; everything he sees
and hears makes an impression on him, he keeps a record
of men's sayings and doings, and his whole environment
is the book from which he unconsciously enriches his
memory, till his judgment is able to profit by it.

. . . . . .

All children learn La Fontaine's fables, but not
one of them understands them. It is just as well that
they do not understand, for the morality of the fables
is so mixed and so unsuitable for their age that it
would be more likely to incline them to vice than to
virtue. "More paradoxes!" you exclaim. Paradoxes they
may be; but let us see if there is not some truth in
them.

I maintain that the child does not understand the
fables he is taught, for however you try to explain
them, the teaching you wish to extract from them demands ideas which he cannot grasp, while the poetical
form which makes it easier to remember makes it harder
to understand, so that clearness is sacrificed to
facility.

. . . . . .

Let us make a bargain, M. de la Fontaine. For my part, I undertake to make your books my favorite study; I undertake to love you, and to learn from your fables, for I hope I shall not mistake their meaning. As to my pupil, permit me to prevent him studying any one of them till you have convinced me that it is good for him to learn things three-fourths of which are unintelligible to him, and until you can convince me that in those fables he can understand he will never reverse the order and imitate the villain instead of taking warning from his dupe.

When I thus get rid of children's lessons, I get rid of the chief cause of their sorrows, namely their books. Reading is the curse of childhood, yet it is almost the only occupation you can find for children. Emile, at twelve years old, will hardly know what a book is. "But," you say, "he must, at least, know how to read." When reading is of use to him, I admit he must learn to read, but till then he will only find it a nuisance.

. . . . . .

People make a great fuss about discovering the best way to teach children to read. They invent "bureaux" and cards, they turn the nursery into a printer's shop. Locke would have them taught to read by means of dice. What a fine idea! And the pity of it! There is a better way than any of those, and one which is generally overlooked - it consists in the desire to learn. Arouse this desire in your scholar and have done with your "bureaux" and your dice - any method will serve.

Present interest, that is the motive power, the only motive power that takes us far and safely. Sometimes Emile receives notes of invitation from his father or mother, his relations or friends; he is invited to a dinner, a walk, a boating expedition, to see some public entertainment. These notes are short, clear, plain, and well written. Some one must read them to him, and he cannot always find anybody when wanted; no more consideration is shown to him than he himself showed to you yesterday. Time passes, the chance is lost. The note is read to him at last, but it is too late. Oh! if only he had known how to read! He receives other notes, so short, so interesting, he would

like to try to read them. Sometimes he gets help, sometimes none. He does his best, and at last he makes out
half the note; it is something about going tomorrow to
drink cream - Where! With whom! He cannot tell - how
hard he tries to make out the rest! I do not think Emile
will need a "bureau." Shall I proceed to the teaching
of writing? No, I am ashamed to toy with these trifles
in a treatise on education.

I will just add a few words which contain a principle of great importance. It is this - What we are in
no hurry to get is usually obtained with speed and certainty. I am pretty sure Emile will learn to read and
write before he is ten, just because I care very little
whether he can do so before he is fifteen; but I would
rather he never learnt to read at all, than that this
art should be acquired at the price of all that makes
reading useful. What is the use of reading to him if
he always hates it?

BOOK III

Our island is this earth; and the most striking
object we behold is the sun. As soon as we pass beyond
our immediate surroundings, one or both of these must
meet our eye. Thus the philosophy of most savage races
is mainly directed to imaginary divisions of the earth
or to the divinity of the sun.

What a sudden change you will say. Just now we
were concerned with what touches ourselves, with our
immediate environment, and all at once we are exploring
the round world and leaping to the bounds of the universe. This change is the result of our growing strength
and of the natural bent of the mind. While we were
weak and feeble, self-preservation concentrated our attention on ourselves; now that we are strong and powerful, the desire for a wider sphere carries us beyond
ourselves as far as our eyes can reach. But as the
intellectual world is still unknown to us, our thoughts
are bounded by the visible horizon, and our understanding only develops within the limits of our vision.

Let us transform our sensations into ideas, but do
not let us jump all at once from the objects of sense
to objects of thought. The latter are attained by means

of the former. Let the senses be the only guide for
the first workings of reason. No book but the world,
no teaching but that of fact. The child, who reads
ceases to think, he only reads. He is acquiring words
not knowledge.

Teach your scholar to observe the phenomena of
nature; you will soon rouse his curiosity, but if you
would have it grow, do not be in too great a hurry to
satisfy this curiosity. Put the problems before him
and let him solve them himself. Let him know nothing
because you have told him, but because he has learnt it
for himself. Let him not be taught science, let him
discover it. If ever you substitute authority for reason he will cease to reason; he will be a mere play-
thing of other people's thought.

You wish to teach this child geography and you
provide him with globes, spheres, and maps. What elaborate preparations! What is the use of all these symbols; why not begin by showing him the real thing so
that he may at least know what you are talking about?

One fine evening we are walking in a suitable
place where the wide horizon gives us a full view of
the setting sun, and we note the objects which mark the
place where it sets. Next morning we return to the
same place for a breath of fresh air before sunrise.
We see the rays of light which announce the sun's approach; the glow increases, the east seems afire, and
long before the sun appears the light leads us to expect its return. Every moment you expect to see it.
There it is at last! A shining point appears like a
flash of lightning and soon fills the whole space; the
veil of darkness rolls away, man perceives his dwelling
place in fresh beauty. During the night the grass has
assumed a fresher green; in the light of early dawn,
and gilded by the first rays of the sun, it seems cov-
ered with a shining network of dew reflecting the light
and colour. The birds raise their chorus of praise to
greet the Father of life; not one of them is mute;
their gentle warbling is softer than by day, it expresses the langour of a peaceful waking. All these
produce an impression of freshness which seems to reach
the very soul. It is a brief hour of enchantment which
no man can resist; a sight so grand, so fair, so delicious, that none can behold it unmoved.

Fired with this enthusiasm, the master wishes to impart it to the child. He expects to rouse his emotion by drawing attention to his own. Mere folly! The splendor of nature lives in man's heart; to be seen, it must be felt. The child sees the objects themselves, but does not perceive their relations, and cannot hear their harmony. It needs knowledge he has not yet acquired, feelings he has not yet experienced, to receive the complex impression which results from all these separate sensations. If he has not wandered over arid plains, if his feet have not been scorched by the burning sands of the desert, if he has not breathed the hot and oppressive air reflected from the glowing rocks, how shall he delight in the fresh air of a fine morning? The scent of flowers, the beauty of foliage, the moistness of the dew, the soft turf beneath his feet, how shall all these delight his senses? How shall the song of the birds arouse voluptuous emotion if love and pleasure are still unknown to him? How shall he behold with rapture the birth of this fair day, if his imagination cannot paint the joys it may bring in its track? How can he feel the beauty of nature, while the hand that formed it is unknown?

Never tell the child what he cannot understand: no descriptions, no eloquence, no figures of speech, no poetry. The time has not come for feeling or taste. Continue to be clear and cold; the time will come only too soon when you must adopt another tone.

Brought up in the spirit of our maxims, accustomed to make his own tools and not to appeal to others until he has tried and failed, he will examine everything he sees carefully and in silence. He thinks rather than questions. Be content, therefore, to show him things at a fit season; then, when you see that his curiosity is thoroughly aroused, put some brief question which will set him trying to discover the answer.

. . . . . .

Should the method of studying science be analytic or synthetic? People dispute over this question, but it is not always necessary to choose between them. Sometimes the same experiments allow one to use both analysis and synthesis, and thus to guide the child by the method of instruction when he fancies he is only analysing. Then, by using both at once, each method

confirms the results of the other. Starting from opposite ends, without thinking of following the same
road, he will unexpectedly reach their meeting place
and this will be a delightful surprise. For example,
I would begin geography at both ends and add to the
study of the earth's revolution the measurement of its
divisions, beginning at home. While the child is studying the sphere and is thus transported to the heavens,
bring him back to the divisions of the globe and show
him his own home.

His geography will begin with the town he lives in
and his father's country house, then the places between
them, the rivers near them, and then the sun's aspect
and how to find one's way by its aid. This is the meeting place. Let him make his own map, a very simple
map, at first containing only two places; others may be
added from time to time, as he is able to estimate
their distance and position. You see at once what a
good start we have given him by making his eye his compass.

No doubt he will require some guidance in spite of
this, but very little, and that little without his
knowing it. If he goes wrong let him alone, do not
correct his mistakes; hold your tongue till he finds
them out for himself and corrects them, or at most arrange something, so opportunity offers, which may show
him his mistakes. If he never makes mistakes he will
never learn anything thoroughly. Moreover, what he
needs is not an exact knowledge of local topography,
but how to find out for himself. No matter whether
he carries maps in his head provided he understands
what they mean, and has a clear idea of the art of making them. See what a difference there is already between the knowledge of your scholars and the ignorance
of mine. They learn maps, he makes them. Here are
fresh ornaments for his room.

Remember that this is the essential point in my
method - Do not teach the child many things, but never
let him form inaccurate or confused ideas. I care
not if he knows nothing provided he is not mistaken,
and I only acquaint him with truths to guard him against
the errors he might put in their place. Reason and
judgment come slowly, prejudices flock to us in crowds,
and from these he must be protected. But if you make
science itself your object, you embark on an unfathom-

able and shoreless ocean, an ocean strewn with reefs from which you will never return. When I see a man in love with knowledge, yielding to its charms and flitting from one branch to another unable to stay his steps, he seems to me like a child gathering shells on the seashore, now picking them up, then throwing them aside for others which he sees beyond them, then taking them again, till overwhelmed by their number and unable to choose between them, he flings them all away and returns empty handed.

Time was long during early childhood; we only tried to pass our time for fear of using it ill; now it is the other way; we have not time enough for all that would be of use. The passions, remember, are drawing near, and when they knock at the door your scholar will have no ear for anything else. The peaceful age of intelligence is so short, it flies so swiftly, there is so much to be done, that it is madness to try to make your child learned. It is not your business to teach him the various sciences, but to give him a taste for them and methods of learning them when this taste is more mature. That is assuredly a fundamental principle of all good education.

This is also the time to train him gradually to prolonged attention to a given object; but this attention should never be the result of constraint, but of interest or desire; you must be very careful that it is not too much for his strength, and that it is not carried to the point of tedium. Watch him, therefore, and whatever happens, stop before he is tired, for it matters little what he learns; it does matter that he should do nothing against his will.

If he asks questions let your answers be enough to whet his curiosity but not enough to satisfy it; above all, when you find him talking at random and overwhelming you with silly questions instead of asking for information, at once refuse to answer; for it is clear that he no longer cares about the matter in hand, but wants to make you a slave to his questions. Consider his motives rather than his words. This warning, which was scarcely needed before, becomes of supreme importance when the child begins to reason.

There is a series of abstract truths by means of which all the sciences are related to common principles

and are developed each in its turn. This relationship
is the method of the philosophers. We are not concerned
with it at present. There is quite another method by
which every concrete example suggests another and always points to the next in the series. This succession,
which stimulates the curiosity and so arouses the attention required by every object in turn, is the order
followed by most men, and it is the right order for all
children. To take our bearings so as to make our maps
we must find meridians. Two points of intersection between the equal shadows morning and evening supply an
excellent meridian for a thirteen-year-old astronomer.
But these meridians disappear, it takes time to trace
them, and you are obliged to work in one place. So
much trouble and attention will at last become irksome.
We foresaw this and are ready for it.

. . . . . .

There are various regions of the earth, and these
regions differ in temperature. The variation is more
evident as we approach the poles; all bodies expand
with heat and contract with cold; this is best measured in liquids and best of all in spirits; hence the
thermometer. The wind strikes the face, then the air
is a body, a fluid; we feel it though we cannot see it.
I invert a glass in water; the water will not fill it
unless you leave a passage for the escape of the air;
so air is capable of resistance. Plunge the glass
further in the water; the water will encroach on the
air space without filling it entirely; so air yeilds
somewhat to pressure. A ball filled with compressed
air bounces better than one filled with anything else;
so air is elastic. Raise your arm horizontally from
the water when you are lying in your bath; you will
feel a terrible weight on it; so air is a heavy body.
By establishing an equilibrium between air and other
fluids its weight can be measured, hence the barometer,
the siphon, the air gun, and the air pump. All the
laws of statics and hydrostatics are discovered by such
rough experiments. For none of these would I take the
child into a physical cabinet; I dislike that array of
instruments and apparatus. The scientific atmosphere
destroys science. Either the child is frightened by
these instruments or his attention, which should be
fixed on their effects, is distracted by their appearance.

We shall make all our apparatus ourselves, and I would not make it beforehand, but having caught a glimpse of the experiment by chance we mean to invent step by step an instrument for its verification. I would rather our apparatus was somewhat clumsy and imperfect, but our ideas clear as to what the apparatus ought to be, and the results to be obtained by means of it. For my first lesson in statics, instead of fetching a balance, I lay a stick across the back of a chair, I measure the two parts when it is balanced; add equal and unequal weights to either end; by pulling or pushing it as required, I find at last that equilibrium is the result of a reciprocal proportion between the amount of the weights and the length of the levers. Thus my little physicist is ready to rectify a balance before ever he sees one.

Undoubtedly the notions of things thus acquired for oneself are clearer and much more convincing than those acquired from the teaching of others; and not only is our reason not accustomed to a slavish submission to authority, but we develop greater ingenuity in discovering relations, connecting ideas and inventing apparatus, than when we merely accept what is given us and allow our minds to be enfeebled by indifference, like the body of a man whose servants always wait on him, dress him and put on his shoes, whose horse carries him, till he loses the use of his limbs. Boileau used to boast that he had taught Racine the art of rhyming with difficulty. Among the many short cuts to science, we badly need some one to teach us the art of learning with difficulty.

The most obvious advantage of these slow and laborious inquiries is this: the scholar, while engaged in speculative studies, is actively using his body, gaining suppleness of limb, and training his hands to labour so that he will be able to make them useful when he is a man. Too much apparatus, designed to guide us in our experiments and to supplement the exactness of our senses, makes us neglect to use those senses. The theodolite makes it unnecessary to estimate the size of angles; the eye which used to judge distances with much precision, trusts to the chain for its measurements; the steel yard dispenses with the need of judging weight by the hand as I used to do. The more ingenious our apparatus, the coarser and more unskillful are our senses.

We surround ourselves with tools and fail to use those with which nature has provided every one of us.

But when we devote to the making of these instruments the skill which did instead of them, when for their construction we use the intelligence which enabled us to dispense with them, this is gain not loss, we add art to nature, we gain ingenuity without loss of skill. If instead of making a child stick to his books I employ him in a workshop, his hands work for the development of his mind. While he fancies himself a workman he is becoming a philosopher. Moreover, this exercise has other advantages of which I shall speak later; and you will see how, through philosophy in sport, one may rise to the real duties of man.

. . . . .

Let the child do nothing because he is told; nothing is good for him but what he recognises as good. When you are always urging him beyond his present understanding, you think you are exercising a foresight which you really lack. To provide him with useless tools which he may never require, you deprive him of man's most useful tool - common-sense. You would have him docile as a child; he will be a credulous dupe when he grows up. You are always saying, "What I ask is for your good, though you cannot understand it. What does it matter to me whether you do it or not; my efforts are entirely on your account." All these fine speeches with which you hope to make him good, are preparing the way, so that the visionary, the tempter, the charlatan, the rascal, and every kind of fool may catch him in his snare or draw him into his folly.

A man must know many things which seem useless to a child, but need the child learn, or can he indeed learn, all that the man must know? Try to teach the child what is of use to a child and you will find that it takes all his time. Why urge him to the studies of an age he may never reach, to the neglect of those studies which meet his present needs? "But," you ask, "will it not be too late to learn what he ought to know when the time comes to use it?" I cannot tell; but this I do know, it is impossible to teach it sooner, for our real teachers are experience and emotion, and man will never learn what befits a man except under its own conditions. A child knows he must become a man;

all the ideas he may have as to man's estate are so
many opportunities for his instruction, but he should
remain in complete ignorance of those ideas which are
beyond his grasp. My whole book is one continued argument in support of this fundamental principle of education.

As soon as we have contrived to give our pupil an
idea of the word "Useful," we have got an additional
means of controlling him, for this word makes a great
impression on him, provided that its meaning for him
is a meaning relative to his own age, and provided he
clearly sees its relation to his own well-being. This
word makes no impression on your scholars because you
have taken no pains to give it a meaning they can understand, and because other people always undertake to
supply their needs so that they never require to think
for themselves, and do not know what utility is.

"What is the use of that?" In the future this is the
sacred formula, the formula by which he and I test every
action of our lives. This is the question with which
I invariably answer all his questions; it serves to
check the stream of foolish and tiresome questions with
which children weary those about them. These incessant
questions produce no result, and their object is rather
to get a hold over you than to gain any real advantage.
A pupil, who has been really taught only to want to
know what is useful, questions like Socrates; he never
asks a question without a reason for it, for he knows
he will be required to give his reason before he gets
an answer.

See what a powerful instrument I have put into
your hands for use with your pupil. As he does not
know the reason for anything you can reduce him to
silence almost at will; and what advantages do your
knowledge and experience give you to show him the usefulness of what you suggest. For, make no mistake
about it, when you put this question to him, you are
teaching him to put it to you, and you must expect that
whatever you suggest to him in the future he will follow your own example and ask, "What is the use of this?"

Perhaps this is the greatest of the tutor's difficulties. If you merely try to put the child off when
he asks a question, and if you give him a single reason
he is not able to understand, if he finds that you rea-

son according to your own ideas, not his, he will think
that what you tell him is good for you but not for him;
you will lose his confidence and all your labour is
thrown away. But what master will stop short and confess his faults to his pupil? We all make it a rule
never to own to the faults we really have. Now I would
make it a rule to admit even the faults I have not, if
I could not make my reasons clear to him; as my conduct
will always be intelligible to him, he will never doubt
me and I shall gain more credit by confessing my imaginary faults than those who conceal their real defects.

. . . . . .

I hate books; they only teach us to talk about
things we know nothing about. Hermes, they say, engraved the elements of science on pillars lest a deluge
should destroy them. Had he imprinted them on men's
hearts they would have been preserved by tradition.
Well-trained minds are the pillars on which human knowledge is most deeply engraved.

Is there no way of correlating so many lessons
scattered through so many books, no way of focusing
them on some common object, easy to see, interesting
to follow, and stimulating even to a child? Could we
but discover a state in which all man's needs appear in
such a way as to appeal to the child's mind, a state in
which the ways of providing for these needs are as easily developed, the simple and stirring portrayal of
this state should form the earliest training of the
child's imagination.

Eager philosopher, I see your own imagination at
work. Spare yourself the trouble; this state is already known, it is described, with due respect to you,
far better than you could describe it, at least with
greater truth and simplicity. Since we must have books,
there is one book which, to my thinking, supplies the
best treatise on an education according to nature.
This is the first book Emile will read; for a long time
it will form his whole library, and it will always retain an honoured place. It will be the text to which
all our talks about natural science are but the commen-
tary. It will serve to test our progress towards a
right judgment, and it will always be read with delight, so long as our taste is unspoilt. What is this

wonderful book? Is it Aristotle? Pliny? Buffon? No; it is *Robinson Crusoe*.

Robinson Crusoe on his island, deprived of the help of his fellowmen, without the means of carrying on the various arts, yet finding food, preserving his life, and procuring a certain amount of comfort; this is the thing to interest people of all ages, and it can be made attractive to children in all sorts of ways. We shall thus make a reality of that desert island which formerly served as an illustration. The condition, I confess, is not that of a social being, nor is it in all probability Emile's own condition, but he should use it as a standard of comparison for all other conditions. The surest way to raise him above prejudice and to base his judgments on the true relations of things, is to put him in the place of a solitary man, and to judge all things as they would be judged by such a man in relation to their own utility.

. . . . . .

At the beginning of this second period we took advantage of the fact that our strength was more than enough for our needs, to enable us to get outside ourselves. We have ranged the heavens and measured the earth; we have sought out the laws of nature; we have explored the whole of our island. Now let us return to ourselves, let us unconsciously approach our own dwelling. We are happy indeed if we do not find it already occupied by the dreaded foe who is preparing to seize it.

What remains to be done when we have observed all that lies around us? We must turn to our own use all that we can get, we must increase our comfort by means of our curiosity. Hitherto we have provided ourselves with tools of all kinds, not knowing which we require. Perhaps those we do not want will be useful to others, and perhaps we may need theirs. Thus we discover the use of exchange; but for this we must know each other's needs, what tools other people use, what they can offer in exchange. Given ten men, each of them has ten different requirements. To get what he needs for himself each must work at ten different trades; but considering our different talents, one will do better at this trade, another at that. Each of them, fitted for one thing, will work at all, and will be badly served. Let us form these ten men into a society, and let each devote himself to the trade for which he is best adapted, and let him work at it for himself and for the rest. Each will reap the advantage of the others' talents, just as if they were his own; by practice each will perfect his own talent, and thus all the ten, well provided for, will still have something to spare for others. This is the plain foundation for all our institutions. It is not my aim to examine its results here; I have done so in another book (*Discours sur l'inegalite*).

According to this principle, any one who wanted to consider himself as an isolated individual, self-sufficing and independent of others, could only be utterly wretched. He could not even continue to exist, for finding the whole earth appropriated by others while he had only himself, how could he get the means of subsistence? When we leave the state of nature we compel others to do the same; no one can remain in a state of nature in spite of his fellow-creatures; and to try to remain in it when it is no longer practicable, would really be to leave it, for self-preservation is nature's first law.

Thus the idea of social relations is gradually developed in the child's mind, before he can really be an active member of human society. Emile sees that to get tools for his own use, other people must have theirs, and that he can exchange what he needs and they possess. I easily bring him to feel the need of such exchange and to take advantage of it.

. . . . . .

Remember I demand no talent, only a trade, a genuine trade, a mere mechanical art, in which the hands work harder than the head, a trade which does not lead to fortune but makes you independent of her. In households far removed from all danger of want I have known fathers carry prudence to such a point as to provide their children not only with ordinary teaching but with knowledge by means of which they could get a living if anything happened. These far-sighted parents thought they were doing a great thing. It is nothing, for the resources they fancy they have secured depend on that very fortune of which they would make their children independent; so that unless they found themselves in circumstances fitted for the display of their talents, they would die of hunger as if they had none.

As soon as it is a question of influence and intrigue you may as well use these means to keep yourself in plenty, as to acquire, in the depths of poverty, the means of returning to your former position. If you cultivate the arts which depend on the artist's reputation, if you fit yourself for posts which are only obtained by favour, how will that help you when, rightly disgusted with the world, you scorn the steps by which you must climb. You have studied politics and state-craft, so far so good; but how will you use this knowledge, if you cannot gain the ear of the ministers, the favourites, or the officials? If you have not the secret of winning their favour, if they fail to find you a rogue to their taste? You are an architect or a painter; well and good; but your talents must be displayed. Do you suppose you can exhibit in the salon without further ado? That is not the way to set about it. Lay aside the rule and the pencil, take a cab and drive from door to door; there is the road to fame. Now you must know that the doors of the great are guarded by porters and flunkeys, who only understand one language, and their ears are in their palms. If you wish to teach what you have learned, geography, mathematics, languages, music, drawing, even to find pupils, you must have friends who will sing your praises. Learning, remember, gains more credit than skill, and with no trade but your own none will believe in your skill. See how little you can depend on these fine "Resources," and how many other resources are required before you can use what you have got. And what will become of you in your degradation? Misfortune will make you worse rather than better. More than ever the sport of public opinion, how will you rise above the prejudices on which your fate depends? How will you despise the vices and the baseness from which you get your living? You were dependent on wealth, now you are dependent on the wealthy; you are still a slave and a poor man in the bargain. Poverty without freedom, can a man sink lower than this!

. . . . . .

When we review with the child the productions of art and nature, when we stimulate his curiosity and follow its lead, we have great opportunities of study-

ing his tastes and inclinations, and perceiving the
first spark of genius, if he has any decided talent in
any direction. You must, however, be on your guard
against the common error which mistakes the effects of
environment for the ardour of genius, or imagines there
is a decided bent towards any one of the arts, when
there is nothing more than that spirit of emulation,
common to men and monkeys, which impels them instinc-
tively to do what they see others doing, without knowing why. The world is full of artisans, and still fuller of artists, who have no native gift for their calling, into which they were driven in early childhood,
either through the conventional ideas of other people,
or because those about them were deceived by an appearance of zeal, which would have led them to take to any
other art they saw practised. One hears a drum and
fancies he is a general; another sees a building and
wants to be an architect. Every one is drawn towards
the trade he sees before him if he thinks it is held in
honour.

. . . . . .

I know I have said too much for my agreeable con-
temporaries, but I sometimes let myself be carried away
by my argument. If any one is ashamed to be seen wearing a leathern apron or handling a plane, I think him
a mere slave of public opinion, ready to blush for what
is right when people poke fun at it. But let us yield
to parents' prejudices so long as they do not hurt the
children. To honour trades we are not obliged to practice every one of them, so long as we do not think them
beneath us. When the choice is ours and we are under
no compulsion, why not choose the pleasanter, more attractive and more suitable trade. Metal work is useful, more useful, perhaps, than the rest, but unless
for some special reason Emile shall not be a blacksmith,
a locksmith nor an ironworker. I do not want to see
him a Cyclops at the forge. Neither would I have him
a mason, still less a shoemaker. All trades must be
carried on, but when the choice is ours, cleanliness
should be taken into account; this is not a matter of
class prejudice, our senses are our guides. In conclusion, I do not like those stupid trades in which the
workmen mechanically perform the same action without
pause and almost without mental effort. Weaving, stock-
ing-knitting, stone-cutting; why employ intelligent men
on such work? It is merely one machine employed on another.

All things considered, the trade I should choose
for my pupil, among the trades he likes, is that of a
carpenter. It is clean and useful; it may be carried
on at home; it gives enough exercise; it calls for
skill and industry, and while fashioning articles for
everyday use, there is scope for elegance and taste.
If your pupil's talents happened to take a scientific
turn, I should not blame you if you gave him a trade
in accordance with his tastes; for instance, he might
learn to make mathematical instruments, glasses, tele-
scopes, etc.

When Emile learns his trade I shall learn it too.
I am convinced he will never learn anything thoroughly
unless we learn it together. So we shall both serve
our apprenticeship, and we do not mean to be treated
as gentlemen, but as real apprentices who are not there
for fun; why should not we actually be apprenticed?
Peter the Great was a ship's carpenter and drummer to
his own troops; was not that prince at least your equal
in birth and merit? You understand this is addressed
not to Emile but to you - to you, whoever you may be.

BOOK IV

We have reached the moral order at last; we have
just taken the second step towards manhood. If this
were the place for it, I would try to show how the
first impulses of the heart give rise to the first
stirrings of conscience, and how from the feelings of
love and hatred spring the first notions of good and
evil. I would show that justice and kindness are no
mere abstract terms, no mere moral conceptions framed
by the understanding, but true affections of the heart
enlightened by reason, the natural outcome of our primitive affections; that by reason alone, unaided by
conscience, we cannot establish any natural law, and
that all natural right is a vain dream if it does not
rest upon some instinctive need of the human heart. But
I do not think it is my business at present to prepare
treatises on metaphysics and morals, nor courses of
study of any kind whatsoever; it is enough if I indicate the order and development of our feelings and our
knowledge in relation to our growth. Others will perhaps work out what I have here merely indicated.

Hitherto my Emile has thought only of himself, so his first glance at his equals leads him to compare himself with them; and the first feeling excited by this comparison is the desire to be first. It is here that self-love is transformed into selfishness, and this is the starting point of all the passions which spring from selfishness. But to determine whether the passions by which his life will be governed shall be humane and gentle or harsh and cruel, whether they shall be the passions of benevolence and pity or those of envy and covetousness, we must know what he believes his place among men to be, and what sort of obstacles he expects to have to overcome in order to attain to the position he seeks.

To guide him in this inquiry, after we have shown him men by means of the accidents common to the species, we must now show him them by means of their differences. This is the time for estimating inequality natural and civil, and for the scheme of the whole social order.

Society must be studied in the individual and the individual in society; those who desire to treat politics and morals apart from one another will never understand either. By confining ourselves at first to the primitive relations, we see how men should be influenced by them and what passions should spring from them; we see that it is in proportion to the development of these passions that a man's relations with others expand or contract. It is not so much strength of arm as moderation of spirit which makes men free and independent. The man whose wants are few is dependent on but few people, but those who constantly confound our vain desires with our bodily needs, those who have made these needs the basis of human society, are continually mistaking effects for causes, and they have only confused themselves by their own reasoning.

. . . . . .

It must be admitted that this method has its drawbacks, and it is not easy to carry it out; for if he becomes too soon engrossed in watching other people, if you train him to mark too closely the actions of others, you will make him spiteful and satirical, quick and decided in his judgments of others; he will find a hateful pleasure in seeking bad motives, and will fail

to see the good even in that which is really good. He
will, at least, get used to the sight of vice, he will
behold the wicked without horror, just as we get used
to seeing the wretched without pity. Soon the perver-
sity of mankind will be not so much a warning as an excuse; he will say, "Man is made so," and he will have
no wish to be different from the rest.

But if you wish to teach him theoretically to make
him acquainted, not only with the heart of man, but also with the application of the external causes which
turn our inclinations into vices; when you thus transport him all at once from the objects of sense to the
objects of reason, you employ a system of metaphysics
which he is not in a position to understand; you fall
back into the error, so carefully avoided hitherto, of
giving him lessons which are like lessons, of substituting in his mind the experience and the authority of
the master for his own experience and the development
of his own reason.

To remove these two obstacles at once, and to
bring the human heart within his reach without risk of
spoiling his own, I would show him men from afar, in
other times or in other places, so that he may behold
the scene but cannot take part in it. This is the time
for history; with its help he will read the hearts of
men without any lessons in philosophy; with its help
he will view them as a mere spectator, dispassionate
and without prejudice; he will view them as their judge,
not as their accomplice or their accuser.

To know men you must behold their actions. In
society we hear them talk; they show their words and
hide their deeds; but in history the veil is drawn
aside, and they are judged by their deeds. Their sayings even help us to understand them; for comparing
what they say and what they do, we see not only what
they are but what they would appear; the more they disguise themselves the more thoroughly they stand revealed.

Unluckily this study has its dangers, its drawbacks of several kinds. It is difficult to adopt a
point of view which will enable one to judge one's fellow-creatures fairly. It is one of the chief defects
of history to paint men's evil deeds rather than their
good ones; it is revolutions and catastrophes that make

history interesting; so long as a nation grows and pros-
pers quietly in the tranquillity of a peaceful government, history says nothing; she only begins to speak of
nations when, no longer able to be self-sufficing, they
interfere with their neighbours' business, or allow
their neighbours to interfere with their own; history
only makes them famous when they are on the downward
path; all our histories begin where they ought to end.
We have very accurate accounts of declining nations;
what we lack is the history of those nations which are
multiplying; they are so happy and so good that history
has nothing to tell us of them; and we see indeed in
our own times that the most successful governments are
least talked of. We only hear what is bad; the good is
scarcely mentioned. Only the wicked become famous, the
good are forgotten or laughed to scorn, and thus history,
like philosophy, is for ever slandering mankind.

Moreover, it is inevitable that the facts described
in history should not give an exact picture of what
really happened; they are transformed in the brain of
the historian, they are moulded by his interests and
coloured by his prejudices. Who can place the reader
precisely in a position to see the event as it really
happened? Ignorance or partiality disguises everything.
What a different impression may be given merely by expanding or contracting the circumstances of the case
without altering a single historical incident. The same
object may be seen from several points of view, and it
will hardly seem the same thing, yet there has been no
change except in the eye that beholds it. Do you indeed do honour to truth when what you tell me is a genuine fact, but you make it appear something quite different? A tree more or less, a rock to the right or to
the left, a cloud of dust raised by the wind, how often
have these decided the result of a battle without any
one knowing it? Does that prevent history from telling
you the cause of defeat or victory with as much assurance as if she had been on the spot? But what are the
facts to me, while I am ignorant of their causes, and
what lessons can I draw from an event, whose true
cause is unknown to me? The historian indeed gives me
a reason, but he invents it; and criticism itself, of
which we hear so much, is only the art of guessing, the
art of choosing from among several lies, the lie that
is most like truth.

Have you ever read Cleopatra or Cassandra or any books of the kind? The author selects some well-known event, he then adapts it to his purpose, adorns it with details of his own invention, with people who never existed, with imaginary portraits; thus he piles fiction on fiction to lend a charm to his story. I see little difference between such romances and your histories, unless it is that the novelist draws more on his own imagination, while the historian slavishly copies what another has imagined; I will also admit, if you please, that the novelist has some moral purpose good or bad, about which the historian scarcely concerns himself.

You will tell me that accuracy in history is of less interest than a true picture of men and manners; provided the human heart is truly portrayed, it matters little that events should be accurately recorded; for after all you say, what does it matter to us what happened two thousand years ago? You are right if the portraits are indeed truly given according to nature; but if the model is to be found for the most part in the historian's imagination, are you not falling into the very error you intended to avoid, and surrendering to the authority of the historian what you would not yield to the authority of the teacher? If my pupil is merely to see fancy pictures, I would rather draw them myself; they will, at least, be better suited to him.

The worst historians for a youth are those who give their opinions. Facts! Facts! And let him decide for himself; this is how he will learn to know mankind. If he is always directed by the opinion of the author, he is only seeing through the eyes of another person, and when those eyes are no longer at his disposal he can see nothing.

I leave modern history on one side, not only because it has no character and all our people are alike, but because our historians, wholly taken up with effect, think of nothing but highly coloured portraits, which often represent nothing. The old historians generally give fewer portraits and bring more intelligence and common-sense to their judgments; but even among them there is plenty of scope for choice, and you must not begin with the wisest but with the simplest. I would not put Polybius or Sallust into the hands of a youth; Tacitus is the author of the old, young men cannot understand him; you must learn to see in human actions

the simplest features of the heart of man before you
try to sound its depths. You must be able to read
facts clearly before you begin to study maxims. Philosophy in the form of maxims is only fit for the experienced. Youth should never deal with the general, all
its teaching should deal with individual instances.

To my mind Thucydides is the true model of historians. He relates facts without giving his opinion; but
he omits no circumstance adapted to make us judge for
ourselves. He puts everything that he relates before
his reader; far from interposing between the facts and
the readers, he conceals himself; we seem not to read
but to see. Unfortunately he speaks of nothing but
war, and in his stories we only see the least instructive part of the world, that is to say the battles. The
virtues and defects of the Retreat of the Ten Thousand
and the Commentaries of Caesar are almost the same. The
kindly Herodotus, without portraits, without maxims,
yet flowing, simple, full of details calculated to delight and interest in the highest degree, would be perhaps the best historian if these very details did not
often degenerate into childish folly, better adapted
to spoil the taste of youth than to form it; we need
discretion before we can read him. I say nothing of
Livy, his turn will come; but he is a statesman, a
rhetorician, he is everything which is unsuitable for
a youth.

History in general is lacking because it only takes
note of striking and clearly marked facts which may be
fixed by names, places, and dates; but the slow evolu-
tion of these facts, which cannot be definitely noted
in this way, still remains unknown. We often find in
some battle, lost or won, the ostensible cause of a
revolution which was inevitable before this battle took
place. War only makes manifest events already determined by moral causes which few historians can perceive.

The philosophic spirit has turned the thoughts of
many of the historians of our times in this direction;
but I doubt whether truth has profited by their labours.
The rage for systems has got possession of all alike,
no one seeks to see things as they are, but only as
they agree with his system.

Add to all these considerations the fact that history shows us actions rather than men, because she only seizes men at certain chosen times in full dress; she only portrays the statesman when he is prepared to be seen; she does not follow him to his home, to his study, among his family and his friends; she only shows him in state; it is his clothes rather than himself that she describes.

I would prefer to begin the study of the human heart with reading the lives of individuals; for then the man hides himself in vain, the historian follows him everywhere; he never gives him a moment's grace nor any corner where he can escape the piercing eye of the spectator; and when he thinks he is concealing himself, then it is that the writer shows him up most plainly.

. . . . .

What then is required for the proper study of men? A great wish to know men, great impartiality of judgment, a heart sufficiently sensitive to understand every human passion, and calm enough to be free from passion. If there is any time in our life when this study is likely to be appreciated, it is this that I have chosen for Emile; before this time men would have been strangers to him; later on he would have been like them. Convention, the effects of which he already perceives, has not yet made him its slave, the passions, whose consequences he realizes, have not yet stirred his heart. He is a man; he takes an interest in his brethren; he is a just man and he judges his peers. Now it is certain that if he judges them rightly he will not want to change places with any one of them, for the goal of all their anxious efforts is the result of prejudices which he does not share, and that goal seems to him a mere dream. For his own part, he has all he wants within his reach. How should he be dependent on any one when he is self-sufficing and free from prejudice? Strong arms, good health, moderation, few needs, together with the means to satisfy those needs, are his. He has been brought up in complete liberty and servitude is the greatest ill he understands. He pities these miserable kings, the slaves of all who obey them; he pities these false prophets fettered by their empty fame; he pities these rich fools, martyrs to their own pomp; he pities these ostentatious voluptuaries, who spend their life in deadly dullness that

they may seem to enjoy its pleasures. He would pity
the very foe who harmed him, for he would discern his
wretchedness beneath his cloak of spite. He would say
to himself, "This man has yielded to his desire to hurt
me, and this need of his places him at my mercy."

One step more and our goal is attained. Selfishness is a dangerous tool though a useful one; it often
wounds the hand that uses it, and it rarely does good
unmixed with evil. When Emile considers his place
among men, when he finds himself so fortunately situ-
ated, he will be tempted to give credit to his own reason for the work of yours, and to attribute to his own
deserts what is really the result of his good fortune.
He will say to himself, "I am wise and other men are
fools." He will pity and despise them and will con-
gratulate himself all the more heartily; and as he
knows he is happier than they, he will think his deserts are greater. This is the fault we have most to
fear, for it is the most difficult to eradicate. If he
remained in this state of mind, he would have profited
little by all our care; and if I had to choose, I hardly know whether I would not rather choose the illusions
of prejudice than those of pride.

Great men are under no illusion with respect to
their superiority; they see it and know it, but they
are none the less modest. The more they have, the better thay know what they lack. They are less vain of
their superiority over us than ashamed by the consciousness of their weakness, and among the good things
they really possess, they are too wise to pride themselves on a gift which is none of their getting. The
good man may be proud of his virtue for it is his own,
but what cause for pride has the man of intellect?
What has Racine done that he is not Pradon, and Boileau
that he is not Cotin?

The circumstances with which we are concerned are
quite different. Let us keep to the common level. I
assumed that my pupil had neither surpassing genius
nor a defective understanding. I chose him of an ordinary mind to show what education could do for a man.
Exceptions defy all rules. If, therefore, as a result
of my care, Emile prefers his way of living, seeing,
and feeling to that of others, he is right; but if he
thinks because of this that he is nobler and better
born than they, he is wrong; he is deceiving himself;

he must be undeceived, or rather let us prevent the mistake, lest it be too late to correct it.

Provided a man is not mad, he can be cured of any folly but vanity; there is no cure for this but experience, if indeed there is any cure for it at all; when it first appears we can at least prevent its further growth. But do not on this account waste your breath on empty arguments to prove to the youth that he is like other men and subject to the same weaknesses. Make him feel it or he will never know it. This is another instance of an exception to my own rules; I must voluntarily expose my pupil to every accident which may convince him that he is no wiser than we. The adventure with the conjurer will be repeated again and again in different ways; I shall let flatterers take advantage of him; if rash comrades draw him into some perilous adventure, I will let him run the risk; if he falls into the hands of sharpers at the card table, I will abandon him to them as their dupe. I will let them flatter him, pluck him, and rob him; and when having sucked him dry they turn and mock him, I will even thank them to his face for the lessons they have been good enough to give him. The only snares from which I will guard him with my utmost care are the wiles of wanton women. The only precaution I shall take will be to share all the dangers I let him run, and all the insults I let him receive. I will bear everything in silence, without a murmur or reproach, without a word to him, and be sure that if this wise conduct is faithfully adhered to, what he sees me endure on his account will make more impression on his heart than what he himself suffers.

. . . . . .

The time of faults is the time for fables. When we blame the guilty under the cover of a story we instruct without offending him; and he then understands that the story is not untrue by means of the truth he finds in its application to himself. The child who has never been deceived by flattery understands nothing of the fable I recently examined; but the rash youth who has just become the dupe of a flatterer perceives only too readily that the crow was a fool. Thus he acquires a maxim from the fact, and the experience he would soon have forgotten is engraved on his mind by means of the fable. There is no knowledge of morals which cannot

be acquired through our own experience or that of others.
When there is danger, instead of letting him try the
experiment himself, we have recourse to history. When
the risk is comparatively slight, it is just as well
that the youth should be exposed to it; then by means
of the apologue the special cases with which the young
man is now acquainted are transformed into maxims.

It is not, however, my intention that these maxims
should be explained, nor even formulated. Nothing is
so foolish and unwise as the moral at the end of most
of the fables; as if the moral was not, or ought not to
be so clear in the fable itself that the reader cannot
fail to perceive it. Why then add the moral at the
end, and so deprive him of the pleasure of discovering
it for himself. The art of teaching consists in making
the pupil wish to learn. But if the pupil is to wish
to learn, his mind must not remain in such a passive
state with regard to what you tell him that there is
really nothing for him to do but listen to you. The
master's vanity must always give way to the scholar's;
he must be able to say, I understand, I see it, I am
getting at it, I am learning something. One of the
things which makes the Pantaloon in the Italian comedies so wearisome is the pains taken by him to explain
to the audience the platitudes they understand only
too well already.

. . . . . .

When I see the studies of young men at the period
of their greatest activity confined to purely speculative matters, while later on they are suddenly plunged,
without any sort of experience, into the world of men
and affairs, it strikes me as contrary alike to reason
and to nature, and I cease to be surprised that so few
men know what to do. How strange a choice to teach us
so many useless things, while the art of doing is never
touched upon! They profess to fit us for society, and
we are taught as if each of us were to live a life of
contemplation in a solitary cell, or to discuss theories with persons whom they did not concern. You think
you are teaching your scholars how to live, and you
teach them certain bodily contortions and certain forms
of words without meaning. I, too, have taught Emile
how to live; for I have taught him to enjoy his own
society and, more than that, to earn his own bread. But
this is not enough. To live in the world he must know

how to get on with other people, he must know what
forces move them, he must calculate the action and reaction of self-interest in civil society, he must estimate the results so accurately that he will rarely fail
in his undertakings, or he will at least have tried in
the best possible way. The law does not allow young
people to manage their own affairs nor to dispose of
their own property; but what would be the use of these
precautions if they never gained any experience until
they were of age. They would have gained nothing by
the delay, and would have no more experience at five-
and-twenty than at fifteen. No doubt we must take precautions, so that a youth, blinded by ignorance or misled by passion, may not hurt himself; but at any age
there are opportunities when deeds of kindness and of
care for the weak may be performed under the direction
of a wise man, on behalf of the unfortunate who need
help.

Mothers and nurses grow fond of children because
of the care they lavish on them; the practice of social
virtues touches the very heart with the love of humanity; by doing good we become good; and I know no surer
way to this end. Keep your pupil busy with the good
deeds that are within his power, let the cause of the
poor be his own, let him help them not merely with his
money, but with his service; let him work for them,
protect them, let his person and his time be at their
disposal; let him be their agent; he will never all
his life long have a more honourable office. How many
of the oppressed, who have never got a hearing, will
obtain justice when he demands it for them with that
courage and firmness which the practice of virtue inspires; when he makes his way into the presence of the
king himself, to plead the cause of the wretched, the
cause of those who find all doors closed to them by
their poverty, those who are so afraid of being punished for their misfortunes that they do not dare to
complain?

But shall we make of Emile a knight-errant, a re-
dresser of wrongs, a paladin? Shall he thrust himself
into public life, play the sage and the defender of the
laws before the great, before the magistrates, before
the king? Shall he lay petitions before the judges
and plead in the law courts? That I cannot say. The
nature of things is not changed by terms of mockery and
scorn. He will do all that he knows to be useful and

good. He will do nothing more, and he knows that nothing is useful and good for him which is unbefitting his
age. He knows that his first duty is to himself; that
young men should distrust themselves; that they should
act circumspectly; that they should show respect to
those older than themselves, reticence and discretion
in talking without cause, modesty in things indifferent,
but courage in well-doing, and boldness to speak the
truth. Such were those illustrious Romans who, having
been admitted into public life, spent their days in
bringing crminals to justice and in protecting the innocent, without any motives beyond those of learning,
and of the furtherance of justice and of the protection
of right conduct.

. . . . . .

So Emile loves peace. He is delighted at the
sight of happiness, and if he can help to bring it
about, this is an additional reason for sharing it. I
do not assume that when he sees the unhappy he will
merely feel for them that barren and cruel pity which
is content to pity the ills it can heal. His kindness
is active and teaches him much he would have learnt
far more slowly, or he would never have learnt at all,
if his heart had been harder. If he finds his comrades at strife, he tries to reconcile them; if he sees
the afflicted, he inquires as to the cause of their
sufferings; if he meets two men who hate each other, he
wants to know the reason of their enmity; if he finds
one who is down-trodden, groaning under the oppression
of the rich and powerful, he tries to discover by what
means he can conteract this oppression, and in the interest he takes with regard to all these unhappy persons, the means of removing their sufferings are never
out of his sight. What use shall we make of this disposition so that it may re-act in a way suited to his
age? Let us direct his efforts and his knowledge, and
use his zeal to increase them.

I am never weary of repeating: let all the lessons
of young people take the form of doing rather than
talking; let them learn nothing from books which they
can learn from experience. How absurd to attempt to
give them practice in speaking when they have nothing
to say, to expect to make them feel, at their school
desks, the vigour of the language of passion and all

the force of the arts of persuasion when they have
nothing and nobody to persuade! All the rules of rhetoric are mere waste of words to those who do not know
how to use them for their own purposes.

. . . . . .

I am aware that many of my readers will be surprised to find me tracing the course of my scholar
through his early years without speaking to him of religion. At fifteen he will not even know that he has
a soul, at eighteen even he may not be ready to learn
about it. For if he learns about it too soon, there
is the risk of his never really knowing anything about
it.

If I had to depict the most heart-breaking stupidity, I would paint a pedant teaching children the catechism; if I wanted to drive a child crazy I would set
him to explain what he learned in his catechism. You
will reply that as most of the Christian doctrines are
mysteries, you must wait, not merely till the child is
a man, but till the man is dead, before the human mind
will understand those doctrines. To that I reply, that
there are mysteries which the heart of man can neither
conceive nor believe, and I see no use in teaching them
to children, unless you want to make liars of them.
Moreover, I assert that to admit that there are mysteries, you must at least realize that they are incompre-
hensible, and children are not even capable of this
conception! At an age when everything is mysterious,
there are no mysteries properly so-called.

"We must believe in God if we would be saved."
This doctrine wrongly understood is the root of blood-
thirsty intolerance and the cause of all the futile
teaching which strikes a deadly blow at human reason
by training it to cheat itself with mere words. No
doubt there is not a moment to be lost if we would deserve eternal salvation; but if the repetition of certain words suffices to obtain it, I do not see why we
should not people heaven with starlings and magpies as
well as with children.

The obligation of faith assumes the possibility of
belief. The philosopher who does not believe is wrong,
for he misuses the reason he has cultivated, and he is
able to understand the truths he rejects. But the child

who professes the Christian faith - what does he believe? Just what he understands; and he understands so
little of what he is made to repeat that if you tell
him to say just the opposite he will be quite ready to
do it. The faith of children and the faith of many men
is a matter of geography. Will they be rewarded for
having been born in Rome rather than in Mecca? One is
told that Mahomet is the prophet of God and he says,
"Mahomet is the prophet God." The other is told that
Mahomet is a rogue and he says, "Mohamet is a rogue."
Either of them would have said just the opposite had
he stood in the other's shoes. When they are so much
alike to begin with, can the one be consigned to Paradise and the other to Hell? When a child says he believes in God, it is not God he believes in, but Peter
or James who told him that there is something called
God, and he believes it after the fashion of Euripides
- "O Jupiter, of whom I know nothing by thy name."

We hold that no child who dies before the age of
reason will be deprived of everlasting happiness; the
Catholics believe the same of all children who have
been baptised, even though they have never heard of
God. There are, therefore, circumstances in which one
can be saved without belief in God, and these circumstances occur in the case of children or madmen when
the human mind is incapable of the operations necessary
to perceive the Godhead. The only difference I see between you and me is that you profess that children of
seven years old are able to do this and I do not think
them ready for it at fifteen. Whether I am right or
wrong depends, not on any article of the creed, but on
a simple observation in natural history.

From the same principle it is plain that any man
having reached old age without faith in God will not,
therefore, be deprived of God's presence in another
life if his blindness was not willful; and I maintain
that it is not always willful. You admit that it is so
in the case of lunatics deprived by disease of their
spiritual faculties, but not of their manhood, and
therefore still entitled to the goodness of their Creator. Why then should we not admit it in the case of
those brought up from infancy in seclusion, those who
have led the life of a savage and are without the knowl-
egde of the true God. Reason tells that man should
only be punished for his willful faults, and that invincible ignorance can never be imputed to him as a

crime. Hence it follows that in the sight of the Eternal Justice every man who would believe if he had the necessary knowledge is counted a believer, and that there will be no unbelievers to be punished except those who have closed their hearts against the truth.

Let us beware of proclaiming the truth to those who cannot as yet comprehend it, for to do so is to try to inculcate error. It would be better to have no idea at all of the Divinity than to have mean, grotesque, harmful, and unworthy ideas; to fail to perceive the Divine is a lesser evil than to insult it. The worthy Plutarch says, "I would rather men said, 'There is no such person as Plutarch,' than that they should say, 'Plutarch is unjust, envious, jealous, and such a tyrant that he demands more than can be performed.' "

The chief harm which results from the monstrous ideas of God which are instilled into the minds of children is that they last all their life long, and as men they understand no more of God than they did as children. In Switzerland, I once saw a good and pious mother who was so convinced of the truth of this maxim that she refused to teach her son religion when he was a little child for fear lest he should be satisfied with this crude teaching and neglect a better teaching when he reached the age of reason. This child never heard the name of God pronounced except with reverence and devotion, and as soon as he attempted to say the word he was told to hold his tongue, as if the subject were too sublime and great for him. This reticence aroused his curiosity and his self-love; he looked forward to the time when he would know this mystery so carefully hidden from him. The less they spoke of God to him, the less he was himself permitted to speak of God, the more he thought about Him; this child beheld God everywhere. What I should most dread as the result of this unwise affectation of mystery is this: by overstimulating the youth's imagination you may turn his head, and make him at the best a fanatic rather than a believer.

But we need fear nothing of the sort for Emile, who always declines to pay attention to what is beyond his reach, and listens with profound indifference to things he does not understand. There are so many things of which he is accustomed to say, "That is no concern of mine," that one more or less makes little difference to him; and when he does begin to perplex himself with these great matters, it is because the natural growth of his knowledge is turning his thoughts that way.

We have seen the road by which the cultivated human mind approaches these mysteries, and I am ready to admit that it would not attain to them naturally, even in the bosom of society, till a much later age. But as there are in this same society inevitable causes which hasten the development of the passions, if we did not also hasten the development of the knowledge which controls those passions we should indeed depart from the path of nature and disturb her equilibrium. When we can no longer restrain a precocious development in one direction we must promote a corresponding development in another direction, so that the order of nature may not be inverted, and so that things should progress together, not separately, so that the man, complete at every moment of his life, may never find himself at one stage in one of his faculties and at another stage in another faculty.

What a difficulty do I see before me! A difficulty all the greater because it depends less on actual facts than on the cowardice of those who dare not look the difficulty in the face. Let us at least venture to state our problem. A child should always be brought up in his father's religion; he is always given plain proofs that this religion, whatever it may be, is the only true religion, that all others are ridiculous and absurd. The force of the argument depends entirely on the country in which it is put forward. Let a Turk, who thinks Christianity so absurd at Constantinople, come to Paris and see what they think of Mahomet. It is in matters of religion more than in anything else that prejudice is triumphant. But when we who profess to shake off its yoke entirely, we who refuse to yield any homage to authority, decline to teach Emile anything which he could not learn for himself in any country, what religion shall we give him, to what sect shall this child of nature belong? The answer strikes me as quite easy. We will not attach him to any sect, but we will give him the means to choose for himself according to the right use of his own reason.

. . . . . .

Remember that to guide a grown man you must reverse all that you did to guide the child. Do not hesitate to speak to him of those dangerous mysteries which
you have so carefully concealed from him hitherto.
Since he must become aware of them, let him not learn
them from another, nor from himself, but from you alone;
since he must henceforth fight against them, let him
know his enemy, that he may not be taken unawares.

. . . . . .

As there is a fitting age for the study of the
sciences, so there is a fitting age for the study of
the ways of the world. Those who learn these too soon,
follow them throughout life, without choice or consideration, and although they follow them fairly well they
never really know what they are about. But he who studies the ways of the world and sees the reason for them,
follows them with more insight, and therefore more
exactly and gracefully. Give me a child of twelve who
knows nothing at all; at fifteen I will restore him to
you knowing as much as those who have been under instruction from infancy; with this difference, that your
scholars only know things by heart, while mine knows
how to use his knowledge. In the same way plunge a
young man of twenty into society; under good guidance,
in a year's time, he will be more charming and more
truly polite than one brought up in society from childhood. For the former is able to perceive the reasons
for all the proceedings relating to age, position, and
sex, on which the customs of society depend, and can
reduce them to general principles, and apply them to
unforeseen emergencies; while the latter, who is guided
solely by habit, is at a loss when habit fails him.

. . . . .

If in order to cultivate my pupil's taste, I were
compelled to choose between a country where this form
of culture has not yet arisen and those in which it has
already degenerated, I would progress backwards. I
would begin his survey with the latter and end with the
former. My reason for this choice is, that taste becomes corrupted through excessive delicacy, which makes
it sensitive to things which most men do not perceive;
this delicacy leads to a spirit of discussion, for the
more subtle is our discrimination of things the more
things there are for us. This subtlety increases the

delicacy and decreases the uniformity of our touch. So
there are as many tastes as there are people. In disputes as to our preferences, philosophy and knowledge
are enlarged, and thus we learn to think. It is only
men accustomed to plenty of society who are capable of
very delicate observations, for these observations do
not occur to us till the last, and people who are un-
used to all sorts of society exhaust their attention in
the consideration of the more conspicuous features.
There is perhaps no civilised place upon earth where
the common taste is so bad as in Paris. Yet it is in
this capital that good taste is cultivated, and it seems
that few books make any impression in Europe whose
authors have not studied in Paris. Those who think it
is enough to read our books are mistaken; there is more
to be learnt from the conversation of authors than from
their books; and it is not from the authors that we
learn most. It is the spirit of social life which develops a thinking mind, and carries the eye as far as
it can reach. If you have a spark of genius, go and
spend a year in Paris; you will soon be all that you
are capable of becoming, or you will never be good for
anything at all.

. . . . . .

I will go still further in order to keep his taste
pure and wholesome. In the tumult of dissipation I
shall find opportunities for useful conversation with
him; and while these conversations are always about
things in which he takes a delight, I shall take care
to make them as amusing as they are instructive. Now is
the time to read pleasant books; now is the time to
teach him to analyse speech and to appreciate all the
beauties of eloquence and diction. It is a small matter
to learn languages, they are less useful than people
think; but the study of languages leads us on to that
of grammar in general. We must learn Latin if we
would have a thorough knowledge of French; these two
languages must be studied and compared if we would understand the rules of the art of speaking.

There is, moreover, a certain simplicity of taste
which goes straight to the heart; and this is only to
be found in the classics. In oratory, poetry, and every
kind of literature, Emile will find the classical
authors as he found them in history, full 'of matter and
sober in their judgment. The authors of our own time,

on the contrary, say little and talk much. To take their judgment as our law is not the way to form our own judgment.

. . . . . .

If I am not mistaken, the attention of my pupil, who sets so small a value upon words, will be directed in the first place to these differences, and they will affect his choice in his reading. He will be carried away by the manly eloquence of Demosthenes, and will say, "This is an orator;" but when he reads Cicero, he will say, "This is a lawyer."

Speaking generally Emile will have more taste for the books of the ancients than for our own, just because they were the first, and therefore the ancients are nearer to nature and their genius is more distinct. Whatever La Motte and the Abbe Terrasson may say, there is no real advance in human reason, for what we gain in one direction we lose in another; for all minds start from the same point, and as the time spent in learning what others have thought is so much time lost in learning to think for ourselves, we have more acquired knowledge and less vigour of mind. Our minds like our arms are accustomed to use tools for everything, and to do nothing for themselves. Fontenelle used to say that all these disputes as to the ancients and the moderns came to this - Were the trees in former times taller than they are now. If agriculture had changed, it would be worth our while to ask this question.

After I have led Emile to the sources of pure literature, I will also show him the channels into the resenvoirs of modern compilers; journals, translations, dictionairies, he shall cast a glance at them all, and then leave them forever. To amuse him he shall hear the chatter of the academies; I will draw his attention to the fact that every member of them is worth more by himself than he is as a member of the society; he will then draw his own conclusions as to the utility of these fine institutions.

I take him to the theatre to study taste, not morals; for in the theatre above all taste is revealed to those who can think. Lay aside precepts and morality, I should say; this is not the place to study them. The stage is not made for truth; its object is to flatter

and amuse; there is no place where one can learn so
completely the art of pleasing and of interesting the
human heart. The study of plays leads to the study of
poetry; both have the same end in view. If he has the
least glimmering of taste for poetry, how eagerly will
he study the languages of the poets, Greek, Latin, and
Italian! These studies will afford him unlimited amusement and will be none the less valuable; they will be a
delight to him at an age and in circumstances when the
heart finds so great a charm in every kind of beauty
which affects it. Picture to yourself on the one hand
Emile, on the other some young rascal from college,
reading the fourth book of the *Aeneid*, or Tibullus, or
the *Banquet* of Plato: what a difference between them!
What stirs the heart of Emile to its depths, makes not
the least impression on the other! Oh, good youth,
stay, make a pause in your reading, you are too deeply
moved; I would have you find pleasure in the language
of love, but I would not have you carried away by it;
be a wise man, but be a good man too. If you are only
one of these, you are nothing. After this let him win
fame or not in dead languages, in literature, in poetry,
I care little. He will be none the worse if he knows
nothing of them, and his education is not concerned
with these mere words.

My main object in teaching him to feel and love
beauty of every kind is to fix his affections and his
taste on these, to prevent the corruption of his natural
appetites, lest he should have to seek some day in the
midst of his wealth for the means of happiness which
should be found close at hand. I have said elsewhere
that taste is only the art of being a connoisseur in
matters of little importance, and this is quite true;
but since the charm of life depends on a tissue of
these matters of little importance, such efforts are no
small thing; through their means we learn how to fill
our life with the good things within our reach, with as
much truth as they may hold for us. I do not refer to
the morally good which depends on a good disposition of
the heart, but only to that which depends on the body,
on real delight, apart from the prejudices of public
opinion.

M. E. de Montaigne, ESSAYS: OF THE EDUCATION
OF CHILDREN

John Milton, ARCOPAGITICA
OF EDUCATION

1. What are some of the shortcomings of teachers and
   the curriculum that Montaigne sees in his day? To
   the extent that they continue today, how might they
   be overcome?

2. What are the proper aims of education as Montaigne
   sees them?

3. What types of educational experiences does Montaigne
   think are important and why?

4. Considering Aristotle's view of education, does
   Montaigne see education's goal to be developing
   goodness of intellect or goodness of character?

5. How would Montaigne define an educated man? How
   would you define an educated man?

6. What segments, if any, of today's society accept
   Montaigne's view of education? Do you see elements
   of Montaigne's theory in the college curriculum?
   Explain.

7. What, according to Milton, is the purpose of learning? How does he describe an "educated man"? How
   does this view compare to that of Newman?

8. What was your reaction to Milton's description of
   the ways in which learning is made disagreeable?

9. Characterize Milton's approach to the process of
   education.

    M. E. de Montaigne (1533-1592) is frequently cited
as the creator of the essay form. His charming wit and
impressive wisdom come through in this delightful essay
which is surprisingly modern, yet clearly shows the influence of Aristotle.

ESSAYS

Of the Institution and Education of Children;
to the Lady Diana of Foix, Countess of Gurson

I NEVER knew father, how crooked and deformed soever his
son were, that would either altogether cast him off or not
acknowledge him for his own; and yet (unless he be merely
besotted or blinded in his affection) it may not be said but he
plainly perceiveth his defects and hath a feeling of his imperfections. But so it is, he is his own. So is it in myself. I
see better than any man else that what I have set down is
nought but the fond imagination of him who in his youth
hath tasted nothing but the paring, and seen but the superficies
of true learning, whereof he hath retained but a general and
shapeless form, a smack of everything in general but nothing
to the purpose in particular, after the French manner. To be
short, I know there is an art of Physic, a course of laws, four
parts of the Mathematics, and I am not altogether ignorant
what they tend unto. And perhaps I also know the scope and

drift of Sciences in general to be for the service of our life. But to wade further, or that ever I tired myself with plodding upon *Aristotle* (the Monarch of our modern doctrine) or obstinately continued in the search of any one science, I confess I never did it. Nor is there any one art whereof I am able so much as to draw the first lineaments. And there is no scholar (be he of the lowest form) that may not repute himself wiser than I, who am not able to appose him in his first lesson; and if I be forced to it, I am constrained very impertinently to draw in matter from some general discourse, whereby I examine and give a guess at his natural judgment, a lesson as much unknown to them as theirs is to me.

I have not dealt or had commerce with any excellent book except *Plutarch* or *Seneca,* from whom (as the *Danaïdes*) I draw my water, incessantly filling and as fast emptying, something whereof I fasten to this paper but to myself nothing at all. And touching books, History is my chief study, Poesy my only delight, to which I am particularly affected. For as *Cleanthes* said, that as the voice being forcibly pent in the narrow gullet of a trumpet at last issueth forth more strong and shriller, so meseems that a sentence cunningly and closely couched in measure-keeping Poesy, darts itself forth more furiously and wounds me even to the quick. And concerning the natural faculties that are in me (whereof behold here an essay), I perceive them to faint under their own burden; my conceits and my judgment march but uncertain and as it were groping, staggering, and stumbling at every rush. And when I have gone as far as I can, I have no whit pleased myself, for the further I sail, the more land I descry, and that so dimmed with fogs and overcast with clouds, that my sight is so weakened I cannot distinguish the same. And then, undertaking to speak indifferently of all that presents itself unto my fantasy and having nothing but mine own natural means to employ therein, if it be my hap (as commonly it is) among good Authors, to light upon those very places which I have undertaken to treat of, as even now I did in *Plutarch,* reading his discourse of the power of imagination, wherein in regard of those wise men I acknowledge myself so weak and so poor, so dull and gross-headed, as I am forced both to pity and disdain myself. Yet am I pleased with this, that my opinions have often the grace to jump with theirs and that I follow them a loof-off and thereby possess at least that which all other men have not, which is that I know the utmost difference between them and myself. All which notwithstanding, I suffer my inventions to run abroad, as weak and faint as I have produced them, without bungling and botching the faults which this comparison hath discovered to me in them.

A man had need have a strong back to undertake to march foot to foot with this kind of men. The indiscreet writers of our age, amidst their trivial compositions, intermingle and wrest in whole sentences taken from ancient Authors, supposing by such filching theft to purchase honor and reputation to themselves, do clean contrary. For this infinite variety and dissemblance of lusters makes a face so wan, so ill-favored, and so ugly, in respect of theirs, that they lose much more than gain thereby. These were two contrary humors: The Philosopher *Chrysippus* was wont to foist in amongst his books not only whole sentences and other long-long discourses, but whole books of other Authors, as in one he brought in *Euripides' Medea*. And *Apollodorus* was wont to say of him that if one should draw from out his books what he had stolen from others, his paper would remain blank. Whereas *Epicurus,* clean contrary to him, in three hundred volumes he left behind him had not made use of one allegation.

It was my fortune not long since to light upon such a place. I had languishingly traced after some French words, so naked and shallow and so void either of sense or matter, that at last I found them to be nought but mere French words; and after a tedious and wearisome travel, I chanced to stumble upon an high, rich, and even to the clouds-raised piece, the descent whereof, had it been somewhat more pleasant or easy, or the ascent reaching a little further, it had been excusable and to be borne withal. But it was such a steep downfall, and by mere strength hewn out of the main rock, that by reading of the first six words, methought I was carried into another world, whereby I perceived the bottom whence

I came to be so low and deep as I durst never more adventure to go through it. For if I did stuff any one of my discourses with those rich spoils, it would manifestly cause the sottishness of others to appear.

To reprove mine own faults in others seems to me no more insufferable than to reprehend (as I do often) those of others in myself. They ought to be accused everywhere, and have all places of Sanctuary taken from them. Yet do I know how overboldly at all times I adventure to equal myself unto my filchings, and to march hand in hand with them, not without a fond-hardy hope that I may perhaps be able to blear the eyes of the Judges from discerning them. But it is as much for the benefit of my application as for the good of mine invention and force. And I do not furiously front, and body to body wrestle with those old champions. It is but by sleights, advantages, and false offers I seek to come within them, and if I can, to give them a fall. I do not rashly take them about the neck; I do but touch them. Nor do I go so far as by my bargain I would seem to do. Could I but keep even with them, I should then be an honest man, for I seek not to venture on them but where they are strongest.

To do as I have seen some, that is to shroud themselves under others' arms, not daring so much as to show their fingers' ends unarmed, and to botch up all their works (as it is an easy matter in a common subject, namely for the wiser sort) with ancient inventions here and there huddled up together. And in those who endeavored to hide what they have filched from others and make it their own, it is first a manifest note of injustice than a plain argument of cowardliness; who, having nothing of any worth in themselves to make show of, will yet, under the countenance of others' sufficiency go about to make a fair offer. Moreover (oh, great foolishness), to seek by such cozening tricks to forestall the ignorant approbation of the common sort, nothing fearing to discover their ignorance to men of understanding (whose praise only is of value), who will soon trace out such borrowed ware.

As for me, there is nothing I will do less. I never speak of others but that I may the more speak of myself. This concerneth not those mingle-mangles of many kinds of stuff, or as the Grecians call them, *Rhapsodies,* that for such are published, of which kind I have (since I came to years of discretion) seen diverse most ingenious and witty; amongst others, one under the name of *Capilupus;* besides many of the ancient stamp. These are wits of such excellence, as both here and elsewhere they will soon be perceived, as our late famous writer *Lipsius,* in his learned and laborious work of the Politics. Yet whatsoever come of it, forsomuch as they are but follies, my intent is not to smother them, no more than a bald or hoary picture of mine where a Painter hath drawn not a perfect visage but mine own. For, howsoever, these are but my humors and opinions, and I deliver them but to show what my conceit is, and not what ought to be believed. Wherein I aim at nothing but to display myself, who peradventure (if a new apprenticeship change me) shall be another tomorrow. I have no authority to purchase belief; neither do I desire it, knowing well that I am not sufficiently taught to instruct others. Some, having read my precedent Chapter, told me not long since in mine own house, I should somewhat more have extended myself in the discourse concerning the institution of children.

Now (Madam), if there were any sufficiency in me touching that subject, I could not better employ the same than to bestow it as a present upon that little lad which ere long threateneth to make a happy issue from out your honorable womb—for (Madam) you are too generous to begin with other than a man child. And having had so great a part in the conduct of your successful marriage, I may challenge some right and interest in the greatness and prosperity of all that shall proceed from it. Moreover, the ancient and rightful possession which you from time to time have ever had and still have over my service, urgeth me with more than ordinary respects to wish all honor, welfare, and advantage to whatsoever may in any sort concern you and yours. And truly, my meaning is but to show that the greatest difficulty, and importing all human knowledge, seemeth to be in this point, where the nurture and institution of young children is in question. For as in matters of husbandry, the labor that must be used before sowing, setting, and planting, yea in planting itself, is most certain and easy. But when that which was sown, set, and planted, cometh to take life, before it come to ripeness, much ado and great variety of proceeding belongeth to it. So in men, it is no great matter to get them, but being born, what continual cares, what diligent attendance, what doubts and fears, do daily wait on their parents and tutors before they can be nurtured and brought to any good! The foreshow of their inclination whilst they are young is so uncertain, their humors so variable, their promises so changing, their hopes so false, and their proceedings so doubtful, that it is very hard (yea for the wisest) to ground any certain judgment or assured success upon them. Behold *Cimon,* view *Themistocles* and a thousand others, how they have differed, and fallen to better from themselves, and deceive the expectation of such as knew them. The young whelps both of Dogs and Bears at first sight show their natural disposition, but men headlong embracing this custom or fashion, following that humor or opinion, admitting this or that passion, allowing of that or this law, are easily changed and soon disguised. Yet is it hard to force the natural propensity or readiness of the mind, whereby it followeth that for want of heedy foresight in those that could not guide their course well, they often employ much time in vain to address young children in those matters whereunto they are not naturally addicted. All which difficulties notwithstanding, mine opinion is to bring them up in the best and profitablest studies, and that a man should slightly pass over those fond presages and deceiving prognostics which we overprecisely gather in their infancy. And (without offense be it said) methinks that *Plato* in his commonwealth alloweth them too-too much authority.

Madam, Learning joined with true knowledge is an especial and graceful ornament, and an implement of wonderful use and consequence, namely in persons raised to that degree of fortune wherein you are. And in good truth, learning hath not her own true form, nor can she make show of her beauteous lineaments if she fall into the hands of base and vile persons. [For as famous *Torquato Tasso* saith: "Philosophy being a rich and noble Queen and knowing her own worth, graciously smileth upon and lovingly embraceth Princes and noble men if they become suitors to her, admitting them as her minions and gently affording them all the favors she can; whereas upon the contrary, if she be wooed and sued unto by clowns, mechanical fellows, and such base kind of people, she holds herself disparaged and disgraced, as holding no proportion with them. And therefore see we by experience that if a true Gentleman or nobleman follow her with any attention, and woo her with importunity, he shall learn and know more of her, and prove a better scholar in one year than an ungentle or base fellow shall in seven, though he pursue her never so attentively."] She is much more ready and fierce to lend her furtherance and direction in the conduct of a war, to attempt honorable actions, to command a people, to treat a peace with a prince of foreign nation, than she is to form an argument in Logic, to devise a Syllogism, to canvass a case at the bar, or to prescribe a receipt of pills. So (noble Lady), forsomuch as I cannot persuade myself that you will either forget or neglect this point concerning the institution of yours, especially having tasted the sweetness thereof and being descended of so noble and learned a race (for we yet possess the learned compositions of the ancient and noble Earls of *Foix,* from out whose heroic loins your husband and you take your offspring, and *Francis,* Lord of *Candale,* your worthy uncle, doth daily bring forth such fruits thereof, as the knowledge of the matchless quality of your house shall hereafter extend itself to many ages), I will therefore make you acquainted with one conceit of mine, which contrary to the common use I hold, and that is all I am able to afford you concerning that matter.

The charge of the Tutor, which you shall appoint your son, in the choice of whom consisteth the whole substance of his education and bringing up, on which are many branches depending, which (forasmuch as I can add nothing of any moment to it) I will not touch at all. And for that point wherein I presume to advise him, he may so far forth give credit unto it as he shall see just cause. To a gentleman born of noble parentage, and heir of a house, that aimeth at true learning and in it would be disciplined, not so much for gain or commodity to himself (because so abject an end is far unworthy the grace and favor of the Muses, and besides, hath a regard or dependency of others) nor for external show and ornament, but to adorn and enrich his inward mind, desiring rather to shape and institute an able and sufficient man than a bare learned man. My desire is therefore that the parents or overseers of such a gentleman be very circumspect and careful in choosing his director, whom I would rather commend for having a well-composed and temperate brain than a full-stuffed head, yet both will do well. And I would rather prefer wisdom, judgment, civil customs, and modest behavior, than bare and mere literal learning; and that in his charge he hold a new course. Some never cease brawling in their scholars' ears (as if they were still pouring in a tun) to follow their book; yet is their charge nothing else but to repeat what hath been told them before. I would have a tutor to correct this part, and that at first entrance, according to the capacity of the wit he hath in hand, he should begin to make show of it, making him to have a smack of all things, and how to choose and distinguish them, without help of others, sometimes opening him the way, other times leaving him to open it by himself. I would not have him to invent and speak alone, but suffer his disciple to speak when his turn cometh. *Socrates*, and after him *Arcesilaus*, made their scholars to speak first, and then would speak themselves. *Most commonly the authority of them that teach, hinders them that would learn* (Cic. *De Nat.* i.).

It is therefore meet that he make him first trot on before him, whereby he may the better judge of his pace and so guess how long he will hold out, that accordingly he may fit his strength, for want of which proportion, we often mar all. And to know how to make a good choice and how far forth one may proceed (still keeping a due measure) is one of the hardest labors I know. It is a sign of a noble, and effect of an undaunted spirit to know how to second, and how far forth he shall condescend to his childish proceedings and how to guide them. As for myself, I can better and with more strength walk up, than down a hill. Those which, according to our common fashion, undertake with one selfsame lesson and like manner of education to direct many spirits of diverse forms and different humors, it is no marvel if among a multitude of children they scarce meet with two or three that reap any good fruit by their discipline or that come to any perfection. I would not only have him to demand an account of the words contained in his lesson, but of the sense and substance thereof, and judge of the profit he hath made of it not by the testimony of his memory, but by the witness of his life. That what he lately learned he cause him to set forth and portray the same into sundry shapes, and then to accommodate it to as many different and several subjects; whereby he shall perceive whether he have yet apprehended the same and therein enfeoffed himself, at due times taking his instruction from the institution given by *Plato*. It is a sign of crudity and indigestion for a man to yield up his meat even as he swallowed the same; the stomach hath not wrought his full operation unless it have changed form and altered fashion of that which was given him to boil and concoct.

[We see men gape after no reputation but learning, and when they say such a one is a learned man, they think they have said enough;] Our mind doth move at others' pleasure, as tied and forced to serve the fantasies of others, being brought under by authority and forced to stoop to the lure of their bare lesson. We have been so subjected to harp upon one string that we have no way left us to descant upon voluntary. Our vigor and liberty is clean extinct. *They never come to their own tuition* [SEN. *Epist.* xxxiii.]. It was my hap to be familiarly acquainted with an honest man at *Pisa*, but such an *Aristotelian* as he held this infallible position, that a conformity to *Aristotle's* doctrine was the true touchstone and squire of all solid imaginations and perfect verity; for whatsoever had no coherency with it was but fond *Chimeras* and idle humors, inasmuch as he had known all, seen all, and said all. This proposition of his, being somewhat overamply and in-

juriously interpreted by some, made him a long time after to
be troubled in the inquisition of *Rome*. I would have him
make his scholar narrowly to sift all things with discretion,
and harbor nothing in his head by mere authority or upon
trust. *Aristotle's* principles shall be no more axioms unto him
than the Stoics' or Epicureans'. Let this diversity of judgments
be proposed unto him; if he can, he shall be able to distinguish the truth from falsehood, if not, he will remain doubtful.

> No less it pleaseth me,
> To doubt, than wise to be.
> DANTE. *Inferno,* cant. xii. 48.

For if by his own discourse he embrace the opinions of
Xenophon or of *Plato,* they shall be no longer theirs but his.
He that merely followeth another, traceth nothing and seeketh
nothing: *We are not under a King's command; everyone may
challenge himself, for let him at least know that he knoweth*
(SEN. *Epist.* xxxiii.). It is requisite he endeavor as much to
feed himself with their conceits as labor to learn their precepts; which, so he know how to apply, let him hardly forget
where or whence he had them. Truth and reason are common to all, and are no more proper unto him that spoke them
heretofore than unto him that shall speak them hereafter.
And it is no more according to *Plato's* opinion than to mine,
since both he and I understand and see alike. The Bees do
here and there suck this and cull that flower, but afterward
they produce the honey which is peculiarly their own; then is
it no more Thyme or Marjoram. So of pieces borrowed of
others he may lawfully alter, transform, and compound them,
to shape out of them a perfect piece of work altogether his
own, always provided his judgment, his travel, study, and institution, tend to nothing but to frame the same perfect. Let
him hardly conceal where or whence he hath had any help,
and make no show of anything but of that which he hath made
himself. Pirates, filchers, and borrowers make a show of their
purchases and buildings, but not of that which they have
taken from others. You see not the secret fees or bribes

Lawyers take of their Clients, but you shall manifestly discover the alliances they make, the honors they get for their children, and the goodly houses they build. No man makes open show of his receipts, but everyone of his gettings. The good that comes of study (or at least should come) is to prove better, wiser, and honester. It is the understanding power (said *Epicharmus*) that seeth and heareth; it is it that profiteth all and disposeth all, that moveth, swayeth, and ruleth all. All things else are but blind, senseless, and without spirit. And truly in barring him of liberty to do anything of himself, we make him thereby more servile and more coward. Who would ever inquire of his scholar what he thinketh of Rhetoric, of Grammar, of this or of that sentence of *Cicero?* Which things, thoroughly feathered (as if they were oracles), are let fly into our memory; in which both letters and syllables are substantial parts of the subject. To know by rote is no perfect knowledge, but to keep what one hath committed to his memory charge is commendable. What a man directly knoweth, that will he dispose of without turning still to his book or looking to his pattern. A mere bookish sufficiency is unpleasant. All I expect of it is an embellishing of my actions, and not a foundation of them, according to *Plato's* mind, who saith, "Constancy, faith, and sincerity are true Philosophy; as for other Sciences, and tending elsewhere, they are but garish paintings."

I would fain have *Paluel* or *Pompey*, those two excellent dancers of our time, with all their nimbleness, teach any man to do their lofty tricks and high capers only with seeing them done and without stirring out of his place, as some Pedantic fellows would instruct our minds without moving or putting it in practise. And glad would I be to find one that would teach us how to manage a horse, to toss a pike, to shoot off a piece, to play upon the lute, or to warble with the voice, without any exercise, as these kind of men would teach us to judge, and how to speak well, without any exercise of speaking or judging.

In which kind of life, or as I may term it, Apprenticeship, what action or object soever presents itself unto our eyes may serve us instead of a sufficient book. A pretty prank of a boy, a knavish trick of a page, a foolish part of a lackey, an idle tale or any discourse else, spoken either in jest or earnest, at the table or in company, are even as new subjects for us to work upon. For furtherance whereof, commerce or common society among men, visiting of foreign countries and observing of strange fashions, are very necessary, not only to be able (after the manner of our young gallants of *France*) to report how many paces the Church of *Santa Rotonda* is in length or breadth, or what rich garments the courtesan *Signora Livia* weareth and the worth of her hose, or as some do, nicely to dispute how much longer or broader the face of *Nero* is, which they have seen in some old ruins of *Italy*, than that which is made for him in other old monuments elsewhere. But they should principally observe and be able to make certain relation of the humors and fashions of those countries they have seen, that they may the better know how to correct and prepare their wits by those of others. I would therefore have him begin even from his infancy to travel abroad; and first, that at one shoot he may hit two marks, he should see neighbor countries, namely where languages are most different from ours; for unless a man's tongue be fashioned unto them in his youth, he shall never attain to the true pronunciation of them if he once grow in years. Moreover, we see it received as a common opinion of the wiser sort that it agreeth not with reason that a child be always nuzzled, cockered, dandled, and brought up in his parents' lap or sight, forsomuch as their natural kindness, or (as I may call it) tender fondness, causeth often even the wisest to prove so idle, so overnice, and so base-minded. For parents are not capable; neither can they find in their hearts to see them checked, corrected, or chastised, nor endure to see them brought up so meanly and so far from daintiness, and many times so dangerously as they must needs be. And it would grieve them to see their children come home from those exercises that a Gentleman must necessarily acquaint himself with, sometimes all wet and bemired, other times sweaty and full of dust, and to drink being either extreme hot, or exceeding cold. And it would trouble them to see him ride a rough untamed horse, or with his weapon furiously encounter a skillful Fencer, or to handle and shoot off a musket. Against which there is no remedy. If he will make him prove a sufficient, complete, or honest man, he must not be spared in his youth, and it will come to pass that he shall many times have occasion and be forced to shock the rules of Physic.

> Lead he his life in open air,
> And in affairs full of despair.
> Hor. i. *Od.* ii. 4.

It is not sufficient to make his mind strong; his muscles must also be strengthened. The mind is overborne if it be not seconded; and it is too much for her alone to discharge two offices. I have a feeling how mine panteth, being joined to so tender and sensible a body, and that lieth so heavy upon it. And in my lecture I often perceive how my Authors in their writings sometimes commend examples for magnanimity and force that rather proceed from a thick skin and hardness of the bones. I have known men, women, and children born of so hard a constitution that a blow with a cudgel would less hurt them than a fillip would do me, and so dull and block-ish that they will neither stir tongue nor eyebrows, beat them never so much. When wrestlers go about to counterfeit the Philosophers' patience, they rather show the vigor of their sinews than of their heart. For the custom to bear travail is to tolerate grief: *Labor worketh a hardness upon sorrow* (Cic. *Tusc. Qu.* ii.). He must be inured to suffer the pain and hard-ness of exercises that so he may be induced to endure the pain of the colic, of cautery, of falls, of sprains, and other diseases incident to man's body: yea, if need require, patiently to bear imprisonment and other tortures, by which sufferance he shall come to be had in more esteem and account. For, ac-cording to time and place, the good as well as the bad man may haply fall into them; we have seen it by experience. Whosoever striveth against the laws threatens good men with mischief and extortion. Moreover, the authority of the Tutor (who should be sovereign over him) is by the cockering and presence of the parents hindered and interrupted. Besides, the awe and respect which the household bears him, and the knowledge of the means, possibilities, and greatness of his house, are in my judgment no small lets in a young Gentleman.

In this school of commerce and society among men, I have often noted this vice, that in lieu of taking acquaintance of others, we only endeavor to make ourselves known to them, and we are more ready to utter such merchandise as we have than to engross and purchase new commodities. Silence and modesty are qualities very convenient to civil conversation. It is also necessary that a young man be rather taught to be discreetly sparing and closehanded, than prodigally wasteful and lavish in his expenses, and moderate in husbanding his wealth when he shall come to possess it. And not to take pepper in the nose for every foolish tale that shall be spoken in his presence, because it is an uncivil importunity to contradict whatsoever is not agreeing to our humor. Let him be pleased to correct himself. And let him not seem to blame that in others which he refuseth to do himself, nor go about to withstand common fashions. *A man may be wise without ostentation, without envy* (SEN. *Epist.* ciii. f.). Let him avoid those imperious images of the world, those uncivil behaviors, and childish ambition, wherewith, God wot, too-too many are possessed; that is, to make a fair show of that which is not in him, endeavoring to be reputed other than indeed he is; and as if reprehension and new devices were hard to come by, he would by that means acquire unto himself the name of some peculiar virtue. As it pertaineth but to great Poets to use the liberty of arts, so is it tolerable but in noble minds and great spirits to have a pre-eminence above ordinary fashions. *If* Socrates *and* Aristippus *have done ought against custom or good manner, let not a man think he may do the same, for they obtained this license by their great and excellent good parts* (CIC. *Off.* i.).

He shall be taught not to enter rashly into discourse or contesting, but when he shall encounter with a Champion worthy his strength. And then would I not have him employ all the tricks that may fit his turn, but only such as may stand him in most stead. That he be taught to be curious in making choice of his reasons, loving pertinency and, by consequence, brevity. That above all he be instructed to yield, yea to quit his weapons unto truth as soon as he shall discern the same, whether it proceed from his adversary or upon better advice from himself, for he shall not be preferred to any place of eminence above others for repeating of a prescribed part, and he is not engaged to defend any cause further than he may approve it. Nor shall he be of that trade where the liberty for a man to repent and readvise himself is sold for ready money. *Nor is he enforced by any necessity to defend and make good all that is prescribed and commanded him* (Cic. *Acad. Qu.* iv.).

If his tutor agree with my humor, he shall frame his affection to be a most loyal and true subject to his Prince, and a most affectionate and courageous Gentleman, in all that may concern the honor of his Sovereign or the good of his country. And endeavor to suppress in him all manner of affection to undertake any action otherwise than for a public good and duty. Besides many inconveniences which greatly prejudice our liberty by reason of these particular bonds, the judgment of a man that is waged and bought, either it is less free and honest or else it is blemished with oversight and ingratitude. A mere and precise Courtier can neither have law nor will to speak or think otherwise than favorably of his Master, who among so many thousands of his subjects hath made choice of him alone to institute and bring him up with his own hand. These favors, with the commodities that follow minion Courtiers, corrupt (not without some color of reason) his liberty and dazzle his judgment. It is therefore commonly seen that the Courtiers' language differs from other men's in the same state, and to be of no great credit in such matters. Let therefore his conscience and virtue shine in his speech, and reason be his chief direction. Let him be taught to confess such faults as he shall discover in his own discourses, albeit none other perceive them but himself, for it is an evident show of judgment and effect of sincerity, which are the chief-

est qualities he aimeth at. That willfully to strive and obstinately to contest in words, are common qualities, most apparent in basest minds. That to readvise and correct himself,
and when one is most earnest, to leave an ill opinion, are
rare, noble, and Philosophical conditions.

Being in company, he shall be put in mind to cast his eyes
round about and everywhere. For I note that the chief places
are usually seized upon by the most unworthy and less
capable, and that height of fortune is seldom joined with
sufficiency. I have seen that whilst they at the upper end of
a board were busy entertaining themselves with talking of the
beauty of the hangings about a chamber or of the taste of some
good cup of wine, many good discourses at the lower end have
utterly been lost. He shall weigh the carriage of every man
in his calling, a Herdsman, a Mason, a Stranger, or a traveler.
All must be employed; every one according to his worth, for
all helps to make up household. Yea, the folly and the simplicity of others shall be as instructions to him. By controlling
the graces and manners of others, he shall acquire into himself
envy of the good and contempt of the bad. Let him hardly be
possessed with an honest curiosity to search out the nature
and causes of all things. Let him survey whatsoever is rare and
singular about him, a building, a fountain, a man, a place
where any battle hath been fought, or the passages of *Caesar*
or *Charlemagne*.

What land is parched with heat, what clogged with frost,
What wind drives kindly to the Italian coast.
Prop. iv. El. iii. 39.

He shall endeavor to be familiarly acquainted with the customs, with the means, with the state, with the dependences
and alliances of all Princes; they are things soon and pleasant
to be learned and most profitable to be known. In this acquaintance of men, my meaning is that he chiefly comprehend
them that live but by the memory of books. He shall, by the
help of Histories, inform himself of the worthiest minds that
were in the best ages. It is a frivolous study, if a man list, but

of invaluable worth to such as can make use of it. And as *Plato* saith, the only study the Lacedemonians reserved for themselves. What profit shall he not reap, touching this point, reading the lives of our *Plutarch?* Always conditioned, the master bethink himself whereto his charge tendeth, and that he imprint not so much in his scholar's mind the date of the ruin of *Carthage,* as the manners of *Hannibal* and *Scipio,* nor so much where *Marcellus* died, as because he was unworthy of his devoir he died there; that he teach him not so much to know Histories as to judge of them. It is, amongst things that best agree with my humor, the subject to which our spirits do most diversely apply themselves. I have read in *Livy* a number of things which peradventure others never read, in whom *Plutarch* haply read a hundred more than ever I could read, and which perhaps the author himself did never intend to set down. To some kind of men, it is a mere grammatical study, but to others a perfect anatomy of Philosophy, by means whereof the secretest part of our nature is searched into.

There are in *Plutarch* many ample discourses most worthy to be known, for in my judgment he is the chief work-master of such works, whereof there are a thousand whereat he hath but slightly glanced. For with his finger he doth but point us out a way to walk in if we list, and is sometimes pleased to give but a touch at the quickest and main point of a discourse, from whence they are by diligent study to be drawn and so brought into open market. As that saying of his, that "the inhabitants of *Asia* served but one alone because they could not pronounce one only syllable, which is *Non,*" gave perhaps both subject and occasion to my friend *Boëtie* to compose his book of voluntary servitude. If it were no more but to see *Plutarch* wrest a slight action to man's life or a word that seemeth to bear no such sense, it will serve for a whole discourse. It is pity men of understanding should so much love brevity. Without doubt their reputation is thereby better, but we the worse. *Plutarch* had rather we should commend him for his judgment than for his knowledge; he loveth better to leave a kind of longing-desire in us of him, than a satiety. He knew very well that even in good things too much may be said, and that *Alexandridas* did justly reprove him who spoke very good sentences to the *Ephors*, but they were overtedious. "O stranger," quoth he, "thou speakest what thou oughtest, otherwise than thou shouldest." Those that have lean and thin bodies stuff them up with bombasting. And such as have but poor matter will puff it up with lofty words.

There is a marvelous clearness, or as I may term it, an enlightening of man's judgment, drawn from the commerce of men and by frequenting abroad in the world. We are all so contrived and compact in ourselves that our sight is made shorter by the length of our nose. When *Socrates* was demanded whence he was, he answered not "Of *Athens*," but "Of the world"; for he, who had his imagination more full and farther stretching, embraced all the world for his native City, and extended his acquaintance, his society, and affections to all mankind, and not as we do, that look no further than our feet. If the frost chance to nip the vines about my village, my Priest doth presently argue that the wrath of God hangs over our head and threateneth all mankind, and judgeth that the Pipe is already fallen upon the Cannibals.

In viewing these intestine and civil broils of ours, who doth not exclaim that this world's vast frame is near unto a dissolution and that the day of judgment is ready to fall on us? never remembering that many worse revolutions have been seen, and that whilst we are plunged in grief and overwhelmed in sorrow, a thousand other parts of the world besides are blessed with all happiness, and wallow in pleasures, and never think on us? Whereas, when I behold our lives, our license, and impunity, I wonder to see them so mild and easy. He on whose head it haileth, thinks all the Hemisphere besides to be in a storm and tempest. And as that dull-pated *Savoyard* said, that if the silly King of *France* could cunningly have managed his fortune, he might very well have made himself chief Steward of his Lord's household, whose imagination conceived no other greatness than his Master's. We are all insensible of this kind of error, an error of great consequence and prejudice. But whosoever shall present unto his inward eyes, as it were in a Table, the Idea of the great image of our universal mother

Nature, attired in her richest robes, sitting in the throne of her Majesty, and in her visage shall read so general and so constant a variety; he that therein shall view himself, not himself alone but a whole Kingdom, to be in respect of a great circle but the smallest point that can be imagined, he only can value things according to their essential greatness and proportion. This great universe (which some multiply as *Species* under one *Genus*) is the true looking glass wherein we must look if we will know whether we be of a good stamp or in the right bias.

To conclude, I would have this world's frame to be my Scholar's choice book. So many strange humors, sundry sects, varying judgments, diverse opinions, different laws, and fantastical customs teach us to judge rightly of ours and instruct our judgment to acknowledge his imperfections and natural weakness, which is no easy an apprenticeship. So many innovations of estates, so many falls of Princes and changes of public fortune, may and ought to teach us not to make so great account of ours. So many names, so many victories, and so many conquests buried in dark oblivion makes the hope to perpetuate our names but ridiculous, by the surprising of ten argoletiers, or of a small cottage which is known but by his fall. The pride and fierceness of so many strange and gorgeous shows, the pride-puffed majesty of so many courts and of their greatness, ought to confirm and assure our sight undauntedly to bear the affronts and thunderclaps of ours without sealing our eyes. So many thousands of men, low-laid in their graves afore us, may encourage us not to fear or be dismayed to go meet so good company in the other world. And so of all things else. Our life (said *Pythagoras*) draws near unto the great and populous assemblies of the Olympic games, wherein some, to get the glory and to win the goal of the games, exercise their bodies with all industry; others, for greediness of gain, bring thither merchandise to sell; others there are (and those be not the worst) that seek after no other good but to mark how, wherefore, and to what end all things are done, and to be spectators or observers of other men's lives and actions that so they may the better judge and direct their own.

Unto examples may all the most profitable Discourses of Philosophy be sorted, which ought to be the touchstone of human actions and a rule to square them by; to whom may be said,

> What thou mayest wish, what profit may come clear,
> From new-stamped coin, to friends and country dear,
> What thou ought'st give: whom God would have thee be,
> And in what part 'mongst men he placed thee.
> What we are, and wherefore,
> To live here we were bore.
> Pers. Sat. iii. 69, 67.

What it is to know, and not to know (which ought to be the scope of study); what valor, what temperance, and what justice is; what difference there is between ambition and avarice, bondage and freedom, subjection and liberty; by which marks a man may distinguish true and perfect contentment; and how far-forth one ought to fear or apprehend death, grief, or shame.

> How every labor he may ply,
> And bear, or every labor fly.
> Virg. Æn. viii. 853.

What wards or springs move us, and the causes of so many motions in us. For meseemeth that the first discourses wherewith his conceit should be sprinkled, ought to be those that rule his manners and direct his sense; which will both teach him to know himself and how to live and how to die well. Among the liberal Sciences, let us begin with that which makes us free. Indeed, they may all in some sort stead us as an instruction to our life and use of it, as all other things else serve the same to some purpose or other. But let us make especial choice of that which may directly and pertinently serve the same. If we could restrain and adapt the appurtenances of our life to their right bias and natural limits, we should find the best part of the Sciences that now are in use clean out of fashion with us; yea, and in those that are most in use, there are certain byways and deep-flows most [un]profitable, which we should do well to leave, and according to the institution of *Socrates*, limit the course of our studies in those where profit is wanting.

> Be bold to be wise: to begin, be strong,
> He that to live well doth the time prolong,
> Clownlike expects, till down the stream he run;
> That runs, and will run, till the world be done.
> HOR. i. Epi. ii. 40.

It is mere simplicity to teach our children,

> What *Pisces* move, or hot-breathed *Leo* beams,
> Or *Capricornus* bathed in western streams.
> PROP. iv. El. i. 85.

The knowledge of the stars and the motion of the eighth sphere, before their own.

> [What matters to me the Pleiades and the Boötes' stare.]
> [ANAC. Odes. xvii. 10.]

Anaximenes, writing to *Pythagoras*, saith, *With what sense can I amuse myself to the secrets of the Stars, having continually death or bondage before mine eyes?* For at that time the Kings of *Persia* were making preparations to war against his Country. All men ought to say so, being beaten with ambition, with avarice, with rashness, and with superstition, and having such other enemies unto life within him: "Wherefore shall I study and take care about the mobility and variation of the world?" When he is once taught what is fit to make him better and wiser, he shall be entertained with Logic, natural Philosophy, Geometry, and Rhetoric. Then having settled his judgment, look what science he doth most addict himself unto; he shall in short time attain to the perfection of it. His lecture shall be sometimes by way of talk and sometimes by book. His tutor may now and then supply him with the Author [himself], as an end and motive of his institution, sometimes giving him the pith and substance of it ready chewed. And if of himself he be not so thoroughly acquainted with books that he may readily find so many notable discourses as are in them to effect his purpose, it shall not be amiss that some learned man being appointed to keep him company, who at any time of need may furnish him with such munition as he shall stand in need of, that he may afterward distribute and dispense them to his best use. And that this kind of lesson be more easy and natural than that of *Gaza*, who will make question? Those are but harsh, thorny, and unpleasant precepts; vain, idle and immaterial words, on which small hold may be taken; wherein is nothing to quicken the mind. In this, the spirit findeth substance to [bite] and feed upon. A fruit without all comparison much better, and that will soon be ripe.

It is a thing worthy consideration to see what state things are brought unto in this our age, and how Philosophy, even to the wisest and men of best understanding, is but an idle, vain, and fantastical name, of small use and less worth, both in opinion and effect. I think these Sophistries are the cause of it, which have forestalled the ways to come unto it. They do very ill that go about to make it seem as it were inaccessible for children to come unto, setting it forth with a wrinkled, ghastly, and frowning visage. Who hath masked her with so counterfeit, pale, and hideous a countenance? There is nothing more beauteous, nothing more delightful, nothing more gamesome; and as I may say, nothing more fondly wanton. For she presenteth nothing to our eyes and preacheth nothing to our ears but sport and pastime. A sad and lowering look plainly declareth that that is not her haunt. *Demetrius* the Grammarian, finding a company of Philosophers sitting close together in the Temple of *Delphi*, said unto them, *Either I am deceived, or by your plausible and pleasant looks, you are not in any serious and earnest discourse amongst yourselves.* To whom one of them, named *Heracleon* the Megarian, answered, *That belongeth to them who busy themselves in seek-*

ing whether future tense of the verb βάλλω hath a double λ
or that labor to find the derivation of the comparatives χείρων,
βέλτιων, and of the superlatives χείριστον, βέλτιστον. It is they
that must chafe in entertaining themselves with their science.
As for discourses of Philosophy, they are wont to glad, rejoice,
and not to vex and molest those that use them.

> You may perceive the torments of the mind,
> Hid in sick body, you the joys may find,
> The face such habit takes in either kind.
> JUVEN. *Sat.* ix. 18.

That mind which harboreth Philosophy ought by reason
of her sound health make that body also sound and healthy;
it ought to make her contentment to through-shine in all exterior parts; it ought to shape and model all outward de-
meanors to the model of it, and by consequence arm him that
doth possess it with a gracious stoutness and lively audacity,
with an active and pleasing gesture, and with a settled and
cheerful countenance. The most evident token and apparent
sign of true wisdom is a constant and unconstrained rejoicing,
whose estate is like unto all things above the Moon, that is,
ever clear, always bright. It is *Baroco* and *Baralipton* that
make their followers prove so base and idle, and not Philosophy. They know her not but by hearsay. What? Is it not
she that cleareth all storms of the mind? And teacheth misery,
famine, and sickness to laugh? Not by reason of some imaginary Epicycles, but by natural and palpable reasons. She
aimeth at nothing but virtue. It is virtue she seeks after,
which, as the school saith, is not pitched on the top of a high,
steep, or inaccessible hill. For they that have come unto her
affirm that, clean contrary, she keeps her stand and holds her
mansion in a fair, flourishing, and pleasant plain, whence, as
from a high watchtower, she surveyeth all things to be subject unto her, to whom any man may with great facility come if
he but know the way or entrance to her palace. For the paths
that lead unto her are certain fresh and shady green alleys,
sweet and flowery ways, whose ascent is even, easy, and

nothing wearisome, like unto that of heaven's vaults. Forsomuch as they have not frequented this virtue, who gloriously, as in a throne of Majesty sits sovereign, goodly, triumphant, lovely, equally delicious and courageous, protesting herself to be a professed and irreconcilable enemy to all sharpness, austerity, fear, and compulsion; having nature for her guide, fortune and voluptuousness for her companions; they according to their weakness have imaginarily fained her to have a foolish, sad, grim, querulous, spiteful, threatening, and disdainful visage, with a horrid and unpleasant look; and have placed her upon a craggy, sharp, and unfrequented rock, amidst desert cliffs, and uncouth crags, as a scarecrow or bugbear to affright the common people with. Now, the tutor, which ought to know that he should rather seek to fill the mind and store the will of his disciple as much, or rather more, with love and affection than with awe and reverence unto virtue, may show and tell him that Poets follow common humors, making him plainly to perceive, and as it were palpably to feel, that the Gods have rather placed labor and sweat at the entrances which lead to *Venus'* chambers than at the doors that direct to *Pallas'* cabinets.

And when he shall perceive his scholar to have a sensible feeling of himself, presenting *Bradamente* or *Angelica* before him as a Mistress to enjoy, embellished with a natural, active, generous, and unspotted beauty, not ugly or Giantlike, but blithe and lively, in respect of a wanton, soft, affected, and artificial-flaring beauty; the one attired like unto a young man, coifed with a bright-shining helmet, the other disguised and dressed about the head like unto an impudent harlot, with embroideries, frizzlings, and carcanets of pearls, he will no doubt deem his own love to be a man and no woman if in his choice he differ from that effeminate shepherd of *Phrygia*.

In this new kind of lesson, he shall declare unto him that the prize, the glory, and height of true virtue consisted in the facility, profit, and pleasure of his exercises, so far from difficulty and encumbrances that children as well as men, the simple as soon as the wise, may come unto her. Discretion and temperance, not force or waywardness, are the instru-

ments to bring him unto her. *Socrates* (virtue's chief favorite),
that he might the better walk in the pleasant, natural, and
open path of her progresses, doth voluntarily and in good
earnest quit all compulsion. She is the nurse and foster mother
of all human pleasures, who in making them just and upright,
she also makes them sure and sincere. By moderating them,
she keepeth them in ure and breath. In limiting and cutting
them off whom she refuseth, she whets us on toward those she
leaveth unto us, and plenteously leaves us them which Nature
pleaseth, and like a kind mother giveth us over unto satiety, if
not unto wearisomeness, unless we will peradventure say that
the rule and bridle which stayeth the drunkard before drunk-
enness, the glutton before surfeiting, and the lecher before
the losing of his hair, be the enemies of our pleasures. If common fortune fail her, it clearly escapes her, or she cares not for
her, or she frames another unto herself, altogether her own,
not so fleeting nor so rolling. She knoweth the way how to be
rich, mighty, and wise, and how to lie in sweet-perfumed
beds. She loveth life; she delights in beauty, in glory, and in
health. But her proper and particular office is first to know
how to use such goods temperately, and how to lose them
constantly. An office much more noble than severe, without
which all course of life is unnatural, turbulent, and deformed,
to which one may lawfully join those rocks, those encumbrances, and those hideous monsters.

If so it happen that his Disciple prove of so different a condition that he rather love to give ear to an idle fable than to
the report of some noble voyage or other notable and wise
discourse when he shall hear it; that at the sound of a Drum
or clang of a Trumpet, which are wont to rouse and arm the
youthly heat of his companions, turneth to another that calleth
him to see a play, tumbling, juggling tricks, or other idle lose-
time sports; and who for pleasure's sake doth not deem it
more delightsome to return all sweaty and weary from a victorious combat, from wrestling, or riding of a horse, than from
a Tennis court, or dancing school, with the prize or honor of
such exercises; the best remedy I know for such a one is to
put him apprentice to some base occupation in some good

town or other, yea were he the son of a Duke; according to *Plato's* rule, who saith that *Children must be placed, not according to their father's condition, but the faculties of their mind.* Since it is Philosophy that teacheth us to live, and that infancy as well as other ages may plainly read her lessons in the same, why should it not be imparted unto young Scholars?

> He's moist and soft mold, and must by and by
> Be cast, made up, while wheel whirls readily.
> PERS. *Sat.* iii. 23.

We are taught to live when our life is well-nigh spent. Many scholars have been infected with that loathsome and marrow-wasting disease before ever they came to read *Aristotle's* treatise of Temperance. *Cicero* was wont to say that *Could he outlive the lives of two men, he should never find leisure to study the Lyric Poets.* And I find these Sophisters both worse and more unprofitable. Our child is engaged in greater matters. And but the first fifteen or sixteen years of his life are due unto Pedantry, the rest unto action. Let us therefore employ so short time as we have to live in more necessary instructions. It is an abuse; remove these thorny quiddities of Logic, whereby our life can no whit be amended, and betake ourselves to the simple discourses of Philosophy. Know how to choose and fitly to make use of them; they are much more easy to be conceived than one of *Boccaccio's* tales. A child coming from nurse is more capable of them than he is to learn to read or write. Philosophy hath discourses whereof infancy as well as decaying old age may make good use. I am of *Plutarch's* mind, which is that *Aristotle* did not so much amuse his great Disciple about the arts how to frame Syllogisms or the principles of Geometry, as he endeavored to instruct him with good precepts concerning valor, prowess, magnanimity, and temperance, and an undaunted assurance not to fear anything. And with such munition he sent him, being yet very young, to subdue the Empire of the world, only with 30,000 footmen, 4,000 horsemen, and 42,000 Crowns in money. As for other arts and sciences, he saith *Alexander* honored them and commended their excellency and comeliness, but for any pleasure he took in them, his affection could not easily be drawn to exercise them.

> Young men and old, draw hence (in your affairs)
> Your minds set mark, provision for gray hairs.
> [*Ibid.*] Sat. v. 64.

It is that which *Epicurus* said in the beginning of his letter to *Meniceus: Neither let the youngest shun nor the oldest weary himself in philosophizing, for who doth otherwise seemeth to say that either the season to live happily is not yet come or is already past.* Yet would I not have this young gentleman pent up nor carelessly cast off to the heedless choler or melancholy humor of the hasty Schoolmaster. I would not have his budding spirit corrupted with keeping him fast-tied, and as it were laboring fourteen or fifteen hours a day poring on his book, as some do, as if he were a day-laboring man. Neither do I think it fit, if at any time, by reason of some solitary or melancholy complexion, he should be seen with an over-indiscreet application given to his book, it should be cherished in him, for that doth often make him both unapt for civil conversation and distracts him from better employments. How many have I seen in my days, by an over-greedy desire of knowledge become as it were foolish? *Carneades* was so deeply plunged, and as I may say besotted in it, that he could never have leisure to cut his hair or pare his nails. Nor would I have his noble manners obscured by the incivility and barbarism of others. The French wisdom hath long since proverbially been spoken of as very apt to conceive study in her youth but most unapt to keep it long. In good truth, we see at this day that there is nothing lovelier to behold than the young children of *France;* but for the most part, they deceive the hope which was foreapprehended of them, for when they once become men, there is no excellency at all in them. I have heard men of understanding hold this opinion, that the Colleges to which they are sent (of which there are store) do thus besot them. Whereas to our scholar, a cabinet, a garden, the table, the bed, a solitariness, a company, morning and evening, and all hours shall be alike unto him, all places shall be a study for him.

For Philosophy (as a former of judgments, and modeler of customs) shall be his principal lesson, having the privilege to intermeddle herself with all things and in all places. *Isocrates* the Orator, being once requested at a great banquet to speak of his art, when all thought he had reason to answer, said, *It is not now time to do what I can, and what should now be done, I cannot do it.* For to present orations or to enter into disputation of Rhetoric before a company assembled together to be merry and make good cheer, would be but a medley of harsh and jarring music. The like may be said of all other Sciences. But touching Philosophy, namely in that point where it treateth of man and of his duties and offices, it hath been the common judgment of the wisest that in regard of the pleasantness of her conversation, she ought not to be rejected, neither at banquets nor at sports. And *Plato* having invited her to his solemn feast, we see how kindly she entertaineth the company with a mild behavior, fitly suiting herself to time and place, notwithstanding it be one of his learnedest and profitable discourses.

> Poor men alike, alike rich men it easeth,
> Alike it scorned, old and young displeaseth.
> HOR. i. *Epi.* i. 25.

So doubtless he shall less be idle than others. For even as the paces we bestow walking in a gallery, although they be twice as many more, weary us not so much as those we spend in going a set journey, so our lesson being passed over, as it were, by chance or way of encounter, without strict observance of time or place, being applied to all our actions, shall be digested, and never felt. All sports and exercises shall be a part of his study; running, wrestling, music, dancing, hunting, and managing of arms and horses. I would have the exterior demeanor or decency and the disposition of his person to be fashioned together with his mind, for it is not a mind, it is not a body, that we erect, but it is a man, and we must not make two parts of him. And as *Plato* saith, *They must not be erected one without another, but equally be directed, no otherwise than a couple of horses matched to draw in one selfsame team.* And to hear him, doth he not seem to employ more time and care in the exercises of his body, and to think that the mind is together with the same exercised, and not the contrary?

As for other matters, this institution ought to be directed by a sweet-severe mildness. Not as some do, who in lieu of gently bidding children to the banquet of letters, present them with nothing but horror and cruelty. Let me have this violence and compulsion removed. There is nothing that, in my seeming, doth more bastardize and dizzy a well-born and gentle nature. If you would have him stand in awe of shame and punishment, do not so much inure him to it. Accustom him patiently to endure sweat and cold, the sharpness of the wind, the heat of the sun, and how to despise all hazards. Remove from him all niceness and quaintness in clothing, in lying, in eating, and in drinking. Fashion him to all things, that he prove not a fair and wanton-puling boy, but a lusty and vigorous boy. When I was a child, being a man, and now am old, I have ever judged and believed the same.

But amongst other things, I could never away with this kind of discipline used in most of our Colleges. It had peradventure been less hurtful if they had somewhat inclined to mildness or gentle entreaty. It is a very prison of captivated youth, and proves dissolute in punishing it before it be so. Come upon them when they are going to their lesson, and you hear nothing but whipping and brawling, both of children tormented and masters besotted with anger and chafing. How wise are they which go about to allure a child's mind to go to his book, being yet but tender and fearful, with a stern-frowning countenance and with handfuls of rods? O wicked and pernicious manner of teaching! Which *Quintilian* hath very well noted, that this imperious kind of authority, namely this way of punishing of children, draws many dangerous inconveniences within. How much more decent were it to see their schoolhouses and forms strewn with green boughs and flow-

ers than with bloody birch twigs? If it lay in me, I would do
as the Philosopher *Speusippus* did, who caused the pictures
of Gladness and Joy, of *Flora,* and of the Graces, to be set up
round about his schoolhouse. Where their profit lieth, there
should also be their recreation. Those meats ought to be
sugared over that are healthful for children's stomachs, and
those made bitter that are hurtful for them. It is strange to see
how careful *Plato* showeth himself in framing of his laws
about the recreation and pastime of the youth of his City, and
how far he extends himself about their exercises, sports, songs,
leaping, and dancing, whereof he saith that severe antiquity
gave the conduct and patronage unto the Gods themselves,
namely to *Apollo,* to the Muses, and to *Minerva.* Mark but
how far-forth he endeavoreth to give a thousand precepts to
be kept in his places of exercises both of body and mind. As
for learned Sciences, he stands not much upon them and
seemeth in particular to commend Poesy, but for Music's sake.

All strangeness and self-particularity in our manners and
conditions is to be shunned as an enemy to society and civil
conversation. Who would not be astonished at *Demophon's*
complexion, chief steward of *Alexander's* household, who was
wont to sweat in the shadow and quiver for cold in the sun?
I have seen some to startle at the smell of an apple more than
at the shot of a piece, some to be frighted with a mouse, some
ready to cast their gorge at the sight of a mess of cream, and
others to be scared with seeing a featherbed shaken, as *Ger-
manicus,* who could not abide to see a cock or hear his crow-
ing. There may haply be some hidden property of nature,
which in my judgment might easily be removed if it were
taken in time. Institution hath gotten this upon me (I must
confess with much ado) for, except beer, all things else that
are man's food agree indifferently with my taste.

The body, being yet supple, ought to be accommodated to
all fashions and customs; and (always provided his appetites
and desires be kept under) let a young man boldly be made
fit for all Nations and companies; yea, if need be, for all disorders and surfeitings. Let him acquaint himself with all
fashions, that he may be able to do all things and love to do

none but those that are commendable. Some strict Philosophers
commend not but rather blame *Callisthenes* for losing the
good favor of his Master *Alexander* only because he would not
pledge him as much as he had drunk to him. He shall laugh,
jest, dally, and debauch himself with his Prince. And in his
debauching, I would have him outgo all his fellows in vigor
and constancy, and that he omit not to do evil, neither for
want of strength or knowledge, but for lack of will. *There is a
great difference whether one have no will or no wit to do
amiss* [SEN. *Epist.* xc.]. I thought to have honored a gentleman (as great a stranger and as far from such riotous disorders
as any is in *France*) by inquiring of him, in very good company, how many times in all his life he had been drunk in *Germany* during the time of his abode there about the necessary
affairs of our King; who took it even as I meant it, and answered, "Three times," telling the time and manner how. I
know some who, for want of that quality, have been much
perplexed when they have had occasion to converse with that
nation. I have often noted with great admiration that wonderful nature of *Alcibiades,* to see how easily he could suit himself to so diverse fashions and different humors without prejudice unto his health; sometimes exceeding the sumptuousness
and pomp of the Persians, and now and then surpassing the
austerity and frugality of the Lacedemonians, as reformed in
Sparta, as voluptuous in *Ionia.*

> All colors, states, and things are fit
> For courtly *Aristippus'* wit.
>> HOR. *Epi.* xvii. 23.

Such a one would I frame my Disciple,

> Whom patience clothes with suits of double kind,
> I muse, if he another way will find.
>> [*Ibid.*] 25.

> He not unfitly may,
> Both parts and persons play.
>> [*Ibid.*] 29.

Lo here my lessons, wherein he that acteth them profiteth more than he that but knoweth them; whom if you see, you hear, and if you hear him, you see him. God forbid, saith somebody in *Plato*, that to Philosophize be to learn many things and to exercise the arts. *This discipline of living well, which is the amplest of all other arts, they followed rather in their lives than in their learning or writing* (CIC. *Tusc. Qu.* iv.). *Leo*, Prince of the Phliasians, inquiring of *Heraclides Ponticus*, what art he professed, he answered, "Sir, I profess neither art nor science, but I am a Philosopher." Some reproved *Diogenes*, that being an ignorant man he did nevertheless meddle with Philosophy, to whom he replied, "So much the more reason have I, and to greater purpose do I meddle with it." *Hegesias* prayed him upon a time to read some book unto him. *You are a merry man*, said he. *As you choose natural and not painted, right and not counterfeit, figs to eat, why do you not likewise choose not the painted and written but the true and natural exercises?*

He shall not so much repeat as act his lesson. In his actions shall he make repetition of the same. We must observe whether there be wisdom in his enterprises, integrity in his demeanor, modesty in his gestures, justice in his actions, judgment and grace in his speech, courage in his sickness, moderation in his sports, temperance in his pleasures, order in the government of his house, and indifference in his taste, whether it be flesh, fish, wine, or water, or whatsoever he feedeth upon. *Who thinks his learning not an ostentation of knowledge but a law of life, himself obeys himself and doth what is decreed* (CIC. *ibid.* ii.).

The true mirror of our discourses is the course of our lives. *Xeuxidamus* answered one that demanded of him why the Lacedemonians did not draw into a book the ordinances of prowess, that so their young men might read them; *It is*, saith he, *because they would rather accustom them to deeds and actions than to books and writings*. Compare at the end of fifteen or sixteen years one of these college Latinizers who hath employed all that while only in learning how to speak, to such a one as I mean. The world is nothing but babbling and words, and I never saw man that doth not rather speak more than he ought, than less. Notwithstanding, half our age is consumed that way. We are kept four or five years learning to understand bare words and to join them into clauses, then as long in proportioning a great body extended into four or five parts, and five more at least ere we can succinctly know how to mingle, join, and interlace them handsomely into a subtle fashion and into one coherent orb. Let us leave it to those whose profession is to do nothing else. Being once on my journey toward *Orleans,* it was my chance to meet, upon that plain that lieth on this side *Cléry,* with two Masters of Arts traveling toward *Bordeaux,* about fifty paces, one from another. Far off behind them, I descried a troupe of horsemen, their Master riding foremost, who was the Earl of *Rochefoucault.* One of my servants inquiring of the first of those Masters of Arts what Gentleman he was that followed him, supposing my servant had meant his fellow scholar, for he had not yet seen the Earl's train, answered pleasantly, *He is no gentleman, Sir, but a Grammarian, and I am a Logician.*

Now, we that contrariwise seek not to frame a Grammarian nor a Logician, but a complete gentleman, let us give them leave to misspend their time. We have elsewhere and somewhat else of more import to do. So that our Disciple be well and sufficiently stored with matter, words will follow apace; and if they will not follow gently, he shall hale them on perforce. I hear some excuse themselves that they cannot express their meaning, and make a semblance that their heads are so full-stuffed with many goodly things, but for want of eloquence they can neither utter nor make show of them. It is a mere foppery. And will you know what, in my seeming, the cause is? They are shadows and *Chimeras,* proceeding of some formless conceptions which they cannot distinguish or resolve within and by consequence are not able to produce them, inasmuch as they understand not themselves. And if you but mark their earnestness and how they stammer and labor at the point of their delivery, you would deem that what they go withal is but a conceiving, and therefore nothing near down-lying, and that they do but lick that imperfect and shapeless lump of matter. As for me, I am of opinion, and *Socrates* would have it so, that he who hath a clear and lively imagination in his mind, may easily produce and utter the same, although it be in *Bergamask* or *Welsh,* and if he be dumb, by signs and tokens.

> When matter we foreknow,
> Words voluntary flow.
>   HOR. *Art. Poet.* 311.

As one said, as poetically in his prose, *When matter hath possessed their minds, they hunt after words* (SEN. *Controv.* vii. Proæ.), and another: *Things themselves will catch and carry words* [CIC. *Finib.* iii. 5.].

He knows neither Ablative, Conjunctive, Substantive, nor Grammar—no more doth his Lackey nor any Oyster wife about the streets—and yet if you have a mind to it, he will entertain you your fill and peradventure stumble as little and as seldom against the rules of his tongue as the best Master of Arts in *France.* He hath no skill in Rhetoric, nor can he with a preface forestall and captivate the Gentle Reader's good will, nor careth he greatly to know it. In good sooth, all this garish painting is easily defaced by the luster of an inbred and simple truth. For these dainties and quaint devices serve but to amuse the vulgar sort, unapt and incapable to taste the most solid and firm meat. As *Afer* very plainly declareth in *Cornelius Tacitus.* The Ambassadors of *Samos* being come to *Cleomenes,* King of *Sparta,* prepared with a long, prolix Oration to stir him up to war against the tyrant *Polycrates,* after he had listened a good while unto them, his answer was: *Touching your Exordium or beginning, I have forgotten it; the middle, I remember not; and for your conclusion, I will do nothing in it.* A fit and (to my thinking) a very good answer. And the Orators were put to such a shift as they knew not what to reply.

And what said another? The *Athenians* from out two of their cunning Architects were to choose one to erect a notable great frame. The one of them more affected and self-presuming, presented himself before them with a smooth forepremeditated discourse about the subject of that piece of work, and thereby drew the judgments of the common people unto his liking. But the other in few words spake thus: *Lords of Athens, what this man hath said, I will perform.*

In the greatest earnestness of *Cicero's* eloquence, many were drawn into a kind of admiration. But *Cato,* jesting at it, said, *Have we not a pleasant Consul?* A quick, cunning Argument and a witty saying, whether it go before or come after, it is never out of season. If it have no coherence with that which goeth before nor with what cometh after, it is good and commendable in itself. I am none of those that think a good Rhyme to make a good Poem. Let him hardly (if so he please) make a short syllable long; it is no great matter. If the invention be rare and good, and his wit and judgment have cunningly played their part, I will say to such a one he is a good Poet but an ill Versifier.

> A man whose sense could finely pierce,
> But harsh and hard to make a verse.
> HOR. i. *Sat.* iv. 8. Lucil.

Let a man (saith *Horace*) make his work lose all seams, measures, and joints.

> Set times and moods, make you the first word last,
> The last word first, as if they were new cast:
> Yet find the unjointed Poets' joints stands fast.
> [*Ibid.*] 58, 62.

He shall, for all that, nothing gainsay himself; every piece will make a good show. To this purpose answered *Menander* those that chided him, the day being at hand in which he had promised a Comedy, and had not begun the same. *Tut-tut,* said he, *it is already finished. There wanteth nothing but to add the verse unto it.* For, having ranged and cast the plot in his mind, he made small account of feet, of measures or cadences of verses, which indeed are but of small import in regard of the rest. Since great *Ronsard* and learned *Bellay* have raised our French Poesy unto that height of honor where it now is, I see not one of these petty ballad makers or apprentice doggerel rhymers that doth not bombast his labors with high-swelling and heaven-disemboweling words, and that doth not marshal his cadences very near as they do. *The sound is more than the weight or worth* (SEN. *Epist.* xl.). And for the vulgar sort, there were never so many Poets, and so few good. But as it hath been easy for them to represent their rhymes, so come they far short in imitating the rich descriptions of the one and rare inventions of the other.

But what shall he do if he be urged with sophistical subtleties about a Syllogism? A gammon of Bacon makes a man drink, drinking quencheth a man's thirst, *Ergo,* a gammon of bacon quencheth a man's thirst. Let him mock at it; it is more witty to be mocked at than to be answered. Let him borrow this pleasant counter-craft of *Aristippus: Why shall I unbind that which, being bound, doth so much trouble me?* Someone proposed certain Logical quiddities against *Cleanthes,* to whom *Chrysippus* said, "Use such juggling tricks to play with children, and divert not the serious thoughts of an aged man to such idle matters." If such foolish wiles, *intricate and stinged sophisms* (CIC. *Acad. Qu.* iv.), must persuade a lie, it is dangerous; but if they prove void of any effect and move him but to laughter, I see not why he shall beware of them. Some there are so foolish that will go a quarter of a mile out of the way to hunt after a quaint new word if they once get in chase: *Or such as fit not words to matter, but fetch matter from abroad, whereto words be fitted* [QUINT. viii. 3.]. And another: *Who are allured by the grace of some pleasing word, to write that they intended not to write* (SEN. *Epist.* lix.). I do more willingly wind up a witty, notable sentence that so I may sew it upon me, than unwind my thread to go fetch it. Contrariwise, it is for words to serve and wait upon the matter and not for matter to attend upon words, and if the French tongue cannot reach unto it, let the Gascon, or any other. I would have the matters to surmount and so fill the imagination of him that harkeneth that he have no remembrance at all of the words. It is a natural, simple, and unaffected speech that I love, so written as it is spoken, and such upon the paper as it is in the mouth; a pithy, sinewy, full, strong, compendious, and material speech, not so delicate and affected as vehement and piercing.

> In fine, that word is wisely fit,
> Which strikes the fence, the mark doth hit.
> [LUCAN. *Epit.* 6.]

Rather difficult than tedious, void of affectation, free, loose, and bold, that every member of it seem to make a body; not Pedantic, nor Friarlike, nor Lawyerlike, but rather downright, Soldierlike, as *Suetonius* calleth that of *Julius Caesar*, which I see no reason wherefore he calleth it.

I have sometimes pleased myself in imitating that licentiousness or wanton humor of our youths in wearing of their garments; as carelessly to let their cloaks hang down over one shoulder, to wear their cloaks scarf or baldricwise, and their stockings loose-hanging about their legs. It represents a kind of disdainful fierceness of these foreign embellishings, and neglect careless of art. But I commend it more being employed in the course and form of speech. All manner of affectation, namely in the liveliness and liberty of *France*, is unseemly in a Courtier. And in a Monarch every Gentleman ought to address himself unto a Courtier's carriage. Therefore do we well somewhat to incline to a native and careless behavior. I like not a contexture where the seams and pieces may be seen. As in a well compact body, what need a man distinguish and number all the bones and veins severally? *The speech that intendeth truth must be plain and unpolished. Who speaketh elaborately but he that means to speak unsavoredly?* (SEN. *Epist.* xl. m. lxxv. p.). That eloquence offereth injury unto things which altogether draws us to observe it. As in apparel, it is a sign of pusillanimity for one to mark himself in some particular and unusual fashion, so likewise in common speech, for one to hunt after new phrases and unaccustomed-quaint words proceedeth of a scholastic and childish ambition. Let me use none other than are spoken in the halls of *Paris*. *Aristophanes* the Grammarian was somewhat out of the way when he reproved *Epicurus* for the simplicity of his words and the end of his art oratory, which was only perspicuity in speech. The imitation of speech, by reason of the facility of it, followeth presently a whole nation. The imitation of judging and inventing comes more slow. The greater number of Readers, because they have found one self-same kind of gown, suppose most falsely to hold one like body. Outward garments and cloaks may be borrowed, but never the sinews and strength of the body. Most of those that converse with me speak like unto these Essays, but I know not whether they think alike. The Athenians (as *Plato* averreth) have for their part great care to be fluent and eloquent in their speech. The Lacedemonians endeavor to be short and compendious. And those of *Crete* labor more to be plentiful in conceits than in language. And these are the best. *Xeno* was wont to say that *he had two sorts of disciples: the one he called* φιλολόγους, *curious to learn things, and those were his darlings; the other he termed* λογοφίλους, *who respected nothing more than the language.* Yet can no man say but that to speak well is most gracious and commendable. But not so excellent as some make it, and I am grieved to see how we employ most part of our time about that only. I would first know mine own tongue perfectly, then my neighbors' with whom I have most commerce. I must needs acknowledge that the Greek and Latin tongues are great ornaments in a Gentleman, but they are purchased at over-high a rate. Use it who list, I will tell you how they may be gotten better cheap and much sooner than is ordinarily used, which was tried in myself.

My late father having, by all the means and industry that is possible for man, sought amongst the wisest and men of best understanding to find a most exquisite and ready way of teaching, being advised of the inconveniences then in use, was given to understand that the lingering while and best part of our youth that we employ in learning the tongues which cost them nothing, is the only cause we can never attain to that absolute perfection of skill and knowledge of the Greeks and Romans. I do not believe that to be the only cause. But so it is the expedient my father found out was this: that being yet at nurse and before the first loosing of my tongue, I was delivered to a German (who died since, a most excellent Physician in *France*), he being then altogether ignorant of the French tongue but exquisitely ready and skillful in the Latin. This man, whom my Father had sent for of purpose and to whom he gave very great entertainment, had me continually in his arms and was mine only overseer. There were also joined unto him two of his countrymen, but not so learned, whose charge was to attend and now and then to play with me. And all these together did never entertain me with other than the Latin tongue. As for others of his household, it was an inviolable rule that neither himself nor my mother, nor man nor maidservant, were suffered to speak one word in my company except such Latin words as everyone had learned to chat and prattle with me. It were strange to tell how everyone in the house profited therein. My Father and my Mother learned so much Latin that for a need they could understand it when they heard it spoken; even so did all the household servants, namely such as were nearest and most about me. To be short, we were all so Latinized that the towns round about us had their share of it, insomuch as even at this day many Latin names both of workmen and of their tools are yet in use among them. And as for myself, I was about six years old and could understand no more French or Périgordine than Arabic, and that without art, without books, rules, or grammar, without whipping or whining. I had gotten as pure a Latin tongue as my Master could speak, the rather because I could neither mingle nor confound the same with other tongues. If for an Essay they would give me a Theme, whereas the fashion in Colleges is to give it in French, I had it in bad Latin, to reduce the same into good. And *Nicholas Grucchi,* who hath written *De Comitiis Romanorum; William Guerenti,* who hath commented *Aristotle; George Buchanan,* that famous Scottish Poet; and *Marke-Antonie Muret,* whom (while he lived) both *France* and *Italy* to this day acknowledge to have been the best Orator, all which have been my familiar tutors, have often told me that in mine infancy I had the Latin tongue so ready and so perfect that themselves feared to take me in hand. And *Buchanan,* who afterward I saw attending on the Marshal of *Brissac,* told me he was about to write a treatise of the institution of children, and that he took the model and pattern from mine; for at that time he had the charge and bringing up of the young Earl of *Brissac,* whom since we have seen prove so worthy and so valiant a Captain.

As for the Greek, wherein I have but small understanding, my father purposed to make me learn it by art, but by new and uncustomed means—that is, by way of recreation and exercise. We did toss our declinations and conjugations to and fro as they do who by way of a certain game at tables learn both Arithmetic and Geometry. For amongst other things he had especially been persuaded to make me taste and apprehend the fruits of duty and science by an unforced kind of will and of mine own choice, and without any compulsion or rigor, to bring me up in all mildness and liberty—yea with such kind of superstition that, whereas some are of opinion that suddenly to awaken young children and as it were by violence to startle and fright them out of their dead sleep in a morning (wherein they are more heavy and deeper plunged than we) doth greatly trouble and distemper their brains, he would every morning cause me to be awakened by the sound of some instrument; and I was never without a servant who to that purpose attended upon me. This example may serve to judge of the rest, as also to commend the judgment and tender affection of so careful and loving a father, who is not to be blamed though he reaped not the fruits answerable to his exquisite toil, and painful manuring. Two things hindered the same: First, the barrenness and unfit soil, for howbeit I were of a sound and strong constitution, and of a tractable and yielding condition, yet was I so heavy, so sluggish, and so dull that I could not be roused (yea were it to go to play) from out mine idle drowsiness. What I saw, I saw it perfectly; and under this heavy and as it were Lethean complexion did I breed hardy imaginations and opinions far above my years. My spirit was very slow and would go no further than it was led by others; my apprehension blockish, my invention poor; and besides, I had a marvelous defect in my weak memory. It is therefore no wonder if my father could never bring me to any perfection. Secondly, as those that in some dangerous sickness, moved with a kind of hopeful and greedy desire of perfect health again, give ear to every Leech or Empiric, and follow all counsels, the good man being exceedingly fearful to commit any oversight in a matter he took so to heart, suffered himself at last to be led away by the common opinion which, like unto the Cranes, followeth ever those that go before, and yielded to custom, having those no longer about him that had given him his first directions and which they had brought out of *Italy*.

Being but six years old, I was sent to the College of *Guienne*, then most flourishing and reputed the best in *France*, where it is impossible to add anything to the great care he had, both to choose the best and most sufficient Masters that could be found, to read unto me, as also for all other circumstances pertaining to my education, wherein, contrary to usual customs of Colleges, he observed many particular rules. But so it is, it was ever a College. My Latin tongue was forthwith corrupted, whereof by reason of discontinuance I afterward lost all manner of use. Which new kind of institution stood me in no other stead but that at my first admittance it made me to overskip some of the lower forms and to be placed in the highest. For at thirteen years of age that I left the College, I had read over the whole course of Philosophy (as they call it), but with so small profit that I can now make no account of it.

The first taste or feeling I had of books was of the pleasure I took in reading the fables of *Ovid's Metamorphoses*. For being but seven or eight years old, I would steal and sequester myself from all other delights only to read them, forsomuch as the tongue wherein they were written was to me natural, and it was the easiest book I knew, and, by reason of the matter therein contained, most agreeing with my young age. For of King *Arthur*, of *Lancelot du Lake*, of *Amadis*, of *Huon of Bordeaux*, and such idle time-consuming and wit-besotting trash of books wherein youth doth commonly amuse itself, I was not so much as acquainted with their names, and to this day know not their bodies nor what they contain, so exact was my discipline. Whereby I became more careless to study my other prescribed lessons. And well did it fall out for my purpose that I had to deal with a very discreet Master, who out of his judgment could with such dexterity wink at and second my untowardliness, and such other faults that were in me. For by that means I read over *Virgil's Æneid, Terence, Plautus,* and other Italian Comedies, allured thereunto by the pleasantness of their several subjects. Had he been so foolishly severe or so severely froward as to cross this course of mine, I think verily I had never brought anything from the College but the hate and contempt of Books, as doth the greatest part of our Nobility. Such was his discretion and so warily did he behave himself, that he saw and would not see. He would foster and increase my longing, suffering me, but by stealth and by snatches, to glut myself with those Books, holding ever a gentle hand over me concerning other regular studies. For the chiefest thing my father required at their hands (unto whose charge he had committed me) was a kind of well-conditioned mildness and facility of complexion. And to say truth, mine had no other fault but a certain dull languishing and heavy slothfulness. The danger was not I should do ill, but that I should do nothing.

No man did ever suspect I would prove a bad, but an unprofitable man, foreseeing in me rather a kind of idleness than a voluntary craftiness. I am not so self-conceited but I perceive what hath followed. The complaints that are daily buzzed in mine ears are these: that I am idle, cold, and negligent in offices of friendship and duty to my parents and kinfolks; and touching public offices, that I am over-singular and disdainful. And those that are most injurious cannot ask. Wherefore I have taken, and why I have not paid? but may rather demand why I do not quit, and wherefore I do not give? I would take it as a favor they should wish such effects of supererogation in me. But they are unjust and over-partial that will go about to exact that from me which I owe not, with more rigor than they will exact from themselves that which they owe. Wherein if they condemn me, they utterly cancel both the gratifying of the action, and the gratitude which thereby would be due to me. Whereas the active well doing should be of more consequence proceeding from my hand, in regard I have no passive at all. Wherefore I may so much the more freely dispose of my fortune by how much more it is mine, and of myself that am most mine own. Notwithstanding, if I were a great blazoner of mine own actions, I might peradventure bar such reproaches, and justly upbraid some that they are not so much offended because I do not enough as for that I may, and it lies in my power to do much more than I do. Yet my mind ceased not at the same time to have peculiar unto itself well-settled notions, true and open judgments concerning the objects which it knew, which alone and without any help or communication it would digest. And amongst other things, I verily believe it would have proved altogether incapable and unfit to yield unto force or stoop unto violence. Shall I account or relate this quality of my infancy, which was a kind of boldness in my looks, and gentle softness in my voice, and affability in my gestures, and a dexterity in conforming myself to the parts I undertook? For before the age of the

> Years had I (to make even)
> Scarce [one] above eleven.
> VIRG. *Buc*. Ecl. viii. 39.

I have undergone and represented the chiefest parts in the Latin Tragedies of *Buchanan, Guerenti* and of *Muret,* which in great state were acted and played in our College of *Guienne.* Wherein *Andreas Goveanus,* our Rector principal, who, as in all other parts belonging to his charge, was without comparison the chiefest Rector of *France,* and myself (without ostentation be it spoken) was reputed, if not a chief master, yet a principal Actor in them. It is an exercise I rather commend than disallow in young Gentlemen, and have seen some of our Princes (in imitation of some of former ages), both commendably and honestly, in their proper persons act and play some parts in Tragedies. It hath heretofore been esteemed a lawful exercise and a tolerable profession in men of honor, namely in *Greece. He imparts the matter to Ariston, a Player of tragedies, whose progeny and fortune were both honest; nor did his profession disgrace them, because no such matter is a disparagement amongst the Grecians* (LIVY. dec. iii. lib. 4.).

And I have ever accused them of impertinency that condemn and disallow such kinds of recreations, and blamed those of injustice that refuse good and honest Comedians, or (as we call them) Players, to enter our good towns, and grudge the common people such public sports. Politic and well-ordered commonwealths endeavor rather carefully to unite and assemble their Citizens together; as in serious offices of devotion, so in honest exercises of recreation. Common society and loving friendship is thereby cherished and increased. And besides, they cannot have more formal and regular pastimes allowed them than such as are acted and represented in open view of all and in the presence of the magistrates themselves. And if I might bear sway, I would think it reasonable that Princes should sometimes, at their proper charges, gratify the common people with them as an argument of a fatherly affection and loving goodness towards them, and that in populous and frequented cities there should be Theaters and places appointed for such spectacles, as a diverting of worse inconveniences and secret actions.

But to come to my intended purpose, there is no better way than to allure the affection and to entice the appetite; otherwise a man shall breed but asses laden with Books. With jerks of rods they have their satchels full of learning given them to keep. Which, to do well, one must not only harbor in himself but wed and marry the same with his mind.

John Milton (1608-1674) occupies a position in English literature perhaps second only to Shakespeare. In addition to his poetry, studied by every school child, Milton left a legacy of letters and essays. His essay *Of Education* was originally a letter to a young friend, advising him on the proper kind of education a young man ought to pursue.

OF EDUCATION

To Master *Samuel Hartlib.*

Mr. *Hartlib,*

I AM long since persuaded, that to say, or do aught worth memory and imitation, no purpose or respect[1] should sooner move us, than simply the love of God, and of mankind. Nevertheless to write now the reforming of education, though it be one of the greatest and noblest designs that can be thought on, and for the want whereof this nation perishes, I had not yet at this time been induced, but by your earnest entreaties, and serious conjurements;[2] as having my mind for the present half diverted in the pursuance of some other assertions,[3] the knowledge and the use of which, can not but be a great furtherance both to the enlargement of truth, and honest living, with much more peace. Nor should the laws of any private friendship have prevailed with me to divide thus, or transpose[4] my former thoughts, but that I see those aims, those actions which have won you with me the esteem[5] of a person sent hither by some good providence from a far country to be the occasion and the incitement of great good to this island. And, as I hear, you have obtained the same repute with men of most approved wisdom, and some of highest authority among us. Not to mention the learned correspondence which you hold in foreign parts, and the extraordinary pains and diligence which you have used in this matter both here, and beyond the seas; either by the definite will of God so ruling, or the peculiar sway of nature, which also is God's working. Neither can I think that so reputed, and so valued as you are, you would to the forfeit of your own discerning ability, impose upon me an unfit and over-ponderous argument, but that the satisfaction which you profess to have received from those incidental discourses

---

[1] Consideration. [2] Appeals. [3] As, *e. g.,* unlicensed printing and divorce.
[4] Change. [5] Reputation.

which we have wandered into, hath pressed and almost constrained you into a persuasion, that what you require from me in this point, I neither ought, nor can in conscience defer beyond this time both of so much need at once, and so much opportunity to try what God hath determined. I will not resist therefore, whatever it is either of divine, or human obligement that you lay upon me; but will forthwith set down in writing, as you request me, that voluntary *Idea,* which hath long in silence presented itself to me, of a better education, in extent and comprehension far more large, and yet of time far shorter, and of attainment far more certain, than hath been yet in practise.

Brief I shall endeavor to be; for that which I have to say, assuredly this nation hath extreme need should be done sooner than spoken. To tell you therefore what I have benefited herein among old renowned authors, I shall spare; and to search what many modern *Januas*[6] and *Didactics*[6] more than ever I shall read, have projected, my inclination leads me not. But if you can accept of these few observations which have flowered off, and are, as it were, the burnishing[7] of many studious and contemplative years altogether spent in the search of religious and civil knowledge, and such as pleased you so well in the relating, I here give you them to dispose of.

The end then of learning is to repair the ruins of our first parents by regaining to know God aright, and out of that knowledge to love him, to imitate him, to be like him, as we may the nearest by possessing our souls of true virtue, which being united to the heavenly grace of faith makes up the highest perfection. But because our understanding can not in this body found itself but on sensible[8] things, nor arrive so clearly to the knowledge of God and things invisible, as by orderly conning over the visible and inferior creature, the same method is necessarily to be followed in all discreet teaching. And seeing every nation affords not experience and tradition enough for all kind of learning, therefore we are chiefly taught the languages of those people who have at any time been most industrious after wisdom; so that language is but the instrument conveying to us things useful to be known. And though a linguist should

[6] Works on education by John Amos Comenius, a great educational reformer and a friend of Hartlib's.
[7] Fragments rubbed off in polishing.   [8] Perceived by the senses.

pride himself to have all the tongues that *Babel* cleft the world into, yet if he have not studied the solid things in them as well as the words and lexicons, he were nothing so much to be esteemed a learned man, as any yoeman or tradesman competently wise in his mother dialect only. Hence appear the many mistakes which have made learning generally so unpleasing and so unsuccessful; first we do amiss to spend seven or eight years merely in scraping together so much miserable Latin and Greek, as might be learned other wise easily and delightfully in one year. And that which casts our proficiency therein so much behind, is our time lost partly in too oft idle vacancies[9] given both to schools and universities, partly in a preposterous[10] exaction, forcing the empty wits of children to compose themes, verses and orations, which are the acts of ripest judgment and the final work of a head filled by long reading and observing, with elegant maxims, and copious invention. These are not matters to be wrung from poor striplings, like blood out of the nose, or the plucking of untimely fruit: besides the ill habit which they get of wretched barbarizing against the Latin and Greek *idiom,* with their untutored *Anglicisms,* odious to be read, yet not to be avoided without a well continued and judicious conversing[11] among pure authors digested, which they scarce taste, whereas, if after some preparatory grounds of speech by their certain forms got into memory, they were led to the praxis[12] thereof in some chosen short books lessoned throughly to them, they might then forthwith proceed to learn the substance of good things, and arts in due order, which would bring the whole language quickly into their power. This I take to be the most rational and most profitable way of learning languages, and whereby we may best hope to give account to God of our youth spent herein: and for the usual method of teaching arts, I deem it to be an old error of universities not yet well recovered from the scholastic grossness of barbarous ages, that instead of beginning with arts most easy, and those be such as are most obvious to the sense, they present their young unmatriculated novices at first coming with the most intellective[13] abstractions of logic and metaphysics; so that they having but newly left those grammatic flats

---

[9] Holidays.　　[10] Lit., in inverted order.　　[11] Familiar intercourse.
[12] Practical application.　　[13] Intellectual.

and shallows where they stuck unreasonably to learn a few words with lamentable construction, and now on the sudden transported under another climate to be tossed and turmoiled with their unballasted wits in fathomless and unquiet deeps of controversy, do for the most part grow into hatred and contempt of learning, mocked and deluded all this while with ragged notions and babblements, while they expected worthy and delightful knowledge; till poverty or youthful years call them importunately their several ways, and hasten them with the sway[14] of friends either to an ambitious and mercenary, or ignorantly zealous divinity; some allured to the trade of law, grounding their purposes not on the prudent and heavenly contemplation of justice and equity which was never taught them, but on the promising and pleasing thoughts of litigious terms, fat contentions and flowing fees; others betake them to State affairs, with souls so unprincipled in virtue and true generous breeding, that flattery, and court shifts[15] and tyrannous aphorisms appear to them the highest points of wisdom; instilling their barren hearts with a conscientious slavery,[16] if, as I rather think, it be not feigned. Others lastly of a more delicious and airy spirit,[17] retire themselves knowing no better, to the enjoyments of ease and luxury, living out their days in feast and jollity; which indeed is the wisest and the safest course of all these, unless they were with more integrity undertaken. And these are the fruits of misspending our prime youth at the schools and universities as we do, either in learning mere words or such things chiefly, as were better unlearned.

I shall detain you no longer in the demonstration of what we should not do, but straight conduct ye to a hill side where I will point ye out the right path of a virtuous and noble education; laborious indeed at the first ascent, but else so smooth, so green, so full of goodly prospect, and melodious sounds on every side, that the harp of *Orpheus*[18] was not more charming. I doubt not but ye shall have more ado to drive our dullest and laziest youth, our stocks and stubs from the infinite desire of such a happy nurture, than we have not to hale and drag our choicest and hopefulest wits to that asinine feast of sowthistles and brambles which is commonly set before them, as

[14] Influence. [15] Tricks. [16] A slavery which they try to believe conscientious.
[17] Delicate and spiritual nature. [18] Which charmed even trees and stones.

all the food and entertainment of their tenderest and most docible[19] age. I call therefore a complete and generous education that which fits a man to perform justly, skilfully and magnanimously all the offices both private and public, of peace and war. And how all this may be done between twelve, and one and twenty, less time than is now bestowed in pure trifling at grammar and *sophistry,* is to be thus ordered.

First to find out a spacious house and ground about it fit for an academy, and big enough to lodge a hundred and fifty persons, whereof twenty or thereabout may be attendants, all under the government of one, who shall be thought of desert sufficient, and ability either to do all, or wisely to direct, and oversee it done. This place should be at once both school and university, not heeding a remove to any other house of scholarship, except it be some peculiar College of Law, or Physic, where they mean to be practitioners; but as for those general studies which take up all our time from *Lilly*[20] to the commencing,[21] as they term it, Master of Art, it should be absolute. After this pattern, as many Edifices may be converted to this use, as shall be needful in every city throughout this land, which would tend much to the increase of learning and civility everywhere. This number, less or more thus collected, to the convenience of a foot company, or interchangeably two troops of cavalry, should divide their day's work into three parts, as it lies orderly. Their studies, their exercise, and their diet.

For the studies, first they should begin with the chief and necessary rules of some good grammar, either that now used, or any better: and while this is doing, their speech is to be fashioned to a distinct and clear pronunciation, as near as may be to the *Italian,* especially in the vowels. For we *Englishmen* being far northerly, do not open our mouths in the cold air, wide enough to grace a southern tongue; but are observed by all other nations to speak exceeding close and inward: So that to smatter Latin with an English mouth, is as ill a hearing as Law-French. Next to make them expert in the usefulest points of grammar, and withal to season[22] them, and win them early to the love of virtue and true labor, ere any flattering seducement, or vain principle seize them wandering, some easy and delight-

---

[19] Docile.   [20] Lilly's "Latin Primer."   [21] Graduation.   [22] Imbue.

ful book of education would be read to them; whereof the Greeks have store, as *Cebes*,[23] *Plutarch*,[24] and other Socratic discourses. But in Latin we have none of classic authority extant, except the two or three first books of *Quintilian*,[25] and some select pieces elsewhere. But here the main skill and groundwork will be, to temper[26] them such lectures and explanations upon every opportunity as may lead and draw them in willing obedience, inflamed with the study of learning, and the admiration of virtue; stirred up with high hopes of living to be brave men, and worthy patriots, dear to God, and famous to all ages. That they may despise and scorn all their childish, and ill-taught qualities, to delight in manly, and liberal exercises: which he who hath the art, and proper eloquence to catch them with, what with mild and effectual persuasions, and what with the intimation of some fear, if need be, but chiefly by his own example, might in a short space gain them to an incredible diligence and courage: infusing into their young breasts such an ingenuous and noble ardor, as would not fail to make many of them renowned and matchless men. At the same time, some other hour of the day, might be taught them the rules of arithmetic, and soon after the elements of geometry even playing, as the old manner was. After evening repast, till bed-time their thoughts will be best taken up in the easy grounds of religion, and the story of Scripture. The next step would be to the authors on *agriculture, Cato, Varro, and Columella,* for the matter is most easy, and if the language be difficult, so much the better, it is not a difficulty above their years. And here will be an occasion of inciting and enabling them hereafter to improve the tillage of their country, to recover the bad soil, and to remedy the waste that is made of good; for this was one of *Hercules'* praises. Ere half these authors be read (which will soon be with plying[27] hard, and daily) they can not choose but be masters of any ordinary prose.[28] So that it will be then seasonable for them to learn in any modern author, the use of the globes, and all the maps; first with the old names, and then with the new: or they might be then capable to read any compendious method of natural philosophy.

[23] A disciple of Socrates, to whom was ascribed a book on the cultivation of virtue. [24] Author of the famous "Lives." He lived about 100 A.D. [25] The Latin rhetorician, b. 42 A.D. [26] Adept. [27] Applying themselves. [28] *I. e.,* Latin prose.

And at the same time might be entering into the Greek tongue, after the same manner as was before prescribed in the Latin: whereby the difficulties of grammar being soon overcome, all the historical physiology of *Aristotle* and *Theophrastus*[29] are open before them, and as I may say, under contribution. The like access will be to *Vitruvius*,[30] to *Seneca's* natural questions,[31] to *Mela*,[32] *Celsus*,[33] *Pliny*,[34] or *Solinus*.[35] And having thus passed the principles of *arithmetic, geometry, astronomy,* and *geography* with a general compact of physics, they may descend in *mathematics* to the instrumental science of *trigonometry* and from thence to fortification, architecture, engineering, or navigation. And in natural philosophy they may proceed leisurely from the history of meteors, minerals, plants and living creatures as far as anatomy. Then also in course might be read to them out of some not tedious writer the institution of physic; that they may know the tempers,[36] the humors,[36] the seasons, and how to manage a crudity;[37] which he who can wisely and timely do, is not only a great physician to himself, and to his friends, but also may at some time or other, save an army by this frugal and expenseless means only; and not let the healthy and stout bodies of young men rot away under him for want of this discipline; which is a great pity, and no less a shame to the commander. To set forward all these proceedings in nature and mathematics, what hinders, but that they may procure, as often as shall be needful, the helpful experiences of hunters, fowlers, fishermen, shepherds, gardeners, apothecaries; and in the other sciences, architects, engineers, mariners, anatomists; who doubtless would be ready some for reward, and some to favor such a hopeful seminary. And this will give them such a real tincture of natural knowledge, as they shall never forget, but daily augment with delight. Then also those poets which are now counted most hard, will be both facile and pleasant, *Orpheus, Hesiod, Theocritus, Aratus, Nicander, Oppian, Dionysius,* and in Latin *Lucretius, Manilius,* and the rural part of *Virgil.*

[29] A pupil of Aristotle's. [30] On architecture. [31] On physics. [32] On geography.
[33] On medicine. [34] On natural history. [35] An abridgement of Pliny.
[36] The temperament was supposed to be due to the predominance of one of the four humors in the body. [37] Indigestion.

By this time, years and good general precepts will have furnished them more distinctly with that act of reason which in *ethics* is called *proairesis*[38] that they may with some judgment contemplate upon moral good and evil. Then will be required a special reenforcement of constant and sound indoctrinating to set them right and firm, instructing them more amply in the knowledge of virtue and the hatred of vice: while their young and pliant affections are led through all the moral works of *Plato, Xenophon, Cicero, Plutarch, Laertius*[39] and those *Locrian* remnants;[40] but still to be reduced[41] in their nightward studies wherewith they close the day's work, under the determinate[42] sentence of *David* or *Solomon,* or the evanges[43] and apostolic scriptures. Being perfect in the knowledge of personal duty, they may then begin the study of economics. And either now, or before this, they may have easily learned at any odd hour the *Italian tongue.* And soon after, but with wariness and good antidote, it would be wholesome enough to let them taste some choice comedies, Greek, Latin, or *Italian:* Those tragedies also that treat of household matters, as Trachiniæ,[44] Alcestis[45] and the like. The next remove must be to the study of politics; to know the beginning, end, and reasons of political societies; that they may not in a dangerous fit of the commonwealth be such poor, shaken, uncertain reeds, of such a tottering conscience, as many of our great counselors have lately shown themselves, but steadfast pillars of the state. After this they are to dive into the ground of law and legal justice; delivered first, and with best warrant by *Moses;* and as far as human prudence can be trusted, in those extolled remains of Grecian lawgivers, *Lycurgus, Solon, Zaleucus, Charondas,*[46] and thence to all the Roman *edicts* and tables with their *Justinian;* and so down to the *Saxon* and common laws of *England,* and the statutes. Sundays also and every evening may be now understandingly spent in the highest matters of *theology,* and church history ancient and modern: and ere this time the Hebrew tongue at a set hour might have been gained, that the Scriptures may be now read in their own original; whereto it would be no impossibility to add

[38] The choice between good and evil. [39] Diogenes Laertius, who wrote a history of philosophy. [40] Ascribed to Timæus. [41] Brought back. [42] Authoritative.
[43] Gospels. [44] By Sophocles. [45] By Euripides. [46] Lawgivers respectively to Sparta, Athens, the Locrians in southern Italy, and certain cities in Sicily.

the *Chaldey*,[47] and the *Syrian*[48] dialect. When all these employments are well conquered, then will the choice histories, *heroic poems*, and *Attic* tragedies of stateliest and most regal argument, with all the famous political orations offer themselves; which if they were not only read; but some of them got by memory, and solemnly pronounced with right accent, and grace, as might be taught, would endow them even with the spirit and vigor of *Demosthenes*, or *Cicero, Euripides*, or *Sophocles*. And now lastly will be the time to read with them those organic[49] arts which enable men to discourse and write perspicuously, elegantly, and according to the fitted style of lofty, mean or lowly. Logic therefore so much as is useful, is to be referred to this due place with all her well couched[50] heads and topics, until to be time to open her contracted palm into a graceful and ornate rhetoric taught out of the rule of *Plato, Aristotle, Phalereus, Cicero, Hermogenes, Longinus.* To which poetry would be made subsequent, or indeed rather precedent, as being less subtle and fine, but more simple, sensuous and passionate. I mean not here the prosody of a verse, which they could not have hit on before among the rudiments of grammar; but that sublime art which in *Aristotle's Poetics,* in *Horace,* and the *Italian* commentaries of *Castelvetro, Tasso, Mazzoni,* and others, teaches what the laws are of a true *epic* poem, what of a *dramatic*, what of a *lyric*, what decorum is, which is the grand masterpiece to observe. This would make them soon perceive what despicable creatures our common rimers and playwriters be, and show them, what religious, what glorious and magnificent use might be made of poetry both in divine and human things. From hence and not till now will be the right season of forming them to be able writers and composers in every excellent matter, when they shall be thus fraught with an universal insight into things. Or whether they be to speak in Parliament or council, honor and attention would be waiting on their lips. There would then also appear in pulpits other visages, other gestures, and stuff otherwise wrought than what we now sit under, ofttimes to as great a trial of our patience as any other that they preach to us. These are the studies wherein our noble and our gentle

---

[47] Chaldean, a language akin to Hebrew. [48] Aramaic, the language of Palestine in the time of Christ. [49] Practical. [50] Arranged.

youth ought to bestow their time in a disciplinary way from twelve to one and twenty; unless they rely more upon their ancestors dead, than upon themselves living. In which methodical course it is so supposed they must proceed by the steady pace of learning onward, as at convenient times for memories' sake to retire back into the middle ward,[51] and sometimes into the rear of what they have been taught, until they have confirmed, and solidly united the whole body of their perfected knowledge, like the last embattling of a Roman legion. Now will be worth the seeing what exercises and recreations may best agree, and become these studies.

Their Exercise.

The course of study hitherto briefly described, is, what I can guess by reading, likest to those ancient and famous schools of *Pythagoras, Plato, Isocrates, Aristotle* and such others, out of which were bred up such a number of renowned philosophers, orators, historians, poets and princes all over *Greece, Italy,* and *Asia,* besides the flourishing studies of *Cyrene* and *Alexandria.* But herein it shall exceed them, and supply a defect as great as that which *Plato* noted in the commonwealth of *Sparta,* whereas that city trained up their youth most for war, and these in their Academies and *Lycæum,* all for the gown,[52] this institution of breeding which I here delineate, shall be equally good both for peace and war. Therefore about an hour and a half ere they eat at noon should be allowed them for exercise and due rest afterward: but the time for this may be enlarged at pleasure, according as their rising in the morning shall be early. The exercise which I commend first, is the exact use of their weapon, to guard and to strike safely with edge, or point; this will keep them healthy, nimble, strong, and well in breath, is also the likeliest means to make them grow large and tall, and to inspire them with a gallant and fearless courage, which being tempered with seasonable lectures and precepts to them of true fortitude and patience, will turn into a native and heroic valor, and make them hate the cowardice of doing wrong. They must be also practised in all the locks and grips of wrestling, wherein Englishmen were wont to excel, as need may often be in fight to tug or grapple, and to close.

[51] Center.   [52] Civil life.

And this perhaps will be enough, wherein to prove and heat their single strength. The interim of unsweating[53] themselves regularly, and convenient rest before meat may both with profit and delight be taken up in recreating and composing their travailed[54] spirits with the solemn and divine harmonies of music heard or learned; either while the skilful *organist plies his grave* and fancied descant, in lofty fugues, or the whole symphony with artful and unimaginable touches adorn and grace the well studied chords of some choice composer, sometimes the lute, or soft organ stop waiting on elegant voices either to religious, martial, or civil ditties; which if wise men and prophets be not extremely out,[55] have a great power over dispositions and manners, to smooth and make them gentle from rustic harshness and distempered passions. The like also would not be unexpedient after meat to assist and cherish Nature in her first concoction,[56] and send their minds back to study in good tune and satisfaction. Where having followed it closer under vigilant eyes till about two hours before supper, they are by a sudden alarum or watchword, to be called out to their military motions, under sky or covert, according to the season, as was the Roman wont: first on foot, then as their age permits, on horseback, to all the art of cavalry; that having in sport, but with much exactness, and daily muster, served out the rudiments of their soldiership in all the skill of embattling, marching, encamping, fortifying, besieging and battering, with all the helps of ancient and modern stratagems, *tactics* and warlike maxims, they may as it were out of a long war come forth renowned and perfect commanders in the service of their country. They would not then, if they were trusted with fair and hopeful armies, suffer them for want of just and wise discipline to shed away from about them like sick feathers, though they never so oft supplied: they would not suffer their empty and unrecruitable[57] colonels of twenty men in a company to quaff out,[58] or convey,[59] into secret hoards, the wages of a delusive list, and a miserable remnant: yet in the meanwhile to be overmastered with a score or two of drunkards, the only soldiery left about them, or else to comply with all rapines and violences. No certainly, if they knew

---

[53] Cooling off.   [54] Tired with exercise.   [55] Mistaken.   [56] Digestion.
[57] Unable to enlist recruits.   [58] Spend in drinking.   [59] Steal.

aught of that knowledge that belongs to good men or good governors, they would not suffer these things. But to return to our own
institute, besides these constant exercises at home, there is another
opportunity of gaining experience to be won from pleasure itself
abroad; in those vernal seasons of the year, when the air is calm
and pleasant, it were an injury and sullenness against nature not to
go out, and see her riches, and partake in her rejoicing with heaven
and earth. I should not therefore be a persuader to them of studying
much then, after two or three years that they have well laid their
grounds, but to ride out in companies with prudent and staid guides,
to all the quarters of the land: learning and observing all places of
strength, all commodities[60] of building and of soil, for towns and
tillage, harbors and ports for trade. Sometimes taking sea as far as
to our navy, to learn there also what they can in the practical knowledge of sailing and of sea-fight. These ways would try all their peculiar gifts of nature, and if there were any secret excellence among
them, would fetch it out, and give it fair opportunities to advance
itself by, which could not but mightily redound to the good of this
nation, and bring into fashion again those old admired virtues and
excellencies, with far more advantage now in this purity of Christian
knowledge. Nor shall we then need the monsieurs of *Paris*, to take
our hopeful youth into their slight[61] and prodigal custodies and send
them over back again transformed into mimics, apes, and kick-
shaws. But if they desire to see other countries at three or four
and twenty years of age, not to learn principles but to enlarge experience, and make wise observation, they will by that time be such
as shall deserve the regard and honor of all men where they pass,
and the society and friendship of those in all places who are best
and most eminent. And perhaps then other nations will be glad to
visit us for their breeding, or else to imitate us in their own country.

Now lastly for their diet there can not be much to say, save only
that it would be best in the same house; for much time else would
be lost abroad, and many ill habits got; and that it should be plain,
healthful, and moderate I suppose is out of controversy. Thus Mr.
Hartlib, you have a general view in writing, as your desire was, of
that which at several times I had discoursed with you concerning

60 Advantages.   61 Evil.

228

the best and noblest way of education; not beginning as some have done from the cradle, which yet might be worth many considerations, if brevity had not been my scope, many other circumstances also I could have mentioned, but this to such as have the worth in them to make trial, for light and direction may be enough. Only I believe that this is not a bow for every man to shoot in that counts himself a teacher; but will require sinews almost equal to those which *Homer* gave *Ulysses,* yet I am withal persuaded that it may prove much more easy in the assay,[62] than it now seems at distance, and much more illustrious: howbeit not more difficult than I imagine, and that imagination presents me with nothing but very happy and very possible according to best wishes; if God have so decreed, and this age have spirit and capacity enough to apprehend.

[62] Attempt.

AREOPAGITICA

A SPEECH FOR THE LIBERTY OF

UNLICENSED PRINTING

TO THE PARLIAMENT OF ENGLAND (1644)

Lords and Commons of England, consider what Nation it is whereof ye are, and whereof ye are the governors: a Nation not slow and dull, but of a quick, ingenious and piercing spirit, acute to invent, subtle and sinewy to discourse, not beneath the reach of any point, the highest that human capacity can soar to. Therefore the studies of Learning in her deepest sciences have been so ancient and so eminent among us, that writers of good antiquity and ablest judgment have been persuaded that even the school of Pythagoras and the Persian wisdom took beginning from the old philosophy of this island. And that wise and civil Roman, Julius Agricola, who governed once here for Cæsar, preferred the natural wits of Britain before the laboured studies of the French. Nor is it for nothing that the grave and frugal Transylvanian sends out yearly from as far as the mountainous borders of Russia, and beyond the Hercynian wilderness, not their youth, but their staid men, to learn our language and our theologic arts.

Yet that which is above all this, the favour and the love of Heaven, we have great argument to think in a peculiar manner propitious and propending towards us. Why else was this Nation chosen before any other, that out of her, as out of Sion, should be proclaimed and sounded forth the first tidings and trumpet of Reformation to all Europe? And had it not been the obstinate perverseness of our prelates against the divine and admirable spirit of Wickliffe, to suppress him as a schismatic and innovator, perhaps neither the Bohemian Huss and Jerome, no nor the name of Luther or of Calvin, had been ever known: the glory of reforming all our neighbours had been completely ours. But now, as our obdurate clergy have with violence demeaned the matter, we are become hitherto the latest and backwardest scholars, of whom God offered to have made us the teachers. Now once again by all concurrence of signs, and by the general instinct of holy and devout men, as they daily and solemnly express their thoughts, God is decreeing to begin some new and great period in His Church, even to the reforming of Reformation itself: what does He then but reveal Himself to His servants, and as His manner is, first to His Englishmen? I say, as His manner is, first to us, though we mark not the method of His counsels, and are unworthy.

Behold now this vast City: a city of refuge, the mansion house of liberty, encompassed and surrounded with His protection; the shop of war hath not there more anvils and hammers waking, to fashion out the plates and instruments of armed Justice in defence of beleaguered Truth, than there be pens and heads there, sitting by their studious lamps, musing, searching, revolving new notions and ideas wherewith to present, as with their homage and their fealty, the approaching Reformation: others as fast reading, trying all things, assenting to the force of reason and convincement. What could a man require more from a Nation so pliant and so prone to seek after knowledge? What wants there to such a towardly and pregnant soil, but wise and faithful labourers, to make a knowing people, a Nation of Prophets, of Sages, and of Worthies? We reckon more than five months yet to harvest; there need not be five weeks; had we but eyes to lift up, the fields are white already.

Where there is much desire to learn, there of necessity will be much arguing, much writing, many opinions; for opinion in good men is but knowledge in the making. Under these fantastic terrors of sect and schism, we wrong the earnest and zealous thirst after knowledge and understanding which God hath stirred up in this city. What some lament of, we rather should rejoice at, should rather praise this pious forwardness among men, to reassume the ill-reputed care of their Religion into their own hands again.

A little generous prudence, a little forbearance of one another, and some grain of charity might win all these diligences to join, and unite in one general and brotherly search after Truth; could we but forego this prelatical tradition of crowding free consciences and Christian liberties into canons and precepts of men. I doubt not, if some great and worthy stranger should come among us, wise to discern the mould and temper of a people, and how to govern it, observing the high hopes and aims, the diligent alacrity of our extended thoughts and reasonings in the pursuance of truth and freedom, but that he would cry out as Pyrrhus did, admiring the Roman docility and courage: If such were my Epirots, I would not despair the greatest design that could be attempted, to make a Church or Kingdom happy.

Yet these are the men cried out against for schismatics and sectaries; as if, while the temple of the Lord was building, some cutting, some squaring the marble, others hewing the cedars, there should be a sort of irrational men who could not consider there must be many schisms and many dissections made in the quarry and in the timber, ere the house of God can be built. And when every stone is laid artfully together, it cannot be united into a continuity, it can but be contiguous in this world; neither can every piece of the building be of one form; nay rather the perfection consists in this, that, out of many moderate varieties and brotherly dissimilitudes that are not vastly disproportional, arises the goodly and the graceful symmetry that commends the whole pile and structure.

Let us therefore be more considerate builders, more wise in spiritual architecture, when great reformation is expected. For now the time seems come, wherein Moses the great prophet may sit in heaven rejoicing to see that memorable and glorious wish of his fulfilled, when not only our seventy Elders, but all the Lord's people, are become prophets. No marvel then though some men, and some good men too perhaps, but young in goodness, as Joshua then was, envy them. They fret, and out of their own weakness are in agony, lest these divisions and subdivisions will undo us. The adversary again applauds, and waits the hour: When they have branched themselves out, saith he, small enough into parties and partitions, then will be our time. Fool! he sees not the firm root, out of which we all grow, though into branches: nor will be ware until he see our small divided maniples cutting through at every angle of his ill-united and unwieldy brigade. And that we are to hope better of all these supposed sects and schisms, and that we shall not need that solicitude, honest perhaps though over-timorous of them that vex in this behalf, but shall laugh in the end at those malicious applauders of our differences, I have these reasons to persuade me.

First, when a City shall be as it were besieged and blocked about, her navigable river infested, inroads and incursions round, defiance and battle oft rumoured to be marching up even to her walls and suburb trenches, that then the people, or the greater part, more than at other times, wholly taken up with the study of highest and most important matters to be reformed, should be disputing, reasoning, read-

ing, inventing, discoursing, even to a rarity and admiration, things not before discoursed or written of,
argues first a singular goodwill, contentedness and
confidence in your prudent foresight and safe government, Lords and Commons; and from thence derives
itself to a gallant bravery and well-grounded contempt
of their enemies, as if there were no small number
of as great spirits among us, as his was, who when
Rome was nigh besieged by Hannibal, being in
the city, bought that piece of ground at no cheap
rate, whereon Hannibal himself encamped his own
regiment.

Next, it is a lively and cheerful presage of our
happy success and victory. For as in a body, when the
blood is fresh, the spirits pure and vigorous, not only
to vital but to rational faculties, and those in the
acutest and the pertest operations of wit and subtlety,
it argues in what good plight and constitution the
body is so when the cheerfulness of the people is so
sprightly up, as that it has not only wherewith to
guard well its own freedom and safety, but to spare,
and to bestow upon the solidest and sublimest points
of controversy and new invention, it betokens us not
degenerated, nor drooping to a fatal decay, but casting off the old and wrinkled skin of corruption to
outlive these pangs and wax young again, entering
the glorious ways of truth and prosperous virtue,
destined to become great and honourable in these
latter ages. Methinks I see in my mind a noble and
puissant nation rousing herself like a strong man after
sleep, and shaking her invincible locks. Methinks I
see her as an eagle mewing her mighty youth, and

kindling her undazzled eyes at the full midday beam; purging and unscaling her long-abused sight at the fountain itself of heavenly radiance; while the whole noise of timorous and flocking birds, with those also that love the twilight, flutter about, amazed at what she means, and in their envious gabble would prognosticate a year of sects and schisms.

What would ye do then? should ye suppress all this flowery crop of knowledge and new light sprung up and yet springing daily in this city? should ye set an oligarchy of twenty engrossers over it, to bring a famine upon our minds again, when we shall know nothing but what is measured to us by their bushel? Believe it, Lords and Commons, they who counsel ye to such a suppressing do as good as bid ye suppress yourselves; and I will soon show how. If it be desired to know the immediate cause of all this free writing and free speaking, there cannot be assigned a truer than your own mild and free and humane government. It is the liberty, Lords and Commons, which your own valorous and happy counsels have purchased us, liberty which is the nurse of all great wits; this is that which hath rarefied and enlightened our spirits like the influence of heaven; this is that which hath enfranchised, enlarged and lifted up our apprehensions degrees above themselves.

Ye cannot make us now less capable, less knowing, less eagerly pursuing of the truth, unless ye first make yourselves, that made us so, less the lovers, less the founders of our true liberty. We can grow ignorant again, brutish, formal and slavish, as ye found us; but you then must first become that which ye cannot be, oppressive, arbitrary and tyrannous, as they were from whom ye have freed us. That our hearts are now more capacious, our thoughts more erected to the search and expectation of greatest and exactest things, is the issue of your own virtue propagated in us; ye cannot suppress that, unless ye reinforce an abrogated and merciless law, that fathers may despatch at will their own children. And who shall then stick closest to ye, and excite others? not he who takes up arms for coat and conduct, and his four nobles of Danegelt. Although I dispraise not the defence of just immunities, yet love my peace better, if that were all. Give me the liberty to know, to utter, and to argue freely according to conscience, above all liberties.

What would be best advised, then, if it be found so hurtful and so unequal to suppress opinions for the newness or the unsuitableness to a customary acceptance, will not be my task to say. I only shall repeat what I have learned from one of your own honourable number, a right noble and pious lord, who, had he not sacrificed his life and fortunes to the Church and Commonwealth, we had not now missed and bewailed a worthy and undoubted patron of this argument. Ye know him, I am sure; yet I for honour's sake, and may it be eternal to him, shall name him, the Lord Brook. He writing of Episcopacy and by the way treating of sects and schisms, left ye his vote, or rather now the last words of his dying charge, which I know will ever be of dear and honoured regard with ye, so full of meekness and breathing charity, that next to His last testament, who bequeathed love and peace to His disciples, I cannot call to mind where I have read or heard words more mild and peaceful. He there exhorts us to hear with patience and humility those, however they be miscalled, that desire to live purely, in such a use of God's ordinances, as the best guidance of their conscience gives them, and to tolerate them, though in some disconformity to ourselves. The book itself will tell us more at large, being published to the world, and dedicated to the Parliament by him who, both for his life and for his death, deserves that what advice he left be not laid by without perusal.

And now the time in special is, by privilege to write and speak what may help to the further discussing of matters in agitation. The temple of Janus with his two controversial faces might now not unsignificantly be set open. And though all the winds of doctrine were let loose to play upon the earth, so Truth be in the field, we do injuriously, by licensing and prohibiting, to misdoubt her strength. Let her and Falsehood grapple; who ever knew Truth put to the worse, in a free and open encounter? Her confuting is the best and surest suppressing. He who hears what praying there is for light and clearer knowledge to be sent down among us, would think of other matters to be constituted beyond the discipline of Geneva, framed and fabricked already to our hands. Yet when the new light which we beg for shines in upon us, there be who envy and oppose, if it come not first in at their casements. What a collusion is this, whenas we are exhorted by the wise man to use diligence, to seek for wisdom as for hidden treasures early and late, that another order shall enjoin us to know nothing but by statute? When a man hath been labouring the hardest labour in the deep mines of knowledge; hath furnished out his findings in all their equipage; drawn forth his reasons as it were a battle ranged; scattered and defeated all objections in his way; calls out his adversary into the plain, offers him the advantage of wind and sun, if he please, only that he may try the matter by dint of argument: for his opponents then to skulk, to lay ambushments, to keep a narrow bridge of licensing where the challenger should pass, though it be valour enough in soldiership, is but weakness and cowardice in the wars of Truth.

For who knows not that Truth is strong, next to the Almighty? She needs no policies, nor stratagems, nor licensings to make her victorious; those are the shifts and the defences that error uses against her power. Give her but room, and do not bind her when she sleeps, for then she speaks not true, as the old Proteus did, who spake oracles only when he was caught and bound, but then rather she turns herself into all shapes, except her own, and perhaps tunes her voice according to the time, as Micaiah did before Ahab, until she be adjured into her own likeness. Yet is it not impossible that she may have more shapes than one. What else is all that rank of things indifferent, wherein Truth may be on this side or on the other, without being unlike herself? What but a vain shadow else is the abolition of those ordinances, that hand-writing nailed to the cross? What great purchase is this Christian liberty which Paul so often boasts of?

His doctrine is, that he who eats or eats not, regards a day or regards it not, may do either to the Lord. How many other things might be tolerated in peace, and left to conscience, had we but charity, and were it not the chief stronghold of our hypocrisy to be ever judging one another?

I fear yet this iron yoke of outward conformity hath left a slavish print upon our necks; the ghost of a linen decency yet haunts us. We stumble and are impatient at the least dividing of one visible congregation from another, though it be not in fundamentals; and through our forwardness to suppress, and our backwardness to recover any enthralled piece of truth out of the gripe of custom, we care not to keep truth separated from truth, which is the fiercest rent and disunion of all. We do not see that, while we still affect by all means a rigid external formality, we may as soon fall again into a gross conforming stupidity, a stark and dead congealment of wood and hay and stubble, forced and frozen together, which is more to the sudden degenerating of a Church than many sub-dichotomies of petty schisms.

Not that I can think well of every light separation, or that all in a Church is to be expected gold and silver and precious stones: it is not possible for man to sever the wheat from the tares, the good fish from the other fry; that must be the Angels' Ministry at the end of mortal things. Yet if all cannot be of one mind —as who looks they should be?—this doubtless is more wholesome, more prudent, and more Christian that many be tolerated, rather than all compelled. I mean not tolerated popery, and open superstition,

which, as it extirpates all religions and civil suprem-
acies, so itself should be extirpate, provided first
that all charitable and compassionate means be used
to win and regain the weak and the misled: that also
which is impious or evil absolutely either against faith
or manners no law can possibly permit, that intends
not to unlaw itself: but those neighbouring differences, or rather indifferences, are what I speak of,
whether in some point of doctrine or of discipline,
which, though they may be many, yet need not inter-
rupt the unity of Spirit, if we could but find among us
the bond of peace.

In the meantime if any one would write, and bring
his helpful hand to the slow-moving Reformation
which we labour under, if Truth have spoken to him
before others, or but seemed at least to speak, who
hath so bejesuited us that we should trouble that man
with asking licence to do so worthy a deed? and not
consider this, that if it come to prohibiting, there is
not aught more likely to be prohibited than truth itself; whose first appearance to our eyes, bleared and
dimmed with prejudice and custom, is more unsightly and unplausible than many errors, even as
the person is of many a great man slight and contemptible to see to. And what do they tell us vainly
of new opinions, when this very opinion of theirs,
that none must be heard, but whom they like, is the
worst and newest opinion of all others; and is the
chief cause why sects and schisms do so much abound,
and true knowledge is kept at distance from us; besides yet a greater danger which is in it?

For when God shakes a Kingdom with strong and

healthful commotions to a general reforming, 'tis not untrue that many sectaries and false teachers are then busiest in seducing; but yet more true it is, that God then raises to His own work men of rare abilities, and more than common industry, not only to look back and revise what hath been taught heretofore, but to gain further and go on some new enlightened steps in the discovery of truth. For such is the order of God's enlightening His Church, to dispense and deal out by degrees His beam, so as our earthly eyes may best sustain it.

Neither is God appointed and confined, where and out of what place these His chosen shall be first heard to speak; for He sees not as man sees, chooses not as man chooses, lest we should devote ourselves again to set places, and assemblies, and outward callings of men; planting our faith one while in the old Convocation house, and another while in the Chapel at Westminster; when all the faith and religion that shall be there canonised is not sufficient without plain convincement, and the charity of patient instruction to supple the least bruise of conscience, to edify the meanest Christian, who desires to walk in the Spirit, and not in the letter of human trust, for all the number of voices that can be there made; no, though Harry VII. himself there, with all his liege tombs about him, should lend them voices from the dead, to swell their number.

And if the men be erroneous who appear to be the leading schismatics, what withholds us but our sloth, our self-will, and distrust in the right cause, that we do not give them gentle meeting and gentle dismissions, that we debate not and examine the matter thoroughly with liberal and frequent audience; if not for their sakes, yet for our own? seeing no man who hath tasted learning, but will confess the many ways of profiting by those who, not contented with stale receipts, are able to manage and set forth new positions to the world. And were they but as the dust and cinders of our feet, so long as in that notion they may yet serve to polish and brighten the armoury of Truth, even for that respect they were not utterly to be cast away. But if they be of those whom God hath fitted for the special use of these times with eminent and ample gifts, and those perhaps neither among the Priests nor among the Pharisees, and we in the haste of a precipitant zeal shall make no distinction, but resolve to stop their mouths, because we fear they come with new and dangerous opinions, as we commonly forejudge them ere we understand them, no less than woe to us, while, thinking thus to defend the Gospel, we are found the persecutors.

There have been not a few since the beginning of this Parliament, both of the Presbytery and others, who by their unlicensed books, to the contempt of an Imprimatur, first broke that triple ice clung about our hearts, and taught the people to see day: I hope that none of those were the persuaders to renew upon us this bondage which they themselves have wrought so much good by contemning. But if neither the check that Moses gave to young Joshua, nor the countermand which our Saviour gave to young John, who was so ready to prohibit those whom he thought unlicensed, be not enough to admonish our Elders how unacceptable to God their testy mood of prohibiting is, if neither their own remembrance what evil hath abounded in the Church by this let of licensing, and what good they themselves have begun by transgressing it, be not enough, but that they will persuade and execute the most Dominican part of the Inquisition over us, and are already with one foot in the stirrup so active at suppressing, it would be no unequal distribution in the first place to suppress the suppressors themselves: whom the change of their condition hath puffed up, more than their late experience of harder times hath made wise.

And as for regulating the Press, let no man think to have the honour of advising ye better than yourselves have done in that Order published next before this, "that no book be Printed, unless the Printer's and the Author's name, or at least the Printer's, be registered." Those which otherwise come forth, if they be found mischievous and libellous, the fire and the executioner will be the timeliest and the most effectual remedy that man's prevention can use. For this authentic Spanish policy of licensing books, if I have said aught, will prove the most unlicensed book itself within a short while; and was the immediate image of a Star Chamber decree to that purpose made in those very times when that Court did the rest of those her pious works, for which she is now fallen from the stars with Lucifer. Whereby ye may guess what kind of state prudence, what love of the people, what care of Religion or good manners there was at the contriving, although with singular hypocrisy it pretended to bind books to their good behaviour.

And how it got the upper hand of your precedent Order so well constituted before, if we may believe those men whose profession gives them cause to enquire most, it may be doubted there was in it the fraud of some old patentees and monopolisers in the trade of bookselling; who under pretence of the poor in their Company not to be defrauded, and the just retaining of each man his several copy, which God forbid should be gainsaid, brought divers glosing colours to the House, which were indeed but colours, and serving to no end except it be to exercise a superiority over their neighbours; men who do not therefore labour in an honest profession to which learning is indebted, that they should be made other men's vassals. Another end is thought was aimed at by some of them in procuring by petition this Order, that, having power in their hands, malignant books might the easier scape abroad, as the event shows.

But of these sophisms and elenchs of merchandise I skill not. This I know, that errors in a good government and in a bad are equally almost incident; for what Magistrate may not be misinformed, and much the sooner, if Liberty of Printing be reduced into the power of a few? But to redress willingly and speedily what hath been erred, and in highest authority to esteem a plain advertisement more than others have done a sumptuous bribe, is a virtue (honoured Lords and Commons) answerable to your highest actions, and whereof none can participate but greatest and wisest men.

Alfred North Whitehead,   THE AIMS OF EDUCATION

1.   What were Whitehead's "educational commandments"?
     Do you think that 20th century public education in
     the U.S. has followed these dicta? Explain.

2.   In this essay, Whitehead presents what one might
     call a "cyclical" model of the educational pro-
     cess. Describe this model and relate it to your
     own education.

3.   How would Whitehead have reacted to the use of
     standardized tests, or competency tests, in to-
     day's schools? Why?

     Alfred North Whitehead (1861-1947), trained as a
mathematician, collaborated with Bertrand Russell to
write the famed *Principia Mathematica* - a milestone of
modern mathematics. At age 63, he became Professor of
Philosophy at Harvard, launching his career as a philosopher. Although known chiefly for his contributions to
mathematics and to the philosophy of science, he was
also an astute observer of the educational structure of
his day.

1. The Aims of Education

CULTURE is activity of thought, and receptiveness to beauty and humane feeling. Scraps of information have nothing to do with it. A merely well-informed man is the most useless bore on God's earth. What we should aim at producing is men who possess both culture and expert knowledge in some special direction. Their expert knowledge will give them the ground to start from, and their culture will lead them as deep as philosophy and as high as art. We have to remember that the valuable intellectual development is self-development, and that it mostly takes place between the ages of sixteen and thirty. As to training, the most important part is given by mothers before the age of twelve. A saying due to Archbishop Temple illustrates my meaning. Surprise was expressed at the success in after-life of a man, who as a boy at Rugby had been somewhat undistinguished. He answered, "It is not what they are at eighteen, it is what they become afterwards that matters."

In training a child to activity of thought, above all things we must beware of what I will call "inert ideas" —that is to say, ideas that are merely received into the mind without being utilised, or tested, or thrown into fresh combinations.

In the history of education, the most striking phenomenon is that schools of learning, which at one epoch are alive with a ferment of genius, in a succeeding generation exhibit merely pedantry and routine. The reason is, that they are overladen with inert ideas. Education with inert ideas is not only useless: it is, above all things, harmful— *Corruptio optimi, pessima.* Except at rare intervals of intellectual ferment, education in the past has been radically infected with inert ideas. That is the reason why uneducated clever women, who have seen much of the world, are in middle life so much the most cultured part of the community. They have been saved from this horrible burden of inert ideas. Every intellectual revolution which has ever stirred humanity into greatness has been a passionate protest against inert ideas. Then, alas, with pathetic ignorance of human psychology, it has proceeded by some edu-

cational scheme to bind humanity afresh with inert ideas
of its own fashioning.

Let us now ask how in our system of education we are
to guard against this mental dryrot. We enunciate two
educational commandments, "Do not teach too many
subjects," and again, "What you teach, teach thoroughly."

The result of teaching small parts of a large number of
subjects is the passive reception of disconnected ideas, not
illumined with any spark of vitality. Let the main ideas
which are introduced into a child's education be few and
important, and let them be thrown into every combination possible. The child should make them his own, and
should understand their application here and now in the
circumstances of his actual life. From the very beginning
of his education, the child should experience the joy of
discovery. The discovery which he has to make, is that
general ideas give an understanding of that stream of
events which pours through his life, which is his life. By
understanding I mean more than a mere logical analysis,
though that is included. I mean "understanding" in the
sense in which it is used in the French proverb, "To understand all, is to forgive all." Pedants sneer at an education which is useful. But if education is not useful, what is
it? Is it a talent, to be hidden away in a napkin? Of course,
education should be useful, whatever your aim in life. It
was useful to Saint Augustine and it was useful to Napo-
leon. It is useful, because understanding is useful.

I pass lightly over that understanding which should be
given by the literary side of education. Nor do I wish to
be supposed to pronounce on the relative merits of a classical or a modern curriculum. I would only remark that the
understanding which we want is an understanding of an
insistent present. The only use of a knowledge of the past
is to equip us for the present. No more deadly harm can
be done to young minds than by depreciation of the present. The present contains all that there is. It is holy
ground; for it is the past, and it is the future. At the same
time it must be observed that an age is no less past if it
existed two hundred years ago than if it existed two thousand years ago. Do not be deceived by the pedantry of
dates. The ages of Shakespeare and of Molière are no less
past than are the ages of Sophocles and of Virgil. The
communion of saints is a great and inspiring assemblage,

but it has only one possible hall of meeting, and that is, the present; and the mere lapse of time through which any particular group of saints must travel to reach that meeting-place, makes very little difference.

Passing now to the scientific and logical side of education, we remember that here also ideas which are not utilised are positively harmful. By utilising an idea, I mean relating it to that stream, compounded of sense perceptions, feelings, hopes, desires, and of mental activities adjusting thought to thought, which forms our life. I can imagine a set of beings which might fortify their souls by passively reviewing disconnected ideas. Humanity is not built that way—except perhaps some editors of newspapers.

In scientific training, the first thing to do with an idea is to prove it. But allow me for one moment to extend the meaning of "prove"; I mean—to prove its worth. Now an idea is not worth much unless the propositions in which it is embodied are true. Accordingly an essential part of the proof of an idea is the proof, either by experiment or by logic, of the truth of the propositions. But it is not essential that this proof of the truth should constitute the first introduction to the idea. After all, its assertion by the authority of respectable teachers is sufficient evidence to begin with. In our first contact with a set of propositions, we commence by appreciating their importance. That is what we all do in after-life. We do not attempt, in the strict sense, to prove or to disprove anything, unless its importance makes it worthy of that honour. These two processes of proof, in the narrow sense, and of appreciation, do not require a rigid separation in time. Both can be proceeded with nearly concurrently. But in so far as either process must have the priority, it should be that of appreciation by use.

Furthermore, we should not endeavour to use propositions in isolation. Emphatically I do not mean, a neat little set of experiments to illustrate Proposition I and then the proof of Proposition I, a neat little set of experiments to illustrate Proposition II and then the proof of Proposition II, and so on to the end of the book. Nothing could be more boring. Interrelated truths are utilised en bloc, and the various propositions are employed in any order, and with any reiteration. Choose some important applications of your theoretical subject; and study them concurrently with the systematic theoretical exposition. Keep the theoretical exposition short and simple, but let it be strict and rigid so far as it goes. It should not be too long for it to be easily known with thoroughness and accuracy. The consequences of a plethora of half-digested theoretical knowledge are deplorable. Also the theory should not be muddled up with the practice. The child should have no doubt when it is proving and when it is utilising. My point is that what is proved should be utilised, and that what is utilised should—so far as is practicable—be proved. I am far from asserting that proof and utilisation are the same thing.

At this point of my discourse, I can most directly carry forward my argument in the outward form of a digression. We are only just realising that the art and science of education require a genius and a study of their own; and that this genius and this science are more than a bare knowledge of some branch of science or of literature. This truth was partially perceived in the past generation; and headmasters, somewhat crudely, were apt to supersede learning in their colleagues by requiring left-hand bowling and a taste for football. But culture is more than cricket, and more than football, and more than extent of knowledge.

Education is the acquisition of the art of the utilisation of knowledge. This is an art very difficult to impart. Whenever a text-book is written of real educational worth, you may be quite certain that some reviewer will say that it will be difficult to teach from it. Of course it will be difficult to teach from it. If it were easy, the book ought to be burned; for it cannot be educational. In education, as elsewhere, the broad primrose path leads to a nasty place. This evil path is represented by a book or a set of lectures which will practically enable the student to learn by heart all the questions likely to be asked at the next external examination. And I may say in passing that no educational system is possible unless every question directly asked of a pupil at any examination is either framed or modified by the actual teacher of that pupil in that subject. The external assessor may report on the curriculum or on the performance of the pupils, but never should be allowed to ask the pupil a question which has not been strictly supervised by the actual teacher, or at least inspired by a long conference with him. There are a few exceptions to this rule, but they are exceptions, and could easily be allowed for under the general rule.

We now return to my previous point, that theoretical ideas should always find important applications within the pupil's curriculum. This is not an easy doctrine to apply, but a very hard one. It contains within itself the problem of keeping knowledge alive, of preventing it from becoming inert, which is the central problem of all education.

The best procedure will depend on several factors, none of which can be neglected, namely, the genius of the teacher, the intellectual type of the pupils, their prospects in life, the opportunities offered by the immediate surroundings of the school, and allied factors of this sort. It is for this reason that the uniform external examination is so deadly. We do not denounce it because we are cranks, and like denouncing established things. We are not so childish. Also, of course, such examinations have their use in testing slackness. Our reason of dislike is very definite and very practical. It kills the best part of culture. When you analyse in the light of experience the central task of education, you find that its successful accomplishment depends on a delicate adjustment of many variable factors. The reason is that we are dealing with human minds, and not with dead matter. The evocation of curiosity, of judgment, of the power of mastering a complicated tangle of circumstances, the use of theory in giving foresight in special cases—all these powers are not to be imparted by a set rule embodied in one schedule of examination subjects.

I appeal to you, as practical teachers. With good discipline, it is always possible to pump into the minds of a class a certain quantity of inert knowledge. You take a text-book and make them learn it. So far, so good. The child then knows how to solve a quadratic equation. But what is the point of teaching a child to solve a quadratic equation? There is a traditional answer to this question. It runs thus: The mind is an instrument, you first sharpen it, and then use it; the acquisition of the power of solving a quadratic equation is part of the process of sharpening the mind. Now there is just enough truth in this answer to have made it live through the ages. But for all its half-truth, it embodies a radical error which bids fair to stifle the genius of the modern world. I do not know who was first responsible for this analogy of the mind to a dead instrument. For aught I know, it may have been one of the seven wise men of Greece, or a committee of the whole lot of them. Whoever was the originator, there can be no doubt of the authority which it has acquired by the continuous approval bestowed upon it by eminent persons. But whatever its weight of authority, whatever the high approval which it can quote, I have no hesitation in denouncing it as one of the most fatal, erroneous, and dangerous conceptions ever introduced into the theory of education. The mind is never passive; it is a perpetual activity, delicate, receptive, responsive to stimulus. You cannot postpone its life until you have sharpened it. Whatever interest attaches to your subject-matter must be evoked here and now; whatever powers you are strengthening in the pupil, must be exercised here and now; whatever possibilities of mental life your teaching should impart, must be exhibited here and now. That is the golden rule of education, and a very difficult rule to follow.

The difficulty is just this: the apprehension of general ideas, intellectual habits of mind, and pleasurable interest in mental achievement can be evoked by no form of words, however accurately adjusted. All practical teachers know that education is a patient process of the mastery of details, minute by minute, hour by hour, day by day. There is no royal road to learning through an airy path of brilliant generalisations. There is a proverb about the difficulty of seeing the wood because of the trees. That difficulty is exactly the point which I am enforcing. The problem of education is to make the pupil see the wood by means of the trees.

The solution which I am urging, is to eradicate the fatal disconnection of subjects which kills the vitality of our modern curriculum. There is only one subject-matter for education, and that is Life in all its manifestations. Instead of this single unity, we offer children—Algebra, from which nothing follows; Geometry, from which nothing follows; Science, from which nothing follows; History, from which nothing follows; a Couple of Languages, never mastered; and lastly, most dreary of all, Literature, represented by plays of Shakespeare, with philological notes and short analyses of plot and character to be in substance committed to memory. Can such a list be said to represent Life, as it is known in the midst of the living of it? The best that can be said of it is, that it is a rapid table of contents which a deity might run over in his mind while he was thinking of creating a world, and had not yet determined how to put it together.

Let us now return to quadratic equations. We still have on hand the unanswered question. Why should children be taught their solution? Unless quadratic equations fit into a connected curriculum, of course there is no reason to teach anything about them. Furthermore, extensive as should be the place of mathematics in a complete culture, I am a little doubtful whether for many types of boys algebraic solutions of quadratic equations do not lie on the specialist side of mathematics. I may here remind you that as yet I have not said anything of the psychology or the content of the specialism, which is so necessary a part of an ideal education. But all that is an evasion of our real question, and I merely state it in order to avoid being misunderstood in my answer.

Quadratic equations are part of algebra, and algebra is the intellectual instrument which has been created for rendering clear the quantitative aspects of the world. There is no getting out of it. Through and through the world is infected with quantity. To talk sense, is to talk in quantities. It is no use saying that the nation is large, —How large? It is no use saying that radium is scarce,— How scarce? You cannot evade quantity. You may fly to poetry and to music, and quantity and number will face you in your rhythms and your octaves. Elegant intellects which despise the theory of quantity, are but half developed. They are more to be pitied than blamed. The scraps of gibberish, which in their school-days were taught to them in the name of algebra, deserve some contempt.

This question of the degeneration of algebra into gibberish, both in word and in fact, affords a pathetic instance of the uselessness of reforming educational schedules without a clear conception of the attributes which you wish to evoke in the living minds of the children. A few years ago there was an outcry that school algebra was in need of reform, but there was a general agreement that graphs would put everything right. So all sorts of things were extruded, and graphs were introduced. So far as I can see, with no sort of idea behind them, but just graphs. Now every examination paper has one or two questions on graphs. Personally, I am an enthusiastic adherent of graphs. But I wonder whether as yet we have gained very much. You cannot put life into any schedule of general education unless you succeed in exhibiting its relation to some essential characteristic of all intelligent or emotional perception. It is a hard saying, but it is true; and I do not see how to make it any easier. In making these little formal alterations you are beaten by the very nature of things. You are pitted against too skilful an adversary, who will see to it that the pea is always under the other thimble.

Reformation must begin at the other end. First, you must make up your mind as to those quantitative aspects of the world which are simple enough to be introduced into general education; then a schedule of algebra should be framed which will about find its exemplification in these applications. We need not fear for our pet graphs, they will be there in plenty when we once begin to treat algebra as a serious means of studying the world. Some of the simplest applications will be found in the quantities which occur in the simplest study of society. The curves of history are more vivid and more informing than the dry catalogues of names and dates which comprise the greater part of that arid school study. What purpose is effected by a catalogue of undistinguished kings and queens? Tom, Dick, or Harry, they are all dead. General resurrections are failures, and are better postponed. The quantitative flux of the forces of modern society is capable of very simple exhibition. Meanwhile, the ideas of the variable, of the function, of rate of change, of equations and their solution, of elimination, are being studied as an abstract science for their own sake. Not, of course, in the pompous phrases with which I am alluding to them, here, but with that iteration of simple special cases proper to teaching.

If this course be followed, the route from Chaucer to the Black Death, from the Black Death to modern Labour troubles, will connect the tales of the mediæval pilgrims with the abstract science of algebra, both yielding diverse aspects of that single theme, Life. I know what most of you are thinking at this point. It is that the exact course which I have sketched out is not the particular one which you would have chosen, or even see how to work. I quite agree. I am not claiming that I could do it myself. But your objection is the precise reason why a common external examination system is fatal to education. The process of exhibiting the applications of knowledge must, for its success, essentially depend on the character of the pupils and the genius of the teacher. Of course I have left out the easiest applications with which most of us are more at home. I mean the quantitative sides of sciences, such as mechanics and physics.

Again, in the same connection we plot the statistics of social phenomena against the time. We then eliminate the time between suitable pairs. We can speculate how far we have exhibited a real causal connection, or how far a mere temporal coincidence. We notice that we might have plotted against the time one set of statistics for one country and another set for another country, and thus, with suitable choice of subjects, have obtained graphs which certainly exhibited mere coincidence. Also other graphs exhibit obvious causal connections. We wonder how to discriminate. And so are drawn on as far as we will.

But in considering this description, I must beg you to remember what I have been insisting on above. In the first place, one train of thought will not suit all groups of children. For example, I should expect that artisan children will want something more concrete and, in a sense, swifter than I have set down here. Perhaps I am wrong, but that is what I should guess. In the second place, I am not contemplating one beautiful lecture stimulating, once and for all, an admiring class. That is not the way in which education proceeds. No; all the time the pupils are hard at work solving examples, drawing graphs, and making experiments, until they have a thorough hold on the whole subject. I am describing the interspersed explanations, the directions which should be given to their thoughts. The pupils have got to be made to feel that they are studying something, and are not merely executing intellectual minuets.

Finally, if you are teaching pupils for some general examination, the problem of sound teaching is greatly complicated. Have you ever noticed the zig-zag moulding round a Norman arch? The ancient work is beautiful, the modern work is hideous. The reason is, that the modern work is done to exact measure, the ancient work is varied according to the idiosyncrasy of the workman. Here it is crowded, and there it is expanded. Now the essence of getting pupils through examinations is to give equal weight to all parts of the schedule. But mankind is naturally specialist. One man sees a whole subject, where another can find only a few detached examples. I know that it seems contradictory to allow for specialism in a curriculum especially designed for a broad culture. Without contradictions the world would be simpler, and perhaps duller. But I am certain that in education wherever you exclude specialism you destroy life.

We now come to the other great branch of a general mathematical education, namely Geometry. The same principles apply. The theoretical part should be clear-cut, rigid, short, and important. Every proposition not absolutely necessary to exhibit the main connection of ideas should be cut out, but the great fundamental ideas should be all there. No omission of concepts, such as those of Similarity and Proportion. We must remember that, owing to the aid rendered by the visual presence of a figure, Geometry is a field of unequalled excellence for the exercise of the deductive faculties of reasoning. Then, of course, there follows Geometrical Drawing, with its training for the hand and eye.

But, like Algebra, Geometry and Geometrical Drawing must be extended beyond the mere circle of geometrical ideas. In an industrial neighbourhood, machinery and workshop practice form the appropriate extension. For example, in the London Polytechnics this has been achieved with conspicuous success. For many secondary schools I suggest that surveying and maps are the natural applications. In particular, plane-table surveying should lead pupils to a vivid apprehension of the immediate application of geometric truths. Simple drawing apparatus, a surveyor's chain, and a surveyor's compass, should enable the pupils to rise from the survey and mensuration of a field to the construction of the map of a small district. The best education is to be found in gaining the utmost information from the simplest apparatus. The provision of elaborate instruments is greatly to be deprecated. To have constructed the map of a small district, to have considered its roads, its contours, its geology, its climate, its relation to other districts, the effects on the status of its inhabitants, will teach more history and geography than any knowledge of Perkin Warbeck or of Behren's Straits. I mean not a nebulous lecture on the subject, but a serious investigation in which the real facts are definitely ascertained by the aid of accurate theoretical knowledge. A typical mathematical problem should be: Survey such and such a field, draw a plan of it to such and such a scale, and find the area. It would be quite a good procedure to impart the necessary geometrical propositions without their proofs. Then, concurrently in the same term, the proofs of the propositions would be learnt while the survey was being made.

Fortunately, the specialist side of education presents an easier problem than does the provision of a general culture. For this there are many reasons. One is that many of the principles of procedure to be observed are the same in both cases, and it is unnecessary to recapitulate. Another reason is that specialist training takes place—or should take place—at a more advanced stage of the pupil's course, and thus there is easier material to work upon. But undoubtedly the chief reason is that the specialist study is normally a study of peculiar interest to the student. He is studying it because, for some reason, he wants to know it. This makes all the difference. The general culture is designed to foster an activity of mind; the specialist course utilises this activity. But it does not do to lay too much stress on these neat antitheses. As we have already seen, in the general course foci of special interest will arise; and similarly in the special study, the external connections of the subject drag thought outwards.

Again, there is not one course of study which merely gives general culture, and another which gives special knowledge. The subjects pursued for the sake of a general education are special subjects specially studied; and, on the other hand, one of the ways of encouraging general mental activity is to foster a special devotion. You may not divide the seamless coat of learning. What education has to impart is an intimate sense for the power of ideas, for the beauty of ideas, and for the structure of ideas, together with a particular body of knowledge which has peculiar reference to the life of the being possessing it.

The appreciation of the structure of ideas is that side of a cultured mind which can only grow under the influence of a special study. I mean that eye for the whole chess-board, for the bearing of one set of ideas on another. Nothing but a special study can give any appreciation for the exact formulation of general ideas, for their relations when formulated, for their service in the comprehension of life. A mind so disciplined should be both more abstract and more concrete. It has been trained in the comprehension of abstract thought and in the analysis of facts.

Finally, there should grow the most austere of all mental qualities; I mean the sense for style. It is an æsthetic sense, based on admiration for the direct attainment of a foreseen end, simply and without waste. Style in art, style in literature, style in science, style in logic, style in practical execution have fundamentally the same æsthetic qualities, namely, attainment and restraint. The love of a subject in itself and for itself, where it is not the sleepy pleasure of pacing a mental quarter-deck, is the love of style as manifested in that study.

Here we are brought back to the position from which we started, the utility of education. Style, in its finest sense, is the last acquirement of the educated mind; it is also the most useful. It pervades the whole being. The administrator with a sense for style hates waste; the engineer with a sense for style economises his material; the artisan with a sense for style prefers good work. Style is the ultimate morality of mind.

But above style, and above knowledge, there is something, a vague shape like fate above the Greek gods. That something is Power. Style is the fashioning of power, the restraining of power. But, after all, the power of attainment of the desired end is fundamental. The first thing is to get there. Do not bother about your style, but solve your problem, justify the ways of God to man, administer your province, or do whatever else is set before you.

Where, then, does style help? In this, with style the end is attained without side issues, without raising undesirable inflammations. With style you attain your end and nothing but your end. With style the effect of your activity is calculable, and foresight is the last gift of gods to men. With style your power is increased, for your mind is not distracted with irrelevancies, and you are more likely to attain your object. Now style is the exclusive privilege of the expert. Whoever heard of the style of an amateur painter, of the style of an amateur poet? Style is always the product of specialist study, the peculiar contribution of specialism to culture.

English education in its present phase suffers from a lack of definite aim, and from an external machinery which kills its vitality. Hitherto in this address I have been considering the aims which should govern education. In this respect England halts between two opinions. It has not decided whether to produce amateurs or experts. The profound change in the world which the nineteenth century has produced is that the growth of knowledge has given foresight. The amateur is essentially a man with appreciation and with immense versatility in mastering a given routine. But he lacks the foresight which comes from special knowledge. The object of this address is to suggest how to produce the expert without loss of the essential virtues of the amateur. The machinery of our secondary education is rigid where it should be yielding, and lax where it should be rigid. Every school is bound on pain of extinction to train its boys for a small set of definite examinations. No headmaster has a free hand to develop his general education or his specialist studies in accordance with the opportunities of his school, which are created by its staff, its environment, its class of boys, and its endowments. I suggest that no system of external tests which aims primarily at examining individual scholars can result in anything but educational waste.

Primarily it is the schools and not the scholars which should be inspected. Each school should grant its own leaving certificates, based on its own curriculum. The standards of these schools should be sampled and corrected. But the first requisite for educational reform is the school as a unit, with its approved curriculum based on its own needs, and evolved by its own staff. If we fail to secure that, we simply fall from one formalism into another, from one dung-hill of inert ideas into another.

In stating that the school is the true educational unit in any national system for the safeguarding of efficiency, I have conceived the alternative system as being the external examination of the individual scholar. But every Scylla is faced by its Charybdis—or, in more homely language, there is a ditch on both sides of the road. It will be equally fatal to education if we fall into the hands of a supervising department which is under the impression that it can divide all schools into two or three rigid categories, each type being forced to adopt a rigid curriculum. When I say that the school is the educational unit, I mean exactly what I say, no larger unit, no smaller unit. Each school must have the claim to be considered in relation to its special circumstances. The classifying of schools for some purposes is necessary. But no absolutely rigid curriculum, not modified by its own staff, should be permissible. Exactly the same principles apply, with the proper modifications, to universities and to technical colleges.

When one considers in its length and in its breadth the importance of this question of the education of a nation's young, the broken lives, the defeated hopes, the national failures, which result from the frivolous inertia with which it is treated, it is difficult to restrain within oneself a savage rage. In the conditions of modern life the rule is absolute, the race which does not value trained intelligence is doomed. Not all your heroism, not all your social charm, not all your wit, not all your victories on land or at sea, can move back the finger of fate. To-day we maintain ourselves. To-morrow science will have moved forward yet one more step, and there will be no appeal from the judgment which will then be pronounced on the uneducated.

We can be content with no less than the old summary of educational ideal which has been current at any time from the dawn of our civilisation. The essence of education is that it be religious.

Pray, what is religious education?

A religious education is an education which inculcates duty and reverence. Duty arises from our potential control over the course of events. Where attainable knowledge could have changed the issue, ignorance has the guilt of vice. And the foundation of reverence is this perception, that the present holds within itself the complete sum of existence, backwards and forwards, that whole amplitude of time, which is eternity.

——Presidential address to the Mathematical Association of England, 1916.

2. The Rhythm of Education

By the Rhythm of Education I denote a certain principle which in its practical application is well known to everyone with educational experience. Accordingly, when I remember that I am speaking to an audience of some of the leading educationalists in England, I have no expectation that I shall be saying anything that is new to you. I do think, however, that the principle has not been subjected to an adequate discussion taking account of all the factors which should guide its application.

I first seek for the baldest statement of what I mean by the Rhythm of Education, a statement so bald as to exhibit the point of this address in its utter obviousness. The principle is merely this—that different subjects and modes of study should be undertaken by pupils at fitting times when they have reached the proper stage of mental development. You will agree with me that this is a truism, never doubted and known to all. I am really anxious to emphasise the obvious character of the foundational idea of my address; for one reason, because this audience will certainly find it out for itself. But the other reason, the reason why I choose this subject for discourse, is that I do not think that this obvious truth has been handled in educational practice with due attention to the psychology of the pupils.

The Tasks of Infancy

I commence by challenging the adequacy of some principles by which the subjects for study are often classified in order. By this I mean that these principles can only be accepted as correct if they are so explained as to be explained away. Consider first the criterion of difficulty. It is not true that the easier subjects should precede the harder. On the contrary, some of the hardest must come first because nature so dictates, and because they are essential to life. The first intellectual task which confronts an infant is the acquirement of spoken language. What an appalling task, the correlation of meanings with sounds! It requires an analysis of ideas and an analysis of sounds. We all know that the infant does it, and that the miracle of his achievement is explicable. But so are all miracles, and yet to the wise they remain miracles. All I ask is that with this example staring us in the face we should cease talking nonsense about postponing the harder subjects.

What is the next subject in the education of the infant minds? The acquirement of written language; that is to say, the correlation of sounds with shapes. Great heavens! Have our educationists gone mad? They are setting babbling mites of six years old to tasks which might daunt a sage after lifelong toil. Again, the hardest task in mathematics is the study of the elements of algebra, and yet this stage must precede the comparative simplicity of the differential calculus.

I will not elaborate my point further; I merely restate it in the form, that the postponement of difficulty is no safe clue for the maze of educational practice.

The alternative principle of order among subjects is that of necessary antecedence. There we are obviously on firmer ground. It is impossible to read *Hamlet* until you can read; and the study of integers must precede the study of fractions. And yet even this firm principle dissolves under scrutiny. It is certainly true, but it is only true if you give an artificial limitation to the concept of a subject for study. The danger of the principle is that it is accepted in one sense, for which it is almost a necessary truth, and that it is applied in another sense for which it is false. You cannot read Homer before you can read; but many a child, and in ages past many a man, has sailed with Odysseus over the seas of Romance by the help of the spoken word of a mother, or of some wandering bard. The uncritical application of the principle of the necessary antecedence of some subjects to others has, in the hands of dull people with a turn for organisation, produced in education the dryness of the Sahara.

Stages of Mental Growth

The reason for the title which I have chosen for this address, the Rhythm of Education, is derived from yet another criticism of current ideas. The pupil's progress is often conceived as a uniform steady advance undifferentiated by change of type or alteration in pace; for example, a boy may be conceived as starting Latin at ten years of age and by a uniform progression steadily developing into a

classical scholar at the age of eighteen or twenty. I hold
that this conception of education is based upon a false
psychology of the process of mental development which
has gravely hindered the effectiveness of our methods. Life
is essentially periodic. It comprises daily periods, with their
alternations of work and play, of activity and of sleep, and
seasonal periods, which dictate our terms and our holidays;
and also it is composed of well-marked yearly periods.
These are the gross obvious periods which no one can overlook. There are also subtler periods of mental growth, with
their cyclic recurrences, yet always different as we pass
from cycle to cycle, though the subordinate stages are repro-
duced in each cycle. That is why I have chosen the term
"rhythmic," as meaning essentially the conveyance of difference within a framework of repetition. Lack of attention
to the rhythm and character of mental growth is a main
source of wooden futility in education. I think that Hegel
was right when he analysed progress into three stages,
which he called Thesis, Antithesis, and Synthesis; though
for the purpose of the application of his idea to educational
theory I do not think that the names he gave are very happily suggestive. In relation to intellectual progress I would
term them, the stage of romance, the stage of precision,
and the stage of generalisation.

The Stage of Romance

The stage of romance is the stage of first apprehension.
The subject-matter has the vividness of novelty; it holds
within itself unexplored connexions with possibilities half-
disclosed by glimpses and half-concealed by the wealth of
material. In this stage knowledge is not dominated by systematic procedure. Such system as there must be is created
piecemeal ad hoc. We are in the presence of immediate
cognisance of fact, only intermittently subjecting fact to
systematic dissection. Romantic emotion is essentially the
excitement consequent on the transition from the bare
facts to the first realisations of the import of their unexplored relationships. For example, Crusoe was a mere
man, the sand was mere sand, the footprint was a mere
footprint, and the island a mere island, and Europe was
the busy world of men. But the sudden perception of the
half-disclosed and half-hidden possibilities relating Crusoe

and the sand and the footprint and the lonely island
secluded from Europe constitutes romance. I have had to
take an extreme case for illustration in order to make my
meaning perfectly plain. But construe it as an allegory
representing the first stage in a cycle of progress. Education
must essentially be a setting in order of a ferment already
stirring in the mind: you cannot educate mind in vacuo.
In our conception of education we tend to confine it to
the second stage of the cycle; namely, to the stage of precision. But we cannot so limit our task without miscon-
ceiving the whole problem. We are concerned alike with
the ferment, with the acquirement of precision, and with
the subsequent fruition.

The Stage of Precision

The stage of precision also represents an addition to
knowledge. In this stage, width of relationship is subordinated to exactness of formulation. It is the stage of grammar, the grammar of language and the grammar of science.
It proceeds by forcing on the students' acceptance a given
way of analysing the facts, bit by bit. New facts are added,
but they are the facts which fit into the analysis.

It is evident that a stage of precision is barren without a
previous stage of romance: unless there are facts which
have already been vaguely apprehended in their broad
generality, the previous analysis is an analysis of nothing.
It is simply a series of meaningless statements about bare
facts, produced artificially and without any further rele-
vance. I repeat that in this stage we do not merely remain
within the circle of the facts elicited in the romantic epoch.
The facts of romance have disclosed ideas with possibilities of wide significance, and in the stage of precise progress we acquire other facts in a systematic order, which
thereby form both a disclosure and an analysis of the general subject-matter of the romance.

The Stage of Generalisation

The final stage of generalisation is Hegel's synthesis. It
is a return to romanticism with added advantage of classified ideas and relevant technique. It is the fruition which
has been the goal of the precise training. It is the final

success. I am afraid that I have had to give a dry analysis of somewhat obvious ideas. It has been necessary to do so because my subsequent remarks presuppose that we have clearly in our minds the essential character of this three-fold cycle.

The Cyclic Processes

Education should consist in a continual repetition of such cycles. Each lesson in its minor way should form an eddy cycle issuing in its own subordinate process. Longer periods should issue in definite attainments, which then form the starting-grounds for fresh cycles. We should banish the idea of a mythical, far-off end of education. The pupils must be continually enjoying some fruition and starting afresh—if the teacher is stimulating in exact proportion to his success in satisfying the rhythmic cravings of his pupils.

An infant's first romance is its awakening to the apprehension of objects and to the appreciation of their connexions. Its growth in mentality takes the exterior form of occupying itself in the co-ordination of its perceptions with its bodily activities. Its first stage of precision is mastering spoken language as an instrument for classifying its contemplation of objects and for strengthening its apprehension of emotional relations with other beings. Its first stage of generalisation is the use of language for a classified and enlarged enjoyment of objects.

This first cycle of intellectual progress from the achievement of perception to the acquirement of language, and from the acquirement of language to classified thought and keener perception, will bear more careful study. It is the only cycle of progress which we can observe in its purely natural state. The later cycles are necessarily tinged by the procedure of the current mode of education. There is a characteristic of it which is often sadly lacking in subsequent education; I mean, that it achieves complete success. At the end of it the child can speak, its ideas are classified, and its perceptions are sharpened. The cycle achieves its object. This is a great deal more than can be said for most systems of education as applied to most pupils. But why should this be so? Certainly, a new-born baby looks a most unpromising subject for intellectual progress when we remember the difficulty of the task before it. I suppose it is because nature, in the form of surrounding circumstances, sets it a task for which the normal development of its brain is exactly fitted. I do not think that there is any particular mystery about the fact of a child learning to speak and in consequence thinking all the better; but it does offer food for reflection.

In the subsequent education we have not sought for cyclic processes which in a finite time run their course and within their own limited sphere achieve a complete success. This completion is one outstanding character in the natural cycle for infants. Later on we start a child on some subject, say Latin, at the age of ten, and hope by a uniform system of formal training to achieve success at the age of twenty. The natural result is failure, both in interest and in acquirement. When I speak of failure, I am comparing our results with the brilliant success of the first natural cycle. I do not think that it is because our tasks are intrinsically too hard, when I remember that the infant's cycle is the hardest of all. It is because our tasks are set in an unnatural way, without rhythm and without the stimulus of intermediate successes and without concentration.

I have not yet spoken of this character of concentration which so conspicuously attaches to the infant's progress. The whole being of the infant is absorbed in the practice of its cycle. It has nothing else to divert its mental development. In this respect there is a striking difference between this natural cycle and the subsequent history of the student's development. It is perfectly obvious that life is very various and that the mind and brain naturally develop so as to adapt themselves to the many-hued world in which their lot is cast. Still, after making allowance for this consideration, we will be wise to preserve some measure of concentration for each of the subsequent cycles. In particular, we should avoid a competition of diverse subjects in the same stage of their cycles. The fault of the older education was unrhythmic concentration on a single undifferentiated subject. Our modern system, with its insistence on a preliminary general education, and with its easy toleration of the analysis of knowledge into distinct subjects, is an equally unrhythmic collection of distracting scraps. I am pleading that we shall endeavour to weave in the learner's mind a harmony of patterns, by co-ordinating the various elements of instruction into subordinate cycles each of intrinsic worth for the immediate apprehension of the pupil. We must garner our crops each in its due season.

The Romance of Adolescence

We will now pass to some concrete applications of the ideas which have been developed in the former part of my address.

The first cycle of infancy is succeeded by the cycle of adolescence, which opens with by far the greatest stage of romance which we ever experience. It is in this stage that the lines of character are graven. How the child emerges from the romantic stage of adolescence is how the subsequent life will be moulded by ideals and coloured by imagination. It rapidly follows on the generalisation of capacity produced by the acquirement of spoken language and of reading. The stage of generalisation belonging to the infantile cycle is comparatively short because the romantic material of infancy is so scanty. The initial knowledge of the world in any developed sense of the word "knowledge" really commences after the achievement of the first cycle, and thus issues in the tremendous age of romance. Ideas, facts, relationships, stories, histories, possibilities, artistry in words, in sounds, in form and in colour, crowd into the child's life, stir his feelings, excite his appreciation, and incite his impulses to kindred activities. It is a saddening thought that on this golden age there falls so often the shadow of the crammer. I am thinking of a period of about four years of the child's life, roughly, in ordinary cases, falling between the age of eight and twelve or thirteen. It is the first great period of the utilisation of the native language, and of developed powers of observation and of manipulation. The infant cannot manipulate, the child can; the infant cannot observe, the child can; the infant cannot retain thoughts by the recollection of words, the child can. The child thus enters upon a new world.

Of course, the stage of precision prolongs itself as recurring in minor cycles which form eddies in the great romance. The perfecting of writing, of spelling, of the elements of arithmetic, and of lists of simple facts, such as the Kings of England, are all elements of precision, very necessary both as training in concentration and as useful acquirements. However, these are essentially fragmentary in character, whereas the great romance is the flood which bears on the child towards the life of the spirit.

The success of the Montessori system is due to its recognition of the dominance of romance at this period of growth. If this be the explanation, it also points to the limitations in the usefulness of that method. It is the system which in some measure is essential for every romantic stage. Its essence is browsing and the encouragement of vivid freshness. But it lacks the restraint which is necessary for the great stages of precision.

The Mastery of Language

As he nears the end of the great romance the cyclic course of growth is swinging the child over towards an aptitude for exact knowledge. Language is now the natural subject-matter for concentrated attack. It is the mode of expression with which he is thoroughly familiar. He is acquainted with stories, histories, and poems illustrating the lives of other people and of other civilisations. Accordingly, from the age of eleven onwards there is wanted a gradually increasing concentration towards precise knowledge of language. Finally, the three years from twelve to fifteen should be dominated by a mass attack upon language, so planned that a definite result, in itself worth having, is thereby achieved. I should guess that within these limits of time, and given adequate concentration, we might ask that at the end of that period the children should have command of English, should be able to read fluently fairly simple French, and should have completed the elementary stage of Latin; I mean, a precise knowledge of the more straightforward parts of Latin grammar, the knowledge of the construction of Latin sentences, and the reading of some parts of appropriate Latin authors, perhaps simplified and largely supplemented by the aid of the best literary translations so that their reading of the original, plus translation, gives them a grip of the book as a literary whole. I conceive that such a measure of attainment in these three languages is well within the reach of the ordinary child, provided that he has not been distracted by the effort at precision in a multiplicity of other subjects. Also some more gifted children could go further. The Latin would come to them easily, so that it would be possible to start Greek before the end of the period, always provided that their bent is literary and that they mean later to pursue that study at least for some years. Other subjects will occupy a subordinate place in the time-table and will be undertaken in a different spirit. In the first place, it must be remembered that the semi-literary subjects, such as history, will largely have been provided in the study of the languages. It will be hardly possible to read some English, French, and Latin literature without imparting some knowledge of European history. I do not mean that all special history teaching should be abandoned. I do, however, suggest that the subject should be exhibited in what I have termed the romantic spirit, and that the pupils should not be subjected to the test of precise recollection of details on any large systematic scale.

At this period of growth science should be in its stage of romance. The pupils should see for themselves, and experiment for themselves, with only fragmentary precision of thought. The essence of the importance of science, both for interest in theory or for technological purposes, lies in its application to concrete detail, and every such application evokes a novel problem for research. Accordingly, all training in science should begin as well as end in research, and in getting hold of the subject-matter as it occurs in nature. The exact form of guidance suitable to this age and the exact limitations of experiment are matters depending on experience. But I plead that this period is the true age for the romance of science.

Concentration on Science

Towards the age of fifteen the age of precision in language and of romance in science draws to its close, to be succeeded by a period of generalisation in language and of precision in science. This should be a short period, but one of vital importance. I am thinking of about one year's work, and I suggest that it would be well decisively to alter the balance of the preceding curriculum. There should be a concentration on science and a decided diminution of the linguistic work. A year's work on science, coming on the top of the previous romantic study, should make everyone understand the main principles which govern the development of mechanics, physics, chemistry, algebra and geometry. Understand that they are not beginning these subjects, but they are putting together a previous discursive study by an exact formulation of their main ideas. For example, take algebra and geometry, which I single out as being subjects with which I have some slight familiarity. In the previous three years there has been work on the applications of the simplest algebraic formulæ and geometrical propositions to problems of surveying, or of some other scientific work involving calculations. In this way arithmetic has been carefully strengthened by the insistence on definite numerical results, and familiarity with the ideas of literal formulæ and of geometrical properties has been gained; also some minor methods of manipulation have been inculcated. There is thus no long time to be wasted in getting used to the ideas of the sciences. The pupils are ready for the small body of algebraic and geometrical truths which they ought to know thoroughly. Furthermore, in the previous period some boys will have shown an aptitude for mathematics and will have pushed on a little more, besides in the final year somewhat emphasising their mathematics at the expense of some of the other subjects. I am simply taking mathematics as an illustration.

Meanwhile, the cycle of language is in its stage of generalisation. In this stage the precise study of grammar and composition is discontinued, and the language study is confined to reading the literature with emphasised attention to its ideas and to the general history in which it is embedded; also the time allotted to history will pass into the precise study of a short definite period, chosen to illustrate exactly what does happen at an important epoch and also to show how to pass the simpler types of judgments on men and policies.

I have now sketched in outline the course of education from babyhood to about sixteen and a half, arranged with some attention to the rhythmic pulses of life. In some such way a general education is possible in which the pupil throughout has the advantage of concentration and of freshness. Thus precision will always illustrate subject-matter already apprehended and crying out for drastic treatment. Every pupil will have concentrated in turn on a variety of different subjects, and will know where his strong points lie. Finally—and this of all the objects to be attained is the most dear to my heart—the science students will have obtained both an invaluable literary education and also at the most impressionable age an early initiation into habits of thinking for themselves in the region of science.

After the age of sixteen new problems arise. For literary students science passes into the stage of generalisation, largely in the form of lectures on its main results and general ideas. New cycles of linguistic, literary, and historical study commence. But further detail is now unnecessary. For the scientists the preceding stage of precision maintains itself to the close of the school period with an increasing apprehension of wider general ideas.

However, at this period of education the problem is too individual, or at least breaks up into too many cases, to be susceptible of broad general treatment. I do suggest, nevertheless, that all scientists should now keep up their French, and initiate the study of German if they have not already acquired it.

University Education

I should now like, if you will bear with me, to make some remarks respecting the import of these ideas for a University education.

The whole period of growth from infancy to manhood forms one grand cycle. Its stage of romance stretches across the first dozen years of its life, its stage of precision comprises the whole school period of secondary education, and its stage of generalisation is the period of entrance into manhood. For those whose formal education is prolonged beyond the school age, the University course or its equivalent is the great period of generalisation. The spirit of generalisation should dominate a University. The lectures should be addressed to those to whom details and procedure are familiar; that is to say, familiar at least in the sense of being so congruous to pre-existing training as to be easily acquirable. During the school period the student has been mentally bending over his desk; at the University he should stand up and look around. For this reason it is fatal if the first year at the university be frittered away in going over the old work in the old spirit. At school the boy painfully rises from the particular towards glimpses at general ideas; at the University he should start from general ideas and study their applications to concrete cases. A well-planned University course is a study of the wide sweep of generality. I do not mean that it should be abstract in the sense of divorce from concrete fact, but that concrete fact should be studied as illustrating the scope of general ideas.

Cultivation of Mental Power

This is the aspect of University training in which theoretical interest and practical utility coincide. Whatever be the detail with which you cram your student, the chance of his meeting in after-life exactly that detail is almost infinitesimal; and if he does meet it, he will probably have forgotten what you taught him about it. The really useful training yields a comprehension of a few general principles with a thorough grounding in the way they apply to a variety of concrete details. In subsequent practice the men will have forgotten your particular details; but they will remember by an unconscious common sense how to apply principles to immediate circumstances. Your learning is useless to you till you have lost your text-books, burnt your lecture notes, and forgotten the minutiæ which you learnt by heart for the examination. What, in the way of detail, you continually require will stick in your memory as obvious facts like the sun and moon; and what you casually require can be looked up in any work of reference. The function of a University is to enable you to shed details in favour of principles. When I speak of principles I am hardly even thinking of verbal formulations. A principle which has thoroughly soaked into you is rather a mental habit than a formal statement. It becomes the way the mind reacts to the appropriate stimulus in the form of illustrative circumstances. Nobody goes about with his knowledge clearly and consciously before him. Mental cultivation is nothing else than the satisfactory way in which the mind will function when it is poked up into activity. Learning is often spoken of as if we are watching the open pages of all the books which we have ever read, and then, when occasion arises, we select the right page to read aloud to the universe.

Luckily, the truth is far otherwise from this crude idea; and for this reason the antagonism between the claims of pure knowledge and professional acquirement should be much less acute than a faulty view of education would lead us to anticipate. I can put my point otherwise by saying that the ideal of a University is not so much knowledge, as power. Its business is to convert the knowledge of a boy into the power of a man.

The Rhythmic Character of Growth

I will conclude with two remarks which I wish to make by way of caution in the interpretation of my meaning. The point of this address is the rhythmic character of growth. The interior spiritual life of man is a web of many strands. They do not all grow together by uniform extension. I have tried to illustrate this truth by considering the normal unfolding of the capacities of a child in somewhat favourable circumstances but otherwise with fair average capacities. Perhaps I have misconstrued the usual phenomena. It is very likely that I have so failed, for the evidence is complex and difficult. But do not let any failure in this respect prejudice the main point which I am here to enforce. It is that the development of mentality exhibits itself as a rhythm involving an interweaving of cycles, the whole process being dominated by a greater cycle of the same general character as its minor eddies. Furthermore, this rhythm exhibits certain ascertainable general laws which are valid·for most pupils, and the quality of our teaching should be so adapted as to suit the stage in the rhythm to which our pupils have advanced. The problem of a curriculum is not so much the succession of subjects; for all subjects should in essence be begun with the dawn of mentality. The truly important order is the order of quality which the educational procedure should assume.

My second caution is to ask you not to exaggerate into sharpness the distinction between the three stages of a cycle. I strongly suspect that many of you, when you heard me detail the three stages in each cycle, said to yourselves—

How like a mathematician to make such formal divisions! I assure you that it is not mathematics but literary incompetence that may have led me into the error against which I am warning you. Of course, I mean throughout a distinction of emphasis, of pervasive quality—romance, precision, generalisation, are all present throughout. But there is an alternation of dominance, and it is this alternation which constitutes the cycles.

——Address to the Training College Association of London, 1922.

4. Technical Education and Its Relation to Science and Literature

THE subject of this address is Technical Education. I wish to examine its essential nature and also its relation to a liberal education. Such an inquiry may help us to realise the conditions for the successful working of a national system of technical training. It is also a very burning question among mathematical teachers; for mathematics is included in most technological courses.

Now it is unpractical to plunge into such a discussion without framing in our own minds the best ideal towards which we desire to work, however modestly we may frame our hopes as to the result which in the near future is likely to be achieved.

People are shy of ideals; and accordingly we find a formulation of the ideal state of mankind placed by a modern dramatist [1] in the mouth of a mad priest: "In my dreams it is a country where the State is the Church and the Church the people: three in one and one in three. It is a commonwealth in which work is play and play is life: three in one and one in three. It is a temple in which the priest is the worshipper and the worshipper the worshipped: three in one and one in three. It is a god-head in which all life is human and all humanity divine: three in one and one in three. It is, in short, the dream of a madman."

Now the part of this speech to which I would direct attention is embodied in the phrase, "It is a commonwealth in which work is play and play is life." This is the ideal of technical education. It sounds very mystical when we confront it with the actual facts, the toiling millions, tired, discontented, mentally indifferent, and then the employers—— I am not undertaking a social analysis, but I shall carry you with me when I admit that the present facts of society are a long way off this ideal. Furthermore, we are agreed that an employer who conducted his workshop on the principle that "work should be play" would be ruined in a week.

The curse that has been laid on humanity, in fable and in fact, is, that by the sweat of its brow shall it live. But reason and moral intuition have seen in this curse the foundation for advance. The early Benedictine monks rejoiced in their labours because they conceived themselves as thereby made fellow-workers with Christ.

Stripped of its theological trappings, the essential idea remains, that work should be transfused with intellectual

1 Cf. BERNARD SHAW: *John Bull's Other Island.*

275

and moral vision and thereby turned into a joy, triumphing over its weariness and its pain. Each of us will restate this abstract formulation in a more concrete shape in accordance with his private outlook. State it how you like, so long as you do not lose the main point in your details. However you phrase it, it remains the sole real hope of toiling humanity; and it is in the hands of technical teachers, and of those who control their spheres of activity, so to mould the nation that daily it may pass to its labours in the spirit of the monks of old.

The immediate need of the nation is a large supply of skilled workmen, of men with inventive genius, and of employers alert in the development of new ideas.

There is one—and only one—way to obtain these admirable results. It is by producing workmen, men of science, and employers who enjoy their work. View the matter practically in the light of our knowledge of average human nature. Is it likely that a tired, bored workman, however skilful his hands, will produce a large output of first-class work? He will limit his production, will scamp his work, and be an adept at evading inspection; he will be slow in adapting himself to new methods; he will be a focus of discontent, full of unpractical revolutionary ideas, controlled by no sympathetic apprehension of the real working of trade conditions. If, in the troubled times which may be before us, you wish appreciably to increase the chance of some savage upheaval, introduce widespread technical education and ignore the Benedictine ideal. Society will then get what it deserves.

Again, inventive genius requires pleasurable mental activity as a condition for its vigorous exercise. "Necessity is the mother of invention" is a silly proverb. "Necessity is the mother of futile dodges" is much nearer to the truth. The basis of the growth of modern invention is science, and science is almost wholly the outgrowth of pleasurable intellectual curiosity.

The third class are the employers, who are to be enterprising. Now it is to be observed that it is the successful employers who are the important people to get at, the men with business connections all over the world, men who are already rich. No doubt there will always be a continuous process of rise and fall of businesses. But it is futile to expect flourishing trade, if in the mass the successful houses of business are suffering from atrophy. Now if these men conceive their businesses as merely indifferent means for acquiring other disconnected opportunities of life, they have no spur to alertness. They are already doing very well, the mere momentum of their present business engagements will carry them on for their time. They are not at all likely to bother themselves with the doubtful chances of new methods. Their real soul is in the other side of their life. Desire for money will produce hard-fistedness and not enterprise. There is much more hope for humanity from manufacturers who enjoy their work than from those who continue in irksome business with the object of founding hospitals.

Finally, there can be no prospect of industrial peace so long as masters and men in the mass conceive themselves as engaged in a soulless operation of extracting money from the public. Enlarged views of the work performed, and of the communal service thereby rendered, can be the only basis on which to found sympathetic co-operation.

The conclusion to be drawn from this discussion is, that alike for masters and for men a technical or technological education, which is to have any chance of satisfying the practical needs of the nation, must be conceived in a liberal spirit as a real intellectual enlightenment in regard to principles applied and services rendered. In such an education geometry and poetry are as essential as turning laths.

The mythical figure of Plato may stand for modern liberal education as does that of St. Benedict for technical education. We need not entangle ourselves in the qualifications necessary for a balanced representation of the actual thoughts of the actual men. They are used here as symbolic figures typical of antithetical notions. We consider Plato in the light of the type of culture he now inspires.

In its essence a liberal education is an education for thought and for æsthetic appreciation. It proceeds by imparting a knowledge of the masterpieces of thought, of imaginative literature, and of art. The action which it contemplates is command. It is an aristocratic education implying leisure. This Platonic ideal has rendered imperishable services to European civilisation. It has encouraged art, it has fostered that spirit of disinterested curiosity which is the origin of science, it has maintained the dignity of mind in the face of material force, a dignity which claims freedom of thought. Plato did not, like St. Benedict, bother himself to be a fellow-worker with his slaves; but he must rank among the emancipators of mankind. His type of culture is the peculiar inspiration of the liberal aristocrat, the class from which Europe derives what ordered liberty it now possesses. For centuries, from Pope Nicholas V to the school of the Jesuits, and from the Jesuits to the modern headmasters of English public schools, this educational ideal has had the strenuous support of the clergy.

For certain people it is a very good education. It suits their type of mind and the circumstances amid which their life is passed. But more has been claimed for it than this. All education has been judged adequate or defective according to its approximation to this sole type.

The essence of the type is a large discursive knowledge of the best literature. The ideal product of the type is the man who is acquainted with the best that has been written. He will have acquired the chief languages, he will have considered the histories of the rise and fall of nations, the poetic expression of human feeling, and have read the great dramas and novels. He will also be well grounded in the chief philosophies, and have attentively read those philosophic authors who are distinguished for lucidity of style.

It is obvious that, except at the close of a long life, he will not have much time for anything else if any approximation is to be made to the fulfilment of this programme. One is reminded of the calculation in a dialogue of Lucian that, before a man could be justified in practising any one of the current ethical systems, he should have spent a hundred and fifty years in examining their credentials.

Such ideals are not for human beings. What is meant by a liberal culture is nothing so ambitious as a full acquaintance with the varied literary expression of civilised mankind from Asia to Europe, and from Europe to America. A small selection only is required; but then, as we are told, it is a selection of the very best. I have my doubts of a selection which includes Xenophon and omits Confucius, but then I have read through neither in the original. The ambitious programme of a liberal education really shrinks to a study of some fragments of literature included in a couple of important languages.

But the expression of the human spirit is not confined to literature. There are the other arts, and there are the sciences. Also education must pass beyond the passive reception of the ideas of others. Powers of initiative must be strengthened. Unfortunately initiative does not mean just one acquirement—there is initiative in thought, initiative in action, and the imaginative initiative of art; and these three categories require many subdivisions.

The field of acquirement is large, and the individual so fleeting and so fragmentary: classical scholars, scientists, headmasters are alike ignoramuses.

There is a curious illusion that a more complete culture was possible when there was less to know. Surely the only gain was, that it was more possible to remain unconscious of ignorance. It cannot have been a gain to Plato to have read neither Shakespeare, nor Newton, nor Darwin. The achievements of a liberal education have in recent times not been worsened. The change is that its pretensions have been found out.

My point is, that no course of study can claim any position of ideal completeness. Nor are the omitted factors of subordinate importance. The insistence in the Platonic culture on disinterested intellectual appreciation is a psychological error. Action and our implication in the transition of events amid the inevitable bond of cause to effect are fundamental. An education which strives to divorce intellectual or æsthetic life from these fundamental facts carries with it the decadence of civilisation. Essentially culture should be for action, and its effect should be to divest labour from the association of aimless toil. Art exists that we may know the deliverances of our senses as good. It heightens the sense-world.

Disinterested scientific curiosity is a passion for an ordered intellectual vision of the connection of events. But the goal of such curiosity is the marriage of action to thought. This essential intervention of action even in abstract science is often overlooked. No man of science wants merely to know. He acquires knowledge to appease his passion for discovery. He does not discover in order to know, he knows in order to discover. The pleasure which art and science can give to toil is the enjoyment which arises from successfully directed intention. Also it is the same pleasure which is yielded to the scientist and to the artist.

The antithesis between a technical and a liberal education is fallacious. There can be no adequate technical education which is not liberal, and no liberal education which is not technical: that is, no education which does not impart both technique and intellectual vision. In simpler language, education should turn out the pupil with something he knows well and something he can do well. This intimate union of practice and theory aids both. The intellect does not work best in a vacuum. The stimulation of creative impulse requires, especially in the case of a child, the quick transition to practice. Geometry and mechanics, followed by workshop practice, gain that reality without which mathematics is verbiage.

There are three main methods which are required in a national system of education, namely, the literary curriculum, the scientific curriculum, the technical curriculum. But each of these curricula should include the other two. What I mean is, that every form of education should give the pupil a technique, a science, an assortment of general ideas, and æsthetic appreciation, and that each of these sides of his training should be illuminated by the others. Lack of time, even for the most favoured pupil, makes it impossible to develop fully each curriculum. Always there must be a dominant emphasis. The most direct æsthetic training naturally falls in the technical curriculum in those cases when the training is that requisite for some art or artistic craft. But it is of high importance in both a literary and a scientific education.

The educational method of the literary curriculum is the study of language, that is, the study of our most habitual method of conveying to others our states of mind. The technique which should be acquired is the technique of verbal expression, the science is the study of the structure of language and the analysis of the relations of language to the states of mind conveyed. Furthermore, the subtle relations of language to feeling, and the high development of the sense organs to which written and spoken words appeal, lead to keen æsthetic appreciations being aroused by the successful employment of language.

Finally, the wisdom of the world is preserved in the masterpieces of linguistic composition.

This curriculum has the merit of homogeneity. All its various parts are co-ordinated and play into each other's hands. We can hardly be surprised that such a curriculum, when once broadly established, should have claimed the position of the sole perfect type of education. Its defect is unduly to emphasise the importance of language. Indeed the varied importance of verbal expression is so overwhelming that its sober estimation is difficult. Recent generations have been witnessing the retreat of literature, and of literary forms of expression, from their position of unique importance in intellectual life. In order truly to become a servant and a minister of nature something more is required than literary aptitudes.

A scientific education is primarily a training in the art of observing natural phenomena, and in the knowledge and deduction of laws concerning the sequence of such phenomena. But here, as in the case of a liberal education, we are met by the limitations imposed by shortness of time. There are many types of natural phenomena, and to each type there corresponds a science with its peculiar modes of observation, and its peculiar types of thought employed in the deduction of laws. A study of science in general is impossible in education, all that can be achieved is the study of two or three allied sciences. Hence the charge of narrow specialism urged against any education which is primarily scientific. It is obvious that the charge is apt to be well-founded; and it is worth considering how, within the limits of a scientific education and to the advantage of such an education, the danger can be avoided.

Such a discussion requires the consideration of technical education. A technical education is in the main a training in the art of utilising knowledge for the manufacture of material products. Such a training emphasises manual skill, and the co-ordinated action of hand and eye, and judgment in the control of the process of construction. But judgment necessitates knowledge of those natural processes of which the manufacture is the utilisation. Thus somewhere in technical training an education in scientific knowledge is required. If you minimize the scientific side, you will confine it to the scientific experts;

if you maximise it, you will impart it in some measure to the men, and—what is of no less importance—to the directors and managers of the businesses.

Technical education is not necessarily allied exclusively to science on its mental side. It may be an education for an artist or for apprentices to an artistic craft. In that case æsthetic appreciation will have to be cultivated in connection with it.

An evil side of the Platonic culture has been its total neglect of technical education as an ingredient in the complete development of ideal human beings. This neglect has arisen from two disastrous antitheses, namely, that between mind and body, and that between thought and action. I will here interject, solely to avoid criticism, that I am well aware that the Greeks highly valued physical beauty and physical activity. They had, however, that perverted sense of values which is the nemesis of slave-owning.

I lay it down as an educational axiom that in teaching you will come to grief as soon as you forget that your pupils have bodies. This is exactly the mistake of the post-renaissance Platonic curriculum. But nature can be kept at bay by no pitchfork; so in English education, being expelled from the classroom, she returned with a cap and bells in the form of all-conquering athleticism.

The connections between intellectual activity and the body, though diffused in every bodily feeling, are focused in the eyes, the ears, the voice, and the hands. There is a co-ordination of senses and thought, and also a reciprocal influence between brain activity and material creative activity. In this reaction the hands are peculiarly important. It is a moot point whether the human hand created the human brain, or the brain created the hand. Certainly the connection is intimate and reciprocal. Such deep-seated relations are not widely atrophied by a few hundred years of disuse in exceptional families.

The disuse of hand-craft is a contributory cause to the brain-lethargy of aristocracies, which is only mitigated by sport where the concurrent brain-activity is reduced to a minimum and the hand-craft lacks subtlety. The necessity for constant writing and vocal exposition is some slight stimulus to the thought-power of the professional classes. Great readers, who exclude other activities, are not distinguished by subtlety of brain. They tend to be timid conventional thinkers. No doubt this is partly due to their excessive knowledge outrunning their powers of thought; but it is partly due to the lack of brain-stimulus from the productive activities of hand or voice.

In estimating the importance of technical education we must rise above the exclusive association of learning with book-learning. First-hand knowledge is the ultimate basis of intellectual life. To a large extent book-learning conveys second-hand information, and as such can never rise to the importance of immediate practice. Our goal is to see the immediate events of our lives as instances of our general ideas. What the learned world tends to offer is one second-hand scrap of information illustrating ideas derived from another second-hand scrap of information. The second-handedness of the learned world is the secret of its mediocrity. It is tame because it has never been scared by facts. The main importance of Francis Bacon's influence does not lie in any peculiar theory of inductive reasoning which he happened to express, but in the revolt against second-hand information of which he was a leader.

The peculiar merit of a scientific education should be, that it bases thought upon first-hand observation; and the corresponding merit of a technical education is, that it follows our deep natural instinct to translate thought into manual skill, and manual activity into thought.

The thought which science evokes is logical thought. Now logic is of two kinds: the logic of discovery and the logic of the discovered.

The logic of discovery consists in the weighing of probabilities, in discarding details deemed to be irrelevant, in divining the general rules according to which events occur, and in testing hypotheses by devising suitable experiments. This is inductive logic.

The logic of the discovered is the deduction of the special events which, under certain circumstances, would happen in obedience to the assumed laws of nature. Thus when the laws are discovered or assumed, their utilisation entirely depends on deductive logic. Without deductive logic science would be entirely useless. It is merely a barren game to ascend from the particular to the general, unless afterwards we can reverse the process and descend from the general to the particular, ascending and descending like the angels on Jacob's ladder. When Newton had divined the law of gravitation he at once proceeded to calculate the earth's attractions on an apple at its surface and on the moon. We may note in passing that inductive logic would be impossible without deductive logic. Thus Newton's calculations were an essential step in his inductive verification of the great law.

Now mathematics is nothing else than the more complicated parts of the art of deductive reasoning, especially where it concerns number, quantity, and space.

In the teaching of science, the art of thought should be taught: namely, the art of forming clear conceptions applying to first-hand experience, the art of divining the general truths which apply, the art of testing divinations, and the art of utilising general truths by reasoning to more particular cases of some peculiar importance. Furthermore, a power of scientific exposition is necessary, so that the relevant issues from a confused mass of ideas can be stated clearly, with due emphasis on important points.

By the time a science, or a small group of sciences, has been taught thus amply, with due regard to the general art of thought, we have gone a long way towards correcting the specialism of science. The worst of a scientific education based, as necessarily must be the case, on one or two particular branches of science, is that the teachers under the influence of the examination system are apt merely to stuff their pupils with the narrow results of these special sciences. It is essential that the generality of the method be continually brought to light and contrasted with the speciality of the particular application. A man who only knows his own science, as a routine peculiar to that science, does not even know that. He has no fertility of thought, no power of quickly seizing the bearing of alien ideas. He will discover nothing, and be stupid in practical applications.

This exhibition of the general in the particular is extremely difficult to effect, especially in the case of younger pupils. The art of education is never easy. To surmount its difficulties, especially those of elementary education, is a task worthy of the highest genius. It is the training of human souls.

Mathematics, well taught, should be the most powerful instrument in gradually implanting this generality of idea. The essence of mathematics is perpetually to be discarding more special ideas in favour of more general ideas, and special methods in favour of general methods. We express the conditions of a special problem in the form of an equation, but that equation will serve for a hundred other problems, scattered through diverse sciences. The general reasoning is always the powerful reasoning, because deductive cogency is the property of abstract form.

Here, again, we must be careful. We shall ruin mathematical education if we use it merely to impress general truths. The general ideas are the means of connecting particular results. After all, it is the concrete special cases which are important. Thus in the handling of mathematics in your results you cannot be too concrete, and in your methods you cannot be too general. The essential course of reasoning is to generalise what is particular, and then to particularise what is general. Without generality there is no reasoning, without concreteness there is no importance.

Concreteness is the strength of technical education. I would remind you that truths which lack the highest generality are not necessarily concrete facts. For example, $x + y = y + x$ is an algebraic truth more general than $2 + 2 = 4$. But "two and two make four" is itself a highly general proposition lacking any element of concreteness. To obtain a concrete proposition immediate intuition of a truth concerning particular objects is requisite; for example, "these two apples and those apples together make four apples" is a concrete proposition, if you have direct perception or immediate memory of the apples.

In order to obtain the full realisation of truths as applying, and not as empty formulæ, there is no alternative to technical education. Mere passive observation is not sufficient. In creation only is there vivid insight into the properties of the object thereby produced. If you want to understand anything, make it yourself, is a sound rule. Your faculties will be alive, your thoughts gain vividness by an immediate translation into acts. Your ideas gain that reality which comes from seeing the limits of their application.

In elementary education this doctrine has long been put into practice. Young children are taught to familiarise themselves with shapes and colours by simple manual operations of cutting out and of sorting. But good though this is, it is not quite what I mean. That is practical experience before you think, experience antecedent to thought in order to create ideas, a very excellent discipline. But technical education should be much more than that: it is creative experience while you think, experience which realises your thought, experience which teaches you to co-ordinate act and thought, experience leading you to associate thought with foresight and foresight with achievement. Technical education gives theory, and a shrewd insight as to where theory fails.

A technical education is not to be conceived as a maimed alternative to the perfect Platonic culture: namely, as a defective training unfortunately made necessary by cramped conditions of life. No human being can attain to anything but fragmentary knowledge and a fragmentary training of his capacities. There are, however, three main roads along which we can proceed with good hope of advancing towards the best balance of intellect and character: these are the way of literary culture, the way of scientific culture, the way of technical culture. No one of these methods can be exclusively followed without grave loss of intellectual activity and of character. But a mere mechanical mixture of the three curricula will produce bad results in the shape of scraps of information never interconnected or utilised. We have already noted as one of the strong points of the traditional literary culture that all its parts are co-ordinated. The problem of education is to retain the dominant emphasis, whether literary, scientific, or technical, and without loss of co-ordination to infuse into each way of education something of the other two.

To make definite the problem of technical education fix attention on two ages: one thirteen, when elementary education ends; and the other seventeen, when technical education ends so far as it is compressed within a school curriculum. I am aware that for artisans in junior technical schools a three-years' course would be more usual. On the other hand, for naval officers, and for directing classes generally, a longer time can be afforded. We want to consider the principles to govern a curriculum which shall land these children at the age of seventeen in the position of having technical skill useful to the community.

Their technical manual training should start at thirteen, bearing a modest proportion to the rest of their work, and should increase in each year finally to attain to a substantial proportion. Above all things it should not be too specialised. Workshop finish and workshop dodges, adapted to one particular job, should be taught in the commercial workshop, and should form no essential part of the school course. A properly trained worker would pick them up in no time. In all education the main cause of failure is staleness. Technical education is doomed if we conceive it as a system for catching children young and for giving them one highly specialised manual aptitude. The nation has need of a fluidity of labour, not merely from place to place, but also within reasonable limits of allied aptitudes, from one special type of work to another special type. I know that here I am on delicate ground, and I am not claiming that men while they are specialising on one sort of work should spasmodically be set to other kinds. That is a question of trade organisation with which educationalists have no concern. I am only asserting the principles that training should be broader than the ultimate specialisation, and that the resulting power of adaptation to varying demands is advantageous to the workers, to the employers, and to the nation.

In considering the intellectual side of the curriculum we must be guided by the principle of the co-ordination of studies. In general, the intellectual studies most immediately related to manual training will be some branches of science. More than one branch will, in fact, be concerned; and even if that be not the case, it is impossible to narrow down scientific study to a single thin line of thought. It is possible, however, provided that we do not press the classification too far, roughly to classify technical pursuits according to the dominant science involved. We thus find a sixfold division, namely, (1) Geometrical techniques, (2) Mechanical techniques, (3) Physical techniques, (4) Chemical techniques, (5) Biological techniques, (6) Techniques of commerce and of social service.

By this division, it is meant that apart from auxiliary sciences some particular science requires emphasis in the training for most occupations. We can, for example, reckon carpentry, ironmongery, and many artistic crafts among geometrical techniques. Similarly agriculture is a biological technique. Probably cookery, if it includes food catering, would fall midway between biological, physical, and chemical sciences, though of this I am not sure.

The sciences associated with commerce and social service would be partly algebra, including arithmetic and statistics, and partly geography and history. But this section is somewhat heterogeneous in its scientific affinities. Anyhow the exact way in which technical pursuits are classified in relation to science is a detail. The essential point is, that with some thought it is possible to find scientific courses which illuminate most occupations. Furthermore, the problem is well understood, and has been brilliantly solved in many of the schools of technology and junior technical schools throughout the country.

In passing from science to literature, in our review of the intellectual elements of technical education, we note that many studies hover between the two: for example, history and geography. They are both of them very essential in education, provided that they are the right history and the right geography. Also books giving descriptive accounts of general results, and trains of thought in various sciences fall in the same category. Such books should be partly historical and partly expository of the main ideas which have finally arisen. Their value in education depends on their quality as mental stimulants. They must not be inflated with gas on the wonders of science, and must be informed with a broad outlook.

It is unfortunate that the literary element in education has rarely been considered apart from grammatical study. The historical reason is, that when the modern Platonic curriculum was being formed Latin and Greek were the sole keys which rendered great literature accessible. But there is no necessary connection between literature and grammar. The great age of Greek literature was already past before the arrival of the grammarians of Alexandria. Of all types of men to-day existing, classical scholars are the most remote from the Greeks of the Periclean times.

Mere literary knowledge is of slight importance. The only thing that matters is, how it is known. The facts related are nothing. Literature only exists to express and develop that imaginative world which is our life, the kingdom which is within us. It follows that the literary side of a technical education should consist in an effort to make the pupils enjoy literature. It does not matter what they know, but the enjoyment is vital. The great English Universities, under whose direct authority school-children are examined in plays of Shakespeare, to the certain destruction of their enjoyment, should be prosecuted for soul murder.

Now there are two kinds of intellectual enjoyment: the enjoyment of creation, and the enjoyment of relaxation. They are not necessarily separated. A change of occupation may give the full tide of happiness which comes from the concurrence of both forms of pleasure. The appreciation of literature is really creation. The written word, its music, and its associations, are only the stimuli. The vision which they evoke is our own doing. No one, no genius other than our own, can make our own life live. But except for those engaged in literary occupations, literature is also a relaxation. It gives exercise to that other side which any occupation must suppress during the working hours. Art also has the same function in life as has literature.

To obtain the pleasure of relaxation requires no help. The pleasure is merely to cease doing. Some such pure relaxation is a necessary condition of health. Its dangers are notorious, and to the greater part of the necessary relaxation nature has affixed, not enjoyment, but the oblivion of sleep. Creative enjoyment is the outcome of successful effort and requires help for its initiation. Such enjoyment is necessary for high-speed work and for original achievement.

To speed up production with unrefreshed workmen is a disastrous economic policy. Temporary success will be at the expense of the nation, which, for long years of their lives, will have to support worn-out artisans—unemployables. Equally disastrous is the alternation of spasms of effort with periods of pure relaxation. Such periods are the seed-times of degeneration, unless rigorously curtailed. The normal recreation should be change of activity, satisfying the cravings of instincts. Games afford such activity. Their disconnection emphasises the relaxation, but their excess leaves us empty.

It is here that literature and art should play an essential part in a healthily organised nation. Their services to economic production would be only second to those of sleep or of food. I am not now talking of the training of an artist, but of the use of art as a condition of healthy life. It is analogous to sunshine in the physical world.

When we have once rid our minds of the idea that

knowledge is to be exacted, there is no especial difficulty or expense involved in helping the growth of artistic enjoyment. All school-children could be sent at regular intervals to neighbouring theatres where suitable plays could be subsidised. Similarly for concerts and cinema films. Pictures are more doubtful in their popular attraction; but interesting representations of scenes or ideas which the children have read about would probably appeal. The pupils themselves should be encouraged in artistic efforts. Above all the art of reading aloud should be cultivated. The Roger de Coverley essays of Addison are perfect examples of readable prose.

Art and literature have not merely an indirect effect on the main energies of life. Directly, they give vision. The world spreads wide beyond the deliverances of material sense, with subtleties of reaction and with pulses of emotion. Vision is the necessary antecedent to control and to direction. In the contest of races which in its final issues will be decided in the workshops and not on the battlefield, the victory will belong to those who are masters of stores of trained nervous energy, working under conditions favourable to growth. One such essential condition is Art.

If there had been time, there are other things which I should like to have said: for example, to advocate the inclusion of one foreign language in all education. From direct observation I know this to be possible for artisan children. But enough has been put before you to make plain the principles with which we should undertake national education.

In conclusion, I recur to the thought of the Benedictines, who saved for mankind the vanishing civilisation of the ancient world by linking together knowledge, labour, and moral energy. Our danger is to conceive practical affairs as the kingdom of evil, in which success is only possible by the extrusion of ideal aims. I believe that such a conception is a fallacy directly negatived by practical experience. In education this error takes the form of a mean view of technical training. Our forefathers in the dark ages saved themselves by embodying high ideals in great organisations. It is our task, without servile imitation, boldly to exercise our creative energies.

——Presidential address to the Mathematical Association of England, 1917.

5. The Place of Classics in Education

THE future of classics in this country is not going mainly to be decided by the joy of classics to a finished scholar, and by the utility of scholarly training for scholarly avocations. The pleasure and the discipline of character to be derived from an education based mainly on classical literature and classical philosophy has been demonstrated by centuries of experience. The danger to classical learning does not arise because classical scholars now love classics less than their predecessors. It arises in this way. In the past classics reigned throughout the whole sphere of higher education. There were no rivals; and accordingly all students were steeped in classics throughout their school life, and its domination at the universities was only challenged by the narrow discipline of mathematics. There were many consequences to this state of things. There was a large demand for classical scholars for the mere purposes of tuition; there was a classical tone in all learned walks of life, so that aptitude for classics was a synonym for ability; and finally every boy who gave the slightest promise in that direction cultivated his natural or acquired interest in classical learning. All this is gone, and gone for ever. Humpty Dumpty was a good egg so long as he was on the top of the wall, but you can never set him up again. There are now other disciplines each involving topics of widespread interest, with complex relationships, and exhibiting in their development the noblest feats of genius in its stretch of imagination and its philosophic intuition. Almost every walk of life is now a learned profession, and demands one or more of these disciplines as the substratum for its technical skill. Life is short, and the plastic period when the brain is apt for acquirement is still shorter. Accordingly, even if all children were fitted for it, it is absolutely impossible to maintain a system of education in which a complete training as a classical scholar is the necessary preliminary to the acquirement of other intellectual disciplines. As a member of the Prime Minister's Committee on the Place of Classics in Education it was my misfortune to listen to much ineffectual wailing from witnesses on the mercenary tendencies of modern parents. I do not believe that the modern parent of any class is more mercenary than his predecessors. When classics was the road to advancement, classics was the popular subject for study. Opportunity has now shifted its location, and classics is in danger. Was it not Aristotle who said that a good income was a desirable adjunct to an intellectual life? I wonder how Aristotle, as a parent, would have struck a headmaster of one of our great public schools. From my slight knowledge of Aristotle, I suspect that there would have been an argument, and that Aristotle would have got the best of it. I have been endeavouring to appreciate at its full value the danger which besets classics in the educational curriculum. The conclusion that I draw is that the future classics will be decided during the next few years in the secondary schools of this country. Within a generation the great public schools will have to follow suit, whether they like it or not.

The situation is dominated by the fact that in the future ninety per cent. of the pupils who leave school at the age of eighteen will never again read a classical book in the original. In the case of pupils leaving at an earlier age, the estimate of ninety per cent. may be changed to one of ninety-nine per cent. I have heard and read many a beautiful exposition of the value of classics to the scholar who reads Plato and Virgil in his armchair. But these people will never read classics either in their armchairs or in any other situation. We have got to produce a defence of classics which applies to this ninety per cent. of the pupils. If classics is swept out of the curriculum for this section, the remaining ten per cent. will soon vanish. No school will have the staff to teach them. The problem is urgent.

It would, however, be a great mistake to conclude that classics is faced with a hostile opinion either in the learned professions or from leaders of industry who have devoted attention to the relation between education and efficiency. The last discussion, public or private, on this subject at which I have been present was a short and vigorous one at one of the leading committees of a great modern university. The three representatives of the Faculty of Science energetically urged the importance of classics on the ground of its value as a preliminary discipline for scientists. I mention this incident because in my experience it is typical.

We must remember that the whole problem of intellectual education is controlled by lack of time. If Methuselah was not a well-educated man, it was his own fault or that of his teachers. But our task is to deal with five years of secondary school-life. Classics can only be defended on the ground that within that period, and sharing that period with other subjects, it can produce a necessary enrichment of intellectual character more quickly than any alternative discipline directed to the same object.

In classics we endeavour by a thorough study of language to develop the mind in the regions of logic, philosophy, history and of æsthetic apprehension of literary beauty. The learning of the languages—Latin or Greek—is a subsidiary means for the furtherance of this ulterior object. When the object has been obtained, the languages can be dropped unless opportunity and choice lead to their further pursuit. There are certain minds, and among them some of the best, for which the analysis of language is not the avenue of approach to the goal of culture. For these a butterfly or a steam-engine has a wider range of significance than a Latin sentence. This is especially the case where there is a touch of genius arising from vivid apprehensions stimulating originality of thought. The assigned verbal sentence almost always says the wrong thing for such people, and confuses them by its trivial irrelevance.

But on the whole the normal avenue is the analysis of language. It represents the greatest common measure for the pupils, and by far the most manageable job for the teachers.

At this point I must cross-question myself. My other self asks me, Why do you not teach the children logic, if you want them to learn that subject? Wouldn't that be the obvious procedure? I answer in the words of a great man who to our infinite loss has recently died, Sanderson, the late headmaster of Oundle. His phrase was, They learn by contact. The meaning to be atached to this saying goes to the root of the true practice of education. It must start from the particular fact, concrete and definite for individual apprehension, and must gradually evolve towards the general idea. The devil to be avoided is the cramming of general statements which have no reference to individual personal experiences.

Now apply this principle to the determination of the best method to help a child towards a philosophical analysis of thought. I will put it in more homely style, What is the best way to make a child clear-headed in its thoughts and its statements? The general statements of a logic book have no reference to anything the child has ever heard of. They belong to the grown-up stage of education at—or not far from—the university. You must begin with the analysis of familiar English sentences. But this grammatical procedure, if prolonged beyond its elementary stages, is horribly dry. Furthermore, it has the disadvantage that it only analyses so far as the English language analyses. It does nothing to throw light upon the complex significance of English phrases, and words, and habits of mental procedure. Your next step is to teach the child a foreign language. Here you gain an enormous advantage. You get away from the nauseating formal drill for the drill's sake. The analysis is now automatic, while the pupil's attention is directed to expressing his wants in the language, or to understanding someone who is speaking to him, or to making out what an author has written. Every language embodies a definite type of mentality, and two languages necessarily display to the pupil some contrast between their two types. Common sense dictates that you start with French as early as possible in the child's life. If you are wealthy, you will provide a French nursery-governess. Less fortunate children will start French in a secondary school about the age of twelve. The direct method is probably used, by which the child is immersed in French throughout the lesson and is taught to think in French without the intervention of English between the French words and their significations. Even an average child will get on well, and soon acquires the power of handling and understanding simple French sentences. As I have said before, the gain is enormous; and, in addition, a useful instrument for after life is acquired. The sense for language grows, a sense which is the subconscious appreciation of language as an instrument of definite structure.

It is exactly now that the initiation of Latin is the best stimulus for mental expansion. The elements of Latin exhibit a peculiarly plain concrete case of language as a structure. Provided that your mind has grown to the level of that idea, the fact stares you in the face. You can miss it over English and French. Good English of a simple kind will go straight into slipshod French , and conversely good French will go into slipshod English. The difference between the slipshod French of the literal translation and the good French, which ought to have been written, is often rather subtle for that stage of mental growth, and is not always easy to explain. Both languages have the same common modernity of expression. But in the case of English and Latin the contrast of structure is obvious, and yet not so wide as to form an insuperable difficulty.

According to the testimony of schoolmasters, Latin is rather a popular subject; I know that as a schoolboy I enjoyed it myself. I believe that this popularity is due to the sense of enlightenment that accompanies its study. You know that you are finding out something. The words somehow stick in the sentences in a different way to what they do either in English or French, with odd queer differences of connotation. Of course in a way Latin is a more barbaric language than English. It is one step nearer to the sentence as the unanalysed unit.

This brings me to my next point. In my catalogue of the gifts of Latin I placed philosophy between logic and history. In this connection, that is its true place. The philosophic instinct which Latin evokes, hovers between the two and enriches both. The analysis of thought involved in translation, English to Latin or Latin to English, imposes that type of experience which is the necessary introduction to philosophic logic. If in after life your job is to think, render thanks to Providence which ordained that, for five years of your youth, you did a Latin prose once a week and daily construed some Latin author. The introduction to any subject is the process of learning by contact. To that majority of people for whom the language is the readiest stimulus to thought-activity, the road towards enlightenment of understanding runs from simple English grammar to French, from French to Latin, and also traverses the elements of Geometry and of Algebra. I need not remind my readers that I can claim Plato's authority for the general principle which I am upholding.

From the philosophy of thought we now pass to the philosophy of history. I again recur to Sanderson's great saying, They learn by contact. How on earth is a child to learn history by contact? The original documents, charters and laws and diplomatic correspondence, are double Dutch to it. A game of football is perhaps a faint reflection of the Battle of Marathon. But that is only to say that human life in all ages and circumstances has common qualities. Furthermore, all this diplomatic and political stuff with which we cram children is a very thin view of history. What is really necessary is that we should have an instinctive grasp of the flux of outlook, and of thought, and of æsthetic and racial impulses, which have controlled the troubled history of mankind. Now the Roman Empire is the bottleneck through which the vintage of the past has passed into modern life. So far as European civilisation is concerned the key to history is a comprehension of the mentality of Rome and the work of its Empire.

In the language of Rome, embodying in literary form the outlook of Rome, we possess the simplest material, by contact with which we can gain appreciation of the tides of change in human affairs. The mere obvious relations of the languages, French and English, to Latin are in themselves a philosophy of history. Consider the contrast which English presents to French: the entire break of English with the civilised past of Britain and the slow creeping back of words and phrases of Mediterranean origin with their cargoes of civilised meaning: in French we have continuity of development, amid obvious traces of rude shock. I am not asking for pretentious abstract lectures on such points. The thing illustrates itself. An elementary knowledge of French and Latin with a mother-tongue of English imparts the requisite atmosphere of reality to the story of the racial wanderings which created our Europe. Language is the incarnation of the mentality of the race which fashioned it. Every phrase and word embodies some habitual idea of men and women as they ploughed their fields, tended their homes, and built their cities. For this reason there are no true synonyms as between words and phrases in different languages. The whole of what I have been saying is merely an embroidery upon this single theme, and our endeavour to emphasise its critical importance. In English, French, and Latin we possess a triangle, such that one pair of vertices, English and French, exhibits a pair of diverse expressions of two chief types of modern mentality, and the relations of these vertices to the third exhibit alternative processes of derivation from the Mediterranean civilisation of the past. This is the essential triangle of literary culture, containing within itself freshness of contrast, embracing both the present and the past. It ranges through space and time. These are the grounds by which we justify the assertion, that in the acquirement of French and Latin is to be found the easiest mode of learning by contact the philosophy of logic and the philosophy of history. Apart from some such intimate experience, your analyses of thought and your histories of actions are mere sounding brasses. I am not claiming, and I do not for a moment believe, that this route of education is more than the simplest, easiest route for the majority of pupils. I am certain that there is a large minority for which the emphasis should be different. But I do believe that it is the route which can give the greatest success for the largest majority. It has also the advantage of having survived the test of experience. I believe that large modifications require to be introduced into existing practice to adapt it for present needs. But on the whole this foundation of literary education involves the best understood tradition and the largest corps of experienced scholarly teachers who can realise it in practice.

The reader has perhaps observed that I have as yet said nothing of the glories of Roman literature. Of course the teaching of Latin must proceed by the means of reading Latin literature with the pupils. This literature possesses vigorous authors who have succeeded in putting across the footlights the Roman mentality on a variety of topics, including its appreciation of Greek thought. One of the merits of Roman literature is its comparative lack of outstanding genius. There is very little aloofness about its authors, they express their race and very little which is beyond all differences of race. With the exception of Lucretius, you always feel the limitations under which they are working. Tacitus expressed the views of the Die-hards of the Roman Senate, and, blind to the achievements of Roman provincial administration, could only see that Greek freedmen were replacing Roman aristocrats. The Roman Empire and the mentality which created it absorbed the genius of Romans. Very little of Roman literature will find its way into the kingdom of heaven, when the events of this world will have lost their importance. The languages of heaven will be Chinese, Greek, French, German, Italian, and English, and the blessed Saints will dwell with delight on these golden expressions of eternal life. They will be wearied with the moral fervour of Hebrew literature in its battle with a vanished evil, and with Roman authors who have mistaken the Forum for the footstool of the living God.

We do not teach Latin in the hope that Roman authors, read in the original, may be for our pupils companions through life. English literature is so much greater: it is richer, deeper, and more subtle. If your tastes are philosophic, would you abandon Bacon and Hobbes, Locke, Berkeley, Hume, and Mill for the sake of Cicero? Not unless your taste among the moderns would lead you to Martin Tupper. Perhaps you crave for reflection on the infinite variety of human existence and the reaction of character to circumstance. Would you exchange Shakespeare and the English novelists for Terence, Plautus, and the banquet of Trimalchio? Then there are our humorists, Sheridan, Dickens, and others. Did anyone ever laugh like that as he read a Latin author? Cicero was a great orator, staged amid the pomp of Empire. England also can show statesmen inspired to expound policies with imagination. I will not weary you with an extended catalogue embracing poetry and history. I simply wish to justify my scepticism as to the claim for Latin literature that it expresses with outstanding perfection the universal element in human life. It cannot laugh, and it can hardly cry.

You must not tear it from its context. It is not a literature in the sense that Greece and England have produced literatures, expressions of universal human feeling. Latin has one theme and that is Rome—Rome, the mother of Europe, and the great Babylon, the harlot whose doom is described by the writer of the Apocalypse:

"Standing afar off for the fear of her torment, saying, Alas, alas, that great city Babylon, that mighty city! for in one hour is thy judgment come. And the merchants of the earth shall weep and mourn over her; for no man buyeth their merchandise any more:

"The merchandise of gold, and silver, and precious stones, and of pearls, and fine linen, and purple, and silk, and scarlet, and all thyine wood, and all manner vessels of ivory, and all manner vessels of most precious wood, and of brass, and iron, and marble;

"And cinnamon, and odours, and ointments, and frankincense, and wine, and oil, and fine flour, and wheat, and beasts, and sheep, and horses, and chariots, and slaves, and souls of men."

This is the way Roman civilisation appeared to an early Christian. But then Christianity itself is part of the out-crop of the ancient world which Rome passed on to Europe. We inherit the dual aspect of the civilisations of the eastern Mediterranean.

The function of Latin literature is its expression of Rome. When to England and France your imagination can add Rome in the background, you have laid firm the foundations of culture. The understanding of Rome leads back to that Mediterranean civilisation of which Rome was the last phase, and it automatically exhibits the geography of Europe, and the functions of seas and rivers and mountains and plains. The merit of this study in the education of youth is its concreteness, its inspiration to action, and the uniform greatness of persons, in their characters and their staging. Their aims were great, their virtues were great, and their vices were great. They had the saving merit of sinning with cart-ropes. Moral education is impossible apart from the habitual vision of greatness. If we are not great, it does not matter what we do or what is the issue. Now the sense of greatness is an immediate intuition and not the conclusion of an argument. It is permissible for youth in the agonies of religious conversion to entertain the feeling of being a worm and no man, so long as there remains the conviction of greatness sufficient to justify the eternal wrath of God. The sense of greatness is the groundwork of morals. We are at the threshold of a democratic age, and it remains to be determined whether the equality of man is to be realised on a high level or a low level. There was never a time in which it was more essential to hold before the young the vision of Rome: in itself a great drama, and with issues greater than itself. We are now already immersed in the topic of æsthetic appreciation of literary quality. It is here that the tradition of classical teaching requires most vigorous reformation for adaptation to new conditions. It is obsessed with the formation of finished classical scholars. The old tradition was remorselessly to devote the initial stages to the acquirement of the languages and then to trust to the current literary atmosphere to secure enjoyment of the literature. During the latter part of the nineteenth century other subjects encroached on the available time. Too often the result has been merely time wasted in the failure to learn the language. I often think that the ruck of pupils from great English schools show a deplorable lack of intellectual zest, arising from this sense of failure. The school course of classics must be planned so that a definite result is clearly achieved. There has been too great a product of failures on the road to an ambitious ideal of scholarship.

In approaching every work of art we have to comport ourselves suitably in regard to two factors, scale and pace. It is not fair to the architect if you examine St. Peter's at Rome with a microscope, and the Odyssey becomes insipid if you read it at the rate of five lines a day. Now the problem before us is exactly this. We are dealing with pupils who will never know Latin well enough to read it quickly, and the vision to be illumed is of vast scale, set in the history of all time. A careful study of scale and pace, and of the correlative functions of various parts of our work, should appear to be essential. I have not succeeded in hitting upon any literature which deals with this question with reference to the psychology of the pupils. Is it a masonic secret?

I have often noticed that, if in an assembly of great scholars the topic of translations be introduced, they function as to their emotions and sentiments in exactly the same way as do decent people in the presence of a nasty sex-problem. A mathematician has no scholastic respectability to lose, so I will face the question.

It follows from the whole line of thought which I have been developing, that an exact appreciation of the meanings of Latin words, of the ways in which ideas are connected in grammatical constructions, and of the whole hang of a Latin sentence with its distribution of emphasis, forms the very backbone of the merits which I ascribe to the study of Latin. Accordingly any woolly vagueness of teaching, slurring over the niceties of language defeats the whole ideal which I have set before you. The use of a translation to enable the pupils to get away from the Latin as quickly as possible, or to avoid the stretch of mind in grappling with construction, is erroneous. Exactness, definiteness, and independent power of analysis are among the main prizes of the whole study.

But we are still confronted with the inexorable problem of pace, and with the short four or five years of the whole course. Every poem is meant to be read within certain limits of time. The contrasts, and the images, and the transition of moods must correspond with the sway of rhythms in the human spirit. These have their periods, which refuse to be stretched beyond certain limits. You may take the noblest poetry in the world, and, if you stumble through it at snail's pace, it collapses from a work of art into a rubbish heap. Think of the child's mind as he pores over his work: he reads "as when," then follows a pause with a reference to the dictionary, then he goes on—"an eagle," then another reference to the dictionary, followed by a period of wonderment over the construction, and so on, and so on. Is that going to help him to the vision of Rome? Surely, surely, common sense dictates that you procure the best literary translation you can, the one which best preserves the charm and vigour of the original, and that you read it aloud at the right pace, and append such comments as will elucidate the comprehension. The attack on the Latin will then be fortified by the sense that it enshrines a living work of art.

But someone objects that a translation is woefully inferior to the original. Of course it is, that is why the boy has to master the Latin original. When the original has been mastered, it can be given its proper pace. I plead for an initial sense of the unity of the whole, to be given by a translation at the right pace, and for a final appreciation of the full value of the whole to be given by the original at the right pace. Wordsworth talks of men of science who "murder to dissect." In the past, classical scholars have been veritable assassins compared to them. The sense of beauty is eager and vehement, and should be treated with the reverence which is its due. But I go further. The total bulk of Latin literature necessary to convey the vision of Rome is much greater than the students can possibly accomplish in the original. They should read more Virgil than they can read in Latin, more Lucretius than they can read in Latin, more history than they can read in Latin, more Cicero than they can read in Latin. In the study of an author the selected portions in Latin should illumine a fuller disclosure of his whole mind, although without the force of his own words in his own language. It is, however, a grave evil if no part of an author be read in his own original words.

The difficulty of scale is largely concerned in the presentation of classical history. Everything set before the young must be rooted in the particular and the individual. Yet we want to illustrate the general characters of whole periods. We must make students learn by contact. We can exhibit the modes of life by visual representations. There are photographs of buildings, casts of statues, and pictures from vases or frescoes illustrating religious myths or domestic scenes. In this way we can compare Rome with the preceding civilisation of the eastern Mediterranean, and with the succeeding period of the Middle Ages. It is essential to get into the children's minds how men altered, in their appearance, their dwellings, their technology, their art, and their religious beliefs. We must imitate the procedure of the zoologists who have the whole of animal creation on their hands. They teach by demonstrating typical examples. We must do likewise, to exhibit the position of Rome in history.

The life of man is founded on Technology, Science, Art and Religion. All four are inter-connected and issue from his total mentality. But there are particular intimacies between Science and Technology, and between Art and Religion. No social organisation can be understood without reference to these four underlying factors. A modern steam-engine does the work of a thousand slaves in the ancient world. Slave-raiding was the key to much of the ancient imperialism. A modern printing-press is an essential adjunct to a modern democracy. The key to modern mentality is the continued advance of science with the consequential shift of ideas and progress of technology. In the ancient world Mesopotamia and Egypt were made possible by irrigation. But the Roman Empire existed by virtue of the grandest application of technology that the world had hitherto seen: its roads, its bridges, its aqueducts, its tunnels, its sewers, its vast buildings, its organised merchant navies, its military science, its metallurgy, and its agriculture. This was the secret of the extension and the unity of Roman civilisation. I have often wondered why Roman engineers did not invent the steam-engine. They might have done it at any time, and then how different would have been the history of the world. I ascribe it to the fact that they lived in a warm climate and had not introduced tea and coffee. In the eighteenth century thousands of men sat by fires and watched their kettles boil. We all know of course that Hicro of Alexandria invented some slight anticipation. All that was wanted was that the Roman engineers should have been impressed with the motive force of steam by the humble process of watching their kettles.

The history of mankind has yet to be set in its proper relation to the gathering momentum of technological advance. Within the last hundred years, a developed science has wedded itself to a developed technology and a new epoch has opened.

Similarly about a thousand years before Christ the first great literary epoch commenced when the art of writing was finally popularised. In its earlier dim origins the art had been used for traditional hieratic formulæ and for the formal purposes of governmental record and chronicle. It is a great mistake to think that in the past the full sweep of a new invention has ever been anticipated at its first introduction. It is not even so at the present day, when we are all trained to meditate on the possibilities of new ideas. But in the past, with its different direction of thought, novelty slowly ate its way into the social system. Accordingly writing, as a stimulus to the preservation of individual novelty of thought, was but slowly grasped on the borders of the eastern Mediterranean. When the realisation of its possibilities was complete, in the hands of the Greeks and the Hebrews, civilisation took a new turn; though the general influence of Hebrew mentality was delayed for a thousand years till the advent of Christianity. But it was now that their prophets were recording their inward thoughts, when Greek civilisation was beginning to take shape.

What I want to illustrate is that in the large scale treatment of history necessary for the background and the foreground of the vision of Rome, the consecutive chronicle of political events on the scale traditional to our histories absolutely vanishes. Even verbal explanations partly go into the background. We must utilise models, and pictures, and diagrams, and charts to exhibit typical examples of the growth of technology and its impact on the current modes of life. In the same way art, in its curious fusion with utility and with religion, both expresses the actual inward life of imagination and changes it by its very expression. The children can see the art of previous epochs in models and pictures, and sometimes the very objects in museums. The treatment of the history of the past must not start with generalised statements, but with concrete examples exhibiting the slow succession of period to period, and of mode of life to mode of life, and of race to race.

The same concreteness of treatment must apply when we come to the literary civilisations of the eastern Mediterranean. When you come to think of it, the whole claim for the importance of classics rests on the basis that there is no substitute for first-hand knowledge. In so far as Greece and Rome are the founders of European civilisation, a knowledge of history means above all things a first-hand knowledge of the thoughts of Greeks and Romans. Accordingly, to put the vision of Rome into its proper setting, I urge that the pupils should read at first hand some few examples of Greek literature. Of course it must be in translation. But I prefer a translation of what a Greek actually said, to any talk about the Greeks written by an Englishman, however well he has done it. Books about Greece should come after some direct knowledge of Greece.

The sort of reading I mean is a verse translation of the Odyssey, some Herodotus, some choruses of plays translated by Gilbert Murray, some lives of Plutarch, especially the part about Archimedes in the life of Marcellus, and the definitions and axioms and one or two propositions from Euclid's Elements in the exact scholarly translation of Heath. In all this, just enough explanation is wanted to give the mental environment of the authors. The marvellous position of Rome in relation to Europe comes from the fact that it has transmitted to us a double inheritance. It received the Hebrew religious thought, and has passed on to Europe its fusion with Greek civilisation. Rome itself stands for the impress of organization and unity upon diverse fermenting elements. Roman Law embodies the secret of Roman greatness in its Stoic respect for intimate rights of human nature within an iron framework of empire. Europe is always flying apart because of the diverse explosive charaoter of its inheritance, and coming together because it can never shake off that impress of unity it has received from Rome. The history of Europe is the history of Rome curbing the Hebrew and the Greek, with their various impulses of religion, and of science, and of art, and of quest for material comfort, and of lust of domination, which are all at daggers drawn with each other. The vision of Rome is the vision of the unity of civilisation.

——Originally published in *The Hibbert Journal*, 1923.

7. Universities and Their Function

THE expansion of universities is one marked feature of the social life in the present age. All countries have shared in this movement, but more especially America, which thereby occupies a position of honor. It is, however, possible to be overwhelmed even by the gifts of good fortune; and this growth of universities, in number of institutions, in size, and in internal complexity of organisation, discloses some danger of destroying the very sources of their usefulness, in the absence of a widespread understanding of the primary functions which universities should perform in the service of a nation. These remarks, as to the necessity for reconsideration of the function of universities, apply to all the more developed countries. They are only more especially applicable to America, because this country has taken the lead in a development which, under wise guidance, may prove to be one of the most fortunate forward steps which civilisation has yet taken.

This article will only deal with the most general principles, though the special problems of the various departments in any university are, of course, innumerable. But generalities require illustration, and for this purpose I choose the business school of a university. This choice is dictated by the fact that business schools represent one of the newer developments of university activity. They are also more particularly relevant to the dominant social activities of modern nations, and for that reason are good examples of the way in which the national life should be affected by the activities of its universities. Also at Harvard, where I have the honour to hold office, the new foundation of a business school on a scale amounting to magnificence has just reached its completion.

There is a certain novelty in the provision of such a school of training, on this scale of magnitude, in one of the few leading universities of the world. It marks the culmination of a movement which for many years past has introduced analogous departments throughout American universities. This is a new fact in the university world; and it alone would justify some general reflections upon the purpose of a university education, and upon the proved importance of that purpose for the welfare of the social organism.

The novelty of business schools must not be exaggerated. At no time have universities been restricted to pure abstract learning. The University of Salerno in Italy, the earliest of European universities, was devoted to medicine. In England, at Cambridge, in the year 1316, a college was founded for the special purpose of providing "clerks for the King's service." Universities have trained clergy, medical men, lawyers, engineers. Business is now a highly intellectualised vocation, so it well fits into the series. There is, however, this novelty: the curriculum suitable for a business school, and the various modes of activity of such a school, are still in the experimental stage. Hence the peculiar importance of recurrence to general principles in connection with the moulding of these schools. It would, however, be an act of presumption on my part if I were to enter upon any consideration of details, or even upon types of policy affecting the balance of the whole training. Upon such questions I have no special knowledge, and therefore have no word of advice.

II

The universities are schools of education, and schools of research. But the primary reason for their existence is not to be found either in the mere knowledge conveyed to the students or in the mere opportunities for research afforded to the members of the faculty.

Both these functions could be performed at a cheaper rate, apart from these very expensive institutions. Books are cheap, and the system of apprenticeship is well understood, So far as the mere imparting of information is concerned, no university has had any justification for existence since the popularisation of printing in the fifteenth century. Yet the chief impetus to the foundation of universities came after that date, and in more recent times has even increased.

The justification for a university is that it preserves the connection between knowledge and the zest of life, by uniting the young and the old in the imaginative consideration of learning. The university imparts information, but it imparts it imaginatively. At least, this is the function which it should perform for society. A university which fails in this respect has no reason for existence. This atmosphere of excitement, arising from imaginative consideration, transforms knowledge. A fact is no longer a bare fact: it is invested with all its possibilities. It is no longer a burden on the memory: it is energising as the poet of our dreams, and as the architect of our purposes.

Imagination is not to be divorced from the facts: it is a way of illuminating the facts. It works by eliciting the general principles which apply to the facts, as they exist, and then by an intellectual survey of alternative possibili-

307

ties which are consistent with those principles. It enables men to construct an intellectual vision of a new world, and it preserves the zest of life by the suggestion of satisfying purposes.

Youth is imaginative, and if the imagination be strengthened by discipline this energy of imagination can in great measure be preserved through life. The tragedy of the world is that those who are imaginative have but slight experience, and those who are experienced have feeble imaginations. Fools act on imagination without knowledge; pedants act on knowledge without imagination. The task of a university is to weld together imagination and experience.

The initial discipline of imagination in its period of youthful vigor requires that there be no responsibility for immediate action. The habit of unbiased thought, whereby the ideal variety of exemplifications is discerned in its derivation from general principles, cannot be acquired when there is the daily task of preserving a concrete organisation. You must be free to think rightly and wrongly, and free to appreciate the variousness of the universe undisturbed by its perils.

These reflections upon the general functions of a university can be at once translated in terms of the particular functions of a business school. We need not flinch from the assertion that the main function of such a school is to produce men with a greater zest for business. It is a libel upon human nature to conceive that zest for life is the product of pedestrian purposes directed toward the narrow routine of material comforts. Mankind by its pioneering instinct, and in a hundred other ways, proclaims falsehood of that lie.

In the modern complex social organism, the adventure of life cannot be disjoined from intellectual adventure. Amid simpler circumstances, the pioneer can follow the urge of his instinct, directed toward the scene of his vision from the mountain top. But in the complex organisations of modern business the intellectual adventure of analysis, and of imaginative reconstruction, must precede any successful reorganisation. In a simpler world, business relations were simpler, being based on the immediate contact of man with man and on immediate confrontation with all relevant material circumstances. To-day business organisation requires an imaginative grasp of the psychologies of populations engaged in differing modes of occupation; of populations scattered through cities, through mountains, through plains; of populations on the ocean, and of populations in mines, and of populations in forests. It requires an imaginative grasp of conditions in the tropics, and of conditions in temperate zones. It requires an imaginative grasp of the interlocking interests of great organisations, and of the reactions of the whole complex to any change in one of its elements. It requires an imaginative understanding of laws of political economy, not merely in the abstract, but also with the power to construe them in terms of the particular circumstances of a concrete business. It requires some knowledge of the habits of government, and of the variations of those habits under diverse conditions. It requires an imaginative vision of the binding forces of any human organisation, a sympathetic vision of the limits of human nature and of the conditions which evoke loyalty of service. It requires some knowledge of the laws of health, and of the laws of fatigue, and of the conditions for sustained reliability. It requires an imaginative understanding of the social effects of the conditions of factories. It requires a sufficient conception of the rôle of applied science in modern society. It requires that discipline of character which can say "yes" and "no" to other men, not by reason of blind obstinacy, but with firmness derived from a conscious evaluation of relevant alternatives.

The universities have trained the intellectual pioneers of our civilisation—the priests, the lawyers, the statesmen, the doctors, the men of science, and the men of letters. They have been the home of those ideals which lead men to confront the confusion of their present times. The Pilgrim Fathers left England to found a state of society according to the ideals of their religious faith; and one of their earlier acts was the foundation of Harvard University in Cambridge, named after that ancient mother of ideals in England, to which so many of them owed their training. The conduct of business now requires intellectual imagination of the same type as that which in former times has mainly passed into those other occupations; and the universities are the organisations which have supplied this type of mentality for the service of the progress of the European races.

In early mediæval history the origin of universities was obscure and almost unnoticed. They were a gradual and natural growth. But their existence is the reason for the sustained, rapid progressiveness of European life in so many fields of activity. By their agency the adventure of action met the adventure of thought. It would not have been possible antecedently to have divined that such organisations would have been successful. Even now, amid the imperfections of all things human, it is sometimes difficult to understand how they succeed in their work. Of course there is much failure in the work of universities. But, if we take a broad view of history, their success has been remarkable and almost uniform. The cultural histories of Italy, of France, of Germany, of Holland, of Scotland, of England, of the United States, bear witness to the influence of universities. By "cultural history" I am not chiefly thinking of the lives of scholars; I mean the energising of the lives of those men who gave to France, to Germany, and to other countries that impress of types of human achievement which, by their addition to the zest of life, form the foundation of our patriotism. We love to be members of society which can do those things.

There is one great difficulty which hampers all the higher types of human endeavour. In modern times this difficulty has even increased in its possibilities for evil. In any large organisation the younger men, who are novices, must be set to jobs which consist in carrying out fixed duties in obedience to orders. No president of a large corporation meets his youngest employee at his office door with the offer of the most responsible job which the work of that corporation includes. The young men are set to work at a fixed routine, and only occasionally even see the president as he passes in and out of the building. Such work is a great discipline. It imparts knowledge, and it produces reliability of character; also it is the only work for which the young men, in that novice stage, are fit, and it is the work for which they are hired. There can be no criticism of the custom, but there may be an unfortunate effect—prolonged routine work dulls the imagination.

The result is that qualities essential at a later stage of a career are apt to be stamped out in an earlier stage. This is only an instance of the more general fact, that necessary technical excellence can only be acquired by a training which is apt to damage those energies of mind which should direct the technical skill. This is the key fact in education, and the reason for most of its difficulties.

The way in which a university should function in the preparation for an intellectual career, such as modern business or one of the older professions, is by promoting the imaginative consideration of the various general principles underlying that career. Its students thus pass into their period of technical apprenticeship with their imaginations already practised in connecting details with general principles. The routine then receives its meaning, and also illuminates the principles which give it that meaning. Hence, instead of a drudgery issuing in a blind rule of thumb, the properly trained man has some hope of obtaining an imagination disciplined by detailed facts and by necessary habits.

Thus the proper function of a university is the imaginative acquisition of knowledge. Apart from this importance of the imagination, there is no reason why business men, and other professional men, should not pick up their facts bit by bit as they want them for particular occasions. A university is imaginative or it is nothing—at least nothing useful.

III

Imagination is a contagious disease. It cannot be measured by the yard, or weighed by the pound, and then delivered to the students by members of the faculty. It can only be communicated by a faculty whose members themselves wear their learning with imagination. In saying this, I am only repeating one of the oldest of observations. More than two thousand years ago the ancients symbolised learning by a torch passing from hand to hand down the generations. That lighted torch is the imagination of which I speak. The whole art in the organisation of a university is the provision of a faculty whose learning is lighted up with imagination. This is the problem of problems in university education; and unless we are careful the recent vast extension of universities in number of students and in variety of activities—of which we are so justly proud—will fail in producing its proper results, by the mishandling of this problem.

The combination of imagination and learning normally requires some leisure, freedom from restraint, freedom from harassing worry, some variety of experiences, and the stimulation of other minds diverse in opinion and diverse in equipment. Also there is required the excitement of curiosity, and the self-confidence derived from pride in the achievements of the surrounding society in procuring the advance of knowledge. Imagination cannot be acquired once and for all, and then kept indefinitely in an ice box to be produced periodically in stated quantities. The learned and imaginative life is a way of living, and is not an article of commerce.

It is in respect to the provision and utilisation of these conditions for an efficient faculty that the two functions of education and research meet together in a university. Do you want your teachers to be imaginative? Then encourage them to research. Do you want your researchers to be imaginative? Then bring them into intellectual sympathy with the young at the most eager, imaginative period of life, when intellects are just entering upon their mature discipline. Make your researchers explain themselves to active minds, plastic and with the world before them; make your young students crown their period of intellectual acquisition by some contact with minds gifted with experience of intellectual adventure. Education is discipline for the adventure of life; research is intellectual adventure; and the universities should be homes of adventure shared in common by young and old. For successful education there must always be a certain freshness in the knowledge dealt with. It must either be new in itself or it must be invested with some novelty of application to the new world of new times. Knowledge does not keep any better than fish. You may be dealing with knowledge of the old species, with some old truth; but somehow or other it must come to the students, as it were, just drawn out of the sea and with the freshness of its immediate importance.

It is the function of the scholar to evoke into life wisdom and beauty which, apart from his magic, would remain lost in the past. A progressive society depends upon its inclusion of three groups—scholars, discoverers, inventors. Its progress also depends upon the fact that its educated masses are composed of members each with a tinge of scholarship, a tinge of discovery, and a tinge of invention. I am here using the term "discovery" to mean the progress of knowledge in respect to truths of some high generality, and the term "invention" to mean the progress of knowledge in respect to the application of general truths in particular ways subservient to present needs. It is evident that these three groups merge into each other, and also that men engaged in practical affairs are properly to be called inventors so far as they contribute to the progress of society. But any one individual has his own limitation of function, and his own peculiar needs. What is important for a nation is that there shall be a very close relation between all types of its progressive elements, so that the study may influence the market place, and the market place the study. Universities are the chief agencies for this fusion of progressive activities into an effective instrument of progress. Of course they are not the only agencies, but it is a fact that to-day the progressive nations are those in which universities flourish.

It must not be supposed that the output of a university in the form of original ideas is solely to be measured by printed papers and books labeled with the names of their authors. Mankind is as individual in its mode of output as in the substance of its thoughts. For some of the most fertile minds composition in writing, or in a form reducible to writing, seems to be an impossibility. In every faculty you will find that some of the more brilliant teachers are not among those who publish. Their originality requires for its expression direct intercourse with their pupils in the form of lectures, or of personal discussion. Such men exercise an immense influence; and yet, after the generation of their pupils has passed away, they sleep among the innumerable unthanked benefactors of humanity. Fortunately, one of them is immortal—Socrates.

Thus it would be the greatest mistake to estimate the value of each member of a faculty by the printed work signed with his name. There is at the present day some tendency to fall into this error; and an emphatic protest is necessary against an attitude on the part of authorities which is damaging to efficiency and unjust to unselfish zeal.

But, when all such allowances have been made, one good

test for the general efficiency of a faculty is that as a whole it shall be producing in published form its quota of contributions of thought. Such a quota is to be estimated in weight of thought, and not in number of words.

This survey shows that the management of a university faculty has no analogy to that of a business organisation. The public opinion of the faculty, and a common zeal for the purposes of the university, form the only effective safeguards for the high level of university work. The faculty should be a band of scholars, stimulating each other, and freely determining their various activities. You can secure certain formal requirements, that lectures are given at stated times and that instructors and students are in attendance. But the heart of the matter lies beyond all regulation.

The question of justice to the teachers has very little to do with the case. It is perfectly just to hire a man to perform any legal services under any legal conditions as to times and salary. No one need accept the post unless he so desires.

The sole question is, What sort of conditions will produce the type of faculty which will run a successful university? The danger is that it is quite easy to produce a faculty entirely unfit—a faculty of very efficient pedants and dullards. The general public will only detect the difference after the university has stunted the promise of youth for scores of years.

The modern university system in the great democratic countries will only be successful if the ultimate authorities exercise singular restraint, so as to remember that universities cannot be dealt with according to the rules and policies which apply to the familiar business corporations. Business schools are no exception to this law of university life. There is really nothing to add to what the presidents of many American universities have recently said in public on this topic. But whether the effective portion of the general public, in America or other countries, will follow their advice appears to be doubtful. The whole point of a university, on its educational side, is to bring the young under the intellectual influence of a band of imaginative scholars. There can be no escape from proper attention to the conditions which—as experience has shown—will produce such a band.

IV

The two premier universities of Europe, in age and in dignity, are the University of Paris and the University of Oxford. I will speak of my own country because I know it best. The University of Oxford may have sinned in many ways. But, for all her deficiencies, she has throughout the ages preserved one supreme merit, beside which all failures in detail are as dust in the balance: for century after century, throughout the long course of her existence, she has produced bands of scholars who treated learning imaginatively. For that service alone, no one who loves culture can think of her without emotion.

But it is quite unnecessary for me to cross the ocean for my examples. The author of the Declaration of Independence, Mr. Jefferson, has some claim to be the greatest American. The perfection of his various achievements certainly places him among the few great men of all ages. He founded a university, and devoted one side of his complex genius to placing that university amid every circumstance which could stimulate the imagination—beauty of buildings, of situation, and every other stimulation of equipment and organisation.

There are many other universities in America which can point my moral, but my final example shall be Harvard—the representative university of the Puritan movement. The New England Puritans of the seventeenth and eighteenth centuries were the most intensely imaginative people, restrained in their outward expression, and fearful of symbolism by physical beauty, but, as it were, racked with the intensity of spiritual truths intellectually imagined. The Puritan faculties of those centuries must have been imaginative indeed, and they produced great men whose names have gone round the world. In later times Puritanism softened, and, in the golden age of literary New England, Emerson, Lowell, and Longfellow set their mark upon Harvard. The modern scientific age then gradually supervenes, and again in William James we find the typical imaginative scholar.

To-day business comes to Harvard; and the gift which the University has to offer is the old one of imagination, the lighted torch which passes from hand to hand. It is a dangerous gift, which has started many a conflagration.

If we are timid as to that danger, the proper course is to shut down our universities. Imagination is a gift which has often been associated with great commercial peoples— with Greece, with Florence, with Venice, with the learning of Holland, and with the poetry of England. Commerce and imagination thrive together. It is a gift which all must pray for their country who desire for it that abiding greatness achieved by Athens:—

> Her citizens, imperial spirits,
> Rule the present from the past.

For American education no smaller ideal can suffice.
——Address to the American Association of the Collegiate Schools of Business, 1927.

John Henry Newman,   THE IDEA OF A UNIVERSITY

1. What does Newman see as the primary function of a university? How might he view modern American higher education? In particular, how would he have viewed the current "cafeteria" style of curriculum? The ever-increasing trend to specialization?

2. Differentiate between "useful" knowledge and "liberal" knowledge. What is the "end" of each? How does the idea of a "liberal arts" education fit into this division of knowledge?

3. Newman sees, based on his division of knowledge into useful and liberal, two methods of education. What are they and how do they currently manifest themselves? What do you see as the proper end for education?

4. What is Newman's criticism of Francis Bacon? Is it justified?

5. According to Newman, what are the uses of knowledge?

6. Discuss Newman's concept of "enlargement" of the mind, as opposed to the acquisition of knowledge. How might Newman have reacted to a course so broad in concept as the Senior Symposium?

7. Compare Whitehead's view of the utility of knowledge to that of Newman.

John Henry Newman (1801-1890) was a prominent British theologian, churchman, educator, and a Cardinal in the Catholic Church. *The Idea of a University*, originally a series of lectures written in conjunction with the development of a new Catholic university in Dublin, addresses many of the fundamental questions which underlie our current educational structure.

THE IDEA OF A UNIVERSITY

I

KNOWLEDGE ITS OWN END

A university may be considered with reference either to its Students or to its Studies; and the principle, that all Knowledge is a whole and the separate Sciences parts of one, which I have hitherto been using in behalf of its studies, is equally important when we direct our attention to its students. Now then I turn to the students, and shall consider the education which, by virtue of this principle, a University will give them; and thus I shall be introduced, Gentlemen, to the second question, which I proposed to discuss, viz. whether and in what
10 sense its teaching, viewed relatively to the taught, carries the attribute of Utility along with it.

1

I have said that all branches of knowledge are connected together, because the subject-matter of knowledge is intimately united in itself, as being the acts and the work of the Creator. Hence it is that the Sciences, into which our knowl edge may be said to be cast, have multiplied bearings one on another, and an internal sympathy, and admit, or rather demand, comparison and adjustment. They complete, correct, balance each other. This consideration, if well-founded, must
20 be taken into account, not only as regards the attainment of truth, which is their common end, but as regards the influence

which they exercise upon those whose education consists in the study of them. I have said already, that to give undue prominence to one is to be unjust to another; to neglect or supersede these is to divert those from their proper object. It is to unsettle the boundary lines between science and science, to disturb their action, to destroy the harmony which binds them together. Such a proceeding will have a corresponding effect when introduced into a place of education. There is no science but tells a different tale, when viewed as a portion of a whole, from what it is likely to suggest when taken by itself, without the safeguard, as I may call it, of others.

Let me make use of an illustration. In the combination of colours, very different effects are produced by a difference in their selection and juxta-position; red, green, and white change their shades, according to the contrast to which they are submitted. And, in like manner, the drift and meaning of a branch of knowledge varies with the company in which it is introduced to the student. If his reading is confined simply to one subject, however such division of labour may favour the advancement of a particular pursuit, a point into which I do not here enter, certainly it has a tendency to contract his mind. If it is incorporated with others, it depends on those others as to the kind of influence which it exerts upon him. Thus the Classics, which in England are the means of refining the taste, have in France subserved the spread of revolutionary and deistical doctrines. In Metaphysics, again, Butler's *Analogy of Religion,* which has had so much to do with the conversion to the Catholic faith of members of the University of Oxford, appeared to Pitt and others, who had received a different training, to operate only in the direction of infidelity. And so again, Watson, Bishop of Llandaff, as I think he tells us in the narrative of his life, felt the science of Mathematics to indispose the mind to religious belief, while others see in its investigations the best parallel, and thereby defence, of the Christian Mysteries. In like manner, I suppose, Arcesilas would not have handled logic as Aristotle, nor Aristotle have criticized poets as Plato; yet reasoning and poetry are subject to scientific rules.

60   It is a great point then to enlarge the range of studies which a University professes, even for the sake of the students; and, though they cannot pursue every subject which is open to them, they will be the gainers by living among those and under those who represent the whole circle. This I conceive to be the advantage of a seat of universal learning, considered as a place of education. An assemblage of learned men, zealous for their own sciences, and rivals of each other, are brought, by familiar intercourse and for the sake of intellectual peace, to adjust together the claims and relations of their respective
70   subjects of investigation. They learn to respect, to consult, to aid each other. Thus is created a pure and clear atmosphere of thought, which the student also breathes, though in his own case he only pursues a few sciences out of the multitude. He profits by an intellectual tradition, which is independent of particular teachers, which guides him in his choice of subjects, and duly interprets for him those which he chooses. He apprehends the great outlines of knowledge, the principles on which it rests, the scale of its parts, its lights and its shades, its great points and its little, as he otherwise cannot apprehend them.
80   Hence it is that his education is called "Liberal." A habit of mind is formed which lasts through life, of which the attributes are, freedom, equitableness, calmness, moderation, and wisdom; or what in a former Discourse I have ventured to call a philosophical habit. This then I would assign as the special fruit of the education furnished at a University, as contrasted with other places of teaching or modes of teaching. This is the main purpose of a University in its treatment of its students.

And now the question is asked me, What is the *use* of it? and my answer will constitute the main subject of the Dis-
90   courses which are to follow.

2

Cautious and practical thinkers, I say, will ask me, what, after all, is the gain of this Philosophy, of which I make such account, and from which I promise so much. Even supposing it to enable us to exercise the degree of trust exactly due to every science respectively, and to estimate precisely the value of every truth which is anywhere to be found, how are we better for this master view of things, which I have been extolling? Does it not reverse the principle of the division of labour? will practical objects be obtained better or worse by its cultivation? to what then does it lead? where does it end? what does it do? how does it profit? what does it promise? Particular sciences are respectively the basis of definite arts, which carry on to results tangible and beneficial the truths which are the subjects of the knowledge attained; what is the Art of this science of sciences? what is the fruit of such a Philosophy? what are we proposing to effect, what inducements do we hold out to the Catholic community, when we set about the enterprise of founding a University?

I am asked what is the end of University Education, and of the Liberal or Philosophical Knowledge which I conceive it to impart: I answer, that what I have already said has been sufficient to show that it has a very tangible, real, and sufficient end, though the end cannot be divided from that knowledge itself. Knowledge is capable of being its own end. Such is the constitution of the human mind, that any kind of knowledge, if it be really such, is its own reward. And if this is true of all knowledge, it is true also of that special Philosophy, which I have made to consist in a comprehensive view of truth in all its branches, of the relations of science to science, of their mutual bearings, and their respective values. What the worth of such an acquirement is, compared with other objects which we seek,—wealth or power or honour or the conveniences and comforts of life, I do not profess here to discuss; but I would maintain, and mean to show, that it is an object, in its own

321

nature so really and undeniably good, as to be the compensa-
tion of a great deal of thought in the compassing, and a great
deal of trouble in the attaining.

Now, when I say that Knowledge is, not merely a means to
something beyond it, or the preliminary of certain arts into
130 which it naturally resolves, but an end sufficient to rest in and
to pursue for its own sake, surely I am uttering no paradox,
for I am stating what is both intelligible in itself, and has ever
been the common judgment of philosophers and the ordinary
feeling of mankind. I am saying what at least the public
opinion of this day ought to be slow to deny, considering how
much we have heard of late years, in opposition to Religion,
of entertaining, curious, and various knowledge. I am but saying what whole volumes have been written to illustrate, viz.,
by a "selection from the records of Philosophy, Literature, and
140 Art, in all ages and countries, of a body of examples, to show
how the most unpropitious circumstances have been unable to
conquer an ardent desire for the acquisition of knowledge." [1]
That further advantages accrue to us and redound to others
by its possession, over and above what it is in itself, I am very
far indeed from denying; but, independent of these, we are
satisfying a direct need of our nature in its very acquisition;
and, whereas our nature, unlike that of the inferior creation,
does not at once reach its perfection, but depends, in order to it,
on a number of external aids and appliances, Knowledge, as
150 one of the principal of these, is valuable for what its very presence in us does for us after the manner of a habit, even though
it be turned to no further account, nor subserve any direct end.

3

Hence it is that Cicero, in enumerating the various heads of
mental excellence, lays down the pursuit of Knowledge for its
own sake, as the first of them. "This pertains most of all to

1. "Pursuit of Knowledge under Difficulties." Introd. By George
Lillie Craik. 2. Cicero. *De Officiis, Initium.*

human nature," he says, "for we are all of us drawn to the pursuit of Knowledge; in which to excel we consider excellent, whereas to mistake, to err, to be ignorant, to be deceived, is both an evil and a disgrace." [2] And he considers Knowledge the very first object to which we are attracted, after the supply of our physical wants. After the calls and duties of our animal existence, as they may be termed, as regards ourselves, our family, and our neighbours, follows, he tells us, "the search after truth. Accordingly, as soon we escape from the pressure of necessary cares, forthwith we desire to see, to hear, and to learn; and consider the knowledge of what is hidden or is wonderful a condition of our happiness."

This passage, though it is but one of many similar passages in a multitude of authors, I take for the very reason that it is so familiarly known to us; and I wish you to observe, Gentlemen, how distinctly it separates the pursuit of Knowledge from those ulterior objects to which certainly it can be made to conduce, and which are, I suppose, solely contemplated by the persons who would ask of me the use of a University or Liberal Education. So far from dreaming of the cultivation of Knowledge directly and mainly in order to our physical comfort and enjoyment, for the sake of life and person, of health, of the conjugal and family union, of the social tie and civil security, the great Orator implies, that it is only after our physical and political needs are supplied, and when we are "free from necessary duties and cares," that we are in a condition for "desiring to see, to hear, and to learn." Nor does he contemplate in the least degree the reflex or subsequent action of Knowledge, when acquired, upon those material goods which we set out by securing before we seek it; on the contrary, he expressly denies its bearing upon social life altogether, strange as such a procedure is to those who live after the rise of the Baconian philosophy, and he cautions us against such a cultivation of it as will interfere with our duties to our fellow-creatures. "All these methods," he says, "are engaged in the investigation of truth; by the pursuit of which to be car-

160

170

180

190

ried off from public occupations is a transgression of duty. For the praise of virtue lies altogether in action; yet intermissions often occur, and then we recur to such pursuits; not to say that the incessant activity of the mind is vigorous enough to carry us on in the pursuit of knowledge, even without any exertion of our own." The idea of benefiting society by means of "the pursuit of science and knowledge" did not enter at all into the motives which he would assign for their cultivation.

200   This was the ground of the opposition which the elder Cato made to the introduction of Greek Philosophy among his countrymen, when Carneades and his companions, on occasion of their embassy, were charming the Roman youth with their eloquent expositions of it. The fit representative of a practical people, Cato estimated every thing by what it produced; whereas the Pursuit of Knowledge promised nothing beyond Knowledge itself. He despised that refinement or enlargement of mind of which he had no experience.

4

Things, which can bear to be cut off from every thing else
210 and yet persist in living, must have life in themselves; pursuits, which issue in nothing, and still maintain their ground for ages, which are regarded as admirable, though they have not as yet proved themselves to be useful, must have their sufficient end in themselves, whatever it turn out to be. And we are brought to the same conclusion by considering the force of the epithet, by which the knowledge under consideration is popularly designated. It is common to speak of *"liberal* knowledge," of the *"liberal* arts and studies," and of a *"liberal* education," as the especial characteristic or property of a Uni-
220 versity and of a gentleman; what is really meant by the word? Now, first, in its grammatical sense it is opposed to *servile;* and by "servile work" is understood, as our catechisms inform us, bodily labour, mechanical employment, and the like, in which the mind has little or no part. Parallel to such servile

works are those arts, if they deserve the name, of which the poet speaks,[3] which owe their origin and their method to hazard, not to skill; as, for instance, the practice and operation of an empiric. As far as this contrast may be considered as a guide into the meaning of the word, liberal education and liberal pursuits are exercises of mind, of reason, of reflection.   230

But we want something more for its explanation, for there are bodily exercises which are liberal, and mental exercises which are not so. For instance, in ancient times the practitioners in medicine were commonly slaves; yet it was an art as intellectual in its nature, in spite of the pretence, fraud, and quackery with which it might then, as now, be debased, as it was heavenly in its aim. And so in like manner, we contrast a liberal education with a commercial education or a professional; yet no one can deny that commerce and the professions afford scope for the highest and most diversified powers of   240 mind. There is then a great variety of intellectual exercises, which are not technically called "liberal;" on the other hand, I say, there are exercises of the body which do receive that appellation. Such, for instance, was the palæstra, in ancient times; such the Olympic games, in which strength and dexterity of body as well as of mind gained the prize. In Xenophon we read of the young Persian nobility being taught to ride on horseback and to speak the truth; both being among the accomplishments of a gentleman. War, too, however rough a profession, has ever been accounted liberal, unless in cases   250 when it becomes heroic, which would introduce us to another subject.

Now comparing these instances together, we shall have no difficulty in determining the principle of this apparent variation in the application of the term which I am examining. Manly games, or games of skill, or military prowess, though bodily, are, it seems, accounted liberal; on the other hand, what is merely professional, though highly intellectual, nay,

3. Art loves fate and fate loves art. Aristotle, *Nicomachean Ethics,* vi.

though liberal in comparison of trade and manual labour, is
260 not simply called liberal, and mercantile occupations are not
liberal at all. Why this distinction? because that alone is liberal
knowledge, which stands on its own pretensions, which is independent of sequel, expects no complement, refuses to be
informed (as it is called) by any end, or absorbed into any
art, in order duly to present itself to our contemplation. The
most ordinary pursuits have this specific character, if they are
self-sufficient and complete; the highest lose it, when they
minister to something beyond them. It is absurd to balance,
in point of worth and importance, a treatise on reducing frac-
270 tures with a game of cricket or a fox-chase; yet of the two the
bodily exercise has that quality which we call "liberal," and
the intellectual has it not. And so of the learned professions
altogether, considered merely as professions; although one of
them be the most popularly beneficial, and another the most
politically important, and the third the most intimately divine
of all human pursuits, yet the very greatness of their end, the
health of the body, or of the commonwealth, or of the soul,
diminishes, not increases, their claim to the appellation "liberal," and that still more, if they are cut down to the strict
280 exigencies of that end. If, for instance, Theology, instead of
being cultivated as a contemplation, be limited to the purposes
of the pulpit or be represented by the catechism, it loses,—
not its usefulness, not its divine character, not its meritorious-
ness (rather it gains a claim upon these titles by such charitable condescension),—but it does lose the particular attribute
which I am illustrating; just as a face worn by tears and fast-
ing loses its beauty, or a labourer's hand loses its delicateness;
—for Theology thus exercised is not simple knowledge, but
rather is an art or a business making use of Theology. And
290 thus it appears that even what is supernatural need not be
liberal, nor need a hero be a gentleman, for the plain reason
that one idea is not another idea. And in like manner the
Baconian Philosophy, by using its physical sciences in the
service of man, does thereby transfer them from the order of

Liberal Pursuits to, I do not say the inferior, but the distinct class of the Useful. And, to take a different instance, hence again, as is evident, whenever personal gain is the motive, still more distinctive an effect has it upon the character of a given pursuit; thus racing, which was a liberal exercise in Greece, forfeits its rank in times like these, so far as it is made the 300 occasion of gambling.

All that I have been now saying is summed up in a few characteristic words of the great Philosopher. "Of possessions," he says, "those rather are useful, which bear fruit; those *liberal, which tend to enjoyment.* By fruitful, I mean, which yield revenue; by enjoyable, where *nothing accrues of consequence beyond the using.*" [4]

5

Do not suppose, that in thus appealing to the ancients, I am throwing back the world two thousand years, and fettering Philosophy with the reasonings of paganism. While the 310 world lasts, will Aristotle's doctrine on these matters last, for he is the oracle of nature and of truth. While we are men, we cannot help, to a great extent, being Aristotelians, for the great Master does but analyze the thoughts, feelings, views, and opinions of human kind. He has told us the meaning of our own words and ideas, before we were born. In many subject-matters, to think correctly, is to think like Aristotle; and we are his disciples whether we will or no, though we may not know it. Now, as to the particular instance before us, the word "liberal" as applied to Knowledge and Education, expresses a 320 specific idea, which ever has been, and ever will be, while the nature of man is the same, just as the idea of the Beautiful is specific, or of the Sublime, or of the Ridiculous, or of the Sordid. It is in the world now, it was in the world then; and, as in the case of the dogmas of faith, it is illustrated by a continuous historical tradition, and never was out of the world,

4. Aristocle, *Rhetoric,* i, 5.

from the time it came into it. There have indeed been differences of opinion from time to time, as to what pursuits and what arts came under that idea, but such differences are but

330 an additional evidence of its reality. That idea must have a substance in it, which has maintained its ground amid these conflicts and changes, which has ever served as a standard to measure things withal, which has passed from mind to mind unchanged, when there was so much to colour, so much to influence any notion or thought whatever, which was not founded in our very nature. Were it a mere generalization, it would have varied with the subjects from which it was generalized; but though its subjects vary with the age, it varies not itself. The palæstra may seem a liberal exercise to Lycurgus,

340 and illiberal to Seneca; coach-driving and prize-fighting may be recognized in Elis, and be condemned in England; music may be despicable in the eyes of certain moderns, and be in the highest place with Aristotle and Plato,—(and the case is the same in the particular application of the idea of Beauty, or of Goodness, or of Moral Virtue, there is a difference of tastes, a difference of judgments)—still these variations imply, instead of discrediting, the archetypal idea, which is but a previous hypothesis or condition, by means of which issue is joined between contending opinions, and without which there would

350 be nothing to dispute about.

I consider, then, that I am chargeable with no paradox, when I speak of a Knowledge which is its own end, when I call it liberal knowledge, or a gentleman's knowledge, when I educate for it, and make it the scope of a University. And still less am I incurring such a charge, when I make this acquisition consist, not in Knowledge in a vague and ordinary sense, but in that Knowledge which I have especially called Philosophy or, in an extended sense of the word, Science; for whatever claims Knowledge has to be considered as a good, these

360 it has in a higher degree when it is viewed not vaguely, not popularly, but precisely and transcendently as Philosophy. Knowledge, I say, is then especially liberal, or sufficient for

itself, apart from every external and ulterior object, when and so far as it is philosophical, and this I proceed to show.

6

Now bear with me, Gentlemen, if what I am about to say, has at first sight a fanciful appearance. Philosophy, then, or Science, is related to Knowledge in this way:—Knowledge is called by the name of Science or Philosophy, when it is acted upon, informed, or if I may use a strong figure, impregnated by Reason. Reason is the principle of that intrinsic fecundity 370 of Knowledge, which, to those who possess it, is its especial value, and which dispenses with the necessity of their looking abroad for any end to rest upon external to itself. Knowledge, indeed, when thus exalted into a scientific form, is also power; not only is it excellent in itself, but whatever such excellence may be, it is something more, it has a result beyond itself. Doubtless; but that is a further consideration, with which I am not concerned. I only say that, prior to its being a power, it is a good; that it is, not only an instrument, but an end. I know well it may resolve itself into an art, and terminate in a me- 380 chanical process, and in tangible fruit; but it also may fall back upon that Reason which informs it, and resolve itself into Philosophy. In one case it is called Useful Knowledge, in the other Liberal. The same person may cultivate it in both ways at once; but this again is a matter foreign to my subject; here I do but say that there are two ways of using Knowledge, and in matter of fact those who use it in one way are not likely to use it in the other, or at least in a very limited measure. You see, then, here are two methods of Education; the end of the one is to be philosophical, of the other to be mechanical; the 390 one rises towards general ideas, the other is exhausted upon what is particular and external. Let me not be thought to deny the necessity, or to decry the benefit, of such attention to what is particular and practical, as belongs to the useful or mechanical arts; life could not go on without them; we owe our daily welfare to them; their exercise is the duty of the many, and we owe to the many a debt of gratitude for fulfilling that duty. I only say that Knowledge, in proportion as it tends more and more to be particular, ceases to be Knowledge. It is a question

400 whether Knowledge can in any proper sense be predicated of the brute creation; without pretending to metaphysical exactness of phraseology, which would be unsuitable to an occasion like this, I say, it seems to me improper to call that passive sensation, or perception of things, which brutes seem to possess, by the name of Knowledge. When I speak of Knowledge, I mean something intellectual, something which grasps what it perceives through the senses; something which takes a view of things; which sees more than the senses convey; which reasons upon what it sees, and while it sees; which invests it with

410 an idea. It expresses itself, not in a mere enunciation, but by an enthymeme: it is of the nature of science from the first, and in this consists its dignity. The principle of real dignity in Knowledge, its worth, its desirableness, considered irrespectively of its results, is this germ within it of a scientific or a philosophical process. This is how it comes to be an end in itself; this is why it admits of being called Liberal. Not to know the relative disposition of things is the state of slaves or children; to have mapped out the Universe is the boast, or at least the ambition, of Philosophy.

420 Moreover, such knowledge is not a mere extrinsic or accidental advantage, which is ours to-day and anothers' to-morrow, which may be got up from a book, and easily forgotten again, which we can command or communicate at our pleasure, which we can borrow for the occasion, carry about in our hand, and take into the market; it is an acquired illumination, it is a habit, a personal possession, and an inward endowment. And this is the reason, why it is more correct, as well as more usual, to speak of a University as a place of education, than of instruction, though, when knowledge is concerned, instruc-

430 tion would at first sight have seemed the more appropriate word. We are instructed, for instance, in manual exercises, in

the fine and useful arts, in trades, and in ways of business; for these are methods, which have little or no effect upon the mind itself, are contained in rules committed to memory, to tradition, or to use, and bear upon an end external to themselves. But education is a higher word; it implies an action upon our mental nature, and the formation of a character; it is something individual and permanent, and is commonly spoken of in connexion with religion and virtue. When, then, we speak of the communication of Knowledge as being Education, we thereby really imply that that Knowledge is a state or condition of mind; and since cultivation of mind is surely worth seeking for its own sake, we are thus brought once more to the conclusion, which the word "Liberal" and the word "Philosophy" have already suggested, that there is a Knowledge, which is desirable, though nothing come of it, as being of itself a treasure, and a sufficient remuneration of years of labour.

7

This, then, is the answer which I am prepared to give to the question with which I opened this Discourse. Before going on to speak of the object of the Church in taking up Philosophy, and the uses to which she puts it, I am prepared to maintain that Philosophy is its own end, and, as I conceive, I have now begun the proof of it. I am prepared to maintain that there is a knowledge worth possessing for what it is, and not merely for what it does; and what minutes remain to me to-day I shall devote to the removal of some portion of the indistinctness and confusion with which the subject may in some minds be surrounded.

It may be objected then, that, when we profess to seek Knowledge for some end or other beyond itself, whatever it be, we speak intelligibly; but that, whatever men may have said, however obstinately the idea may have kept its ground from age to age, still it is simply unmeaning to say that we seek Knowledge for its own sake, and for nothing else; for that it ever leads to something beyond itself, which therefore is its end, and the cause why it is desirable;—moreover, that this end is twofold, either of this world or of the next; that all knowledge is cultivated either for secular objects or for eternal; that if it is directed to secular objects, it is called Useful Knowledge, if to eternal, Religious or Christian Knowledge;—in consequence, that if, as I have allowed, this Liberal Knowledge does not benefit the body or estate, it ought to benefit the soul; but if the fact be really so, that it is neither a physical or a secular good on the one hand, nor a moral good on the other, it cannot be a good at all, and is not worth the trouble which is necessary for its acquisition.

And then I may be reminded that the professors of this Liberal or Philosophical Knowledge have themselves, in every age, recognized this exposition of the matter, and have submitted to the issue in which it terminates; for they have ever been attempting to make men virtuous; or, if not, at least have assumed that refinement of mind was virtue, and that they themselves were the virtuous portion of mankind. This they have professed on the one hand; and on the other, they have utterly failed in .their professions, so as ever to make themselves a proverb among men, and a laughing-stock both to the grave and the dissipated portion of mankind, in consequence of them. Thus they have furnished against themselves both the ground and the means of their own exposure, without any trouble at all to any one else. In a word, from the time that Athens was the University of the world, what has Philosophy taught men, but to promise without practising, and to aspire without attaining? What has the deep and lofty thought of its disciples ended in but eloquent words? Nay, what has its teaching ever meditated, when it was boldest in its remedies for human ill, beyond charming us to sleep by its lessons, that we might feel nothing at all? like some melodious air, or rather like those strong and transporting perfumes, which at first spread their sweetness over every thing they touch, but in a little while do but offend in proportion as they once pleased us. Did Philosophy support Cicero under the disfavour of the fickle populace, or nerve Seneca to oppose an imperial tyrant? It abandoned Brutus, as he sorrowfully confessed, in his greatest need, and it forced Cato, as his panegyrist strangely boasts, into the false position of defying heaven. How few can be counted among its professors, who, like Polemo, were thereby converted from a profligate course, or like Anaxagoras, thought the world well lost in exchange for its possession? The philosopher in *Rasselas*[5] taught a superhuman doctrine, and 510 then succumbed without an effort to a trial of human affection.

"He discoursed," we are told, "with great energy on the government of the passions. His look was venerable, his action graceful, his pronunciation clear, and his diction elegant. He showed, with great strength of sentiment and variety of illustration, that human nature is degraded and debased, when the lower faculties predominate over the higher. He communicated the various precepts given, from time to time, for the conquest of passion, and displayed the happiness of those who had obtained the important victory, after which man is no 520 longer the slave of fear, nor the fool of hope . . . He enumerated many examples of heroes immoveable by pain or pleasure, who looked with indifference on those modes or accidents to which the vulgar give the names of good and evil."

Rasselas in a few days found the philosopher in a room half darkened, with his eyes misty, and his face pale. "Sir," said he, "you have come at a time when all human friendship is useless; what I suffer cannot be remedied, what I have lost cannot be supplied. My daughter, my only daughter, from whose tenderness I expected all the comforts of my age, died 530 last night of a fever." "Sir," said the prince, "mortality is an event by which a wise man can never be surprised; we know that death is always near, and it should therefore always be expected." "Young man," answered the philosopher, "you speak like one who has never felt the pangs of separation."

5. A philosophical novel, by Samuel Johnson.

"Have you, then, forgot the precept," said Rasselas, "which you so powerfully enforced? . . . consider that external things are naturally variable, but truth and reason are always the same." "What comfort," said the mourner, "can truth and
540 reason afford me? Of what effect are they now, but to tell me that my daughter will not be restored?"

8

Better, far better, to make no professions, you will say, than to cheat others with what we are not, and to scandalize them with what we are. The sensualist, or the man of the world, at any rate is not the victim of fine words, but pursues a reality and gains it. The Philosophy of Utility, you will say, Gentlemen, has at least done its work; and I grant it,—it aimed low, but it has fulfilled its aim. If that man of great intellect who has been its Prophet [6] in the conduct of life played false to his
550 own professions, he was not bound by his philosophy to be true to his friend or faithful in his trust. Moral virtue was not the line in which he undertook to instruct men; and though, as the poet [7] calls him, he were the "meanest" of mankind, he was so in what may be called his private capacity and without any prejudice to the theory of induction. He had a right to be so, if he chose, for any thing that the Idols [8] of the den or the theatre had to say to the contrary. His mission was the increase of physical enjoyment and social comfort; [9] and most wonderfully, most awfully has he fulfilled his conception and his
560 design. Almost day by day have we fresh and fresh shoots, and buds, and blossoms, which are to ripen into fruit, on that magical tree of Knowledge which he planted, and to which none of us perhaps, except the very poor, but owes, if not his present life, at least his daily food, his health, and general well-being.

6. Francis Bacon.   7. Alexander Pope, "An Essay on Man," iv.
8. Bacon, *Novum Organum,* vi, 553.   9. [Newman's note: It will be seen that on the whole I agree with Lord Macaulay in his Essay on Bacon's Philosophy. I do not know whether he would agree with me.]

He was the divinely provided minister of temporal benefits to all of us so great, that, whatever I am forced to think of him as a man, I have not the heart, from mere gratitude, to speak of him severely. And, in spite of the tendencies of his philosophy, which are, as we see at this day, to depreciate, or to trample on Theology, he has himself, in his writings, gone out of his 570 way, as if with a prophetic misgiving of those tendencies, to insist on it as the instrument of that beneficent Father,[10] who, when He came on earth in visible form, took on Him first and most prominently the office of assuaging the bodily wounds of human nature. And truly, like the old mediciner in the tale, "he sat diligently at his work, and hummed, with cheerful countenance, a pious song;" and then in turn "went out singing into the meadows so gaily, that those who had seen him from afar might well have thought it was a youth gathering flowers for his beloved, instead of an old physician gathering 580 healing herbs in the morning dew."[11]

Alas, that men, in the action of life or in their heart of hearts, are not what they seem to be in their moments of excitement, or in their trances or intoxications of genius,—so good, so noble, so serene! Alas, that Bacon too in his own way should after all be but the fellow of those heathen philosophers who in their disadvantages had some excuse for their inconsistency, and who surprise us rather in what they did say than in what they did not do! Alas, that he too, like Socrates or Seneca, must be stripped of his holy-day coat, which looks so fair, and should 590 be but a mockery amid his most majestic gravity of phrase; and, for all his vast abilities, should, in the littleness of his own moral being, but typify the intellectual narrowness of his school! However, granting all this, heroism after all was not his philosophy:—I cannot deny he has abundantly achieved what he proposed. His is simply a Method whereby bodily discomforts and temporal wants are to be most effectually removed from the greatest number; and already, before it has

10. Bacon, *De Augmentis Scientiarum*, iv. 2; Macaulay, "Lord Bacon"; Bacon, *Praef. Instauratio Magna.* 11. Fouqué's *Unknown Patient.*

shown any signs of exhaustion, the gifts of nature, in their
600 most artificial shapes and luxurious profusion and diversity,
from all quarters of the earth, are, it is undeniable, by its
means brought even to our doors, and we rejoice in them.

9

Useful Knowledge then, I grant, has done its work; and
Liberal Knowledge as certainly has not done its work,—that
is, supposing, as the objectors assume, its direct end, like Religious Knowledge, is to make men better; but this I will not
for an instant allow, and, unless I allow it, those objectors have
said nothing to the purpose. I admit, rather I maintain, what
they have been urging, for I consider Knowledge to have its
610 end in itself. For all its friends, or its enemies, may say, I insist
upon it, that it is as real a mistake to burden it with virtue or
religion as with the mechanical arts. Its direct business is not
to steel the soul against temptation or to console it in affliction,
any more than to set the loom in motion, or to direct the
steam carriage; be it ever so much the means or the condition
of both material and moral advancement, still, taken by and in
itself, it as little mends our hearts as it improves our temporal
circumstances. And if its eulogists claim for it such a power,
they commit the very same kind of encroachment on a prov-
620 ince not their own as the political economist who should
maintain that his science educated him for casuistry or diplo-
macy. Knowledge is one thing, virtue is another; good sense
is not conscience, refinement is not humility, nor is largeness
and justness of view faith. Philosophy, however enlightened,
however profound, gives no command over the passions, no
influential motives, no vivifying principles. Liberal Education
makes not the Christian, not the Catholic, but the gentleman.
It is well to be a gentleman, it is well to have a cultivated intellect, a delicate taste, a candid, equitable, dispassionate mind, a
630 noble and courteous bearing in the conduct of life;—these are
the connatural qualities of a large knowledge; they are the

objects of a University; I am advocating, I shall illustrate and insist upon them; but still, I repeat, they are no guarantee for sanctity or even for conscientiousness, they may attach to the man of the world, to the profligate, to the heartless,—pleasant, alas, and attractive as he shows when decked out in them. Taken by themselves, they do but seem to be what they are not; they look like virtue at a distance, but they are detected by close observers, and on the long run; and hence it is that they are popularly accused of pretence and hypocrisy, not, I 640 repeat, from their own fault, but because their professors and their admirers persist in taking them for what they are not, and are officious in arrogating for them a praise to which they have no claim. Quarry the granite rock with razors, or moor the vessel with a thread of silk; then may you hope with such keen and delicate instruments as human knowledge and human reason to contend against those giants, the passion and the pride of man.

Surely we are not driven to theories of this kind, in order to vindicate the value and dignity of Liberal Knowledge. Surely 650 the real grounds on which its pretensions rest are not so very subtle or abstruse, so very strange or improbable. Surely it is very intelligible to say, and that is what I say here, that Liberal Education, viewed in itself, is simply the cultivation of the intellect, as such, and its object is nothing more or less than intellectual excellence. Every thing has its own perfection, be it higher or lower in the scale of things; and the perfection of one is not the perfection of another. Things animate, inanimate, visible, invisible, all are good in their kind, and have a *best* of themselves, which is an object of pursuit. Why do you 660 take such pains with your garden or your park? You see to your walks and turf and shrubberies; to your trees and drives; not as if you meant to make an orchard of the one, or corn or pasture land of the other, but because there is a special beauty in all that is goodly in wood, water, plain, and slope, brought all together by art into one shape, and grouped into one whole. Your cities are beautiful, your palaces, your public buildings,

337

your territorial mansions, your churches; and their beauty
leads to nothing beyond itself. There is a physical beauty and a
670 moral: there is a beauty of person, there is a beauty of our
moral being, which is natural virtue; and in like manner
there is a beauty, there is a perfection, of the intellect. There
is an ideal perfection in these various subject-matters,
towards which individual instances are seen to rise, and
which are the standards for all instances whatever. The
Greek divinities and demigods, as the statuary has moulded
them, with their symmetry of figure, and their high fore-
head and their regular features, are the perfection of physical beauty. The heroes, of whom history tells, Alexander,
680 or Cæsar, or Scipio, or Saladin, are the representatives of
that magnanimity or self-mastery which is the greatness of
human nature. Christianity too has its heroes, and in the
supernatural order, and we call them Saints. The artist puts
before him beauty of feature and form; the poet, beauty
of mind; the preacher, the beauty of grace: then intellect too, I
repeat, has its beauty, and it has those who aim at it. To open
the mind, to correct it, to refine it, to enable it to know, and to
digest, master, rule, and use its knowledge, to give it power
over its own faculties, application, flexibility, method, critical
690 exactness, sagacity, resource, address, eloquent expression, is
an object as intelligible (for here we are inquiring, not what
the object of a Liberal Education is worth, nor what use the
Church makes of it, but what it is in itself), I say, an object
as intelligible as the cultivation of virtue, while, at the same
time, it is absolutely distinct from it.

10

This indeed is but a temporal object, and a transitory possession; but so are other things in themselves which we make
much of and pursue. The moralist will tell us that man, in all
his functions, is but a flower which blossoms and fades, except
700 so far as a higher principle breathes upon him, and makes him

and what he is immortal. Body and mind are carried on into an eternal state of being by the gifts of Divine Munificence; but at first they do but fail in a failing world; and if the powers of intellect decay, the powers of the body have decayed before them, and, as an Hospital or an Almshouse, though its end be ephemeral, may be sanctified to the service of religion, so surely may a University, even were it nothing more than I have as yet described it. We attain to heaven by using this world well, though it is to pass away; we perfect our nature, not by undoing it, but by adding to it what is more than 710 nature, and directing it towards aims higher than its own.

II

KNOWLEDGE VIEWED IN RELATION TO LEARNING

I

It were well if the English, like the Greek language, possessed some definite word to express, simply and generally, intellectual proficiency or perfection, such as "health," as used with reference to the animal frame, and "virtue," with reference to our moral nature. I am not able to find such a term;— talent, ability, genius, belong distinctly to the raw material, which is the subject-matter, not to that excellence which is the result of excercise and training. When we turn, indeed, to the particular kinds of intellectual perfection, words are forthcoming for our purpose, as, for instance, judgment, taste, and skill; 10 yet even these belong, for the most part, to powers or habits bearing upon practice or upon art, and not to any perfect condition of the intellect, considered in itself. Wisdom, again, is certainly a more comprehensive word than any other, but it

has a direct relation to conduct, and to human life. Knowledge, indeed, and Science express purely intellectual ideas, but
still not a state or quality of the intellect; for knowledge, in its
ordinary sense, is but one of its circumstances, denoting a
possession or a habit; and science has been appropriated to the
20 subject-matter of the intellect, instead of belonging in English,
as it ought to do, to the intellect itself. The consequence is that,
on an occasion like this, many words are necessary, in order,
first, to bring out and convey what surely is no difficult idea in
itself,—that of the cultivation of the intellect as an end; next,
in order to recommend what surely is no unreasonable object;
and lastly, to describe and make the mind realize the particular
perfection in which that object consists. Every one knows practically what are the constituents of health or virtue; and every
one recognizes health and virtue as ends to be pursued; it is
30 otherwise with intellectual excellence, and this must be my
excuse, if I seem to any one to be bestowing a good deal of
labour on a preliminary matter.

In default of a recognized term, I have called the perfection
or virtue of the intellect by the name of philosophy, philosophical knowledge, enlargement of mind, or illumination; terms
which are not commonly given to it by writers of this day: but,
whatever name we bestow on it, it is, I believe, as a matter of
history, the business of a University to make this intellectual
culture its direct scope, or to employ itself in the education of
40 the intellect,—just as the work of a Hospital lies in healing
the sick or wounded, of a Riding or Fencing School, or of a
Gymnasium, in exercising the limbs, of an Almshouse, in aiding and solacing the old, of an Orphanage, in protecting innocence, of a Penitentiary, in restoring the guilty. I say, a
University, taken in its bare idea, and before we view it as an
instrument of the Church, has this object and this mission; it
contemplates neither moral impression nor mechanical production; it professes to exercise the mind neither in art nor in
duty; its function is intellectual culture; here it may leave its
50 scholars, and it has done its work when it has done as much

as this. It educates the intellect to reason well in all matters, to reach out towards truth, and to grasp it.

2

This, I said in my foregoing Discourse, was the object of a University, viewed in itself, and apart from the Catholic Church, or from the State, or from any other power which may use it; and I illustrated this in various ways. I said that the intellect must have an excellence of its own, for there was nothing which had not its specific good; that the word "educate" would not be used of intellectual culture, as it is used, had not the intellect had an end of its own; that, had it not 60 such an end, there would be no meaning in calling certain intellectual exercises "liberal," in contrast with "useful," as is commonly done; that the very notion of a philosophical temper implied it, for it threw us back upon research and system as ends in themselves, distinct from effects and works of any kind; that a philosophical scheme of knowledge, or system of sciences, could not, from the nature of the case, issue in any one definite art or pursuit, as its end; and that, on the other hand, the discovery and contemplation of truth, to which research and systematizing led, were surely sufficient ends, 70 though nothing beyond them were added, and that they had ever been accounted sufficient by mankind.

Here then I take up the subject; and, having determined that the cultivation of the intellect is an end distinct and sufficient in itself, and that, so far as words go it is an enlargement or illumination, I proceed to inquire what this mental breadth, or power, or light, or philosophy consists in. A Hospital heals a broken limb or cures a fever: what does an Institution effect, which professes the health, not of the body, not of the soul, but of the intellect? What is this good, which in 80 former times, as well as our own, has been found worth the notice, the appropriation, of the Catholic Church?

I have then to investigate, in the Discourses which follow,

those qualities and characteristics of the intellect in which its cultivation issues or rather consists; and, with a view of assisting myself in this undertaking, I shall recur to certain questions which have already been touched upon. These questions are three: viz. the relation of intellectual culture, first, to *mere* knowledge; secondly, to *professional* knowledge; and thirdly,
90 to *religious* knowledge. In other words, are *acquirements* and *attainments* the scope of a University Education? or *expertness in particular arts and pursuits*? or *moral and religious proficiency*? or something besides these three? These questions I shall examine in succession, with the purpose I have mentioned; and I hope to be excused, if, in this anxious undertaking, I am led to repeat what, either in these Discourses or elsewhere,[1] I have already put upon paper. And first, of *Mere Knowledge,* or Learning, and its connexion with intellectual illumination or Philosophy.

3

100   I suppose the *primâ-facie* view which the public at large would take of a University, considering it as a place of Education, is nothing more or less than a place for acquiring a great deal of knowledge on a great many subjects. Memory is one of the first developed of the mental faculties; a boy's business when he goes to school is to learn, that is, to store up things in his memory. For some years his intellect is little more than an instrument for taking in facts, or a receptacle for storing them; he welcomes them as fast as they come to him; he lives on what is without; he has his eyes ever about him; he has a lively
110 susceptibility of impressions; he imbibes information of every kind; and little does he make his own in a true sense of the word, living rather upon his neighbours all around him. He has opinions, religious, political, and literary, and, for a boy, is very positive in them and sure about them; but he gets them

1. Newman's Oxford University Sermons.

from his schoolfellows, or his masters, or his parents, as the case may be. Such as he is in his other relations, such also is he in his school exercises; his mind is observant, sharp, ready, retentive; he is almost passive in the acquisition of knowledge. I say this in no disparagement of the idea of a clever boy. Geography, chronology, history, language, natural history, he 120 heaps up the matter of these studies as treasures for a future day. It is the seven years of plenty with him: he gathers in by handfuls, like the Egyptians, without counting; and though, as time goes on, there is exercise for his argumentative powers in the Elements of Mathematics, and for his taste in the Poets and Orators, still, while at school, or at least, till quite the last years of his time, he acquires, and little more; and when he is leaving for the University, he is mainly the creature of foreign influences and circumstances, and made up of accidents, homogeneous or not, as the case may be. Moreover, the moral 130 habits, which are a boy's praise, encourage and assist this result; that is, diligence, assiduity, regularity, despatch, persevering application; for these are the direct conditions of acquisition, and naturally lead to it. Acquirements, again, are emphatically producible, and at a moment; they are a something to show, both for master and scholar; an audience, even though ignorant themselves of the subjects of an examination, can comprehend when questions are answered and when they are not. Here again is a reason why mental culture is in the minds of men identified with the acquisition of knowledge. 140

The same notion possesses the public mind, when it passes on from the thought of a school to that of a University: and with the best of reasons so far as this, that there is no true culture without requirements, and that philosophy presupposes knowledge. It requires a great deal of reading, or a wide range of information, to warrant us in putting forth our opinions on any serious subject; and without such learning the most original mind may be able indeed to dazzle, to amuse, to refute, to perplex, but not to come to any useful result or any trustworthy conclusion. There are indeed persons who 150 profess a different view of the matter, and even act upon it. Every now and then you will find a person of vigorous or fertile mind, who relies upon his own resources, despises all former authors, and gives the world, with the utmost fearlessness, his views upon religion, or history, or any other popular subject. And his works may sell for a while; he may get a name in his day; but this will be all. His readers are sure to find on the long run that his doctrines are mere theories, and not the expression of facts, that they are chaff instead of bread, 160 and then his popularity drops as suddenly as it rose.

Knowledge then is the indispensable condition of expansion of mind, and the instrument of attaining to it; this cannot be denied, it is ever to be insisted on; I begin with it as a first principle; however, the very truth of it carries men too far, and confirms to them the notion that it is the whole of the matter. A narrow mind is thought to be that which contains little•knowledge; and an enlarged mind, that which holds a great deal; and what seems to put the matter beyond dispute is, the fact of the great number of studies which are pursued 170 in a University, by its very profession. Lectures are given on every kind of subject; examinations are held; prizes awarded. There are moral, metaphysical, physical Professors; Professors of languages, of history, of mathematics, of experimental science. Lists of questions are published, wonderful for their range and depth, variety and difficulty; treatises are written, which carry upon their very face the evidence of extensive reading or multifarious information; what then is wanting for mental culture to a person of large reading and scientific attainments? what is grasp of mind but acquirement? where 180 shall philosophical repose be found, but in the consciousness and enjoyment of large intellectual possessions?

And yet this notion is, I conceive, a mistake, and my present business is to show that it is one, and that the end of a Liberal Education is not mere knowledge, or knowledge considered in its *matter;* and I shall best attain my object, by actually setting down some cases, which will be generally granted to be instances of the process of enlightenment or enlargement of mind, and others which are not, and thus, by the comparison, you will be able to judge for yourselves, Gentlemen, whether Knowledge, that is, acquirement, is after all the real 190 principle of the enlargement, or whether that principle is not rather something beyond it.

4

For instance,[2] let a person, whose experience has hitherto been confined to the more calm and unpretending scenery of these islands, whether here or in England, go for the first time into parts where physical nature puts on her wilder and more awful forms, whether at home or abroad, as into mountainous districts; or let one, who has ever lived in a quiet village, go for the first time to a great metropolis,—then I suppose he will have a sensation which perhaps he never had before. He has a 200 feeling not in addition or increase of former feelings, but of something different in its nature. He will perhaps be borne forward, and find for a time that he has lost his bearings. He has made a certain progress, and he has a consciousness of mental enlargement; he does not stand where he did, he has a new centre, and a range of thoughts to which he was before a stranger.

Again, the view of the heavens which the telescope opens upon us, if allowed to fill and possess the mind, may almost whirl it round and make it dizzy. It brings in a flood of ideas, 210 and is rightly called an intellectual enlargement, whatever is meant by the term.

And so again, the sight of beasts of prey and other foreign animals, their strangeness, the originality (if I may use the term) of their forms and gestures and habits and their variety and independence of each other, throw us out of ourselves

2. The pages which follow are taken almost *verbatim* from the author's 14th (Oxford) University Sermon, which, at the time of writing this Discourse, he did not expect ever to reprint.

into another creation, and as if under another Creator, if I may so express the temptation which may come on the mind. We seem to have new faculties, or a new exercise for our faculties, 220 by this addition to our knowledge; like a prisoner, who, having been accustomed to wear manacles or fetters, suddenly finds his arms and legs free.

Hence Physical Science generally, in all its departments, as bringing before us the exuberant riches and resources, yet the orderly course, of the Universe, elevates and excites the student, and at first, I may say, almost takes away his breath, while in time it exercises a tranquilizing influence upon him.

Again, the study of history is said to enlarge and enlighten the mind, and why? because, as I conceive, it gives it a power 230 of judging of passing events, and of all events, and a conscious superiority over them, which before it did not possess.

And in like manner, what is called seeing the world, entering into active life, going into society, travelling, gaining acquaintance with the various classes of the community, coming into contact with the principles and modes of thought of various parties, interests, and races, their views, aims, habits and manners, their religious creeds and forms of worship—gaining experience how various yet how alike men are, how low-minded, how bad, how opposed, yet how confident in their 240 opinions; all this exerts a perceptible influence upon the mind, which it is impossible to mistake, be it good or be it bad, and is popularly called its enlargement.

And then again, the first time the mind comes across the arguments and speculations of unbelievers, and feels what a novel light they cast upon what he has hitherto accounted sacred; and still more, if it gives in to them and embraces them, and throws off as so much prejudice what it has hitherto held, and, as if waking from a dream, begins to realize to its imagination that there is now no such thing as law and the 250 transgression of law, that sin is a phantom, and punishment a bugbear, that it is free to sin, free to enjoy the world and the flesh; and still further, when it does enjoy them, and reflects that it may think and hold just what it will, that "the world is all before it where to choose," [3] and what system to build up as its own private persuasion; when this torrent of wilful thoughts rushes over and inundates it, who will deny that the fruit of the tree of knowledge, or what the mind takes for knowledge, has made it one of the gods, with a sense of expansion and elevation,—an intoxication in reality, still, so far as the subjective state of the mind goes, an illumination? Hence 260 the fanaticism of individuals or nations, who suddenly cast off their Maker. Their eyes are opened; and, like the judgment-stricken king in the Tragedy,[4] they see two suns, and a magic universe, out of which they look back upon their former state of faith and innocence with a sort of contempt and indignation, as if they were then but fools, and the dupes of imposture.

On the other hand, Religion has its own enlargement, and an enlargement, not of tumult, but of peace. It is often remarked of uneducated persons, who have hitherto thought 270 little of the unseen world, that, on their turning to God, looking into themselves, regulating their hearts, reforming their conduct, and meditating on death and judgment, heaven and hell, they seem to become, in point of intellect, different beings from what they were. Before, they took things as they came, and thought no more of one thing than another. But now every event has a meaning; they have their own estimate of whatever happens to them; they are mindful of times and seasons, and compare the present with the past; and the world, no longer dull, monotonous, unprofitable, and hopeless, is a 280 various and complicated drama, with parts and an object, and an awful moral.

5

Now from these instances, to which many more might be added, it is plain, first, that the communication of knowledge

3. *Paradise Lost,* xii, 646. 4. Euripides, *Bacchae.*

certainly is either a condition or the means of that sense of enlargement or enlightenment, of which at this day we hear so
much in certain quarters: this cannot be denied; but next, it
is equally plain, that such communication is not the whole of
the process. The enlargement consists, not merely in the pas-
290 sive reception into the mind of a number of ideas hitherto unknown to it, but in the mind's energetic and simultaneous
action upon and towards and among those new ideas, which
are rushing in upon it. It is the action of a formative power,
reducing to order and meaning the matter of our acquirements; it is a making the objects of our knowledge subjectively
our own, or, to use a familiar word, it is a digestion of what
we receive, into the substance of our previous state of thought;
and without this no enlargement is said to follow. There is no
enlargement, unless there be a comparison of ideas one with
300 another, as they come before the mind, and a systematizing
of them. We feel our minds to be growing and expanding
then, when we not only learn, but refer what we learn to what
we know already. It is not the mere addition to our knowledge
that is the illumination; but the locomotion, the movement onwards, of that mental centre, to which both what we know,
and what we are learning, the accumulating mass of our acquirements, gravitates. And therefore a truly great intellect,
and recognized to be such by the common opinion of mankind, such as the intellect of Aristotle, or of St. Thomas, or of
310 Newton, or of Goethe, (I purposely take instances within and
without the Catholic pale, when I would speak of the intellect
as such,) is one which takes a connected view of old and new,
past and present, far and near, and which has an insight into
the influence of all these one on another; without which there
is no whole, and no centre. It possesses the knowledge, not only
of things, but also of their mutual and true relations; knowledge, not merely considered as acquirement, but as philosophy.
　　Accordingly, when this analytical, distributive, harmonizing
process is away, the mind experiences no enlargement, and is
320 not reckoned as enlightened or comprehensive, whatever it

may add to its knowledge. For instance, a great memory, as I have already said, does not make a philosopher, any more than a dictionary can be called a grammar. There are men who embrace in their minds a vast multitude of ideas, but with little sensibility about their real relations towards each other. These may be antiquarians, annalists, naturalists; they may be learned in the law; they may be versed in statistics; they are most useful in their own place; I should shrink from speaking disrespectfully of them; still, there is nothing in such attainments to guarantee the absence of narrowness of mind. If they 330 are nothing more than well-read men, or men of information, they have not what specially deserves the name of culture of mind, or fulfils the type of Liberal Education.

In like manner, we sometimes fall in with persons who have seen much of the world, and of the men who, in their day, have played a conspicuous part in it, but who generalize nothing, and have no observation, in the true sense of the word. They abound in information in detail, curious and entertaining, about men and things; and, having lived under the influence of no very clear or settled principles, religious or political, 340 they speak of every one and every thing, only as so many phenomena, which are complete in themselves, and lead to nothing, not discussing them, or teaching any truth, or instructing the hearer, but simply talking. No one would say that these persons, well informed as they are, had attained to any great culture of intellect or to philosophy.

The case is the same still more strikingly where the persons in question are beyond dispute men of inferior powers and deficient education. Perhaps they have been much in foreign countries, and they receive, in a passive, otiose, unfruitful way, 350 the various facts which are forced upon them there. Seafaring men, for example, range from one end of the earth to the other; but the multiplicity of external objects, which they have encountered, forms no symmetrical and consistent picture upon their imagination; they see the tapestry of human life, as it were on the wrong side, and it tells no story. They sleep, and they rise up, and they find themselves, now in Europe, now in Asia; they see visions of great cities and wild regions; they are in the marts of commerce, or amid the islands of the South; they gaze on Pompey's Pillar, or on the Andes; and nothing which meets them carries them forward or backward, to any idea beyond itself. Nothing has a drift or relation; nothing has a history or a promise. Every thing stands by itself, and comes and goes in its turn, like the shifting scenes of a show, which leave the spectator where he was. Perhaps you are near such a man on a particular occasion, and expect him to be shocked or perplexed at something which occurs; but one thing is much the same to him as another, or, if he is perplexed, it is as not knowing what to say, whether it is right to admire, or to ridicule, or to disapprove, while conscious that some expression of opinion is expected from him; for in fact he has no standard of judgment at all, and no landmarks to guide him to a conclusion. Such is mere acquisition, and, I repeat, no one would dream of calling it philosophy.

6

Instances, such as these, confirm, by the contrast, the conclusion I have already drawn from those which preceded them. That only is true enlargement of mind which is the power of viewing many things at once as one whole, of referring them severally to their true place in the universal system, of understanding their respective values, and determining their mutual dependence. Thus is that form of Universal Knowledge, of which I have on a former occasion spoken, set up in the individual intellect, and constitutes its perfection. Possessed of this real illumination, the mind never views any part of the extended subject-matter of Knowledge without recollecting that it is but a part, or without the associations which spring from this recollection. It makes every thing in some sort lead to every thing else; it would communicate the image of the whole to every separate portion, till that whole becomes in imagination like a spirit, everywhere pervading and penetrating its 390 component parts, and giving them one definite meaning. Just as our bodily organs, when mentioned, recall their function in the body, as the word "creation" suggests the Creator, and "subjects" a sovereign, so, in the mind of the Philosopher, as we are abstractedly conceiving of him, the elements of the physical and moral world, sciences, arts, pursuits, ranks, offices, events, opinions, individualities, are all viewed as one, with correlative functions, and as gradually by successive combinations converging, one and all, to the true centre.

To have even a portion of this illuminative reason and true 400 philosophy is the highest state to which nature can aspire, in the way of intellect; it puts the mind above the influences of chance and necessity, above anxiety, suspense, unsettlement, and superstition, which is the lot of the many. Men, whose minds are possessed with some one object, take exaggerated views of its importance, are feverish in the pursuit of it, make it the measure of things which are utterly foreign to it, and are startled and despond if it happens to fail them. They are ever in alarm or in transport. Those on the other hand who have no object or principle whatever to hold by, lose their way, every 410 step they take. They are thrown out, and do not know what to think or say, at every fresh juncture; they have no view of persons, or occurrences, or facts, which come suddenly upon them, and they hang upon the opinion of others, for want of internal resources. But the intellect, which has been disciplined to the perfection of its powers, which knows, and thinks while it knows, which has learned to leaven the dense mass of facts and events with the elastic force of reason, such an intellect cannot be partial, cannot be exclusive, cannot be impetuous, cannot be at a loss, cannot but be patient, collected, and majes- 420 tically calm, because it discerns the end in every beginning, the origin in every end, the law in every interruption, the limit in each delay; because it ever knows where it stands, and how its path lies from one point to another. It is the τετράγωνος[5] of the Peripatetic, and has the "nil admirari"[6] of the Stoic,—

> *Felix qui potuit rerum cognoscere causas,*
> *Atque metus omnes, et inexorabile fatum*
> *Subjecit pedibus, strepitumque Acherontis avari.*[7]

There are men who, when in difficulties, originate at the
430 moment vast ideas or dazzling projects; who, under the influence of excitement, are able to cast a light, almost as if from inspiration, on a subject or course of action which comes before them; who have a sudden presence of mind equal to any emergency, rising with the occasion, and an undaunted magnanimous bearing, and an energy and keenness which is but made intense by opposition. This is genius, this is heroism; it is the exhibition of a natural gift, which no culture can teach, at which no Institution can aim; here, on the contrary, we are concerned, not with mere nature, but with training and teach-
440 ing. That perfection of the Intellect, which is the result of Education, and its *beau ideal,* to be imparted to individuals in their respective measures, is the clear, calm, accurate vision and comprehension of all things, as far as the finite mind can embrace them, each in its place, and with its own characteristics upon it. It is almost prophetic from its knowledge of history; it is almost heart-searching from its knowledge of human nature; it has almost supernatural charity from its freedom from littleness and prejudice; it has almost the repose of faith, because nothing can startle it; it has almost the beauty
450 and harmony of heavenly contemplation, so intimate is it with the eternal order of things and the music of the spheres.

5. four-square man. Aristotle, *Nicomachean Ethics,* I, x, 11. 6. to wonder at nothing. Horace, *Epistles,* I, vi, i. 7. Happy is he who is able to know the sequence of things, and thus triumphs over all fear, and inexorable fate, and the roar of greedy Acheron. Vergil, *Georgics,* ii, 490-492.

7

And now, if I may take for granted that the true and adequate end of intellectual training and of a University is not Learning or Acquirement, but rather, is Thought or Reason exercised upon Knowledge, or what may be called Philosophy, I shall be in a position to explain the various mistakes which at the present day beset the subject of University Education.

I say then, if we would improve the intellect, first of all, we must ascend; we cannot gain real knowledge on a level; we must generalize, we must reduce to method, we must have a 460 grasp of principles, and group and shape our acquisitions by means of them. It matters not whether our field of operation be wide or limited; in every case, to command it, is to mount above it. Who has not felt the irritation of mind and impatience created by a deep, rich country, visited for the first time, with winding lanes, and high hedges, and green steeps, and tangled woods, and every thing smiling indeed, but in a maze? The same feeling comes upon us in a strange city, when we have no map of its streets. Hence you hear of practised travellers, when they first come into a place, mounting some high 470 hill or church tower, by way of reconnoitring its neighbourhood. In like manner, you must be above your knowledge, not under it, or it will oppress you; and the more you have of it, the greater will be the load. The learning of a Salmasius or a Burman, unless you are its master, will be your tyrant. "Imperat aut servit!" [8] if you can wield it with a strong arm, it is a great weapon; otherwise,

> *Vis consili expers*
> *Mole ruit suâ.*[9]

You will be overwhelmed, like Tarpeia, by the heavy wealth 480 which you have exacted from tributary generations.

8. It either commands or serves. Horace, *Epistles,* I, x, 48.   9. Force without discretion falls of its own weight. Horace, *Odes,* III, iv, 65.

Instances abound; there are authors who are as pointless as they are inexhaustible in their literary resources. They measure knowledge by bulk, as it lies in the rude block, without symmetry, without design. How many commentators are there on the Classics, how many on Holy Scripture, from whom we rise up, wondering at the learning which has passed before us, and wondering why it passed! How many writers are there of Ecclesiastical History, such as Mosheim or Du Pin, who, 490 breaking up their subject into details, destroy its life, and defraud us of the whole by their anxiety about the parts! The Sermons, again, of the English Divines in the seventeenth century, how often are they mere repertories of miscellaneous and officious learning! Of course Catholics also may read without thinking; and in their case, equally as with Protestants, it holds good, that such knowledge is unworthy of the name, knowledge which they have not thought through, and thought out. Such readers are only possessed by their knowledge, not possessed of it; nay, in matter of fact they are often even carried 500 ried away by it, without any volition of their own. Recollect, the Memory can tyrannize, as well as the Imagination. Derangement, I believe, has been considered as a loss of control over the sequence of ideas. The mind, once set in motion, is henceforth deprived of the power of initiation, and becomes the victim of a train of associations, one thought suggesting another, in the way of cause and effect, as if by a mechanical process, or some physical necessity. No one, who has had experience of men of studious habits, but must recognize the existence of a parallel phenomenon in the case of those who 510 have over-stimulated the Memory. In such persons Reason acts almost as feebly and as impotently as in the madman; once fairly started on any subject whatever, they have no power of self-control; they passively endure the succession of impulses which are evolved out of the original exciting cause; they are passed on from one idea to another and go steadily forward, plodding along one line of thought in spite of the amplest concessions of the hearer, or wandering from it in endless digression in spite of his remonstrances. Now, if, as is very certain, no one would envy the madman the glow and originality of his conceptions, why must we extol the cultivation of that in- 520 tellect, which is the prey, not indeed of barren fancies but of barren facts, of random intrusions from without, though not of morbid imaginations from within? And in thus speaking, I am not denying that a strong and ready memory is in itself a real treasure; I am not disparaging a well-stored mind, though it be nothing besides, provided it be sober, any more than I would despise a bookseller's shop:—it is of great value to others, even when not so to the owner. Nor am I banishing, far from it, the possessors of deep and multifarious learning from my ideal University; they adorn it in the eyes of men; I do but 530 say that they constitute no type of the results at which it aims; that it is no great gain to the intellect to have enlarged the memory at the expense of faculties which are indisputably higher.

8

Nor indeed am I supposing that there is any great danger, at least in this day, of over-education; the danger is on the other side. I will tell you, Gentlemen, what has been the practical error of the last twenty years,—not to load the memory of the student with a mass of undigested knowledge, but to force upon him so much that he has rejected all. It has been 540 the error of distracting and enfeebling the mind by an unmeaning profusion of subjects; of implying that a smattering in a dozen branches of study is not shallowness, which it really is, but enlargement, which it is not; of considering an acquaintance with the learned names of things and persons, and the possession of clever duodecimos, and attendance on eloquent lecturers, and membership with scientific institutions, and the sight of the experiments on a platform and the specimens of a museum, that all this was not dissipation of mind, but progress. All things now are to be learned at once, not first 550 one thing, then another, not one well, but many badly. Learn-

ing is to be without exertion, without attention, without toil; without grounding, without advance, without finishing. There is to be nothing individual in it; and this, forsooth, is the wonder of the age. What the steam engine does with matter, the printing press is to do with mind; it is to act mechanically, and the population is to be passively, almost unconsciously enlightened, by the mere multiplication and dissemination of volumes. Whether it be the school boy, or the
560 school girl, or the youth at college, or the mechanic in the town, or the politician in the senate, all have been the victims in one way or other of this most preposterous and pernicious of delusions. Wise men have lifted up their voices in vain; and at length, lest their own institutions should be outshone and should disappear in the folly of the hour, they have been obliged, as far as they could with a good conscience, to humour a spirit which they could not withstand, and make temporizing concessions at which they could not but inwardly smile.

It must not be supposed that, because I so speak, therefore I
570 have some sort of fear of the education of the people: on the contrary, the more education they have, the better, so that it is really education. Nor am I an enemy to the cheap publication of scientific and literary works, which is now in vogue: on the contrary, I consider it a great advantage, convenience, and gain; that is, to those to whom education has given a capacity for using them. Further, I consider such innocent recreations as science and literature are able to furnish will be a very fit occupation of the thoughts and the leisure of young persons, and may be made the means of keeping them from bad
580 employments and bad companions. Moreover, as to that superficial acquaintance with chemistry, and geology, and astronomy, and political economy, and modern history, and biography, and other branches of knowledge, which periodical literature and occasional lectures and scientific institutions diffuse through the community, I think it a graceful accomplishment, and a suitable, nay, in this day a necessary accomplishment, in the case of educated men. Nor, lastly, am I

disparaging or discouraging the thorough acquisition of any one of these studies, or denying that, as far as it goes, such thorough acquisition is a real education of the mind. All I say 590 is, call things by their right names, and do not confuse together ideas which are essentially different. A thorough knowledge of one science and a superficial acquaintance with many, are not the same thing; a smattering of a hundred things or a memory for detail, is not a philosophical or comprehensive view. Recreations are not education; accomplishments are not education. Do not say, the people must be educated, when, after all, you only mean, amused, refreshed, soothed, put into good spirits and good humour, or kept from vicious excesses. I do not say that such amusements, such occupations of mind, 600 are not a great gain; but they are not education. You may as well call drawing and fencing education, as a general knowledge of botany or conchology. Stuffing birds or playing stringed instruments is an elegant pastime, and a resource to the idle, but it is not education; it does not form or cultivate the intellect. Education is a high word; it is the preparation for knowledge, and it is the imparting of knowledge in proportion to that preparation. We require intellectual eyes to know withal, as bodily eyes for sight. We need both objects and organs intellectual; we cannot gain them without setting 610 about it; we cannot gain them in our sleep, or by hap-hazard. The best telescope does not dispense with eyes; the printing press or the lecture room will assist us greatly, but we must be true to ourselves, we must be parties in the work. A University is, according to the usual designation, an Alma Mater, knowing her children one by one, not a foundry, or a mint, or a treadmill.

9

I protest to you, Gentlemen, that if I had to choose between a so-called University, which dispensed with residence and tutorial superintendence, and gave its degrees to any person 620 who passed an examination in a wide range of subjects, and a

University which had no professors or examinations at all, but merely brought a number of young men together for three or four years and then sent them away as the University of Oxford is said to have done some sixty years since, if I were asked which of these two methods was the better discipline of the intellect,—mind, I do not say which is *morally* the better, for it is plain that compulsory study must be a good and idleness an intolerable mischief,—but if I must determine which of the 630 two courses was the more successful in training, moulding, enlarging the mind, which sent out men the more fitted for their secular duties, which produced better public men, men of the world, men whose names would descend to posterity, I have no hesitation in giving the preference to that University which did nothing, over that which exacted of its members an acquaintance with every science under the sun. And, paradox as this may seem, still if results be the test of systems, the influence of the public schools and colleges of England, in the course of the last century, at least will bear out one side of the 640 contrast as I have drawn it. What would come, on the other hand, of the ideal systems of education which have fascinated the imagination of this age, could they ever take effect, and whether they would not produce a generation frivolous, narrow-minded, and resourceless, intellectually considered, is a fair subject for debate; but so far is certain, that the Universities and scholastic establishments, to which I refer, and which did little more than bring together first boys and then youths in large numbers, these institutions, with miserable deformities on the side of morals, with a hollow profession of 650 Christianity, and a heathen code of ethics,—I say, at least they can boast of a succession of heroes and statesmen, of literary men and philosophers, of men conspicuous for great natural virtues, for habits of business, for knowledge of life, for practical judgment, for cultivated tastes, for accomplishments, who have made England what it is,—able to subdue the earth, able to domineer over Catholics.

How is this to be explained? I suppose as follows: When a

multitude of young men, keen, open-hearted, sympathetic, and observant, as young men are, come together and freely mix with each other, they are sure to learn one from another, 660 even if there be no one to teach them; the conversation of all is a series of lectures to each, and they gain for themselves new ideas and views, fresh matter of thought, and distinct principles for judging and acting, day by day. An infant has to learn the meaning of the information which its senses convey to it, and this seems to be its employment. It fancies all that the eye presents to it to be close to it, till it actually learns the contrary, and thus by practice does it ascertain the relations and uses of those first elements of knowledge which are necessary for its animal existence. A parallel teaching is necessary 670 for our social being, and it is secured by a large school or a college; and this effect may be fairly called in its own department an enlargement of mind. It is seeing the world on a small field with little trouble; for the pupils or students come from very different places, and with widely different notions, and there is much to generalize, much to adjust, much to eliminate, there are inter-relations to be defined, and conventional rules to be established, in the process, by which the whole assemblage is moulded together, and gains one tone and one character. 680

I et it be clearly understood, I repeat it, that I am not taking into account moral or religious considerations; I am but saying that that youthful community will constitute a whole, it will embody a specific idea, it will represent a doctrine, it will administer a code of conduct, and it will furnish principles of thought and action. It will give birth to a living teaching, which in course of time will take the shape of a self-perpetuating tradition, or a *genius loci,* as it is sometimes called; which haunts the home where it has been born, and which imbues and forms, more or less, and one by one, every indi- 690 vidual who is successively brought under its shadow. Thus it is that, independent of direct instruction on the part of Superiors, there is a sort of self-education in the academic institu-

tions of Protestant England; a characteristic tone of thought, a recognized standard of judgment is found in them, which, as developed in the individual who is submitted to it, becomes a twofold source of strength to him, both from the distinct stamp it impresses on his mind, and from the bond of union which it creates between him and others,—effects which are
700 shared by the authorities of the place, for they themselves have been educated in it, and at all times are exposed to the influence of its ethical atmosphere. Here then is a real teaching, whatever be its standards and principles, true or false; and it at least tends towards cultivation of the intellect; it at least recognizes that knowledge is something more than a sort of passive reception of scraps and details; it is a something, and it does a something, which never will issue from the most strenuous efforts of a set of teachers, with no mutual sympathies and no inter-communion, of a set of examiners with no opinions
710 which they dare profess, and with no common principles, who are teaching or questioning a set of youths who do not know them, and do not know each other, on a large number of subjects, different in kind, and connected by no wide philosophy, three times a week, or three times a year, or once in three years, in chill lecture-rooms or on a pompous anniversary.

10

Nay, self-education in any shape, in the most restricted sense, is preferable to a system of teaching which, professing so much, really does so little for the mind. Shut your College gates against the votary of knowledge, throw him back upon
720 the searchings and the efforts of his own mind; he will gain by being spared an entrance into your Babel. Few indeed there are who can dispense with the stimulus and support of instructors, or will do any thing at all, if left to themselves. And fewer still (though such great minds are to be found), who will not, from such unassisted attempts, contract a self-reliance and a self-esteem, which are not only moral evils, but serious hin-

drances to the attainment of truth. And next to none, perhaps, or none, who will not be reminded from time to time of the disadvantage under which they lie, by their imperfect ground- 730 ing, by the breaks, deficiencies, and irregularities of their knowledge, by the eccentricity of opinion and the confusion of principle which they exhibit. They will be too often ignorant of what every one knows and takes for granted, of that multitude of small truths which fall upon the mind like dust, impalpable and ever accumulating; they may be unable to converse, they may argue perversely, they may pride themselves on their worst paradoxes or their grossest truisms, they may be full of their own mode of viewing things, unwilling to be put out of their way, slow to enter into the minds of others;—but, with these and whatever other liabilities upon their heads, they are 740 likely to have more thought, more mind, more philosophy, more true enlargement, than those earnest but ill-used persons, who are forced to load their minds with a score of subjects against an examination, who have too much on their hands to indulge themselves in thinking or investigation, who devour premiss and conclusion together with indiscriminate greediness, who hold whole sciences on faith, and commit demonstrations to memory, and who too often, as might be expected, when their period of education is passed, throw up all they have learned in disgust, having gained nothing really by their 750 anxious labours, except perhaps the habit of application.

Yet such is the better specimen of the fruit of that ambitious system which has of late years been making way among us: for its result on ordinary minds, and on the common run of students, is less satisfactory still; they leave their place of education simply dissipated and relaxed by the multiplicity of subjects, which they have never really mastered, and so shallow as not even to know their shallowness. How much better, I say, is it for the active and thoughtful intellect, where such is to be found, to eschew the College and the University alto- 760 gether, than to submit to a drudgery so ignoble, a mockery so contumelious How much more profitable for the independent mind, after the mere rudiments of education, to range through a library at random, taking down books as they meet him, and pursuing the trains of thought which his mother wit suggests! How much healthier to wander into the fields, and there with the exiled Prince to find "tongues in the trees, books in the running brooks!" [9] How much more genuine an education is that of the poor boy in the Poem [10]—a Poem, whether in conception or in execution, one of the most touching in our language—who, not in the wide world, but ranging day by day around his widowed mother's home, "a dexterous gleaner" in a narrow field, and with only such slender outfit

> as the village schools and books a few
> Supplied,

contrived from the beach, and the quay, and the fisher's boat, and the inn's fireside, and the tradesman's shop, and the shepherd's walk, and the smuggler's hut, and the mossy moor, and the screaming gulls, and the restless waves, to fashion for himself a philosophy and a poetry of his own!

But in a large subject, I am exceeding my necessary limits. Gentlemen, I must conclude abruptly; and postpone any summing up of my argument, should that be necessary, to another day.

9. Shakespeare, *As You Like It,* Act II, Scene 1. 10. Crabbe's "Tales of the Hall." This Poem, let me say, I read on its first publication, above thirty years ago, with extreme delight, and have never lost my love of it; and on taking it up lately, found I was even more touched by it than heretofore. A work which can please in youth and age, seems to fulfil (in logical language) the *accidental definition* of a Classic.

III

KNOWLEDGE VIEWED IN RELATION
TO PROFESSIONAL SKILL

I

I have been insisting, in my two preceding Discourses, first, on the cultivation of the intellect, as an end which may reasonably be pursued for its own sake; and next, on the nature of that cultivation, or what that cultivation consists in. Truth of whatever kind is the proper object of the intellect; its cultivation then lies in fitting it to apprehend and contemplate truth. Now the intellect in its present state, with exceptions which need not here be specified, does not discern truth intuitively, or as a whole. We know, not by a direct and simple vision, not at a glance, but, as it were, by piecemeal and accumulation, by a mental process, by going round an object, by the comparison, the combination, the mutual correction, the continual adaptation, of many partial notions, by the employment, concentration, and joint action of many faculties and exercises of mind. Such a union and concert of the intellectual powers, such an enlargement and development, such a comprehensiveness, is necessarily a matter of training. And again, such a training is a matter of rule; it is not mere application, however exemplary, which introduces the mind to truth, nor the reading many books, nor the getting up many subjects, nor the witnessing many experiments, nor the attending many lectures. All this is short of enough; a man may have done it all, yet be lingering in the vestibule of knowledge:— he may not realize what his mouth utters; he may not see with his mental eye what confronts him; he may have no grasp of things as they are; or at least he may have no power at all of advancing one step forward of himself, in consequence of

what he has already acquired, no power of discriminating between truth and falsehood, of sifting out the grains of truth
30 from the mass, of arranging things according to their real value, and, if I may use the phrase, of building up ideas. Such a power is the result of a scientific formation of mind; it is an acquired faculty of judgment, of clearsightedness, of sagacity, of wisdom, of philosophical reach of mind, and of intellectual self-possession and repose,—qualities which do not come of mere acquirement. The bodily eye, the organ for apprehending material objects, is provided by nature; the eye of the mind, of which the object is truth, is the work of discipline and habit.

40   This process of training, by which the intellect, instead of being formed or sacrificed to some particular or accidental purpose, some specific trade or profession, or study or science, is disciplined for its own sake, for the perception of its own proper object, and for its own highest culture, is called Liberal Education; and though there is no one in whom it is carried as far as is conceivable, or whose intellect would be a pattern of what intellects should be made, yet there is scarcely any one but may gain an idea of what real training is, and at least look towards it, and make its true scope and result, not some-
50 thing else, his standard of excellence; and numbers there are who may submit themselves to it, and secure it to themselves in good measure. And to set forth the right standard, and to train according to it, and to help forward all students toward it according to their various capacities, this I conceive to be the business of a University.

2

Now this is what some great men are very slow to allow; they insist that Education should be confined to some particular and narrow end, and should issue in some definite work, which can be weighed and measured. They argue as if every
60 thing, as well as every person, had its price; and that where

there has been a great outlay, they have a right to expect a return in kind. This they call making Education and Instruction
"useful," and "Utility" becomes their watchword. With a fundamental principle of this nature, they very naturally go on to
ask, what there is to show for the expense of a University;
what is the real worth in the market of the article called "a
Liberal Education," on the supposition that it does not teach us
definitely how to advance our manufactures, or to improve our
lands, or to better our civil economy; or again, if it does not at
once make this man a lawyer, that an engineer, and that a   70
surgeon; or at least if it does not lead to discoveries in chemistry, astronomy, geology, magnetism, and science of every kind.

This question, as might have been expected, has been keenly
debated in the present age, and formed one main subject of
the controversy, to which I referred in the Introduction to the
present Discourses, as having been sustained in the first decade
of this century by a celebrated Northern Review[1] on the one
hand, and defenders of the University of Oxford on the other.
Hardly had the authorities of that ancient seat of learning,
waking from their long neglect, set on foot a plan for the edu-   80
cation of the youth committed to them, than the representatives of science and literature in the city, which has sometimes
been called the Northern Athens,[2] remonstrated, with their
gravest arguments and their most brilliant satire, against the
direction and shape which the reform was taking. Nothing
would content them, but that the University should be set to
rights on the basis of the philosophy of Utility; a philosophy,
as they seem to have thought, which needed but to be proclaimed in order to be embraced. In truth, they were little
aware of the depth and force of the principles on which the   90
academical authorities were proceeding, and, this being so, it
was not to be expected that they would be allowed to walk
at leisure over the field of controversy which they had selected.
Accordingly they were encountered in behalf of the Univer-

1. *The Edinburgh Review.*   2. Edinburgh.

sity by two men of great name and influence in their day, of
very different minds, but united, as by Collegiate ties, so in the
clear-sighted and large view which they took of the whole
subject of Liberal Education; and the defence thus provided
for the Oxford studies has kept its ground to this day.

3

100   Let me be allowed to devote a few words to the memory
of distinguished persons, under the shadow of whose name I
once lived, and by whose doctrine I am now profiting. In the
heart of Oxford there is a small plot of ground hemmed in by
public thoroughfares, which has been the possession and the
home of one Society for above five hundred years. In the old
time of Boniface the Eighth and John the Twenty-second, in
the age of Scotus and Occam and Dante, before Wiclif or Huss
had kindled those miserable fires which are still raging to the
ruin of the highest interests of man, an unfortunate king of
110 England, Edward the Second, flying from the field of Ban-
nockburn, is said to have made a vow to the Blessed Virgin to
found a religious house in her honour, if he got back in safety.
Prompted and aided by his Almoner, he decided on placing
this house in the city of Alfred; and the Image of Our Lady,
which is opposite its entrance-gate, is to this day the token of
the vow and its fulfilment. King and Almoner have long been
in the dust, and strangers have entered into their inheritance,
and their creed has been forgotten, and their holy rites dis-
owned; but day by day a memento is still made in the holy
120 Sacrifice by at least one Catholic Priest, once a member of that
College, for the souls of those Catholic benefactors who fed
him there for so many years. The visitor, whose curiosity has
been excited by its present fame, gazes perhaps with something of disappointment on a collection of buildings which
have with them so few of the circumstances of dignity or
wealth. Broad quadrangles, high halls and chambers, orna-
mented cloisters, stately walks, or umbrageous gardens, a

throng of students, ample revenues, or a glorious history, none of these things were the portion of that old Catholic foundation; nothing in short which to the common eye sixty years 130 ago would have given tokens of what it was to be. But it had at that time a spirit working within it, which enabled its inmates to do, amid its seeming insignificance, what no other body in the place could equal; not a very abstruse gift or extraordinary boast, but a rare one, the honest purpose to administer the trust committed to them in such a way as their conscience pointed out as best. So, whereas the Colleges of Oxford are self-electing bodies, the fellows in each perpetually filling up for themselves the vacancies which occur in their number, the members of this foundation determined, at a time 140 when, either from evil custom or from ancient statute, such a thing was not known elsewhere, to throw open their fellowships to the competition of all comers, and, in the choice of associates henceforth, to cast to the winds every personal motive and feeling, family connexion, and friendship, and patronage, and political interest, and local claim, and prejudice, and party jealousy, and to elect solely on public and patriotic grounds. Nay, with a remarkable independence of mind, they resolved that even the table of honours, awarded to literary merit by the University in its new system of examination for 150 degrees, should not fetter their judgment as electors; but that at all risks, and whatever criticism it might cause, and whatever odium they might incur, they would select the men, whoever they were, to be children of their Founder, whom they thought in their consciences to be most likely from their intellectual and moral qualities to please him, if (as they expressed it) he were still upon earth, most likely to do honour to his College, most likely to promote the objects which they believed he had at heart. Such persons did not promise to be the disciples of a low Utilitarianism; and consequently, as their 160 collegiate reform synchronized with that reform of the Academical body, in which they bore a principal part, it was not unnatural that, when the storm broke upon the University from the North, their Alma Mater, whom they loved, should have found her first defenders within the walls of that small College, which had first put itself into a condition to be her champion.

These defenders, I have said, were two, of whom the more distinguished was the late Dr. Copleston, then a Fellow of the College, successively its Provost, and Protestant Bishop of Llandaff. In that Society, which owes so much to him, his name lives, and ever will live, for the distinction which his talents bestowed on it, for the academical importance to which he raised it, for the generosity of spirit, the liberality of sentiment, and the kindness of heart, with which he adorned it, and which even those who had least sympathy with some aspects of his mind and character could not but admire and love. Men come to their meridian at various periods of their lives; the last years of the eminent person I am speaking of were given to duties which, I am told, have been the means of endearing him to numbers, but which afforded no scope for that peculiar vigour and keenness of mind which enabled him, when a young man, single-handed, with easy gallantry, to encounter and overthrow the charge of three giants of the North combined against him. I believe I am right in saying that, in the progress of the controversy, the most scientific, the most critical, and the most witty, of that literary company, all of them now, as he himself, removed from this visible scene, Professor Playfair, Lord Jeffrey, and the Rev. Sydney Smith, threw together their several efforts into one article of their Review, in order to crush and pound to dust the audacious controvertist who had come out against them in defence of his own Institutions. To have even contended with such men was a sufficient voucher for his ability, even before we open his pamphlets, and have actual evidence of the good sense, the spirit, the scholar-like taste, and the purity of style, by which they are distinguished.

He was supported in the controversy, on the same general principles, but with more of method and distinctness, and, I will add, with greater force and beauty and perfection, both of thought and of language, by the other distinguished writer, to whom I have already referred, Mr. Davison; who, though not so well known to the world in his day, has left more behind him than the Provost of Oriel, to make his name remembered by posterity. This thoughtful man, who was the admired and intimate friend of a very remarkable person, whom, whether he wish it or not, numbers revere and love as the first author of the subsequent movement in the Protestant Church towards Catholicism,[3] this grave and philosophical writer, whose works I can never look into without sighing that such a man was lost to the Catholic Church, as Dr. Butler[4] before him, by some early bias or some fault of self-education—he, in a review of a work by Mr. Edgeworth on Professional Education, which attracted a good deal of attention in its day, goes leisurely over the same ground, which had already been rapidly traversed by Dr. Copleston, and, though professedly employed upon Mr. Edgeworth, is really replying to the northern critic who had brought that writer's work into notice, and to a far greater author than either of them, who in a past age had argued on the same side.

200

210

220

4

The author to whom I allude is no other than Locke.[5] That celebrated philosopher has preceded the Edinburgh Reviewers in condemning the ordinary subjects in which boys are instructed at school, on the ground that they are not needed by them in after life; and before quoting what his disciples have said in the present century, I will refer to a few passages of the master. " 'Tis matter of astonishment," he says in his work on Education, "that men of quality and parts should suffer

3. Mr. Keble, Vicar of Hursley, late Fellow of Oriel, and Professor of Poetry in the University of Oxford.   4. Joseph Butler, English bishop, author of *Analogy of Religion*.   5. John Locke, author of *Essay Concerning the Human Understanding*.

themselves to be so far misled by custom and implicit faith.
230 Reason, if consulted with, would advise, that their children's
time should be spent in acquiring what might be *useful* to
them, when they come to be men, rather than that their heads
should be stuffed with a deal of trash, a great part whereof
they usually never do ('tis certain they never need to) think
on again as long as they live; and so much of it as does stick by
them they are only the worse for."

And so again, speaking of verse-making, he says, "I know
not what reason a father can have to wish his son a poet, who
does not desire him to *bid defiance to all other callings and*
240 *business;* which is not yet the worst of the case; for, if he
proves a successful rhymer, and gets once the reputation of a
wit, I desire it to be considered, what company and places he
is likely to spend his time in, nay, and estate too; for it is very
seldom seen that any one discovers *mines of gold or silver in
Parnassus.* 'Tis a pleasant air, but a barren soil."

In another passage he distinctly limits utility in education
to its bearing on the future profession or trade of the pupil,
that is, he scorns the idea of any education of the intellect,
simply as such. "Can there be any thing more ridiculous," he
250 asks, "than that a father should waste his own money, and his
son's time, in setting him to *learn the Roman language,* when
at the same time he *designs him for a trade,* wherein he, having no use of Latin, fails not to forget that little which he
brought from school, and which 'tis ten to one he abhors for
the ill-usage it procured him? Could it be believed, unless we
have every where amongst us examples of it, that a child
should be forced to learn the rudiments of a language, which
he is never to use in the course of life that he is designed to,
and neglect all the while the writing a good hand, and casting
260 accounts, which are of great advantage in all conditions of
life, and to most trades indispensably necessary?"[6] Nothing
of course can be more absurd than to neglect in education

6. Locke, *Of Education,* Sections 94, 174, 164.

those matters which are necessary for a boy's future calling; but the tone of Locke's remarks evidently implies more than this, and is condemnatory of any teaching which tends to the general cultivation of the mind.

Now to turn to his modern disciples. The study of the Classics had been made the basis of the Oxford education, in the reforms which I have spoken of, and the Edinburgh Reviewers protested, after the manner of Locke, that no good 270 could come of a system which was not based upon the principle of Utility.

"Classical Literature," they said, "is the great object at Oxford. Many minds, so employed, have produced many works and much fame in that department; but if all liberal arts and sciences, *useful to human life,* had been taught there, if *some* had dedicated themselves to *chemistry, some to mathematics, some* to *experimental philosophy,* and if *every* attainment had been honoured in the mixt ratio of its difficulty and *utility,* the system of such a University would have been much more valu- 280 able, but the splendour of its name something less."

Utility may be made the end of education, in two respects: either as regards the individual educated, or the community at large. In which light do these writers regard it? in the latter. So far they differ from Locke, for they consider the advancement of science as the supreme and real end of a University. This is brought into view in the sentences which follow.

"When a University has been doing *useless* things for a long time, it appears at first degrading to them to be *useful.* A set of Lectures on Political Economy would be discouraged in 290 Oxford, probably despised, probably not permitted. To discuss the inclosure of commons, and to dwell upon imports and exports, to come so near to common life, would seem to be undignified and contemptible. In the same manner, the Parr or the Bentley [7] of the day would be scandalized, in a University, to be put on a level with the discoverer of a neutral salt;

7. Classical scholars.

and yet, *what other measure is there of dignity in intellectual labour but usefulness?* And what ought the term University to mean, but a place where every science is taught which is liberal, and at the same time useful to mankind? Nothing would so much tend to bring classical literature within proper bounds as *a steady and invariable appeal to utility* in our appreciation of all human knowledge. . . . *Looking always to real utility as our guide,* we should see, with equal pleasure, a studious and inquisitive mind arranging the productions of nature, investigating the qualities of bodies, or mastering the difficulties of the learned languages. We should not care whether he was chemist, naturalist, or scholar, because we know it to be as *necessary* that matter should be studied and subdued *to the use of man,* as that taste should be gratified, and imagination inflamed."

Such then is the enunciation, as far as words go, of the theory of Utility in Education; and both on its own account, and for the sake of the able men who have advocated it, it has a claim on the attention of those whose principles I am here representing. Certainly it is specious to contend that nothing is worth pursuing but what is useful; and that life is not long enough to expend upon interesting, or curious, or brilliant trifles. Nay, in one sense, I will grant it is more than specious, it is true; but, if so, how do I propose directly to meet the objection? Why, Gentlemen, I have really met it already, viz., in laying down, that intellectual culture is its own end; for what has its *end* in itself, has its *use* in itself also. I say, if a Liberal Education consists in the culture of the intellect, and if that culture be in itself a good, here, without going further, is an answer to Locke's question; for if a helathy body is a good in itself, why is not a healthy intellect? and if a College of Physicians is a useful institution, because it contemplates bodily health, why is not an Academical Body, though it were simply and solely engaged in imparting vigour and beauty and grasp to the intellectual portion of our nature? And the Reviewers I am quoting seem to allow this in their better moments, in a passage which, putting aside the question of its justice in fact, is sound and true in the principles to which it appeals:—

"The present state of classical education," they say, "cultivates the *imagination* a great deal too much, and other *habits of mind* a great deal too little, and trains up many young men in a style of elegant imbecility, utterly unworthy of the talents with which nature has endowed them. . . . The matter of fact is, that a classical scholar of twenty-three or twenty-four is a man principally conversant with works of imagination. His feelings are quick, his fancy lively, and his taste good. Talents for *speculation* and *original inquiry* he has none, nor has he formed the invaluable *habit of pushing things up to their first principles,* or of collecting dry and unamusing facts as the materials for reasoning. All the solid and masculine parts of his *understanding* are left wholly without cultivation; he hates the pain of thinking, and suspects every man whose boldness and originality call upon him to defend his opinions and prove his assertions."

5

Now, I am not at present concerned with the specific question of classical education; else, I might reasonably question the justice of calling an intellectual discipline, which embraces the study of Aristotle, Thucydides, and Tacitus, which involves Scholarship and Antiquities, *imaginative;* still so far I readily grant, that the cutivation of the "understanding," of a "talent for speculation and original inquiry," and of "the habit of pushing things up to their first principles," is a principal portion of a *good* or *liberal* education. If then the Reviewers consider such cultivation the characteristic of a *useful* education, as they seem to do in the foregoing passage, it follows, that what they mean by "useful" is just what I mean by "good" or "liberal:" and Locke's question becomes a verbal one. Whether youths are to be taught Latin or verse-making will depend on the *fact,* whether these studies tend to mental culture; but, however this is determined, so far is clear, that in that mental culture consists what I have called a liberal or non-professional, and what the Reviewers call a useful education.

370 This is the obvious answer which may be made to those who urge upon us the claims of Utility in our plans of Education; but I am not going to leave the subject here: I mean to take a wider view of it. Let us take "useful," as Locke takes it, in its proper and popular sense, and then we enter upon a large field of thought, to which I cannot do justice in one Discourse, though to-day's is all the space that I can give to it. I say, let us take "useful" to mean, not what is simply good, but what *tends* to good, or is the *instrument* of good; and in this sense also, Gentlemen, I will show you how a liberal education is 380 truly and fully a useful, though it be not a professional, education. "Good" indeed means one thing, and "useful" means another; but I lay it down as a principle, which will save us a great deal of anxiety, that, though the useful is not always good, the good is always useful. Good is not only good, but reproductive of good; this is one of its attributes; nothing is excellent, beautiful, perfect, desirable for its own sake, but it overflows, and spreads the likeness of itself all around it. Good is prolific; it is not only good to the eye, but to the taste; it not only attracts us, but it communicates itself; it excites first our 390 admiration and love, then our desire and our gratitude, and that, in proportion to its intenseness and fulness in particular instances. A great good will impart great good. If then the intellect is so excellent a portion of us, and its cultivation so excellent, it is not only beautiful, perfect, admirable, and noble in itself, but in a true and high sense it must be useful to the possessor and to all around him; not useful in any low, mechanical, mercantile sense, but as diffusing good, or as a blessing, or a gift, or power, or a treasure, first to the owner, then through him to the world. I say then, if a liberal education be 400 good, it must necessarily be useful too.

6

You will see what I mean by the parallel of bodily health. Health is a good in itself, though nothing came of it, and is especially worth seeking and cherishing; yet, after all, the blessings which attend its presence are so great, while they are so close to it and so redound back upon it and encircle it, that we never think of it except as useful as well as good, and praise and prize it for what it does, as well as for what it is, though at the same time we cannot point out any definite and distinct work or production which it can be said to effect. And so as regards intellectual culture, I am far from denying utility in this large sense as the end of Education, when I lay it down, that the culture of the intellect is a good in itself and its own end; I do not exclude from the idea of intellectual culture what it cannot but be, from the very nature of things; I only deny that we must be able to point out, before we have any right to call it useful, some art, or business, or profession, or trade, or work, as resulting from it, and as its real and complete end. The parallel is exact:—As the body may be sacrificed to some manual or other toil, whether moderate or oppressive, so may the intellect be devoted to some specific profession; and I do not call *this* the culture of the intellect. Again, as some member or organ of the body may be inordinately used and developed, so may memory, or imagination, or the reasoning faculty; and *this* again is not intellectual culture. On the other hand, as the body may be tended, cherished, and exercised with a simple view to its general health, so may the intellect also be generally exercised in order to its perfect state; and this *is* its cultivation.

Again, as health ought to precede labour of the body, and as a man in health can do what an unhealthy man cannot do, and as of this health the properties are strength, energy, agility, graceful carriage and action, manual dexterity, and endurance of fatigue, so in like manner general culture of mind is the best aid to professional and scientific study, and educated men can

410

420

43c

do what illiterate cannot; and the man who has learned to think and to reason and to compare and to discriminate and to analyze, who has refined his taste, and formed his judgment, and sharpened his mental vision, will not indeed at once be a lawyer, or a pleader, or an orator, or a statesman, or a physi-
440 cian, or a good landlord, or a man of business, or a soldier, or an engineer, or a chemist, or a geologist, or an antiquarian, but he will be placed in that state of intellect in which he can take up any one of the sciences or callings I have referred to, or any other for which he has a taste or special talent, with an ease, a grace, a versatility, and a success, to which another is a stranger. In this sense then, and as yet I have said but a very few words on a large subject, mental culture is emphatically *useful*.

If then I am arguing, and shall argue, against Professional
450 or Scientific knowledge as the sufficient end of a University Education, let me not be supposed, Gentlemen, to be disrespectful towards particular studies, or arts, or vocations, and those who are engaged in them. In saying that Law or Medicine is not the end of a University course, I do not mean to imply that the University does not teach Law or Medicine. What indeed can it teach at all, if it does not teach something particular? It teaches *all* knowledge by teaching all *branches* of knowledge, and in no other way. I do but say that there will be this distinction as regards a Professor or Law, or of
460 Medicine, or of Geology, or of Political Economy, in a University and out of it, that out of a University he is in danger of being absorbed and narrowed by his pursuit, and of giving Lectures which are the Lectures of nothing more than a lawyer, physician, geologist, or political economist; whereas in a University he will just know where he and his science stand, he has come to it, as it were, from a height, he has taken a survey of all knowledge, he is kept from extravagance by the very rivalry of other studies, he has gained from them a special illumination and largeness of mind and freedom and self-
470 possession, and he treats his own in consequence with a

philosophy and a resource, which belongs not to the study itself, but to his liberal education.

This then is how I should solve the fallacy, for so I must call it, by which Locke and his disciples would frighten us from cultivating the intellect, under the notion that no education is useful which does not teach us some temporal calling, or some mechanical art, or some physical secret, I say that a cultivated intellect, because it is a good in itself, brings with it a power and a grace to every work and occupation which it undertakes, and enables us to be more useful, and to a greater 480 number. There is a duty we owe to human society as such, to the state to which we belong, to the sphere in which we move, to the individuals towards whom we are variously related, and whom we successively encounter in life; and that philosophical or liberal education, as I have called it, which is the proper function of a University, if it refuses the foremost place to professional interests, does but postpone them to the formation of the citizen, and, while it subserves the larger interests of philanthropy, prepares also for the successful prosecution of those merely personal objects, which at first sight it seems 490 to disparage.

7

And now, Gentlemen, I wish to be allowed to enforce in detail what I have been saying, by some extracts from the writings to which I have already alluded, and to which I am so greaty indebted.

"It is an undisputed maxim in Political Economy," says Dr. Copleston, "that the separation of professions and the division of labour tend to the perfection of every art, to the wealth of nations, to the general comfort and well-being of the community. This principle of division is in some instances pur- 500 sued so far as to excite the wonder of people to whose notice it is for the first time pointed out. There is no saying to what extent it may not be carried; and the more the powers of each individual are concentrated in one employment, the greater

skill and quickness will he naturally display in performing it. But, while he thus contributes more effectually to the accumulation of national wealth, he becomes himself more and more degraded as a rational being. In proportion as his sphere of action is narrowed his mental powers and habits become con-
510 tracted; and he resembles a subordinate part of some powerful machinery, useful in its place, but insignificant and worthless out of it. If it be necessary, as it is beyond all question necessary, that society should be split into divisions and subdivisions, in order that its several duties may be well performed, yet we must be careful not to yield up ourselves wholly and exclusively to the guidance of this system; we must observe what its evils are, and we should modify and restrain it, by bringing into action other principles, which may serve as a check and counterpoise to the main force.

520 "There can be no doubt that every art is improved by confining the professor of it to that single study. But, *although the art itself is advanced by this concentration of mind in its service, the individual who is confined to it goes back*. The advantage of the community is nearly in an inverse ratio with his own.

"Society itself requires some other contribution from each individual, besides the particular duties of his profession. And, if no such liberal intercourse be established, it is the common failing of human nature, to be engrossed with petty views
530 and interests, to underrate the importance of all in which we are not concerned, and to carry our partial notions into cases where they are inapplicable, to act, in short, as so many unconnected units, displacing and repelling one another.

"In the cultivation of literature is found that common link, which, among the higher and middling departments of life, unites the jarring sects and subdivisions into one interest, which supplies common topics, and kindles common feelings, unmixed with those narrow prejudices with which all professions are more or less infected. The knowledge, too,
540 which is thus acquired, expands and enlarges the mind, excites

its faculties, and calls those limbs and muscles into freer exercise which, by too constant use in one direction, not only acquire an illiberal air, but are apt also to lose somewhat of their native play and energy. And thus, without directly qualifying a man for any of the employments of life, it enriches an*d* ennobles all. Without teaching him the peculiar business of any one office or calling, it enables him to act his part in each of them with better grace and more elevated carriage; and, if happily planned and conducted, is a main ingredient in that complete and generous education which fits a man 'to perform justly, skilfully, and magnanimously, all the offices, both private and public, of peace and war.' " [8]

550

8

The view of liberal education, advocated in these extracts, is expanded by Mr. Davison in the Essay to which I have already referred. He lays more stress on the "usefulness" of Liberal Education in the larger sense of the word than his predecessor in the controversy. Instead of arguing that the Utility of knowledge to the individual varies inversely with its Utility to the public, he chiefly employs himself on the suggestions contained in Dr. Copleston's last sentences. He shows, first, that a Liberal Education is something far higher, even in the scale of Utility, than what is commonly called a Useful Education, and next, that it is necessary or useful for the purposes even of that Professional Education which commonly engrosses the title of Useful. The former of these two theses he recommends to us in an argument from which the following passages are selected:—

560

"It is to take a very contracted view of life," he says, "to think with great anxiety how persons may be educated to superior skill in their department, comparatively neglecting or excluding the more liberal and enlarged cultivation. In his

570

8. John Milton, "Of Education."

(Mr. Edgeworth's) system, the value of every attainment is to be measured by its subserviency to a calling. The specific duties of that calling are exalted at the cost of those free and independent tastes and virtues which come in to sustain the common relations of society, and raise the individual in them. In short, a man is to be usurped by his profession. He is to be clothed in its garb from head to foot. His virtues, his science, and his ideas are all to be put into a gown or uniform, and the 580 whole man to be shaped, pressed, and stiffened, in the exact mould of his technical character. Any interloping accomplishments, or a faculty which cannot be taken into public pay, if they are to be indulged in him at all, must creep along under the cloak of his more serviceable privileged merits. Such is the state of perfection to which the spirit and general tendency of this system would lead us.

"But the professional character is not the only one which a person engaged in a profession has to support. He is not always upon duty. There are services he owes, which are neither 590 parochial, nor forensic, nor military, nor to be described by any such epithet of civil regulation, and yet are in no wise inferior to those that bear these authoritative titles; inferior neither in their intrinsic value, nor their moral import, nor their impression upon society. As a friend, as a companion, as a citizen at large; in the connections of domestic life; in the improvement and embellishment of his leisure, he has a sphere of action, revolving, if you please, within the sphere of his profession, but not clashing with it; in which if he can show none of the advantages of an improved understanding, what- 600 ever may be his skill or proficiency in the other, he is no more than an ill-educated man.

"There is a certain faculty in which all nations of any re- finement are great practitioners. It is not taught at school or college as a distinct science; though it deserves that what is taught there should be made to have some reference to it; nor is it endowed at all by the public; everybody being obliged to exercise it for himself in person, which he does to the best of his skill. But in nothing is there a greater difference than in the manner of doing it. The advocates of professional learning will smile when we tell them that this same faculty which we 610 would have encouraged, is simply that of speaking good sense in English, without fee or reward, in common conversation. They will smile when we lay some stress upon it; but in reality it is no such trifle as they imagine. Look into the huts of savages, and see, for there is nothing to listen to, the dismal blank of their stupid hours of silence; their professional avocations of war and hunting are over; and, having nothing to do, they have nothing to say. Turn to improved life, and you find conversation in all its forms the medium of something more than an idle pleasure; indeed, a very active agent in circulating 620 and forming the opinions, tastes, and feelings of a whole people. It makes of itself a considerable affair. Its topics are the most promiscuous—all those which do not belong to any particular province. As for its power and influence, we may fairly say that it is of just the same consequence to a man's immediate society, how he talks, as how he acts. Now of all those who furnish their share to rational conversation, a mere adept in his own art is universally admitted to be the worst. The sterility and uninstructiveness of such a person's social hours are quite proverbial. Or if he escape being dull, it is 630 only by launching into ill-timed, learned loquacity. We do not desire of him lectures or speeches; and he has nothing else to give. Among benches he may be powerful; but seated on a chair he is quite another person. On the other hand, we may affirm, that one of the best companions is a man who, to the accuracy and research of a profession, has joined a free excursive acquaintance with various learning, and caught from it the spirit of general observation."

9

Having thus shown that a liberal education is a real benefit to the subjects of it, as members of society, in the various duties 640 and circumstances and accidents of life, he goes on, in the next place, to show that, over and above those direct services which might fairly be expected of it, it actually subserves the discharge of those particular functions, and the pursuit of those particular advantages, which are connected with profes-sional exertion, and to which Professional Education is directed.

"We admit," he observes, "that when a person makes a busi-ness of one pursuit, he is in the right way to eminence in it;
650 and that divided attention will rarely give excellence in many. But our assent will go no further. For, to think that the way to prepare a person for excelling in any one pursuit (and that is the only point in hand), is to fetter his early studies, and cramp the first development of his mind, by a reference to the exigencies of that pursuit barely, is a very different notion, and one which, we apprehend, deserves to be exploded rather than received. Possibly a few of the abstract, insulated kinds of learning might be approached in that way. The exceptions to be made are very few, and need not be recited. But for the
660 acquisition of professional and practical ability such maxims are death to it. The main ingredients of that ability are requi-site knowledge and cultivated faculties; but, of the two, the latter is by far the chief. A man of well improved faculties has the command of another's knowledge. A man without them, has not the command of his own.

"Of the intellectual powers, the judgment is that which takes the foremost lead in life. How to form it to the two habits it ought to possess, of exactness and vigour, is the problem. It would be ignorant presumption so much as to hint at any
670 routine of method by which these qualities may with certainty be imparted to every or any understanding. Still, however, we may safely lay it down that they are not to be got 'by a gatherer of simples,' but are the combined essence and extracts of many different things, drawn from much varied reading and disci-pline, first, and observation afterwards. For if there be a single intelligible point on this head, it is that a man who has

been trained to think upon one subject or for one subject only, will never be a good judge even in that one: whereas the enlargement of his circle gives him increased knowledge and power in a rapidly increasing ratio. So much do ideas act, not 680 as solitary units, but by grouping and combination; and so clearly do all the things that fall within the proper province of the same faculty of the mind, intertwine with and support each other. Judgment lives as it were by comparison and discrimination. Can it be doubted, then, whether the range and extent of that assemblage of things upon which it is practised in its first essays are of use to its power?

"To open our way a little further on this matter, we will define what we mean by the power of judgment; and then try to ascertain among what kind of studies the improvement of 690 it may be expected at all.

"Judgment does not stand here for a certain homely, useful quality of intellect, that guards a person from committing mistakes to the injury of his fortunes or common reputation; but for that master-principle of business, literature, and talent, which gives him strength in any subject he chooses to grapple with, and enables him to *seize the strong point* in it. Whether this definition be metaphysically correct or not, it comes home to the substance of our inquiry. It describes the power that every one desires to possess when he comes to act in a profes- 700 sion, or elsewhere; and corresponds with our best idea of a cultivated mind.

"Next, it will not be denied, that in order to do any good to the judgment, the mind must be employed upon such subjects as come within the cognizance of that faculty, and give some real exercise to its perceptions. Here we have a rule of selection by which the different parts of learning may be classed for our purpose. Those which belong to the province of the judgment are religion (in its evidences and interpretation), ethics, history, eloquence, poetry, theories of general 710 speculation, the fine arts, and works of wit. Great as the variety of these large divisions of learning may appear, they are all held in union by two capital principles of connexion. First, they are all quarried out of one and the same great subject of man's moral, social, and feeling nature. And secondly, they are all under the control (more or less strict) of the same power of moral reason."

"If these studies," he continues, "be such as give a direct play and exercise to the faculty of the judgment, then they are the true basis of education for the active and inventive powers, whether destined for a profession or any other use. Miscellaneous as the assemblage may appear, of history, eloquence, poetry, ethics, etc., blended together, they will all conspire in an union of effect. They are necessary mutually to explain and interpret each other. The knowledge derived from them all will amalgamate, and the habits of a mind versed and practised in them by turns will join to produce a richer vein of thought and of more general and practical application than could be obtained of any single one, as the fusion of the metals into Corinthian brass gave the artist his most ductile and perfect material. Might we venture to imitate an author (whom indeed it is much safer to take as an authority than to attempt to copy), Lord Bacon, in some of his concise illustrations of the comparative utility of the different studies,[9] we should say that history would give fulness, moral philosophy strength, and poetry elevation to the understanding. Such in reality is the natural force and tendency of the studies; but there are few minds susceptible enough to derive from them any sort of virtue adequate to those high expressions. We must be contented therefore to lower our panegyric to this, that a person cannot avoid receiving some infusion and tincture, at least, of those several qualities, from that course of diversified reading. One thing is unquestionable, that the elements of general reason are not to be found fully and truly expressed in any one kind of study; and that he who would wish to know her idiom, must read it in many books.

9. Bacon, "Of Studies."

"If different studies are useful for aiding, they are still more useful for correcting each other; for as they have their particular merits severally, so they have their defects, and the most extensive acquaintance with one can produce only an 750 intellect either too flashy or too jejune, or infected with some other fault of confined reading. History, for example, shows things as they are, that is, the morals and interests of men disfigured and perverted by all their imperfections of passion, folly, and ambition; philosophy strips the picture too much; poetry adorns it too much; the concentrated lights of the three correct the false peculiar colouring of each, and show us the truth. The right mode of thinking upon it is to be had from them taken all together, as every one must know who has seen their united contributions of thought and feeling expressed in 760 the masculine sentiment of our immortal statesman, Mr. Burke, whose eloquence is inferior only to his more admirable wisdom. If any mind improved like his, is to be our instructor, we must go to the fountain head of things as he did, and study not his works but his method; by the one we may become feeble imitators, by the other arrive at some ability of our own. But, as all biography assures us, he, and every other able thinker, has been formed, not by a parsimonious admeasurement of studies to some definite future object (which is Mr. Edgeworth's maxim), but by taking a wide and liberal com- 770 pass, and thinking a great deal on many subjects with no better end in view than because the exercise was one which made them more rational and intelligent beings."

10

But I must bring these extracts to an end. To-day I have confined myself to saying that that training of the intellect, which is best for the individual himself, best enables him to discharge his duties to society. The Philosopher, indeed, and the man of the world differ in their very notion, but the methods, by which they are respectively formed, are pretty

780 much the same. The Philosopher has the same command of matters of thought, which the true citizen and gentleman has of matters of business and conduct. If then a practical end must be assigned to a University course, I say it is that of training good members of society. Its art is the art of social life, and its end is fitness for the world. It neither confines its views to particular professions on the one hand, nor creates heroes or inspires genius on the other. Works indeed of genius fall under no art; heroic minds come under no rule; a University is not a birthplace of poets or of immortal authors, of

790 founders of schools, leaders of colonies, or conquerors of nations. It does not promise a generation of Aristotles or Newtons, of Napoleons or Washingtons, of Raphaels or Shakespeares, though such miracles of nature it has before now contained within its precincts. Nor is it content on the other hand with forming the critic or the experimentalist, the economist or the engineer, though such too it includes within its scope. But a University training is the great ordinary means to a great but ordinary end; it aims at raising the intellectual tone of society, at cultivating the public mind, at purifying

800 the national taste, at supplying true principles to popular enthusiasm and fixed aims to popular aspiration, at giving enlargement and sobriety to the ideas of the age, at facilitating the exercise of political power, and refining the intercourse of private life. It is the education which gives a man a clear conscious view of his own opinions and judgments, a truth in developing them, an eloquence in expressing them, and a force in urging them. It teaches him to see things as they are, to go right to the point, to disentangle a skein of thought, to detect what is sophistical, and to discard what is irrelevant.

810 It prepares him to fill any post with credit, and to master any subject with facility. It shows him how to accommodate himself to others, how to throw himself into their state of mind, how to bring before them his own, how to influence them, how to come to an understanding with them, how to bear with them. He is at home in any society, he has common

ground with every class; he knows when to speak and when to be silent; he is able to converse, he is able to listen; he can ask a question pertinently, and gain a lesson seasonably, when he has nothing to impart himself; he is ever ready, yet never in the way; he is a pleasant companion, and a comrade you can 820 depend upon; he knows when to be serious and when to trifle, and he has a sure tact which enables him to trifle with gracefulness and to be serious with effect. He has the repose of a mind which lives in itself, while it lives in the world, and which has resources for its happiness at home when it cannot go abroad. He has a gift which serves him in public, and supports him in retirement, without which good fortune is but vulgar, and with which failure and disappointment have a charm. The art which tends to make a man all this, is in the object which it pursues as useful as the art of wealth or the 830 art of health, though it is less susceptible of method, and less tangible, less certain, less complete in its result.

Thomas Jefferson,   LETTER TO BERNARD MOORE
                      REPORT ON THE UNIVERSITY
                         OF VIRGINIA

John Locke,   THOUGHTS ON EDUCATION

1. Why did Jefferson believe that the state should accept responsibility for education of citizens?

2. With which of Jefferson's objectives for a university education do you agree? With which do you disagree? Why?

3. Do Jefferson's objectives for education and for curriculum design appear to support Aristotle's goodness of intellect or his goodness of character?

4. Compare and contrast Jefferson's view of education with Montaigne's.

5. Does Jefferson's theory of education agree more with Locke's or Rousseau's? Explain.

6. How would you react if you received a letter similar to Jefferson's letter to Bernard Moore? Can you figure out any way to find out how Moore reacted to it?

7. What evaluation could you make of Jefferson's view of education as expressed in his letter to Moore?

8. What does Locke consider to be the "end of education"? Elaborate upon this "end".

9. Does Locke consider process or content to be more important to learning?

10. Which would be the child's first books according to Locke? Would Rousseau concur in this selection? Why or why not?

11. Are Rousseau and Locke in agreement as to when the child should begin reading? What do you think? Justify your position.

12. Compare and contrast Rousseau and Locke on relig-
    ious education.

13. Define Locke's concept of "tabula rasa". What are
    the implications for education?

14. Analyze Locke's curriculum. Do you agree with it?
    Why or why not?

    Thomas Jefferson (1743-1826), because of his ex-
ploits as a political leader, is seldom thought of as
an educator. Yet his efforts to create a public school
system in Virginia and his founding of the University
of Virginia, were in his own view among the most significant contributions of his life.

TO BERNARD MOORE

c.1767 [1]

Before you enter on the study of the law a sufficient groundwork must be laid. For this purpose an acquaintance with the Latin and French languages is absolutely necessary. The former you have; the latter must now be acquired. Mathematics and Natural Philosophy are so useful in the most familiar occurrences of life, and are so peculiarly engaging and delightful as would induce everyone to wish an acquaintance with them. Besides this, the faculties of the mind, like the members of the body, are strengthened and improved by exercise. Mathematical reasonings and deductions are therefore a fine preparation for investigating the abstruse speculations of the law. In these and the analogous branches of science the following books are recommended:

Mathematics.—Beyzout, Cours de Mathématiques—the best for a student ever published; Montucla or Bossut, Histoire des Mathématiques.

Astronomy.—Ferguson, and le Monnier or de Lalande.

Geography.—Pinkerton.

Natural Philosophy.—Joyce's Scientific Dialogues; Martin's Philosophia Britannica, Muschenbroek's Cours de Physique.

This foundation being laid, you may enter regularly on the study of the law, taking with it such of its kindred sciences as will contribute to eminence in its attainment. The principal of these are Physics, Ethics, Religion, Natural Law, Belles Lettres, Criticism, Rhetoric, and Oratory. The carrying on several studies at a time is attended with advantage. Variety relieves the mind as well as the eye, palled with too long attention to a single object, but, with both, transitions from one object to another may be so frequent and transitory as to leave no impression. The mean is therefore to be steered, and a competent space of time allotted to each branch of study. Again, a great inequality is observable in the vigor of the mind at different periods of the day. Its powers at these periods should therefore be attended to, in marshalling the business of the day. For these reasons I should recommend the following distribution of your time:

[1] In August, 1814, Jefferson sent this letter to John Minor. "I shall give it to you without change," he wrote, "except as to the books recommended to be read; later publications enabling me in some of the departments of science to substitute better, for the less perfect publications we then possessed. In this the modern student has great advantage." *The Federalist* was one of the works inserted in 1814.

Till Eight o'clock in the morning, employ yourself in Physical Studies

Ethics, Religion, natural and sectarian, and Natural Law, reading the following books:

Agriculture.—Dickson's Husbandry of the Ancients; Tull's Horse-hoeing Husbandry; Lord Kames' Gentleman Farmer; Young's Rural Economy; Hale's Body of Husbandry; De Serres's Théâtre d'Agriculture.

Chemistry.—Lavoisier, Conversations in Chemistry.

Anatomy.—John and James Bell's Anatomy.

Zoology.—Abrégé du Système de la nature de Linné par Gilibert; Manuel d'Histoire Naturelle by Blumenbach, Buffon, including Montbeiliard and La Cepède; Wilson's American Ornithology.

Botany.—Barton's Elements of Botany; Turton's Linneus; Persoon's Synopsis Plantarum.

Ethics and Natural Religion.—Locke's Essay; Locke's Conduct of the Mind in the Search after Truth; Stewart's Philosophy of the Human Mind; Enfield's History of Philosophy; Condorcet, Progrès de l'Esprit Humain; Cicerio de Officiis, Tusculanae, de Senectute, Somnia Scipionis; Senecae Philosophica; Hutchinson's Introduction to Moral Philosophy; Lord Kames' Natural Religion; Traité Elémentaire de Morale et Bonheur; La Sagesse de Charron.

Religion, Sectarian.—Bible: New Testament, Commentaries on them by Middleton in his Works, and by Priestley in his Corruptions of Christianity and Early Opinions of Christ; The Sermons of Sterne, Massillon and Bourdaloue.

Natural Law.—Vattel, Droit des Gens; Rayneval, Institutions du Droit de la Nature et des Gens.

From Eight to Twelve read Law

The general course of this reading may be formed on the following grounds. Lord Coke has given us the first views of the whole body of law worthy now of being studied; for so much of the admirable work of Bracton is now obsolete that the students should turn to it occasionally only, when tracing the history of particular portions of the law. Coke's Institutes are a perfect digest of the law in his day. After this, new laws were added by the Legislature, and new developments of the old law by the judges, until they had become so voluminous as to require a new digest. This was ably executed by Matthew Bacon, although unfortunately under an alphabetical instead of analytical arrangement of matter. The same process of new laws and new decisions on the old laws going on, called at length for the same operation again, and produced the inimitable Commentaries of

Blackstone. In the department of the Chancery, a similar progress has taken place. Lord Kames has given us the first digest of the principles of that branch of our jurisprudence, more valuable for the arrangement of matter than for its exact conformity with the English decisions. The reporters from the early times of that branch to that of the same Matthew Bacon are well digested, but alphabetically also in the abridgement of the cases in equity, the second volume of which is said to be done by him. This was followed by a number of able reporters, of which Fonblanque has given us a summary digest by commentaries on the text of the earlier work, ascribed to Ballow, entitled "A Treatise on Equity." The course of reading recommended then in these two branches of law is the following:

Common Law.—Coke's Institutes; Select Cases from the Subsequent Reporters to the time of Matthew Bacon; Bacon's Abridgment; Select Cases from the Subsequent Reporters to the Present Day; Select Tracts on Law, among which those of Baron Gilbert are all of the first merit; the Virginia Laws; Reports on them.

Chancery.—Lord Kames' Principles of Equity, 3d edition; Select Cases from the Chancery Reporters to the time of Matthew Bacon; the Abridgment of Cases in Equity; Select Cases from the Subsequent Reporters to the Present Day; Fonblanque's Treatise of Equity.

Blackstone's Commentaries (Tucker's edition) as the best perfect digest of both branches of law.

In reading the Reporters, enter in a common-place book every case of value, condensed into the narrowest compass possible, which will admit of presenting distinctly the principles of the case. This operation is doubly useful, insomuch as it obliges the student to seek out the pith of the case, and habituates him to a condensation of thought, and to an acquisition of the most valuable of all talents, that of never using two words where one will do. It fixes the case, too, more indelibly in the mind.

From Twelve to One read Politics

Politics, General.—Locke on Government, Sidney on Government, Priestley's First Principles of Government, Review of Montesquieu's Spirit of Laws. De Lolme sur la constitution d'Angleterre; De Burgh's Political Disquisitions; Hatsell's Precedents of the House of Commons; Select Parliamentary Debates of England and Ireland; Chipman's Sketches of the Principles of Government; The Federalist.

Political Economy.—Say's Economie Politique; Malthus on the Principles of Population; de Tracy's work on Political Economy, now about to be printed, 1814.

In the Afternoon read History

History, Ancient.—The Greek and Latin originals; select histories from the Universal History; Gibbon's Decline of the Roman Empire; Histoire ancienne de Millot.

Modern.—Histoire moderne de Millot; Russel's History of Modern Europe; Robertson's Charles V.

English.—The original historians, *to wit:* The History of Edward 2nd, by E. F.; Habington's Edward 4th; More's Richard 3rd; Lord Bacon's Henry 7th; Lord Herbert's Henry 8th; Goodwin's Henry 8th, Edward 7th, Mary; Camden's Elizabeth, James, Ludlow; Macaulay [Catharine]; Fox; Belsham; Baxter's History of England; Hume republicanized and abridged; Robertson's History of Scotland.

American.—Robertson's History of America; Gordon's History of the Independence of the U.S.; Ramsay's History of the American Revolution; Burk's History of Virginia; Continuation of dº., by Jones and Girardin, nearly ready for the press.

From Dark to Bedtime

Belles Lettres; Criticism; Rhetoric; Oratory, *to wit:*

Belles Lettres.—Read the best of the poets, epic, didactic, dramatic, pastoral, lyric, etc.; but among these, Shakespeare must be singled out by one who wishes to learn the full powers of the English language. Of him we must declare as Horace did of the Grecian models, *"Vos exemplaria Graeca nocturna versate manu, versate diurna."*

Criticism.—Lord Kames' Elements of Criticism; Tooke's Diversions of Purley. Of Bibliographical criticism, the Edinburgh Review furnishes the finest models extant.

Rhetoric.—Blair's Rhetoric; Sheridan on Elocution; Mason on Poetic and Prosaic Numbers.

Oratory.—This portion of time (borrowing some of the afternoon when the days are long and the nights short) is to be applied also to acquiring the art of writing and speaking correctly by the following exercises: Criticize the style of any book whatsoever, committing the criticism to writing. Translate into the different styles, *to wit,* the elevated, the middling, and the familiar. Orators and poets will furnish subjects of the first, historians of the second, and epistolary and comic writers of the third. Undertake, at first, short compositions as themes, letters, etc., paying great attention to the elegance and correctness of your language. Read the orations of Demosthenes and Cicero; analyze these orations, and examine the correctness of the disposition, language, figures, state of the cases, arguments, etc.; read good samples also of English eloquence. Some of these may be found in Small's American Speaker, and some in Carey's Criminal Recorder; in which last the defence of Eugene Aram is distinguished as a model of logic, condensation of matter and classical purity of style. Exercise yourself afterwards in preparing orations on feigned cases. In this, observe rigorously the disposition of Blair into introduction, narration, etc. Adapt your language to the several parts of the oration, and suit your arguments to the audience before which it is supposed to be delivered. This is your last and most important exercise. No trouble should therefore be spared. If you have any person in your neighborhood engaged in the same study, take each of you different sides of the same cause, and prepare pleadings according to the custom of the bar, where the plaintiff opens, the defendant answers, and the plaintiff replies..It will further be of great service to pronounce your oration (having before you only short notes to assist the memory) in the presence of some person who may be considered as your judge.

NOTE.—Under each of the preceding heads, the books are to be read in the order in which they are named. These by no means constitute the whole of what might be usefully read in each of these branches of science. The mass of excellent works going more into detail is great indeed. But those here noted will enable the student to select for himself such others of detail as may suit his particular views and dispositions. They will give him a respectable, an useful and satisfactory degree of knowledge in these branches, and will themselves form a valuable and sufficient library for a lawyer who is at the same time a lover of science.

EXCERPTS FROM THE REPORT TO THE LEGISLATURE OF VIRGINIA RELATIVE TO THE UNIVERSITY OF VIRGINIA[1]

August, 1818

In proceeding to the third and fourth duties prescribed by the Legislature, of reporting "the branches of learning, which should be taught in the University, and the number and description of the professorships they will require," the Commissioners were first to consider at what point it was understood that university education should commence. Certainly not with the alphabet, for reasons of expediency and impractability, as well from the obvious sense of the Legislature, who, in the same act, make other provision for the primary instruction of the poor children, expecting, doubtless, that in other cases it would be provided by the parent, or become, perhaps, subject to future and further attention of the Legislature. The objects of this primary education determine its character and limits. These objects would be,

To give to every citizen the information he needs for the transaction of his own business;

---

[1] The report was written by Jefferson. It appeared originally in the *Analectic Magazine,* vol. XIII (February, 1819), pp. 104-116.

To enable him to calculate for himself, and to express and preserve his ideas, his contracts and accounts, in writing;

To improve, by reading, his morals and faculties;

To understand his duties to his neighbors and country, and to discharge with competence the functions confided to him by either;

To know his rights; to exercise with order and justice those he retains; to choose with discretion the fiduciary of those he delegates; and to notice their conduct with diligence, with candor, and judgment;

And, in general, to observe with intelligence and faithfulness all the social relations under which he shall be placed.

To instruct the mass of our citizens in these, their rights, interests and duties, as men and citizens, being then the objects of education in the primary schools, whether private or public, in them should be taught reading, writing and numerical arithmetic, the elements of mensuration (useful in so many callings), and the outlines of geography and history. And this brings us to the point at which are to commence the higher branches of education, of which the Legislature require the development; those, for example, which are,

To form the statesmen, legislators and judges, on whom public prosperity and individual happiness are so much to depend;

To expound the principles and structure of government, the laws which regulate the intercourse of nations, those formed municipally for our own government, and a sound spirit of legislation, which, banishing all arbitrary and unnecessary restraint on individual action, shall leave us free to do whatever does not violate the equal rights of another;

To harmonize and promote the interests of agriculture, manufactures and commerce, and by well informed views of political economy to give a free scope to the public industry;

To develop the reasoning faculties of our youth, enlarge their minds, cultivate their morals, and instill into them the precepts of virtue and order;

To enlighten them with mathematical and physical sciences, which advance the arts, and administer to the health, the subsistence, and comforts of human life;

And, generally, to form them to habits of reflection and correct action, rendering them examples of virtue to others, and of happiness within themselves.

These are the objects of that higher grade of education, the benefits and blessings of which the Legislature now propose to provide for the good and ornament of their country, the gratification and happiness of their fellow-citizens, of the parent especially, and his progeny, on which all his affections are concentrated.

In entering on this field, the Commissioners are aware that they have to encounter much difference of opinion as to the extent which it is expedient that this institution should occupy. Some good men, and even of respectable information, consider the learned sciences as useless acquirements; some think they do not better the condition of man; and others that education, like private and individual concerns, should be left to private individual effort; not reflecting that an establishment embracing all the sciences which may be useful and even necessary in the various vocations of life, with the buildings and apparatus belonging to each, are far beyond the reach of individual means, and must either derive existence from public patronage, or not exist at all. This would leave us, then, without those callings which depend on education, or send us to other countries to seek the instruction they require. But the Commissioners are happy in considering the statute under which they are assembled as proof that the Legislature is far from the abandonment of objects so interesting. They are sensible that the advantages of well-directed education, moral, political and economical, are truly above all estimate. Education generates habits of application, of order, and the love of virtue; and controls, by the force of habit, any innate obliquities in our moral organization. We should be far, too, from the discouraging persuasion that man is fixed, by the law of his nature, at a given point; that his improvement is a chimera, and the hope delusive of rendering ourselves wiser, happier or better than our forefathers were. As well might it be urged that the wild and uncultivated tree, hitherto yielding sour and bitter fruit only, can never be made to yield better; yet we know that the grafting art implants a new tree on the savage stock, producing what is most estimable both in kind and degree. Education, in like manner, engrafts a new man on the native stock, and improves what in his nature was vicious and perverse into qualities of virtue and social worth. And it cannot be but that each generation succeeding to the knoweldge acquired by all those who preceded it, adding to it their own acquisitions and discoveries, and handing the mass down for successive and constant accumulation, must advance the knowledge and well-being of mankind, not *infinitely,* as some have said, but *indefinitely,* and to a term which no one can fix and foresee. Indeed, we need look back half a century, to times which many now living remember well, and see the wonderful advances in the sciences and arts which have been made within that period. Some of these have rendered the elements themselves subservient to the purposes of man, have harnessed them to the yoke of his labors, and effected the great blessings of moderating his own, of accompanying what was beyond his feeble force, and extending the comforts of life to a much enlarged circle, to those who had before known its necessaries only. That these are not the vain dreams of sanguine hope, we have before our eyes real and living examples. What, but education, has advanced us beyond the condition of our indigenous neighbors? And what chains them to their present state of barbarism and wretchedness, but a bigoted veneration for the supposed superlative wisdom of their fathers, and the preposterous idea that they are to look backward for better things, and not forward, longing, as it should seem, to return to the days of eating acorns and roots, rather than indulgence in the degeneracies of civilization? And how much more encouraging to the achievement of science and improvement is this, than the desponding view that the condition of man cannot be ameliorated, that what has been must ever be, and that to secure ourselves where we are, we must tread with awful reverence in the footsteps of our fathers. This doctrine is the genuine fruit of the alliance between Church and State; the tenants of which, finding themselves but too well in their present condition, oppose all advances which might unmask their usurpations, and monopolies of honors, wealth, and power, and fear every change, as endangering the comforts they now hold. Nor must we omit to mention, among the benefits of education, the incalculable advantage of training up able counsellors to administer the affairs of our country in all its departments, legislative, executive and judiciary, and to bear their proper share in the councils of our national government; nothing more than education advancing the prosperity, the power, and the happiness of a nation.

Encouraged, therefore, by the sentiments of the Legislature, manifested in this statute, we present the following tabular statement of the branches of learning which we think should be taught in the University, forming them into groups, each of which are within the powers of a single professor:

I. Languages, ancient:
    Latin
    Greek
    Hebrew
II. Languages, modern:
    French
    Spanish
    Italian
    German
    Anglo-Saxon
III. Mathematics, pure:
    Algebra
    Fluxions
    Geometry, Elementary
        Transcendental
    Architecture, Military
        Naval
IV. Physico-Mathematics:
    Mechanics

Statics
Dynamics
Pneumatics
Acoustics
Optics
Astronomy
Geography
V. Physics, or Natural Philosophy:
    Chemistry
    Mineralogy
VI. Botany
    Zoology
VII. Anatomy
    Medicine
VIII. Government
    Political Economy
    Law of Nature and Nations
    History, being interwoven
        with Politics and Law

IX. Law, municipal Ethics
X. Idealogy Rhetoric
    General Grammar Belles Lettres and the fine arts.

Some of the terms used in this table being subject to a difference of acceptation, it is proper to define the meaning and comprehension intended to be given them here:

Geometry, Elementary, is that of straight lines and of the circle.
    Transcendental, is that of all other curves; it includes, of course, *Projectiles,* a leading branch of military art.
Military Architecture includes Fortification, another branch of that art.
Statics respect matter generally, in a state of rest, and include Hydrostatics,
   · or the laws of fluids particularly, at rest or in equilibrio.
Dynamics, used as a general term, include
    Dynamics proper, or the laws of *solids* in motion; and
    Hydrodynamics, or Hydraulics, those of *fluids* in motion.
Pneumatics teach the theory or air, its weight, motion, condensation, rarefaction, &c.
Acoustics, or Phonics, the theory of sound.
Optics, the laws of light and vision.
Physics, or Physiology, in a general sense, mean the doctrine of the physical objects of our senses.
Chemistry is meant, with its other usual branches, to comprehend the theory of agriculture.
Mineralogy, in addition to its peculiar subjects, is here understood to embrace what is real in geology.
Ideology is the doctrine of thought.
General Grammar explains the construction of language.

Some articles in this distribution of sciences will need observation. A professor is proposed for ancient languages, the Latin, Greek, and Hebrew, particularly; but these languages being the foundation common to all the sciences, it is difficult to foresee what may be the extent of this school. At the same time, no greater obstruction to industrious study could be proposed than the presence, the intrusions and the noisy turbulence of a multitude of small boys; and if they are to be placed here for the rudiments of the languages, they may be so numerous that its character and value as an University will be merged in those of a Grammar school. It is, therefore, greatly to be wished, that preliminary schools, either on private or public establishment, could be distributed in districts through the State, as preparatory to the entrance of students into the University. The tender age at which his part of education commences, generally about the tenth year, would weigh heavily with parents in sending their sons to a school so distant as the central establishment would be from most of them. Districts of such extent as that every parent should be within a day's journey of his son at school, would be desirable in cases of sickness, and convenient for supplying their ordinary wants, and might be made to lessen sensibly the expense of this part of their education. And where a sparse population would not, within such a compass, furnish subjects sufficient to maintain a school, a competent enlargement of district must, of necessity, there be submitted to. At these district schools or colleges, boys should be rendered able to read the easier authors, Latin and Greek. This would be useful and sufficient for many not intended for an University education. At these, too, might be taught English grammar, the higher branches of numerical arithmetic, the geometry of straight lines and of the circle, the elements of navigation, and geography to a sufficient degree, and thus afford to greater numbers the means of being qualified for the various vocations of life, needing more instruction than merely menial or praedial labor, and the same advantages to youths whose education may have been neglected until too late to lay a foundation in the learned languages. These institutions, intermediate between the primary schools and University, might then be the passage of entrance for youths into the University, where their classical learning might be critically completed, by a study of the authors of highest degree; and it is at this stage only that they should be received at the University. Giving then a portion of their time to a finished knowledge of the Latin and Greek, the rest might be appropriated to the modern languages, or to the commencement of the course of science for which they should be destined. This would generally be about the fifteenth year of their age, when they might go with more safety and contentment to that distance from their parents. Until this preparatory provision shall be made, either the University will be overwhelmed with the grammar school, or a separate establishment, under one or more ushers, for its lower classes, will be advisable, at a mile or two distant from the general one; where, too, may be exercised the stricter government necessary for young boys, but unsuitable for youths arrived at years of discretion.

The considerations which have governed the specification of languages to be taught by the professor of modern languages were, that the French is the language of general intercourse among nations, and as a depository of human science, is unsurpassed by any other language, living or dead; that the Spanish is highly interesting to us, as the language spoken by so great a portion of the inhabitants of our continents, with whom we shall probably have great intercourse ere long, and is that also in which is written the greater part of the earlier history of America. The Italian abounds with works of very superior order, valuable for their matter, and still more distinguished as models of the finest taste in style and composition. And the German now stands in a line with that of the most learned nations in richness and erudtion and advance in the sciences. It is too of common descent with the language of our own country, a branch of the same original Gothic stock, and furnishes valuable illustrations for us. But in this point of view, the Anglo-Saxon is of peculiar value. We have placed it among the modern languages, because it is in fact that which we speak, in the earliest form in which we have knowledge of it. It has been undergoing, with time, those gradual changes which all languages, ancient and modern, have experienced; and even now needs only to be printed in the modern character and orthography to be intelligible, in a considerable degree, to an English reader. It has this value, too, above the Greek and Latin, that while it gives the radix of the mass of our language, they explain its innovations only. Obvious proofs of this have been presented to the modern reader in the disquisitions of Horn Tooke; and Fortescue Aland has well explained the great instruction which may be derived from it to a full understanding of our ancient common law, on which, as a stock, our whole system of law is engrafted. It will form the first link in the chain of an historical review of our language through all its successive changes to the present day, will constitute the foundation of that critical instruction in it which ought to be found in a seminary of general learning, and thus reward amply the few weeks of attention which would alone be requisite for its attainment; a language already fraught with all the eminent science of our parent country, the future vehicle of whatever we may ourselves achieve, and destined to occupy so much space on the globe, claims distinguished attention in American education.

Medicine, where fully taught, is usually subdivided into several professorships, but this cannot well be without the accessory of an hospital, where the student can have the benefit of attending clinical lectures, and of assisting at operations of surgery. With this accessory, the seat of our University is not yet prepared, either by its population or by the numbers of poor who would leave their own houses, and accept of the charities of an hospital. For the present, therefore, we propose but a single professor for both medicine and anatomy. By him the medical science may be taught, with a history and explanations of all its successive theories from Hippocrates to the present day; and anatomy may be fully treated. Vegetable pharmacy will make a part of the botanical course, and mineral and chemical pharmacy of those of mineralogy and chemistry. This degree of medical information is such as the mass of scientific students would wish to possess, as enabling them in their course through life, to estimate with satisfaction the extent and limits of the aid to human life and health, which they may understandingly expect from that art; and constitutes such a foundation for those intended for the profession, that the finishing course of practice at the bedsides of the sick, and at the operations of surgery in a hospital, can neither be long nor expensive. To seek this finishing elsewhere, must therefore be submitted to for a while.

In conformity with the principles of our Constitution, which places all sects of religion on an equal footing, with the jealousies of the different sects in guarding that equality from encroachment and surprise, and with the sentiments of the Legislature in favor of freedom of religion, manifested on former occasions, we have proposed no professor of divinity; and the rather as the proofs of the being of a God, the creator, preserver, and supreme ruler of the universe, the author of all the relations of morality, and of the laws and obligations these infer, will be within the province of the professor of ethics; to which adding the developments of these moral obligations, of those in which all sects agree, with a knowledge of the languages, Hebrew, Greek, and Latin, a basis will be formed common to all sects. Proceeding thus far without offence to the Constitution, we have thought it proper at this point to leave every sect to provide, as they think fittest, the means of further instruction in their own peculiar tenets.

We are further of opinion, that after declaring by law that certain sciences shall be taught in the University, fixing the number of professors they require, which we think should, at present, be ten, limiting (except as to the professors who shall be first engaged in each branch) a maximum for their salaries (which should be a certain but moderate subsistence, to be made up by liberal tuition fees, as an excitement to assiduity), it will be best to leave to the discretion of the visitors, the grouping of these sciences together, according to the accidental qualifications of the professors; and the introduction also of other branches of science, when enabled by private donations, or by public provision, and called for by the increase of population, or other change of circumstances; to establish beginnings, in short, to be developed by time, as those who come after us shall find expedient. They will be more advanced than we are in science and in useful arts, and will know best what will suit the circumstances of their day.

We have proposed no formal provision for the gymnastics of the school, although a proper object of attention for every institution of youth. These exercises with ancient nations, constituted the principal part of the education of their youth. Their arms and mode of warfare rendered them severe in the extreme; ours, on the same correct principle, should be adapted to our arms and warfare; and the manual exercise, military manoeuvres, and tactics generally, should be the frequent exercises of the students, in their hours of recreation. It is at that age of aptness, docility, and emulation of the practices of manhood, that such things are soonest learnt and longest remembered. The use of tools too in the manual arts is worthy of encouragement, by facilitating to such as choose it, an admission into the neighboring workshops. To these should be added the arts which embellish life, dancing, music, and drawing; the last more especially, as an important part of military education. These innocent arts furnish amusement and happiness to those who, having time on their hands, might less inoffensively employ it. Needing, at the same time, no regular incorporation with the institution, they may be left to accessory teachers, who will be paid by the individuals employing them, the University only providing proper apartments for their exercise.

The fifth duty prescribed to the Commissioners, is to propose such general provisions as may be properly enacted by the Legislature, for the better organizing and governing the University.

In the education of youth, provision is to be made for, 1, tuition; 2, diet; 3, lodging; 4, government; and 5, honorary excitements. The first of these constitutes the proper functions of the professors; 2, the dieting of the students should be left to private boarding houses of their own choice, and at their own expense; to be regulated by the Visitors from time to time, the house only being provided by the University within its own precincts, and thereby of course subjected to the general regimen, moral or sumptuary, which they shall prescribe. 3. They should be lodged in dormitories, making a part of the general system of buildings. 4. The best mode of government for youth, in large collections, is certainly a desideratum not yet attained with us. It may be well questioned whether *fear* after a certain age, is a motive to which we should have ordinary recourse. The human character is susceptible of other incitements to correct conduct, more worthy of employ, and of better effect. Pride of character, laudable ambition, and moral dispositions are innate correctives of the indiscretions of that lively age; and when strengthened by habitual appeal and exercise, have a happier effect on future character than the degrading motive of fear. Hardening them to disgrace, to corporal punishments, and servile humiliations cannot be the best process for producing erect character. The affectionate deportment between father and son, offers in truth the best example for that of tutor and pupil; and the experience and practice of other [1] countries, in this respect, may be worthy of enquiry and consideration with us. It will then be for the wisdom and discretion of the Visitors to devise and perfect a proper system of government, which, if it be founded in reason and comity, will be more likely to nourish in the minds of our youth the combined spirit of order and self-respect, so congenial with our political institutions, and so important to be woven into the American character.

[1] A police exercised by the students themselves, under proper discretion, has been tried with success in some countries, and the rather as forming them for initiation into the duties and practices of civil life.—T. J.

John Locke (1632-1704) was born in Wrington, England, educated at Oxford University, and later studied medicine. He has sometimes been called the intellectual ruler of the 18th century for his educational, political, philosophical, and psychological theories which widely influenced the thinkers of his day - and are still generally considered to be significant.

SOME THOUGHTS
CONCERNING EDUCATION

§ 1.   **A** SOUND mind in a sound body, is a short, but full description of a happy state in this world. He that has these two, has little more to wish for; and he that wants either of them, will be but little the better for any thing else. Men's happiness or misery is most part of their own making. He, whose mind directs not wisely, will never take the right way; and he, whose body is crazy and feeble, will never be able to advance in it. I confess, there are some men's constitutions of body and mind so vigorous, and well fram'd by nature, that they need not much assistance from others; but by the strength of their natural genius, they are from their cradles carried towards what is excellent; and by the privilege of their happy constitutions, are able to do wonders. But examples of this kind are but few; and I think I may say, that of all the men we meet with, nine parts of ten are what they are, good or evil, useful or not, by their education. 'Tis that which makes the great difference in mankind. The little, or almost insensible impressions on our tender infancies, have very important and lasting consequences: and there 'tis, as in the fountains of some rivers, where a gentle application of the hand turns the flexible waters in channels, that make them take quite contrary courses; and by this direction given them at first in the source, they receive different tendencies, and arrive at last at very remote and distant places.

§ 2. I imagine the minds of children as easily turn'd this or that way, as water it self: and though this be the principal part, and our main care should be about the inside, yet the clay-cottage is not to be neglected. I shall therefore begin with the case, and consider first the *health* of the body, as that which perhaps you may rather expect from that study I have been thought more peculiarly to have apply'd my self to; and that also which will be soonest dispatch'd, as lying, if I guess not amiss, in a very little compass.

§ 3. How necessary *health* is to our business and happiness; and how requisite a strong constitution, able to endure hardships and fatigue, is to one that will make any figure in the world, is too obvious to need any proof.

§ 4. The consideration I shall here have of *health,* shall be, not what a physician ought to do with a sick and crazy child; but what the parents, without the help of physick, should do for the *preservation and improvement of an healthy,* or at least *not sickly constitution* in their children. And this perhaps might be all dispatch'd in this one short rule, *viz.* That gentlemen should use their children, as the honest farmers and substantial yeomen do theirs. But because the mothers possibly may think this a little too hard, and the fathers too short, I shall explain my self more particularly; only laying down this as a general and certain observation for the women to consider, *viz.* That most children's constitutions are either spoil'd, or at least harm'd, by *cockering* and *tenderness.*

§ 5. The first thing to be taken care of, is, that children be not too *warmly clad or cover'd,* winter or summer. The face when we are born, is no less tender than any other part of the body. 'Tis use alone hardens it, and makes it more able to endure the cold. And therefore the *Scythian* philosopher gave a very significant answer to the *Athenian,* who wonder'd how he could go naked in frost and snow. *How,* said the *Scythian, can you endure your face expos'd to the sharp winter air? My face is us'd to it,* said the *Athenian. Think me all face,* reply'd the *Scythian.* Our bodies will endure any thing, that from the beginning they are accustom'd to.

§ 31. Due care being had to keep the body in strength and vigour, so that it may be able to obey and execute the orders of the *mind;* the next and principal business is, to set the *mind* right, that on all occasions it may be dispos'd to consent to nothing but what may be suitable to the dignity and excellency of a rational creature.

§ 32. If what I have said in the beginning of this discourse be true, as I do not doubt but it is, *viz.* That the difference to be found in the manners and abilities of men is owing more to their *education* than to any thing else, we have reason to conclude, that great care is to be had of the forming children's *minds,* and giving them that seasoning early, which shall influence their lives always after: For when they do well or ill, the praise and blame will be laid there; and when any thing is done awkwardly, the common saying will pass upon them, that it's suitable to their *breeding.*

§ 33. As the strength of the body lies chiefly in being able to endure hardships, so also does that of the mind. And the great principle and foundation of all virtue and worth is plac'd in this: that a man is able to *deny himself* his own desires, cross his own inclinations, and purely follow what reason directs as best, tho' the appetite lean the other way.

§ 34. The great mistake I have observ'd in people's breeding their children, has been, that this has not been taken care enough of in its *due season:* that the mind has not been made obedient to discipline, and pliant to reason, when at first it was most tender, most easy to be bow'd. Parents being wisely ordain'd by nature to love their children, are very apt, if reason watch not that natural affection very warily, are apt, I say, to let it run into fondness. They love their little ones and it is their duty; but they often, with them, cherish their faults too. They must not be cross'd, forsooth; they must be permitted to have their wills in all things; and they being in their infancies not capable of great vices, their parents think they may safe enough indulge their irregularities, and make themselves sport with that pretty perverseness which they think well enough becomes that innocent age. But to a fond parent, that would not have his child corrected for a perverse trick, but excus'd it, saying it was a small matter, *Solon* very well reply'd, *aye, but custom is a great one.*

§ 47. The usual lazy and short way by chastisement and the rod, which is the only instrument of government that tutors generally know, or ever think of, is the most unfit of any to be us'd in education, because it tends to both those mischiefs; which, as we have shewn, are the *Scylla* and *Charybdis,* which on the one hand or the other ruin all that miscarry.

§ 48. 1. This kind of punishment contributes not at all to the mastery of our natural propensity to indulge corporal and present pleasure, and to avoid pain at any rate, but rather encourages it, and thereby strengthens that in us, which is the root from whence spring all vicious actions, and the irregularities of life. For what other motive, but of sensual pleasure and pain, does a child act by, who drudges at his book against his inclination, or abstains from eating unwholesome fruit, that he takes pleasure in, only out of fear of *whipping?* He in this only prefers the greater *corporal pleasure,* or avoids the greater *corporal pain.* And what is it, to govern his actions, and direct his conduct by such motives as these? What is it, I say, but to cherish that principle in him, which it is our business to root out and destroy? And therefore I cannot think any correction useful to a child, where the shame of suffering for having done amiss, does not work more upon him than the pain.

§ 49. 2. This sort of correction naturally breeds an aversion to that which 'tis the tutor's business to create a liking to. How obvious is it to observe, that children come to hate things which were at first acceptable to them, when they find themselves *whipp'd,* and *chid,* and teas'd about them? And it is not to be wonder'd at in them, when grown men would not be able to be reconcil'd to any thing by such ways. Who is there that would not be disgusted with any innocent recreation, in itself indifferent to him, if he should with *blows* or ill language be *haled* to it, when he had no mind? Or be constantly so treated, for some circumstances in his application to it? This is natural to be so. Offensive circumstances ordinarily infect innocent things which they are join'd with; and the very sight of a cup wherein any one uses to take nauseous physick, turns his stomach, so that nothing will relish well out of it, tho' the cup be never so clean and well-shap'd, and of the richest materials.

§ 50. 3. Such a sort of *slavish discipline* makes a *slavish temper.*

The child submits, and dissembles obedience, whilst the fear of the rod hangs over him; but when that is remov'd, and by being out of sight, he can promise himself impunity, he gives the greater scope to his natural inclination; which by this way is not at all alter'd, but, on the contrary, heighten'd and increas'd in him; and after such restraint, breaks out usually with the more violence; or,

§ 51. 4. If *severity* carry'd to the highest pitch does prevail, and works a cure upon the present unruly distemper, it often brings in the room of it a worse and more dangerous disease, by breaking the mind; and then, in the place of a disorderly young fellow, you have a *low spirited moap'd* creature, who, however with his unnatural sobriety he may please silly people, who commend tame unactive children, because they make no noise, nor give them any trouble; yet at last, will probably prove as uncomfortable a thing to his friends, as he will be all his life an useless thing to himself and others.

§ 52. Beating them, and all other sorts of slavish and corporal punishments, are not the discipline fit to be used in the education of those we would have wise, good, and ingenuous men; and therefore very rarely to be apply'd, and that only in great occasions, and cases of extremity. On the other side, to flatter children by *rewards* of things that are pleasant to them, is as carefully to be avoided. He that will give to his son *apples* or *sugar-plumbs,* or what else of this kind he is most delighted with, to make him learn his book, does but authorize his love of pleasure, and cocker up that dangerous propensity, which he ought by all means to subdue and stifle in him. You can never hope to teach him to master it, whilst you compound for the check you gave his inclination in one place, by the satisfaction you propose to it in another. To make a good, a wise, and a virtuous man, 'tis fit he should learn to cross his appetite, and deny his inclination to *riches, finery,* or *pleasing his palate,* &c. whenever his reason advises the contrary, and his duty requires it. But when you draw him to do any thing that is fit by the offer of *money,* or reward the pains of learning his book by the pleasure of a luscious morsel; when you promise him a *lace-cravat* or a *fine new suit,* upon performance of some of his little tasks; what do you by proposing these as *rewards,* but allow them to be the good things he should aim at, and thereby encourage his longing for 'em, and accustom him to place his happiness in them? Thus people, to prevail with children to be industrious about their grammar, dancing, or some other such matter, of no great moment to the happiness or usefulness of their lives, by misapply'd *rewards* and *punishments,* sacrifice their virtue, invert the order of their education, and teach them luxury, pride, or covetousness, &c. For in this way, flattering those wrong inclinations which they should restrain and suppress, they lay the foundations of those future vices, which cannot be avoided but by curbing our desires and accustoming them early to submit to reason.

§ 53. I say not this, that I would have children kept from the conveniences or pleasures of life, that are not injurious to their health or virtue. On the contrary, I would have their lives made as pleasant and as agreeable to them as may be, in a plentiful enjoyment of whatsoever might innocently delight them; provided it be with this caution, that they have those enjoyments, only as the consequences of the state of esteem and acceptation they are in with their parents and governors; but they should never be offer'd or bestow'd on them, as the *rewards of this or that particular performance,* that they shew an aversion to, or to which they would not have apply'd themselves without that temptation.

§ 54. But if you take away the rod on one hand, and these little encouragements which they are taken with, on the other, how then (will you say) shall children be govern'd? Remove hope and fear, and there is an end of all discipline. I grant that good and evil, *reward* and *punishment,* are the only motives to a rational creature: these are the spur and reins whereby all mankind are set on work, and guided, and therefore they are to be made use of to children too. For I advise their parents and governors always to carry this in their minds, that children are to be treated as rational creatures.

§ 55. *Rewards,* I grant, and *punishments* must be proposed to children, if we intend to work upon them. The mistake I imagine is, that those that are generally made use of, are *ill chosen.* The pains and pleasures of the body are, I think, of ill consequence, when made the rewards and punishments whereby men would prevail on their children; for, as I said before, they serve but to increase and strengthen those inclinations, which 'tis our business to subdue and master. What principle of virtue do you lay in a child, if you will redeem his desires of one pleasure, by the proposal of another? This is but to enlarge his appetite, and instruct it to wander. If a child cries for an unwholesome and dangerous fruit, you purchase his quiet by giving him a less hurtful sweet-meat. This perhaps may preserve his health, but spoils his mind, and sets that farther out of order. For here you only change the object, but flatter still his *appetite,* and allow that must be satisfy'd, wherein, as I have shew'd, lies the root of the mischief; and till you bring him to be able to bear a denial of that satisfaction, the child may at present be quiet and orderly, but the disease is not cured. By this way of proceeding, you foment and cherish in him that which is the spring from whence all the evil flows, which will be sure on the next occasion to break out again with more violence, give him stronger longings, and you more trouble.

§ 56. The *rewards* and *punishments* then, whereby we should keep children in order, are quite of another kind, and of that force, that when we can get them once to work, the business, I think, is done, and the difficulty is over. *Esteem* and *disgrace* are, of all others, the most powerful incentives to the mind, when once it is brought to relish them. If you can once get into children a love of credit, and an apprehension of shame and disgrace, you have put into 'em the true principle, which will constantly work and incline them to the right. But it will be ask'd, How shall this be done?

I confess it does not at first appearance want some difficulty; but yet I think it worth our while to seek the ways (and practise them when found) to attain this, which I look on as the great secret of education.

§ 57. *First,* children (earlier perhaps than we think) are very sensible of *praise* and commendation. They find a pleasure in being esteem'd and valu'd, especially by their parents and those whom they depend on. If therefore the father *caress and commend them when they do well, shew a cold and neglectful countenance to them upon doing ill,* and this accompany'd by a like carriage of the mother and all others that are about them, it will, in a little time, make them sensible of the difference; and this, if constantly observ'd, I doubt not but will of itself work more than threats or blows, which lose their force when once grown common, and are of no use when shame does not attend them; and therefore are to be forborne, and never to be us'd, but in the case hereafter-mention'd, when it is brought to extremity.

§ 58. But *secondly,* to make the sense of *esteem* or *disgrace* sink the deeper, and be of the more weight, *other agreeable or disagreeable things should constantly accompany these different states;* not as particular rewards and punishments of this or that particular action, but as necessarily belonging to, and constantly attending one, who by his carriage has brought himself into a state of disgrace or commendation. By which way of treating them, children may as much as possible be brought to conceive, that those that are commended, and in esteem for doing well, will necessarily be belov'd and cherish'd by every body, and have all other good things as a consequence of it; and on the other side, when any one by miscarriage falls into disesteem, and cares not to preserve his credit, he will unavoidably fall under neglect and contempt; and in that state, the want of whatever might satisfy or delight him will follow. In this way the objects of their desires are made assisting to virtue, when a settled experience from the beginning teaches children that the things they delight in, belong to, and are to be enjoy'd by those only who are in a state of reputation. If by these means you can come once to shame them out of their faults, (for besides that, I would willingly have no punishment) and make them in love with the pleasure of being well thought on, you may turn them as you please, and they will be in love with all the ways of virtue.

§ 59. The great difficulty here is, I imagine, from the folly and perverseness of servants, who are hardly to be hinder'd from crossing herein the design of the father and mother. Children discountenanc'd by their parents for any fault, find usually a refuge and relief in the caresses of those foolish flatterers, who thereby undo whatever the parents endeavour to establish. When the father or mother looks sowre on the child, everybody else should put on the same coldness to him, and nobody give him countenance, 'till forgiveness ask'd, and a reformation of his fault has set him right again, and restor'd him to his former credit.

§ 147. You will wonder, perhaps, that I put *learning* last, especially if I tell you I think it the least part. This may seem strange in the mouth of a bookish man; and this making usually the chief, if not only bustle and stir about children, this being almost that alone which is thought on, when people talk of education, makes it the greater paradox. When I consider, what ado is made about a little *Latin* and *Greek,* how many years are spent in it, and what a noise and business it makes to no purpose, I can hardly forbear thinking that the parents of children still live in fear of the school-master's rod, which they look on as the only instrument of education; as a language or two to be its whole business. How else is it possible that a child should be chain'd to the oar seven, eight, or ten of the best years of his life, to get a language or two, which, I think, might be had at a great deal cheaper rate of pains and time, and be learn'd almost in playing?

Forgive me therefore if I say, I cannot with patience think, that a young gentleman should be put into the herd, and be driven with a whip and scourge, as if he were to run the gantlet through the several classes, *ad capiendum ingenii cultum*. What then? say you, would you not have him write and read? Shall he be more ignorant than the clerk of our parish, who takes *Hopkins* and *Sternhold* for the best poets in the world, whom yet he makes worse than they are by his ill reading? Not so, not so fast, I beseech you. Reading and writing and *learning* I allow to be necessary, but yet not the chief business. I imagine you would think him a very foolish fellow, that should not value a virtuous or a wise man infinitely before a great scholar. Not but that I think *learning* a great help to both in well-dispos'd minds; but yet it must be confess'd also, that in others not so dispos'd, it helps them only to be the more foolish, or worse men. I say this, that when you consider the breeding of your son, and are looking out for a school-master or a tutor, you would not have (as is usual) Latin and *logick* only in your thoughts. *Learning* must be had, but in the second place, as subservient only to greater qualities. Seek out somebody that may know how discreetly to frame his manners: place him in hands where you may, as much as possible, secure his innocence, cherish and nurse up the good, and gently correct and weed out any bad inclinations, and settle in him good habits. This is the main point, and this being provided for, *learning* may be had into the bargain, and that, as I think, at a very easy rate, by methods that may be thought on.

§ 148. When he can talk, 'tis time he should begin to *learn to read*. But as to this, give me leave here to inculcate again, what is very apt to be forgotten, *viz*. That great care is to be taken, that it be never made as a business to him, nor he look on it as a task. We naturally, as I said, even from our cradles, love liberty, and have therefore an aversion to many things for no other reason but because they are enjoin'd us. I have always had a fancy that *learning* might be made a play and recreation to children: and that they might be brought to desire to be taught, if it were proposed to them as a thing of honour, credit, delight, and recreation, or as a reward for doing something else; and if they were never chid or corrected for the neglect of it. That which confirms me in this opinion is, that amongst the *Portuguese,* 'tis so much a fashion and emulation amongst their children, to *learn to read* and write, that they cannot hinder them from it: they will learn it one from another, and are as intent on it, as if it were forbidden them. I remember that being at a friend's house, whose younger son, a child in coats, was not easily *brought* to his book (being taught *to read* at home by his mother) I advised to try another way, than requiring it of him as his duty; we therefore, in a discourse on purpose amongst our selves, in his hearing, but without taking any notice of him, declared, that it was the privilege and advantage of heirs and elder brothers, to be scholars; that this made them fine gentlemen, and beloved by every body: and that for younger brothers, 'twas a favour to admit them to breeding; to be taught to *read* and write, was more than came to their share; they might be ignorant bumpkins and clowns, if they pleased. This so wrought upon the child, that afterwards he desired to be taught; would come himself to his mother to *learn,* and would not let his maid be quiet till she heard him his lesson. I doubt not but some way like this might be taken with other children; and when their tempers are found, some thoughts be instill'd into them, that might set them upon desiring of *learning,* themselves, and make them seek it as another sort of play or recreation. But then, as I said before, it must never be imposed as a task, nor made a trouble to them. There may be dice and play-things, with the letters on them to teach children the *alphabet* by playing; and twenty other ways may be found, suitable to their particular tempers, to make this kind of *learning a sport* to them.

§ 149. Thus children may be cozen'd into a knowledge of the letters; be *taught to read,* without perceiving it to be any thing but a sport, and play themselves into that which others are whipp'd for. Children should not have any thing like work, or serious, laid on them; neither their minds, nor bodies will bear it. It injures their healths; and their being forced and tied down to their books in an age at enmity with all such restraint, has, I doubt not, been the reason, why a great many have hated books and learning all their lives after. 'Tis like a surfeit, that leaves an aversion behind not to be removed.

§ 150. I have therefore thought, that if *play-things* were fitted to this purpose, as they are usually to none, contrivances might be made to *teach children to read,* whilst they thought they were only playing. For example, what if an *ivory-ball* were made like that of the royal-oak lottery, with thirty two sides, or one rather of twenty four or twenty five sides; and upon several of those sides pasted on an A, upon several others B, on others C, and on others D? I would have you begin with but these four letters, or perhaps only two at first; and when he is perfect in them, then add another; and so on till each side having one letter, there be on it the whole alphabet. This I would have others play with before him, it being as good a sort of play to lay a stake who shall first throw an A or B, as who upon dice shall throw six or seven. This being a play amongst you, tempt him not to it, lest you make it business; for I would not have him understand 'tis any thing but a play of older people, and I doubt not but he will take to it of himself. And that he may have the more reason to think it is a play, that he is sometimes in favour admitted to, when the play is done the ball should be laid up safe out of his reach, that so it may not, by his having it in his keeping at any time, grow stale to him.

§ 151. To keep up his eagerness to it, let him think it a game belonging to those above him: and when, by this means, he knows the letters, by changing them into syllables, he may *learn to read,* without knowing how he did so, and never have any chiding or trouble about it, nor fall out with books because of the hard usage and vexation they have caus'd him. Children, if you observe them, take abundance of pains to learn several games, which, if they should be enjoined them, they would abhor as a task and business. I know a person of great quality (more yet to be honoured for his learning and virtue than for his rank and high place) who by pasting on the six vowels (for in our language Y is one) on the six sides of a die, and the remaining eighteen consonants on the sides of three other dice, has made this a play for his children, that he shall win who, at one cast, throws most words on these four dice; whereby his eldest son, yet in coats, has *play'd* himself *into spelling,* with great eagerness, and without once having been chid for it or forced to it.

§ 152. I have seen little girls exercise whole hours together and take abundance of pains to be expert at *dibstones* as they call it. Whilst I have been looking on, I have thought it wanted only some good contrivance to make them employ all that industry about something that might be more useful to them; and methinks 'tis only the fault and negligence of elder people that it is not so. Children are much less apt to be idle than men; and men are to be blamed if some part of that busy humour be not turned to useful things; which might be made usually as delightful to them as those they are employed in, if men would be but half so forward to lead the way, as these little apes would be to follow. I imagine some wise *Portuguese* heretofore began this fashion amongst the children of his country, where I have been told, as I said, it is impossible to hinder the children from *learning to read and write:* and in some parts of *France* they teach one another to sing and dance from the cradle.

§ 153. The *letters* pasted upon the sides of the dice, or polygon, were best to be of the size of those of the folio Bible, to begin with, and none of them capital letters; when once he can read what is printed in such letters, he will not long be ignorant of the great ones: and in the beginning he should not be perplexed with variety. With this die also, you might have a play just like the royal oak, which would be another variety, and play for cherries or apples, &c.

§ 154. Besides these, twenty other plays might be invented depending on *letters,* which those who like this way, may easily contrive and get made to this use if they will. But the four dice abovemention'd I think so easy and useful, that it will be hard to find any better, and there will be scarce need of any other.

§ 155. Thus much for *learning to read,* which let him never be driven to, nor chid for; cheat him into it if you can, but make it not a business for him. 'Tis better it be a year later *before he can read,* than that he should this way get an aversion to learning. If you have any contest with him, let it be in matters of moment, of truth, and good nature; but lay no task on him about A B C. Use your skill to make his will supple and pliant to reason: teach him to love credit and commendation; to abhor being thought ill or meanly of, especially by you and his mother, and then the rest will come all easily. But I think if you will do that, you must not shackle and tie him up with rules about indifferent matters, nor rebuke him for every little fault, or perhaps some that to others would seem great ones; but of this I have said enough already.

§ 156. When by these gentle ways he begins to *read,* some easy pleasant book, suited to his capacity, should be put into his hands, wherein the entertainment that he finds might draw him on, and reward his pains in reading, and yet not such as should fill his head with perfectly useless trumpery, or lay the principles of vice and folly. To this purpose, I think *Æsop's Fables* the best, which being stories apt to delight and entertain a child, may yet afford useful reflections to a grown man; and if his memory retain them all his life after, he will not repent to find them there, amongst his manly thoughts and serious business. If his *Æsop* has *pictures* in it, it will entertain him much the better, and encourage him to read, when it carries the increase of knowledge with it: for such visible objects children hear talked of in vain and without any satisfaction whilst they have no ideas of them; those ideas being not to be had from sounds, but from the things themselves or their pictures. And therefore I think as soon as he begins to spell, as many pictures of animals should be got him as can be found, with the printed names to them, which at the same time will invite him to read, and afford him matter of enquiry and knowledge. *Reynard the Fox* is another book I think may be made use of to the same purpose. And if those about him will talk to him often about the stories he has read, and hear him tell them, it will, besides other advantages, add encouragement and delight to his *reading,* when he finds there is some use and pleasure in it. These baits seem wholly neglected in the ordinary method; and 'tis usually long before learners find any use or pleasure in reading, which may tempt them to it, and so take books only for fashionable amusements, or impertinent troubles, good for nothing.

§ 157. The Lord's Prayer, the Creeds, and Ten Commandments, 'tis necessary he should learn perfectly by heart; but, I think, not by reading them himself in his primer, but by somebody's repeating them to him, even before he can read. But learning by heart, and *learning to read,* should not I think be mix'd, and so one made to clog the other. But his *learning to read* should be made as little trouble or business to him as might be.

What other books there are in *English* of the kind of those above-mentioned, fit to engage the liking of children, and tempt them to *read,* I do not know: but am apt to think, that children being generally delivered over to the method of schools, where the fear of the rod is to inforce, and not any pleasure of the employment to invite them to learn, this sort of useful books, amongst the number of silly ones that are of all sorts, have yet had the fate to be neglected; and nothing that I know has been considered of this kind out of the ordinary road of the horn-book, primer, psalter, Testament, and Bible.

§ 158. As for the *Bible,* which children are usually employ'd in to exercise and improve their talent *in reading,* I think the promiscuous reading of it through by chapters as they lie in order, is so far from being of any advantage to children, either for the perfecting their *reading,* or principling their religion, that perhaps a worse could not be found. For what pleasure or encouragement can it be to a child to exercise himself in reading those parts of a book where he understands nothing? And how little are the law of *Moses,* the song of *Solomon,* the prophecies in the Old, and the Epistles and *Apocalypse* in the New Testament, suited to a child's capacity? And though the history of the Evangelists and the *Acts* have something easier, yet, taken altogether, it is very disproportional to the understanding of childhood. I grant that the principles of religion are to be drawn from thence, and in the words of the scripture; yet none should be propos'd to a child, but such as are suited to a child's capacity and notions. But 'tis far from this to read through *the whole Bible,* and that for reading's sake. And what an odd jumble of thoughts must a child have in his head, if he have any at all, such as he should have concerning religion, who in his tender age reads all the parts of the *Bible* indifferently as the word of God without any other distinction! I am apt to think, that this in some men has been the very reason why they never had clear and distinct thoughts of it all their lifetime.

§ 159. And now I am by chance fallen on this subject, give me leave to say, that there are some parts of the *Scripture* which may be proper to be put into the hands of a child to engage him to read; such as are the story of *Joseph* and his brethren, of *David* and *Goliath,* of *David* and *Jonathan,* &c. and others that he should be made to read for his instruction, as that, *What you would have others do unto you, do you the same unto them;* and such other easy and plain moral rules, which being fitly chosen, might often be made use of, both for reading and instruction together; and so often read till they are throughly fixed in the memory; and then afterwards, as he grows ripe for them, may in their turns on fit occasions be inculcated as the standing and sacred rules of his life and actions. But the reading of the whole Scripture indifferently, is what I think very inconvenient for children, till after having been made acquainted with the plainest fundamental parts of it, they have got some kind of general view of what they ought principally to believe and practise; which yet, I think, they ought to receive in the very words of the scripture, and not in such as men prepossess'd by systems and analogies are apt in this case to make use of and force upon them. Dr. *Worthington,* to avoid this, has made a catechism, which has all its answers in the precise words of the Scripture; a thing of good example, and such a sound form of words as no Christian can except against as not fit for his child to learn. Of this, as soon as he can say the Lord's Prayer, Creed, the Ten Commandments, by heart, it may be fit for him to learn a question every day, or every week, as his understanding is able to receive and his memory to retain them. And when he has this catechism perfectly by heart, so as readily and roundly to answer to any question in the whole book, it may be convenient to lodge in his mind the remaining moral rules scatter'd up and down in the Bible, as the best *exercise of his memory,* and that which may be always a rule to him, ready at hand, in the whole conduct of his life.

§ 160. When he can read *English* well, it will be seasonable to enter him in *writing:* and here the first thing should be taught him is to *hold his pen right;* and this he should be perfect in before he should be suffered to put it to paper: For not only children but any body else that would do any thing well, should never be put upon too much of it at once, or be set to perfect themselves in two parts of an action at the same time, if they can possibly be separated. I think the *Italian* way of holding the pen between the thumb and the fore-finger alone, may be best; but in this you may consult some good writing-master, or any other person who writes well and quick. When he has learn'd to hold his pen right, in the next place he should learn how to *lay his paper, and place his arm and body to it.* These practices being got over, the way to teach him to write without much trouble, is to get a plate graved with the characters of such a hand as you like best: but you must remember to have them a pretty deal bigger than he should ordinarily write; for every one naturally comes by degrees to write a less hand than he at first was taught, but never a bigger. Such a plate being graved, let several sheets of good writ-ing-paper be printed off with red ink, which he has nothing to do but go over with a good pen fill'd with black ink, which will quickly bring his hand to the formation of those characters, being at first shewed where to begin, and how to form every letter. And when he can do that well, he must then exercise on fair paper; and so may easily be brought to write the hand you desire.

§ 161. When he can write well and quick, I think it may be convenient not only to continue the exercise of his hand in writing, but also to improve the use of it farther in *drawing;* a thing very useful to a gentleman in several occasions; but especially if he travel, as that which helps a man often to express, in a few lines well put together, what a whole sheet of paper in writing would not be able to represent and make intelligible. How many buildings may a man see, how many machines and habits meet with, the ideas whereof would be easily retain'd and communicated by a little skill in *drawing;* which being committed to words, are in danger to be lost, or at best but ill retained in the most exact descriptions? I do not mean that I would have your son a *perfect painter;* to be that to any tolerable degree, will require more time than a young gentleman can spare from his other improvements of greater moment. But so much insight into *perspective* and skill in *drawing,* as will enable him to represent tolerably on paper any thing he sees, except faces, may, I think, be got in a little time, especially if he have a genius to it; but where that is wanting, unless it be in the things absolutely necessary, it is better to let him pass them by quietly, than to vex him about them to no purpose: and therefore in this, as in all other things not absolutely necessary, the rule holds, *nil invita Minerva.*

¶ 1. *Short-hand,* an art, as I have been told, known only in *England,* may perhaps be thought worth the learning, both for dispatch in what men write for their own memory, and concealment of what they would not have lie open to every eye. For he that has once learn'd any sort of character, may easily vary it to his own private use or fancy, and with more contraction suit it to the business he would employ it in. Mr. *Rich's,* the best contriv'd of any I have seen, may, as I think, by one who knows and considers grammar well, be made much easier and shorter. But for the learning this compendious way of writing, there will be no need hastily to look out a master; it will be early enough when any convenient opportunity offers itself at any time, after his hand is well settled in fair and quick writing. For boys have but little use of *short hand,* and should by no means practise it till they write perfectly well, and have throughly fixed the habit of doing so.

§ 162. As soon as he can speak *English,* 'tis time for him to learn some other language. This no body doubts of, when *French* is propos'd. And the reason is, because people are accustomed to the right way of teaching that language, which is by talking it into children in constant conversation, and not by grammatical rules. The *Latin* tongue would easily be taught the same way, if his tutor, being constantly with him, would talk nothing else to him, and make him answer still in the same language. But because *French* is a living language, and to be used more in speaking, that should be first learned, that the yet pliant organs of speech might be accustomed to a due formation of those sounds, and he get the habit of pronouncing *French* well, which is the harder to be done the longer it is delay'd.

§ 163. When he can speak and read *French* well, which in this method is usually in a year or two, he should proceed to *Latin,* which 'tis a wonder parents, when they have had the experiment in *French,* should not think ought to be learned the same way, by talking and reading. Only care is to be taken whilst he is learning these foreign languages, by speaking and reading nothing else with his tutor, that he do not forget to read *English,* which may be preserved by his mother or some body else hearing him read some chosen parts of the scripture or other *English* book every day.

§ 164. *Latin* I look upon as absolutely necessary to a gentleman; and indeed custom, which prevails over every thing, has made it so much a part of education, that even those children are whipp'd to it, and made spend many hours of their precious time uneasily in *Latin,* who after they are once gone from school, are never to have more to do with it as long as they live. Can there be any thing more ridiculous, than that a father should waste his own money and his son's time in setting him to learn the *Roman language,* when at the same time he designs him for a trade, wherein he having no use of *Latin,* fails not to forget that little which he brought from school, and which 'tis ten to one he abhors for the ill usage it procured him? Could it be believed, unless we had every where amongst us examples of it, that a child should be forced to learn the rudiments of a language which he is never to use in the course of life that he is designed to, and neglect all the while the writing a good hand and casting accounts, which are of great advantage in all conditions of life, and to most trades indispensably necessary? But though these qualifications, requisite to trade and commerce and the business of the world, are seldom or never to be had at grammar-schools, yet thither not only gentlemen send their younger sons, intended for trades, but even tradesmen and farmers fail not to send their children, though they have neither intention nor ability to make them scholars. If you ask them why they do this, they think it as strange a question as if you should ask them, why they go to church. Custom serves for reason, and has, to those who take it for reason, so consecrated this method, that it is almost religiously observed by them, and they stick to it, as if their children had scarce an orthodox education unless they learned *Lilly's* grammar.

§ 165. But how necessary soever *Latin* be to some, and is thought to be to others to whom it is of no manner of use and service; yet the ordinary way of learning it in a grammar-school is that which having had thoughts about I cannot be forward to encourage. The reasons against it are so evident and cogent, that they have prevailed with some intelligent persons to quit the ordinary road, not without success, though the method made use of was not exactly what I imagine the easiest, and in short is this. To trouble the child with no *grammar* at all, but to have *Latin,* as *English* has been, without the perplexity of rules, talked into him; for if you will consider it, *Latin* is no more unknown to a child, when he comes into the world, than *English:* and yet he learns *English* without master, rule, or grammar; and so might he *Latin* too, as *Tully* did, if he had some body always to talk to him in this language. And when we so often see a *French* woman teach an *English* girl to speak and read *French* perfectly in a year or two, without any rule of grammar, or any thing else but prattling to her, I cannot but wonder how gentlemen have overseen this way for their sons, and thought them more dull or incapable than their daughters.

§ 166. If therefore a man could be got, who himself speaking good *Latin,* would always be about your son, talk constantly to him, and suffer him to speak or read nothing else, this would be the true and genuine way, and that which I would propose, not only as the easiest and best, wherein a child might, without pains or chiding, get a language, which others are wont to be whipt for at school six or seven years together: but also as that, wherein at the same time he might have his mind and manners formed, and he be instructed to boot in several sciences, such as are a good part of *geography, astronomy, chronology, anatomy,* besides some parts of *history,* and all other parts of knowledge of things that fall under the senses and require little more than memory. For there, if we would take the true way, our knowledge should begin, and in those things be laid the foundation; and not in the abstract notions of *logick* and *metaphysicks,* which are fitter to amuse than inform the understanding in its first setting out towards knowledge. When young men have had their heads employ'd a while in those abstract speculations without finding the success and improvement, or that use of them, which they expected, they are apt to have mean thoughts either of learning or themselves; they are tempted to quit their studies, and throw away their books as containing nothing but hard words and empty sounds; or else, to conclude, that if there be any real knowledge in them, they themselves have not understandings capable of it. That this is so, perhaps I could assure you upon my own experience. Amongst other things to be learned by a young gentleman in this method, whilst others of his age are wholly taken up with *Latin* and languages, I may also set down *geometry* for one; having known a young gentleman, bred something after this way, able to demonstrate several propositions in *Euclid* before he was thirteen.

§ 167. But if such a man cannot be got, who speaks good *Latin,* and being able to instruct your son in all these parts of knowledge, will undertake it by this method; the next best is to have him taught as near this way as may be, which is by taking some easy and pleasant book, such as *Æsop's Fables,* and writing the *English* translation (made as literal as it can be) in one line, and the *Latin* words which answer each of them, just over it in another. These let him read every day over and over again, till he perfectly understands the *Latin;* and then go on to another fable, till he be also perfect in that, not omitting what he is already perfect in, but sometimes reviewing that, to keep it in his memory. And when he comes to write, let these be set him for copies, which with the exercise of his hand will also advance him to *Latin*. This being a more imperfect way than by talking *Latin* unto him; the formation of the verbs first, and afterwards the declensions of the nouns and pronouns perfectly learned by heart, may facilitate his acquaintance with the genius and manner of the *Latin tongue,* which varies the signification of verbs and nouns, not as the modern languages do by particles prefix'd, but by changing the last syllables. More than this of grammar, I think he need not have, till he can read himself *Sanctii Minerva,* with *Scioppius* and *Perizonius's* notes.

In teaching of children, this too, I think, is to be observed, that in most cases where they stick, they are not to be farther puzzled by putting them upon finding it out themselves; as by asking such questions as these, (*viz.*) which is the nominative case, in the sentence they are to construe; or demanding what *aufero* signifies, to lead them to the knowledge what *abstlere* signifies, &c., when they cannot readily tell. This wastes time only in disturbing them; for whilst they are learning, and apply themselves with attention, they are to be kept in good humour, and every thing made easy to them, and as pleasant as possible. Therefore, wherever they are at a stand, and are willing to go forwards, help them presently over the difficulty, without any rebuke or chiding, remembering, that where harsher ways are taken, they are the effect only of pride and peevishness in the teacher, who expects children should instantly be masters of as much as he knows; whereas he should rather consider, that his business is to settle in them habits, not angrily to inculcate rules, which serve for little in the conduct of our lives; at least are of no use to children, who forget them as soon as given. In sciences where their reason is to be exercised, I will not deny but this method may sometimes be varied, and difficulties proposed on purpose to excite industry, and accustom the mind to employ its own strength and sagacity in reasoning. But yet, I guess, this is not to be done to children, whilst very young, nor at their entrance upon any sort of knowledge: then every thing of itself is difficult, and the great use and skill of a teacher is to make all as easy as he can: but particularly in learning of languages there is least occasion for posing of children. For languages being to be learned by rote, custom and memory, are then spoken in greatest perfection, when all rules of grammar are utterly forgotten. I grant the grammar of a language is sometimes very carefully to be studied, but it is not to be studied but by a grown man, when he applies himself to the understanding of any language critically, which is seldom the business of any but professed scholars. This I think will be agreed to, that if a gentleman be to study any language, it ought to be that of his own country, that he may understand the language which he has constant use of, with the utmost accuracy.

There is yet a further reason, why masters and teachers should raise no difficulties to their scholars; but on the contrary should smooth their way, and readily help them forwards, where they find them stop. Children's minds are narrow and weak, and usually susceptible but of one thought at once. Whatever is in a child's head, fills it for the time, especially if set on with any passion. It should therefore be the skill and art of the teacher to clear their heads of all other thoughts whilst they are learning of any thing, the better to make room for what he would instill into them, that it may be received with attention and application, without which it leaves no impression. The natural temper of children disposes their minds to wander. Novelty alone takes them; whatever that presents, they are presently eager to have a taste of, and are as soon satiated with it. They quickly grow weary of the same thing, and so have almost their whole delight in change and variety. It is a contradiction to the natural state of childhood for them to fix their fleeting thoughts. Whether this be owing to the temper of their brains, or the quickness or instability of their animal spirits, over which the mind has not yet got a full command; this is visible, that it is a pain to children to keep their thoughts steady to any thing. A lasting continued attention is one of the hardest tasks can be imposed on them; and therefore, he that requires their application, should endeavour to make what he proposes as grateful and agreeable as possible; at least he ought to take care not to join any displeasing or frightful idea with it. If they come not to their books with some kind of liking and relish, 'tis no wonder their thoughts should be perpetually shifting from what disgusts them; and seek better entertainment in more pleasing objects, after which they will unavoidably be gadding.

'Tis, I know, the usual method of tutors, to endeavour to procure attention in their scholars, and to fix their minds to the business in hand, by rebukes and corrections, if they find them ever so little wandering. But such treatment is sure to produce the quite contrary effect. Passionate words or blows from the tutor fill the child's mind with terror and affrightment, which immediately takes it wholly up, and leaves no room for other impressions. I believe there is nobody that reads this, but may recollect what disorder hasty or imperious words from his parents or teachers have caused in his thoughts; how for the time it has turned his brains, so that he scarce knew what was said by or to him. He presently lost the sight of what he was upon, his mind was filled with disorder and confusion, and in that state was no longer capable of attention to any thing else.

'Tis true, parents and governors ought to settle and establish their authority by an awe over the minds of those under their tuition; and to rule them by that: but when they have got an ascendant over them, they should use it with great moderation, and not make themselves such scare-crows that their scholars should always tremble in their sight. Such an austerity may make their government easy to themselves, but of very little use to their pupils. 'Tis impossible children should learn any thing whilst their thoughts are possessed and disturbed with any passion, especially fear, which makes the strongest impression on their yet tender and weak spirits. Keep the mind in an easy calm temper, when you would have it receive your instructions or any increase of knowledge. 'Tis as impossible to draw fair and regular characters on a trembling mind as on a shaking paper.

The great skill of a teacher is to get and keep the attention of his scholar; whilst he has that, he is sure to advance as fast as the learner's abilities will carry him; and without that, all his bustle and pother will be to little or no purpose. To attain this, he should make the child comprehend (as much as may be) the usefulness of what he teaches him, and let him see, by what he has learnt, that he can do something which he could not do before; something, which gives him some power and real advantage above others who are ignorant of it. To this he should add sweetness in all his instructions, and by a certain tenderness in his whole carriage, make the child sensible that he loves him and designs nothing but his good, the only way to beget love in the child, which will make him hearken to his lessons, and relish what he teaches him.

Nothing but obstinacy should meet with any imperiousness or rough usage. All other faults should be corrected with a gentle hand; and kind engaging words will work better and more effectually upon a willing mind, and even prevent a good deal of that perverseness which rough and imperious usage often produces in well disposed and generous minds. 'Tis true, obstinacy and wilful neglects must be mastered, even though it cost blows to do it: but I am apt to think perverseness in the pupils is often the effect of frowardness in the *tutor;* and that most children would seldom have deserved blows, if needless and misapplied roughness had not taught them ill-nature, and given them an aversion for their teacher and all that comes from him.

Inadvertency, forgetfulness, unsteadiness, and wandering of thought, are the natural faults of childhood; and therefore, where they are not observed to be wilful, are to be mention'd softly, and gain'd upon by time. If every slip of this kind produces anger and rating, the occasions of rebuke and corrections will return so often, that the tutor will be a constant terror and uneasiness to his pupils. Which one thing is enough to hinder their profiting by his lessons, and to defeat all his methods of instruction.

Let the awe he has got upon their minds be so tempered with the constant marks of tenderness and good will, that affection may spur them to their duty, and make them find a pleasure in complying with his dictates. This will bring them with satisfaction to their tutor; make them hearken to him, as to one who is their friend, that cherishes them, and takes pains for their good: this will keep their thoughts easy and free whilst they are with him, the only temper wherein the mind is capable of receiving new informations, and of admitting into itself those impressions, which, if not taken and retain'd, all that they and their teachers do together is lost labour; there is much uneasiness and little learning.

• • • • •

§ 177. But under whose care soever a child is put to be taught during the tender and flexible years of his life, this is certain, it should be one who thinks *Latin* and *language* the least part of education; one who knowing how much virtue and a well-temper'd soul is to be preferred to any sort of *learning* or *language,* makes it his chief business to form the mind of his scholars, and give that a right disposition; which if once got, though all the rest should be neglected, would in due time produce all the rest; and which, if it be not got and settled so as to keep out ill and vicious habits, *languages* and *sciences* and all the other accomplishments of education, will be to no purpose but to make the worse or more dangerous man. And indeed whatever stir there is made about getting of *Latin* as the great and difficult business, his mother may teach it him herself, if she will but spend two or three hours in a day with him, and make him read the Evangelists in *Latin* to her: for she need but buy a *Latin* Testament, and having got some body to mark the last syllable but one where it is long in words above two syllables, (which is enough to regulate her pronunciation, and accenting the words) read daily in the *Gospels,* and then let her avoid understanding them in *Latin* if she can. And when she understands the Evangelists in *Latin,* let her, in the same manner, read *Æsop's* Fables, and so proceed on to *Eutropius, Justin,* and other such books. I do not mention this, as an imagination of what I fancy may do, but as of a thing I have known done, and the *Latin* tongue with ease got this way.

But, to return to what I was saying: he that takes on him the charge of bringing up young men, especially young gentlemen, should have something more in him than *Latin,* more than even a knowledge in the liberal sciences: he should be a person of eminent virtue and prudence, and with good sense, have good humour, and the skill to carry himself with gravity, ease and kindness, in a constant conversation with his pupils. But of this I have spoken at large in another place.

§ 178. At the same time that he is learning *French* and *Latin,* a child, as has been said, may also be enter'd in *Arithmetick, Geography, Chronology, History* and *Geometry* too. For if these be taught him in *French* or *Latin,* when he begins once to understand either of these tongues, he will get a knowledge in these sciences, and the language to boot.

Geography I think should be begun with: for the learning of the figure of the *globe,* the situation and boundaries of the four parts of the world, and that of particular kingdoms and countries, being only an exercise of the eyes and memory, a child with pleasure will learn and retain them. And this is so certain, that I now live in the house with a child whom his mother has so well instructed this way in *geography,* that he knew the limits of the four parts of the world, could readily point, being ask'd, to any country upon the globe, or any county in the map of *England;* knew all the great rivers, prom-ontories, straits and bays in the world, and could find the longitude and latitude of any place, before he was six years old. These things, that he will thus learn by sight, and have by rote in his memory, are not all, I confess, that he is to learn upon the *globes.* But yet it is a good step and preparation to it, and will make the remainder much easier, when his judgment is grown ripe enough for it: besides that, it gets so much time now; and by the pleasure of knowing things, leads him on insensibly to the gaining of languages.

§ 179. When he has the natural parts of the globe well fix'd in his memory, it may then be time to begin *arithmetick.* By the natural parts of the globe, I mean the several positions of the parts of the earth and sea, under different names and distinctions of countries, not coming yet to those artificial and imaginary lines which have been invented, and are only suppos'd for the better improvement of that science.

§ 180. *Arithmetick* is the easiest, and consequently the first sort of abstract reasoning, which the mind commonly bears or accustoms itself to: and is of so general use in all parts of life and business, that scarce any thing is to be done without it. This is certain, a man can-not have too much of it, nor too perfectly: he should therefore be-gin to be exercis'd in *counting,* as soon, and as far, as he is capable of it; and do something in it every day, till he is master of the art of *numbers.* When he understands *addition* and *subtraction,* he then may be advanced farther in *geography,* after he is acquainted with the *poles, zones, parallel circles,* and *meridians,* be taught *longitude* and *latitude*, and by them be made to understand the use of maps, and by the numbers placed on their sides, to know the respective situation of countries, and how to find them out on the terrestrial globe. Which when he can readily do, he may then be entered in the celestial; and there going over all the circles again, with a more particular observation of the Ecliptick, or Zodiack, to fix them all very clearly and distinctly in his mind, he may be taught the figure and position of the several constellations, which may be shewed him first upon the globe, and then in the heavens.

When that is done, and he knows pretty well the constellations of this our hemisphere, it may be time to give him some notions of this our planetary world; and to that purpose, it may not be amiss to make him a draught of the *Copernican* system, and therein explain to him the situation of the planets, their respective distances from the sun, the centre of their revolutions. This will prepare him to understand the motion and theory of the planets, the most easy and natural way. For since astronomers no longer doubt of the motion of the planets about the sun, it is fit he should proceed upon that hypothesis, which is not only the simplest and least perplexed for a learner, but also the likeliest to be true in itself. But in this, as in all other parts of instruction, great care must be taken with children, to begin with that which is plain and simple, and to teach them as little as can be at once, and settle that well in their heads before you proceed to the next, or any thing new in that science. Give them first one simple idea, and see that they take it right, and perfectly comprehend it before you go any farther, and then add some other simple idea which lies next in your way to what you aim at; and so proceeding by gentle and insensible steps, children without confusion and amazement will have their understandings opened and their thoughts extended farther than could have been expected. And when any one has learn'd any thing himself, there is no such way to fix it in his memory, and to encourage him to go on, as to set him to teach it others.

§ 181. When he has once got such an acquaintance with the globes, as is above mentioned, he may be fit to be tried in a little *geometry;* wherein I think the first six books of *Euclid* enough for him to be taught. For I am in some doubt, whether more to a man of business be necessary or useful. At least, if he have a genius and inclination to it, being enter'd so far by his tutor, he will be able to go on of himself without a teacher.

The *globes* therefore must be studied, and that diligently; and I think may be begun betimes, if the tutor will be but careful to distinguish what the child is capable of knowing, and what not; for which this may be a rule that perhaps will go a pretty way, *viz.* that children may be taught anything that falls under their senses, especially their sight, as far as their memories only are exercised: and thus a child very young may learn, which is the *Æquator,* which the *Meridian,* &c. which *Europe,* and which *England,* upon the globes, as soon almost as he knows the rooms of the house he lives in, if care be taken not to teach him too much at once, nor to set him upon a new part, till that which he is upon be perfectly learned and fixed in his memory.

§ 182. With geography, *chronology* ought to go hand in hand. I mean the general part of it, so that he may have in his mind a view of the whole current of time, and the several considerable *epochs* that are made use of in history. Without these two, history, which is the great mistress of prudence and civil knowledge, and ought to be the proper study of a gentleman, or man of business in the world; without geography and *chronology,* I say, history will be very ill retain'd, and very little useful; but be only a jumble of matters of fact, confusedly heaped together without order or instruction. 'Tis by these two that the actions of mankind are ranked into their proper places of time and countries, under which circumstances they are not only much easier kept in the memory, but in that natural order, are only capable to afford those observations which make a man the better and the abler for reading them.

§ 183. When I speak of *chronology* as a science he should be perfect in, I do not mean the little controversies that are in it. These are endless, and most of them of so little importance to a gentleman, as not to deserve to be enquir'd into, were they capable of an easy decision. And therefore all that learned noise and dust of the chronologist is wholly to be avoided. The most useful book I have seen in that part of learning, is a small treatise of *Strauchius,* which is printed in twelves, under the title of *Breviarium Chronologicum,* out of which may be selected all that is necessary to be taught a young gentleman concerning *chronology;* for all that is in that treatise a learner need not be cumbred with. He has in him the most remarkable or useful *epochs* reduced all to that of the *Julian Period,* which is the easiest and plainest and surest method that can be made use of in *chronology.* To this treatise of *Strauchius, Helvicus's* tables may be added, as a book to be turned to on all occasions.

§ 184. As nothing teaches, so nothing delights more than history. The first of these recommends it to the study of grown men, the latter makes me think it the fittest for a young lad, who as soon as he is instructed in chronology, and acquainted with the several *epochs* in use in this part of the world, and can reduce them to the *Julian Period,* should then have some *Latin history* put into his hand. The choice should be directed by the easiness of the stile; for wherever he begins, chronology will keep it from confusion; and the pleasantness of the subject inviting him to read, the language will insensibly be got without that terrible vexation and uneasiness which children suffer where they are put into books beyond their capacity; such as are the *Roman* orators and poets, only to learn the *Roman* language. When he has by reading master'd the easier, such perhaps as *Justin, Eutropius, Quintius Curtius, &c.* the next degree to these will give him no great trouble: and thus by a gradual progress from the plainest and easiest *historians,* he may at last come to read the most difficult and sublime of the *Latin* authors, such as are *Tully, Virgil,* and *Horace.*

§ 185. The knowledge of *virtue,* all along from the beginning, in all the instances he is capable of, being taught him more by practice than rules; and the love of reputation, instead of satisfying his appetite, being made habitual in him, I know not whether he should read any other discourses of morality but what he finds in the Bible; or have any system of *ethicks* put into his hand till he can read *Tully's Offices* not as a school-boy to learn *Latin,* but as one that would be informed in the principles and precepts of virtue for the conduct of his life.

§ 186. When he has pretty well digested *Tully's Offices,* and added to it, *Puffendorf de Officio Hominis & Civis,* it may be seasonable to set him upon *Grotius de Jure Belli & Pacis,* or, which perhaps is the better of the two, *Puffendorf de Jure naturali & Gen-*

tium; wherein he will be instructed in the natural rights of men, and the original and foundations of society, and the duties resulting from thence. This *general part of civil-law* and history, are studies which a gentleman should not barely touch at, but constantly dwell upon, and never have done with. A virtuous and well-behaved young man, that is well-versed in the *general part of the civil-law* (which concerns not the chicane of private cases, but the affairs and intercourse of civilized nations in general, grounded upon principles of reason) understands *Latin* well, and can write a good hand, one may turn loose into the world with great assurance that he will find employment and esteem every where.

§ 187. It would be strange to suppose an *English* gentleman should be ignorant of the *law* of his country. This, whatever station he is in, is so requisite, that from a Justice of the Peace to a Minister of State I know no place he can well fill without it. I do not mean the chicane or wrangling and captious part of the law: a gentleman, whose business is to seek the true measures of right and wrong, and not the arts how to avoid doing the one, and secure himself in doing the other, ought to be as far from such a study of the *law,* as he is concerned diligently to apply himself to that wherein he may be serviceable to his country. And to that purpose, I think the right way for a gentleman to study *our law,* which he does not design for his calling, is to take a view of our *English* constitution and government in the antient books of the *common-law,* and some more modern writers, who out of them have given an account of this government. And having got a true idea of that, then to read our history, and with it join in every king's reign the *laws* then made. This will give an insight into the reason of our *statutes,* and shew the true ground upon which they came to be made, and what weight they ought to have.

§ 188. *Rhetorick* and *logick* being the arts that in the ordinary method usually follow immediately after grammar, it may perhaps be wondered that I have said so little of them. The reason is, because of the little advantage young people receive by them: for I have seldom or never observed any one to get the skill of reasoning well, or speaking handsomely, by studying those rules which pretend to reach it: and therefore I would have a young gentleman take a view of them in the shortest systems could be found, without dwelling long on the contemplation and study of those formalities. Right reasoning is founded on something else than the *predicaments* and *predicables,* and does not consist in talking in *mode* and *figure* it self. But 'tis beside my present business to enlarge upon this speculation. To come therefore to what we have in hand; if you would have your son *reason well,* let him read *Chillingworth;* and if you would have him speak well, let him be conversant in *Tully,* to give him the true *idea* of *eloquence;* and let him read those things that are well writ in *English,* to perfect his style in the purity of our language.

§ 189. If the use and end of right reasoning be to have right notions and a right judgment of things, to distinguish betwixt truth and falsehood, right and wrong, and to act accordingly; be sure not to let your son be bred up in the art and formality of disputing, either practising it himself, or admiring it in others; unless instead of an able man, you desire to have him an insignificant wrangler, opiniator in discourse, and priding himself in contradicting others; or, which is worse, questioning every thing, and thinking there is no such thing as truth to be sought, but only victory, in disputing. There cannot be any thing so disingenuous, so misbecoming a gentleman or any one who pretends to be a rational creature, as not to yield to plain reason and the conviction of clear arguments. Is there any thing more consistent with civil conversation, and the end of all debate, than not to take an answer, though never so full and satisfactory, but still to go on with the dispute as long as equivocal sounds can furnish (a *medius terminus*) a term to wrangle with on the one side, or a distinction on the other; whether pertinent or impertinent, sense or nonsense, agreeing with or contrary to what he had said before, it matters not. For this, in short, is the way and perfection of logical disputes, that the opponent never takes any answer, nor the respondent ever yields to any argument. This neither of them must do, whatever becomes of truth or knowledge, unless he will pass for a poor baffled wretch, and lie under the disgrace of not being able to maintain whatever he has once affirm'd, which is the great aim and glory in disputing. Truth is to be found and supported by a mature and due consideration of things themselves, and not by artificial terms and ways of arguing: these lead not men so much into the discovery of truth, as into a captious and fallacious use of doubtful words, which is the most useless and most offensive way of talking, and such as least suits a gentleman or a lover of truth of any thing in the world.

There can scarce be a greater defect in a gentleman than not to express himself well either in writing or speaking. But yet I think I may ask my reader, whether he doth not know a great many, who live upon their estates, and so with the name should have the qualities of gentlemen, who cannot so much as tell a story as they should, much less speak clearly and persuasively in any business. This I think not to be so much their fault, as the fault of their education; for I must, without partiality, do my countrymen this right, that where they apply themselves, I see none of their neighbours outgo them. They have been taught *rhetorick*, but yet never taught how to express themselves handsomely with their tongues or pens in the language they are always to use; as if the names of the figures that embellish'd the discourses of those who understood the art of speaking, were the very art and skill of speaking well. This, as all other things of practice, is to be learn'd not by a few or a great many rules given, but by exercise and application according to good rules, or rather patterns, till habits are got, and a facility of doing it well.

Agreeable hereunto, perhaps it might not be amiss to make children, as soon as they are capable of it, often to tell a story of any thing they know; and to correct at first the most remarkable fault they are guilty of in their way of putting it together. When that fault is cured, then to shew them the next, and so on, till one after another, all, at least the gross ones, are mended. When they can tell tales pretty well, then it may be the time to make them write them. The Fables of *Æsop*, the only book almost that I know fit for children, may afford them matter for this exercise of writing *English*, as well as for reading and translating, to enter them in the *Latin* tongue. When they have got past the faults of grammar, and can join in a continued coherent discourse the several parts of a story, without bald and unhandsome forms of transition (as is usual) often repeated, he that desires to perfect them yet farther in this, which is the first step to speaking well and needs no invention, may have recourse to *Tully*, and by putting in practice those rules which that master of eloquence gives in his first book *de inventione,* § 20, make them know wherein the skill and graces of an handsome narrative, according to the several subjects and designs of it, lie. Of each of which rules fit examples may be found out, and therein they may be shewn how others have practised them. The antient classick authors afford plenty of such examples, which they should be made not only to translate, but have set before them as patterns for their daily imitation.

When they understand how to write *English* with due connexion, propriety and order, and are pretty well masters of a tolerable narrative style, they may be advanced to writing of letters; wherein they should not be put upon any strains of wit or compliment, but taught to express their own plain easy sense, without any incoherence, confusion or roughness. And when they are perfect in this, they may, to raise their thoughts, have set before them the examples of *Voitures,* for the entertainment of their friends at a distance, with letters of compliment, mirth, raillery or diversion; and *Tully's Epistles,* as the best pattern whether for business or conversation. The writing of letters has so much to do in all the occurrences of human life, that no gentleman can avoid shewing himself in this kind of writing. Occasions will daily force him to make this use of his pen, which, besides the consequences that, in his affairs, his well or ill managing of it often draws after it, always lays him open to a severer examination of his breeding, sense, and abilities, than oral discourses; whose transient faults dying for the most part with the sound that gives them life, and so not subject to a strict review, more easily escape observation and censure.

Had the methods of education been directed to their right end, one would have thought this so necessary a part could not have been neglected whilst themes and verses in *Latin,* of no use at all, were so constantly every where pressed, to the racking of children's inventions beyond their strength and hindering their chearful progress in learning the tongues by unnatural difficulties. But custom has so ordain'd it, and who dares disobey? And would it not be very unreasonable to require of a learned country school-master (who has all the tropes and figures in *Farnaby's Rhetorick* at his fingers' ends) to teach his scholar to express himself handsomely in *English,* when it appears to be so little his business or thought, that the boy's mother (despised, 'tis like, as illiterate for not having read a system of *logick* and *rhetorick*) outdoes him in it?

To write and speak correctly gives a grace and gains a favourable attention to what one has to say: and since 'tis *English* that an *English* gentleman will have constant use of, that is the language he should chiefly cultivate, and wherein most care should be taken to polish and perfect his style. To speak or write better *Latin* than *English,* may make a man be talk'd of, but he would find it more to his purpose to express himself well in his own tongue, that he uses every moment, than to have the vain commendation of others for a very insignificant quality. This I find universally neglected, and no care taken any where to improve young men in their own language, that they may thoroughly understand and be masters of it. If any one among us have a facility or purity more than ordinary in his mother tongue, it is owing to chance, or his genius, or any thing rather than to his education or any care of his teacher. To mind what *English* his pupil speaks or writes, is below the dignity of one bred up amongst *Greek* and *Latin,* though he have but little of them himself. These are the learned languages fit only for learned men to meddle with and teach; *English* is the language of the illiterate vulgar: tho' yet we see the polity of some of our neighbours hath not thought it beneath the publick care to promote and reward the improvement of their own language. Polishing and enriching their tongue is no small business amongst them; it hath colleges and stipends appointed it, and there is raised amongst them a great ambition and emulation of writing correctly: and we see what they are come to by it, and how far they have spread one of the worst languages possibly in this part of the world, if we look upon it as it was in some few reigns backwards, whatever it be now. The great men among the *Romans* were daily exercising themselves in their own language; and we find yet upon record the names of orators, who taught some of their emperors *Latin,* though it were their mother tongue.

'Tis plain the *Greeks* were yet more nice in theirs. All other speech was barbarous to them but their own, and no foreign language appears to have been studied or valued amongst that learned and acute people; tho' it be past doubt that they borrowed their learning and philosophy from abroad.

I am not here speaking against *Greek* and *Latin;* I think they ought to be studied, and the *Latin* at least understood well by every gentleman. But whatever foreign languages a young man meddles with (and the more he knows the better) that which he should critically study, and labour to get a facility, clearness and elegancy to express himself in, should be his own; and to this purpose he should daily be exercised in it.

§ 190. *Natural philosophy,* as a speculative science, I imagine we have none, and perhaps I may think I have reason to say we never shall be able to make a science of it. The works of nature are contrived by a wisdom, and operate by ways too far surpassing our faculties to discover or capacities to conceive, for us ever to be able to reduce them into a science. *Natural philosophy* being the knowledge of the principles, properties and operations of things as they are in themselves, I imagine there are two parts of it, one comprehending *spirits,* with their nature and qualities, and the other *bodies.* The first of these is usually referred to *metaphysicks:* but under what title soever the consideration of *spirits* comes, I think it ought to go before the study of matter and body, not as a science that can be methodized into a system, and treated of upon principles of knowledge; but as an enlargement of our minds towards a truer and fuller comprehension of the intellectual world to which we are led both by reason and revelation. And since the clearest and largest discoveries we have of other *spirits,* besides God and our own souls, is imparted to us from heaven by revelation, I think the information that at least young people should have of them, should be taken from that revelation. To this purpose, I conclude, it would be well, if there were made a good history of the Bible, for young people to read; wherein if every thing that is fit to be put into it, were laid down in its due order of time, and several things omitted which are suited only to riper age, that confusion which is usually produced by promiscuous reading of the Scripture, as it lies now bound up in our Bibles, would be avoided. And also this other good obtained, that by reading of it constantly, there would be instilled into the minds of children a notion and belief of *spirits,* they having so much to do in all the transactions of that history, which will be a good preparation to the study of *bodies*. For without the notion and allowance of *spirit,* our philosophy will be lame and defective in one main part of it, when it leaves out the contemplation of the most excellent and powerful part of the creation.

§ 191. Of this *History of the Bible,* I think too it would be well if there were a short and plain epitome made, containing the chief and most material heads, for children to be conversant in as soon as they can read. This, though it will lead them early into some notion of *spirits,* yet it is not contrary to what I said above, that I would not have children troubled, whilst young, with notions of *spirits;* whereby my meaning was, that I think it inconvenient that their yet tender minds should receive early impressions of *goblins, spectres,* and *apparitions,* wherewith their maids and those about them are apt to fright them into a compliance with their orders, which often proves a great inconvenience to them all their lives after, by subjecting their minds to frights, fearful apprehensions, weakness and superstition; which when coming abroad into the world and conversation they grow weary and ashamed of, it not seldom happens, that to make, as they think, a thorough cure, and ease themselves of a load which has sat so heavy on them, they throw away the thoughts of all *spirits* together, and so run into the other, but worse, extream.

§ 200. These are my present thoughts concerning *learning* and *accomplishments.* The great business of all is virtue and *wisdom*:

Nullum numen abest si sit Prudentia.

Teach him to get a mastery over his inclinations, and *submit his appetite to reason.* This being obtained, and by constant practice settled into habit, the hardest part of the task is over. To bring a young man to this, I know nothing which so much contributes as the love of praise and commendation, which should therefore be instilled into him by all arts imaginable. Make his mind as sensible of credit and shame as may be; and when you have done that, you have put a principle into him, which will influence his actions when you are not by, to which the fear of a little smart of a rod is not comparable, and which will be the proper stock whereon afterwards to graff the true principles of morality and religion.

§ 201. I have one thing more to add, which as soon as I mention I shall run the danger of being suspected to have forgot what I am about, and what I have above written concerning education all tending towards a gentleman's calling, with which a trade seems wholly inconsistent. And yet I cannot forbear to say, I would have him *learn a trade, a manual trade;* nay two or three, but one more particularly.

§ 202. The busy inclination of children being always to be directed to something that may be useful to them, the advantages proposed from what they are set about may be considered of two kinds: 1. Where the skill itself that is got by exercise is worth the having. Thus skill not only in languages and learned sciences, but in painting, turning, gardening, tempering and working in iron, and all other useful arts is worth the having. 2. Where the exercise itself, without any consideration, is necessary or useful for health. Knowledge in some things is so necessary to be got by children whilst they are young, that some part of their time is to be allotted to their improvement in them, though those employments contribute nothing at all to their health. Such are reading and writing and all other sedentary studies for the cultivating of the mind, which unavoidably take up a great part of a gentleman's time, quite from their cradles. *Other manual arts,* which are both got and exercised by labour, do many of them by that exercise not only increase our dexterity and skill, but contribute to our health too, especially such as employ us in the open air. In these, then, health and improvement may be join'd together; and of these should some fit ones be chosen, to be made the recreations of one whose chief business is with books and study. In this choice the age and inclination of the person is to be considered, and constraint always to be avoided in bringing him to it. For command and force may often create, but can never cure, an aversion: and whatever any one is brought to by compulsion, he will leave as soon as he can, and be little profited and less recreated by, whilst he is at it.

John Dewey,   EXPERIENCE AND EDUCATION

1. Compare and contrast Dewey's views of "traditional" and "progressive" education. Does he subscribe to the "either-or" philosophy? Explain.

2. What reasons does Dewey give to support his statement that experience and education cannot be directly equated to each other? How might Rousseau react to this?

3. Why does Dewey say that the "traditional" school can get along without a consistently developed philosophy of education whereas this statement is not so for the "progressive" school?

4. How does Dewey explain his statement that the new education is simpler in principle than the old? Do you agree or disagree with his explanation?

5. Why does Dewey stress the need for forming a "theory of experience"? What are the principles that are most significant in framing this theory? Indicate your understanding of these principles by application in original examples.

6. Do you agree with Dewey that the principle of continuity is easily misunderstood and is badly distorted in traditional education? Explain your response. Give examples where appropriate for clarification.

7. What is the true meaning of preparation in Dewey's education scheme?

8. Define Dewey's concept of collateral learning. Draw on your own experiences to give examples of positive and negative collateral learning.

9. How does Dewey explain the nature of freedom as applied to the classroom?

10. What does Dewey mean by the progressive organization of subject matter?

John Dewey (1859-1952) graduated from the University of Vermont and received a Ph.D. from The Johns Hopkins University. While he taught at a number of universities, he is identified mostly with the University of Chicago and Columbia. Dewey believed in the unity of theory and practice. The selected readings are from a book written <u>after</u> his experience with progressive schools and more than two decades after he wrote *Democracy and Education* (1916). Dewey had reformulated his ideas in the light of the criticisms his theories had stimulated and as a result of his experience.

Chapter 1

Traditional vs. Progressive Education

MANKIND likes to think in terms of extreme opposites. It is given to formulating its beliefs in terms of *Either-Ors,* between which it recognizes no intermediate possibilities. When forced to recognize that the extremes cannot be acted upon, it is still inclined to hold that they are all right in theory but that when it comes to practical matters circumstances compel us to compromise. Educational philosophy is no exception. The history of educational theory is marked by opposition between the idea that education is development from within and that it is for- mation from without; that it is based upon natural en- dowments and that education is a process of overcoming natural inclination and substituting in its place habits acquired under external pressure.

At present, the opposition, so far as practical affairs of the school are concerned, tends to take the form of contrast between traditional and progressive education. If the underlying ideas of the former are formulated broadly, without the qualifications required for accurate state- ment, they are found to be about as follows: The subject- matter of education consists of bodies of information and of skills that have been worked out in the past; therefore, the chief business of the school is to transmit them to the new generation. In the past, there have also been devel- oped standards and rules of conduct; moral training con- sists in forming habits of action in conformity with these rules and standards. Finally, the general pattern of school organization (by which I mean the relations of pupils to one another and to the teachers) constitutes the school a kind of institution sharply marked off from other social institutions. Call up in imagination the ordinary school-room, its time-schedules, schemes of classification, of ex-amination and promotion, of rules of order, and I think you will grasp what is meant by "pattern of organization." If then you contrast this scene with what goes on in the family, for example, you will appreciate what is meant by the school being a kind of institution sharply marked off from any other form of social organization.

The three characteristics just mentioned fix the aims and methods of instruction and discipline. The main pur-pose or objective is to prepare the young for future re-sponsibilities and for success in life, by means of ac-quisition of the organized bodies of information and prepared forms of skill which comprehend the material of instruction. Since the subject-matter as well as stand-ards of proper conduct are handed down from the past, the attitude of pupils must, upon the whole, be one of docility, receptivity, and obedience. Books, especially textbooks, are the chief representatives of the lore and wisdom of the past, while teachers are the organs through which pupils are brought into effective connection with the material. Teachers are the agents through which knowl-edge and skills are communicated and rules of conduct enforced.

I have not made this brief summary for the purpose of criticizing the underlying philosophy. The rise of what is called new education and progressive schools is of itself a product of discontent with traditional education. In effect it is a criticism of the latter. When the implied criticism is made explicit it reads somewhat as follows: The traditional scheme is, in essence, one of imposition from above and from outside. It imposes adult standards, subject-matter, and methods upon those who are only growing slowly toward maturity. The gap is so great that the required subject-matter, the methods of learning and of behaving are foreign to the existing capacities of the young. They are beyond the reach of the experience the young learners already possess. Consequently, they must be imposed; even though good teachers will use devices of art to cover up the imposition so as to relieve it of obviously brutal features.

But the gulf between the mature or adult products and the experience and abilities of the young is so wide that the very situation forbids much active participation by pupils in the development of what is taught. Theirs is to do—and learn, as it was the part of the six hundred to do and die. Learning here means acquisition of what already is incorporated in books and in the heads of the elders. Moreover, that which is taught is thought of as essentially static. It is taught as a finished product, with little regard either to the ways in which it was originally built up or to changes that will surely occur in the future. It is to a large extent the cultural product of societies that assumed the future would be much like the past, and yet it is used as educational food in a society where change is the rule, not the exception.

If one attempts to formulate the philosophy of education implicit in the practices of the new education, we may, I think, discover certain common principles amid the variety of progressive schools now existing. To imposition from above is opposed expression and cultivation of individuality; to external discipline is opposed free activity; to learning from texts and teachers, learning through experience; to acquisition of isolated skills and techniques by drill, is opposed acquisition of them as means of attaining ends which make direct vital appeal; to preparation for a more or less remote future is opposed making the most of the opportunities of present life; to static aims and materials is opposed acquaintance with a changing world.

Now, all principles by themselves are abstract. They become concrete only in the consequences which result from their application. Just because the principles set forth are so fundamental and far-reaching, everything depends upon the interpretation given them as they are put into practice in the school and the home. It is at this point that the reference made earlier to *Either-Or* philosophies becomes peculiarly pertinent. The general philosophy of the new education may be sound, and yet the difference in abstract principles will not decide the way in which the moral and intellectual preference involved shall be worked out in practice. There is always the danger in a new movement that in rejecting the aims and methods of that which it would supplant, it may develop its principles negatively rather than positively and constructively. Then it takes its clew in practice from that which is rejected instead of from the constructive development of its own philosophy.

I take it that the fundamental unity of the newer philosophy is found in the idea that there is an intimate and necessary relation between the processes of actual experience and education. If this be true, then a positive and constructive development of its own basic idea depends upon having a correct idea of experience. Take, for example, the question of organized subject-matter—which will be discussed in some detail later. The problem for progressive education is: What is the place and meaning of subject-matter and of organization *within* experience? How does subject-matter function? Is there anything inherent in experience which tends towards progressive organization of its contents? What results follow when the materials of experience are not progressively organ-

ized? A philosophy which proceeds on the basis of rejection, of sheer opposition, will neglect these questions.
It will tend to suppose that because the old education was
based on ready-made organization, therefore it suffices
to reject the principle of organization *in toto,* instead of
striving to discover what it means and how it is to be
attained on the basis of experience. We might go through
all the points of difference between the new and the old
education and reach similar conclusions. When external
control is rejected, the problem becomes that of finding
the factors of control that are inherent within experience.
When external authority is rejected, it does not follow that
all authority should be rejected, but rather that there is
need to search for a more effective source of authority.
Because the older education imposed the knowledge,
methods, and the rules of conduct of the mature person
upon the young, it does not follow, except upon the basis
of the extreme *Either-Or* philosophy, that the knowledge
and skill of the mature person has no directive value for
the experience of the immature. On the contrary, basing
education upon personal experience may mean more multiplied and more intimate contacts between the mature
and the immature than ever existed in the traditional
school, and consequently more, rather than less, guidance
by others. The problem, then, is: how these contacts
can be established without violating the principle of learning through personal experience. The solution of this
problem requires a well thought-out philosophy of the
social factors that operate in the constitution of individual experience.

What is indicated in the foregoing remarks is that the
general principles of the new education do not of themselves solve any of the problems of the actual or practical
conduct and management of progressive schools. Rather,
they set new problems which have to be worked out on

the basis of a new philosophy of experience. The problems are not even recognized, to say nothing of being solved, when it is assumed that it suffices to reject the ideas and practices of the old education and then go to the opposite extreme. Yet I am sure that you will appreciate what is meant when I say that many of the newer schools tend to make little or nothing of organized subject-matter of study; to proceed as if any form of direction and guidance by adults were an invasion of individual freedom, and as if the idea that education should be concerned with the present and future meant that acquaintance with the past has little or no role to play in education. Without pressing these defects to the point of exaggeration, they at least illustrate what is meant by a theory and practice of education which proceeds negatively or by reaction against what has been current in education rather than by a positive and constructive development of purposes, methods, and subject-matter on the foundation of a theory of experience and its educational potentialities.

It is not too much to say that an educational philosophy which professes to be based on the idea of freedom may become as dogmatic as ever was the traditional education which is reacted against. For any theory and set of practices is dogmatic which is not based upon critical examination of its own underlying principles. Let us say that the new education emphasizes the freedom of the learner. Very well. A problem is now set. What does freedom mean and what are the conditions under which it is capable of realization? Let us say that the kind of external imposition which was so common in the traditional school limited rather than promoted the intellectual and moral development of the young. Again, very well. Recognition of this serious defect sets a problem. Just what is the role of the teacher and of books in promoting the educational development of the immature? Admit that traditional education employed as the subject-matter for study facts and ideas so bound up with the past as to give little help in dealing with the issues of the present and future. Very well. Now we have the problem of discovering the connection which actually exists *within* experience between the achievements of the past and the issues of the present. We have the problem of ascertaining how acquaintance with the past may be translated into a potent instrumentality for dealing effectively with the future. We may reject knowledge of the past as the *end* of education and thereby only emphasize its importance as a *means*. When we do that we have a problem that is new in the story of education: How shall the young become acquainted with the past in such a way that the acquaintance is a potent agent in appreciation of the living present?

Chapter 5

The Nature of Freedom

AT THE RISK of repeating what has been often said by me I want to say something about the other side of the problem of social control, namely, the nature of freedom. The only freedom that is of enduring importance is freedom of intelligence, that is to say, freedom of observation and of judgment exercised in behalf of purposes that are intrinsically worth while. The commonest mistake made about freedom is, I think, to identify it with freedom of movement, or with the external or physical side of activity. Now, this external and physical side of activity cannot be separated from the internal side of activity; from freedom of thought, desire, and purpose. The limitation that was put upon outward action by the fixed arrangements of the typical traditional schoolroom, with its fixed rows of desks and its military regimen of pupils who were permitted to move only at certain fixed signals, put a great restriction upon intellectual and moral freedom. Straitjacket and chain-gang procedures had to be done away with if there was to be a chance for growth of individuals in the intellectual springs of freedom without which there is no assurance of genuine and continued normal growth.

But the fact still remains that an increased measure of freedom of outer movement is a *means,* not an end. The educational problem is not solved when this aspect of freedom is obtained. Everything then depends, so far as education is concerned, upon what is done with this added liberty. What end does it serve? What consequences flow from it? Let me speak first of the advantages which reside potentially in increase of outward freedom. In the first place, without its existence it is practically impossible for a teacher to gain knowledge of the individuals with whom he is concerned. Enforced quiet and acquiescence prevent pupils from disclosing their real natures. They enforce artificial uniformity. They put seeming before being. They place a premium upon preserving the outward appearance of attention, decorum, and obedience. And everyone who is acquainted with schools in which this system prevailed well knows that thoughts, imaginations, desires, and sly activities ran their own unchecked course behind this façade. They were disclosed to the teacher only when some untoward act led to their detection. One has only to contrast this highly artificial situation with normal human relations outside the schoolroom, say in a well-conducted home, to appreciate how fatal it is to the teacher's acquaintance with and understanding of the individuals who are, supposedly, being educated. Yet without this insight there is only an accidental chance that the material of study and the methods used in instruction will so come home to an individual that his development of mind and character is actually directed. There is a vicious circle. Mechanical uniformity of studies and methods creates a kind of uniform immobility and this reacts to perpetuate uniformity of studies and of recitations, while behind this enforced uniformity individual tendencies operate in irregular and more or less forbidden ways.

The other important advantage of increased outward freedom is found in the very nature of the learning process. That the older methods set a premium upon passivity and receptivity has been pointed out. Physical quiescence puts a tremendous premium upon these traits. The only escape from them in the standardized school is an activity which is irregular and perhaps disobedient. There cannot be complete quietude in a laboratory or workshop. The non-social character of the traditional school is seen in the fact that it erected silence into one of its prime virtues. There is, of course, such a thing as intense intellectual activity without overt bodily activity. But capacity for such intellectual activity marks a comparatively late achievement when it is continued for a long period. There should be brief intervals of time for quiet reflection provided for even the young. But they are periods of genuine reflection only when they follow after times of more overt action and are used to organize what has been gained in periods of activity in which the hands and other parts of the body beside the brain are used. Freedom of movement is also important as a means of maintaining normal physical and mental health. We have still to learn from the example of the Greeks who saw clearly the relation between a sound body and a sound mind. But in all the respects mentioned freedom of outward action is a means to freedom of judgment and of power to carry deliberately chosen ends into execution. The amount of external freedom which is needed varies from individual to individual. It naturally tends to decrease with increasing maturity, though its complete absence prevents even a mature individual from having the contacts which will provide him with new materials upon which his intelligence may exercise itself. The amount and the quality of this kind of free activity as a means of growth is a problem that must engage the thought of the educator at every stage of development.

There can be no greater mistake, however, than to treat such freedom as an end in itself. It then tends to be destructive of the shared cooperative activities which are the normal source of order. But, on the other hand, it turns freedom which should be positive into something negative. For freedom from restriction, the negative side, is to be prized only as a means to a freedom which is power: power to frame purposes, to judge wisely, to evaluate desires by the consequences which will result from acting upon them; power to select and order means to carry chosen ends into operation.

Natural impulses and desires constitute in any case the starting point. But there is no intellectual growth without some reconstruction, some remaking, of impulses and desires in the form in which they first show themselves. This remaking involves inhibition of impulse in its first estate. The alternative to externally imposed inhibition is inhibition through an individual's own reflection and judgment. The old phrase "stop and think" is sound psychology. For thinking is stoppage of the immediate manifestation of impulse until that impulse has been brought into connection with other possible tendencies to action so that a more comprehensive and coherent plan of activity is formed. Some of the other tendencies to action lead to use of eye, ear, and hand to observe objective conditions; others result in recall of what has happened in the past. Thinking is thus a postponement of immediate action, while it effects internal control of impulse through a union of observation and memory, this union being the heart of reflection. What has been said explains the meaning of the well-worn phrase "self-control." The ideal aim of education is creation of power of self-control. But the mere removal of external control is no guarantee for the production of self-control. It is easy to jump out of the frying-pan into the fire. It is easy, in other words, to escape one form of external control only to find oneself in another and more dangerous form of external control. Impulses and desires that are not ordered by intelligence are under the control of accidental circumstances. It may be a loss rather than a gain to escape from the control of another person only to find one's conduct dictated by immediate whim and caprice; that is, at the mercy of impulses into whose formation intelligent judgment has not entered. A person whose conduct is controlled in this way has at most only the illusion of freedom. Actually he is directed by forces over which he has no command.

Chapter 6

The Meaning of Purpose

IT IS, then, a sound instinct which identifies freedom with power to frame purposes and to execute or carry into effect purposes so framed. Such freedom is in turn identical with self-control; for the formation of purposes and the organization of means to execute them are the work of intelligence. Plato once defined a slave as the person who executes the purposes of another, and, as has just been said, a person is also a slave who is enslaved to his own blind desires. There is, I think, no point in the philosophy of progressive education which is sounder than its emphasis upon the importance of the participation of the learner in the formation of the purposes which direct his activities in the learning process, just as there is no defect in traditional education greater than its failure to secure the active co-operation of the pupil in construction of the purposes involved in his studying. But the meaning of purposes and ends is not self-evident and self-explanatory. The more their educational importance is emphasized, the more important it is to understand what a purpose is; how it arises and how it functions in experience.

A genuine purpose always starts with an impulse. Obstruction of the immediate execution of an impulse converts it into a desire. Nevertheless neither impulse nor desire is itself a purpose. A purpose is an end-view. That is, it involves foresight of the consequences which will result from acting upon impulse. Foresight of consequences involves the operation of intelligence. It demands, in the first place, observation of objective conditions and circumstances. For impulse and desire produce consequences not by themselves alone but through their interaction or co-operation with surrounding conditions. The impulse for such a simple action as walking is executed only in active conjunction with the ground on which one stands. Under ordinary circumstances, we do not have to pay much attention to the ground. In a ticklish situation we have to observe very carefully just what the conditions are, as in climbing a steep and rough mountain where no trail has been laid out. Exercise of observation is, then, one condition of transformation of impulse into a purpose. As in the sign by a railway crossing, we have to stop, look, listen.

But observation alone is not enough. We have to understand the *significance* of what we see, hear, and touch. This significance consists of the consequences that will result when what is seen is acted upon. A baby may *see* the brightness of a flame and be attracted thereby to reach for it. The significance of the flame is then not its brightness but its power to burn, as the consequence that will result from touching it. We can be aware of consequences only because of previous experiences. In cases that are familiar because of many prior experiences we do not have to stop to remember just what those experiences were. A flame comes to signify light and heat without our having expressly to think of previous experiences of heat and burning. But in unfamiliar cases, we cannot tell just what the consequences of observed conditions will be unless we go over past experiences in our mind, unless we reflect upon them and by seeing what is similar in them to those now present, go on to form a judgment of what may be expected in the present situation.

The formation of purposes is, then, a rather complex

intellectual operation. It involves (1) observation of surrounding conditions; (2) knowledge of what has happened in similar situations in the past, a knowledge obtained partly by recollection and partly from the information, advice, and warning of those who have had a wider experience; and (3) judgment which puts together what is observed and what is recalled to see what they signify. A purpose differs from an original impulse and desire through its translation into a plan and method of action based upon foresight of the consequences of acting under given observed conditions in a certain way. "If wishes were horses, beggars would ride." Desire for something may be intense. It may be so strong as to override estimation of the consequences that will follow acting upon it. Such occurrences do not provide the model for education. The crucial educational problem is that of procuring the postponement of immediate action upon desire until observation and judgment have intervened. Unless I am mistaken, this point is definitely relevant to the conduct of progressive schools. Overemphasis upon activity as an end, instead of upon *intelligent* activity, leads to identification of freedom with immediate execution of impulses and desires. This identification is justified by a confusion of impulse with purpose; although, as has just been said, there is no purpose unless overt action is postponed until there is foresight of the consequences of carrying the impulse into execution—a foresight that is impossible without observation, information, and judgment. Mere foresight, even if it takes the form of accurate prediction, is not, of course, enough. The intellectual anticipation, the idea of consequences, must blend with desire and impulse to acquire moving force. It then gives direction to what otherwise is blind, while desire gives ideas impetus and momentum. An idea then becomes a plan in and for an activity to be carried out. Suppose a man has a desire to secure a new home, say by building a house. No matter how strong his desire, it cannot be directly executed. The man must form an idea of what kind of house he wants, including the number and arrangement of rooms, etc. He has to draw a plan, and have blue prints and specifications made. All this might be an idle amusement for spare time unless he also took stock of his resources. He must consider the relation of his funds and available credit to the execution of the plan. He has to investigate available sites, their price, their nearness to his place of business, to a congenial neighborhood, to school facilities, and so on and so on. All of the things reckoned with: his ability to pay, size and needs of family, possible locations, etc., etc., are objective facts. They are no part of the original desire. But they have to be viewed and judged in order that a desire may be converted into a purpose and a purpose into a plan of action.

All of us have desires, all at least who have not become so pathological that they are completely apathetic. These desires are the ultimate moving springs of action. A professional businessman wishes to succeed in his career; a general wishes to win the battle; a parent to have a comfortable home for his family, and to educate his children, and so on indefinitely. The intensity of the desire measures the strength of the efforts that will be put forth. But the wishes are empty castles in the air unless they are translated into the means by which they may be realized. The question of *how soon* or of means takes the place of a projected imaginative end, and, since means are objective, they have to be studied and understood if a genuine purpose is to be formed.

Traditional education tended to ignore the importance of personal impulse and desire as moving springs. But this is no reason why progressive education should identify impulse and desire with purpose and thereby pass lightly over the need for careful observation, for wide range of information, and for judgment if students are to share in the formation of the purposes which activate them. In an *educational* scheme, the occurrence of a desire and impulse is not the final end. It is an occasion and a demand for the formation of a plan and method of activity. Such a plan, to repeat, can be formed only by study of conditions and by securing all relevant information.

The teacher's business is to see that the occasion is taken advantage of. Since freedom resides in the operations of intelligent observation and judgment by which a purpose is developed, guidance given by the teacher to the exercise of the pupils' intelligence is an aid to freedom, not a restriction upon it. Sometimes teachers seem to be afraid even to make suggestions to the members of a group as to what they should do. I have heard of cases in which children are surrounded with objects and materials and then left entirely to themselves, the teacher being loath to suggest even what might be done with the materials lest freedom be infringed upon. Why, then, even supply materials, since they are a source of some suggestion or other? But what is more important is that the suggestion upon which pupils act must in any case come from somewhere. It is impossible to understand why a suggestion from one who has a larger experience and a wider horizon should not be at least as valid as a suggestion arising from some more or less accidental source.

It is possible of course to abuse the office, and to force the activity of the young into channels which express the teacher's purpose rather than that of the pupils. But the way to avoid this danger is not for the adult to withdraw entirely. The way is, first, for the teacher to be intelligently aware of the capacities, needs, and past experiences of those under instruction, and, secondly, to allow the suggestion made to develop into a plan and project by means of the further suggestions contributed and organized into a whole by the members of the group. The plan, in other words, is a co-operative enterprise, not a dictation. The teacher's suggestion is not a mold for a cast-iron result but is a starting point to be developed into a plan through contributions from the experience of all engaged in the learning process. The development occurs through reciprocal give-and-take, the teacher taking but not being afraid also to give. The essential point is that the purpose grow and take shape through the process of social intelligence.

Chapter 7

Progressive Organization
of Subject-Matter

ALLUSION HAS been made in passing a number of times to objective conditions involved in experience and to their function in promoting or failing to promote the enriched growth of further experience. By implication, these objective conditions, whether those of observation, of memory, of information procured from others, or of imagination, have been identified with the subject-matter of study and learning; or, speaking more generally, with the stuff of the course of study. Nothing, however, has been said explicitly so far about subject-matter as such. That topic will now be discussed. One consideration stands out clearly when education is conceived in terms of experience. Anything which can be called a study, whether arithmetic, history, geography, or one of the natural sciences, must be derived from materials which at the outset fall within the scope of ordinary life-experience. In this respect the newer education contrasts sharply with procedures which start with facts and truths that are outside the range of the experience of those taught, and which, therefore, have the problem of discovering ways and means of bringing them within experience. Undoubtedly one chief cause for the great success of newer methods in early elementary education has been its observance of the contrary principle.

But finding the material for learning within experience is only the first step. The next step is the progressive development of what is already experienced into a fuller and richer and also more organized form, a form that gradually approximates that in which subject-matter is presented to the skilled, mature person. That this change is possible without departing from the organic connection of education with experience is shown by the fact that this change takes place outside of the school and apart from formal education. The infant, for example, begins with an environment of objects that is very restricted in space and time. That environment steadily expands by the momentum inherent in experience itself without aid from scholastic instruction. As the infant learns to reach, creep, walk, and talk, the intrinsic subject-matter of its experience widens and deepens. It comes into connection with new objects and events which call out new powers, while the exercise of these powers refines and enlarges the content of its experience. Life-space and life-durations are expanded. The environment, the world of experience, constantly grows larger and, so to speak, thicker. The educator who receives the child at the end of this period has to find ways for doing consciously and deliberately what "nature" accomplishes in the earlier years.

It is hardly necessary to insist upon the first of the two conditions which have been specified. It is a cardinal precept of the newer school of education that the beginning of instruction shall be made with the experience learners already have; that this experience and the capacities that have been developed during its course provide the starting point for all further learning. I am not so sure that the other condition, that of orderly development toward expansion and organization of subject-matter through growth of experience, receives as much attention. Yet the principle of continuity of educative experience requires that equal thought and attention be given to solution of this aspect of the educational problem. Undoubtedly this phase of the problem is more difficult than the other. Those who deal with the pre-school child, with the kindergarten child, and with the boy and girl of the early primary years do not have much difficulty in determining the range of past experience or in finding activities that connect in vital ways with it. With older children both factors of the problem offer increased difficulties to the educator. It is harder to find out the background of the experience of individuals and harder to find out just how the subject-matters already contained in that experience shall be directed so as to lead out to larger and better organized fields.

It is a mistake to suppose that the principle of the leading on of experience to something different is adequately satisfied simply by giving pupils some new experiences any more than it is by seeing to it that they have greater skill and ease in dealing with things with which they are already familiar. It is also essential that the new objects and events be related intellectually to those of earlier experiences, and this means that there be some advance made in conscious articulation of facts and ideas. It thus becomes the office of the educator to select those things within the range of existing experience that have the promise and potentiality of presenting new problems which by stimulating new ways of observation and judgment will expand the area of further experience. He must constantly regard what is already won not as a fixed possession but as an agency and instrumentality for opening new fields which make new demands upon existing powers of observation and of intelligent use of memory. Connectedness in growth must be his constant watchword.

The educator more than the member of any other profession is concerned to have a long look ahead. The physician may feel his job done when he has restored a patient to health. He has undoubtedly the obligation of advising him how to live so as to avoid similar troubles in the future. But, after all, the conduct of his life is his own affair, not the physician's; and what is more important for the present point is that as far as the physician does occupy himself with instruction and advice as to the future of his patient he takes upon himself the function of an educator. The lawyer is occupied with winning a suit for his client or getting the latter out of some complication into which he has got himself. If it goes beyond the case presented to him he too becomes an educator. The educator by the very nature of his work is obliged to see his present work in terms of what it accomplishes, or fails to accomplish, for a future whose objects are linked with those of the present.

Here, again, the problem for the progressive educator is more difficult than for the teacher in the traditional school. The latter had indeed to look ahead. But unless his personality and enthusiasm took him beyond the limits that hedged in the traditional school, he could content himself with thinking of the next examination period or the promotion to the next class. He could envisage the future in terms of factors that lay within the requirements of the school system as that conventionally existed. There is incumbent upon the teacher who links education and actual experience together a more serious and a harder business. He must be aware of the potentialities for leading students into new fields which belong to experiences already had, and must use this knowledge as his criterion for selection and arrangement of the conditions that influence their present experience.

Because the studies of the traditional school consisted of subject-matter that was selected and arranged on the basis of the judgment of adults as to what would be useful for the young sometime in the future, the material to be learned was settled upon outside the present life-experience of the learner. In consequence, it had to do with the past;

465

it was such as had proved useful to men in past ages. By reaction to an opposite extreme, as unfortunate as it was probably natural under the circumstances, the sound idea that education should derive its materials from present experience and should enable the learner to cope with the problems of the present and future has often been converted into the idea that progressive schools can to a very large extent ignore the past. If the present could be cut off from the past, this conclusion would be sound. But the achievements of the past provide the only means at command for understanding the present. Just as the individual has to draw in memory upon his own past to understand the conditions in which he individually finds himself, so the issues and problems of present *social* life are in such intimate and direct connection with the past that students cannot be prepared to understand either these problems or the best way of dealing with them without delving into their roots in the past. In other words, the sound principle that the objectives of learning are in the future and its immediate materials are in present experience can be carried into effect only in the degree that present experience is stretched, as it were, backward. It can expand into the future only as it is also enlarged to take in the past.

If time permitted, discussion of the political and economic issues which the present generation will be compelled to face in the future would render this general statement definite and concrete. The nature of the issues cannot be understood save as we know how they came about. The institutions and customs that exist in the present and that give rise to present social ills and dislocations did not arise overnight. They have a long history behind them. Attempt to deal with them simply on the basis of what is obvious in the present is bound to result in adoption of superficial measures which in the end will only render existing problems more acute and more difficult to solve.

Policies framed simply upon the ground of knowledge of the present cut off from the past is the counterpart of heedless carelessness in individual conduct. The way out of scholastic systems that made the past an end in itself is to make acquaintance with the past a *means* of understanding the present. Until this problem is worked out, the present clash of educational ideas and practices will continue. On the one hand, there will be reactionaries that claim that the main, if not the sole, business of education is transmission of the cultural heritage. On the other hand, there will be those who hold that we should ignore the past and deal only with the present and future.

That up to the present time the weakest point in progressive schools is in the matter of selection and organization of intellectual subject-matter is, I think, inevitable under the circumstances. It is as inevitable as it is right and proper that they should break loose from the cut and dried material which formed the staple of the old education. In addition, the field of experience is very wide and it varies in its contents from place to place and from time to time. A single course of studies for all progressive schools is out of the question; it would mean abandoning the fundamental principle of connection with life-experiences. Moreover, progressive schools are new. They have had hardly more than a generation in which to develop. A certain amount of uncertainty and of laxity in choice and organization of subject-matter is, therefore, what was to be expected. It is no ground for fundamental criticism or complaint.

It is a ground for legitimate criticism, however, when the ongoing movement of progressive education fails to recognize that the problem of selection and organization of subject-matter for study and learning is fundamental. Improvisation that takes advantage of special occasions prevents teaching and learning from being stereotyped and dead. But the basic material of study cannot be picked up in a cursory manner. Occasions which are not and cannot be foreseen are bound to arise wherever there is intellectual freedom. They should be utilized. But there is a decided difference between using them in the development of a continuing line of activity and trusting to them to provide the chief material of learning.

Unless a given experience leads out into a field previously unfamiliar no problems arise, while problems are the stimulus to thinking. That the conditions found in present experience should be used as sources of problems is a characteristic which differentiates education based upon experience from traditional education. For in the latter, problems were set from outside. Nonetheless, growth depends upon the presence of difficulty to be overcome by the exercise of intelligence. Once more, it is part of the educator's responsibility to see equally to two things: First, that the problem grows out of the conditions of the experience being had in the present, and that it is within the range of the capacity of students; and, secondly, that it is such that it arouses in the learner an active quest for information and for production of new ideas. The new facts and new ideas thus obtained become the ground for further experiences in which new problems are presented. The process is a continuous spiral. The inescapable linkage of the present with the past is a principle whose application is not restricted to a study of history. Take natural science, for example. Contemporary social life is what it is in very large measure because of the results of application of physical science. The experience of every child and youth, in the country and the city, is what it is in its present actuality because of appliances which utilize electricity, heat, and chemical processes. A child does not eat a meal that does not involve in its preparation and assimilation chemical and physiological principles. He does not read by artificial light or take a ride in a motor car or on a train without coming into contact with operations and processes which science has engendered.

It is a sound educational principle that students should be introduced to scientific subject-matter and be initiated into its facts and laws through acquaintance with everyday social applications. Adherence to this method is not only the most direct avenue to understanding of science itself but as the pupils grow more mature it is also the surest road to the understanding of the economic and industrial problems of present society. For they are the products to a very large extent of the application of science in production and distribution of commodities and services, while the latter processes are the most important factor in determining the present relations of human beings and social groups to one another. It is absurd, then, to argue that processes similar to those studied in laboratories and institutes of research are not a part of the daily life-experience of the young and hence do not come within the scope of education based upon experience. That the immature cannot study scientific facts and principles in the way in which mature experts study them goes without saying. But this fact, instead of exempting the educator from responsibility for using present experiences so that learners may gradually be led, through extraction of facts and laws, to experience of a scientific order, sets one of his main problems.

For if it is true that existing experience in detail and also on a wide scale is what it is because of the application of science, first, to processes of production and distribution of goods and services, and then to the relations which human beings sustain socially to one another, it is impossible to obtain an understanding of present social forces (without which they cannot be mastered and directed) apart from an education which leads learners into knowledge of the very same facts and principles which in their final organization constitute the sciences. Nor does the importance of the principle that learners should be led to acquaintance with scientific subject-matter cease with the insight thereby given into present social issues. The methods of science also point the way to the measures and policies by means of which a better social order can be brought into existence. The applications of science which have produced in large measure the social conditions which now exist do not exhaust the possible field of their application. For so far science has been applied more or less casually and under the influence of ends, such as private advantage and power, which are a heritage from the institutions of a prescientific age.

We are told almost daily and from many sources that it is impossible for human beings to direct their common life intelligently. We are told, on one hand, that the complexity of human relations, domestic and international, and on the other hand, the fact that human beings are so largely creatures of emotion and habit, make impossible large-scale social planning and direction by intelligence. This view would be more credible if any systematic effort, beginning with early education and carried on through the continuous study and learning of the young, had ever been undertaken with a view to making the method of intelligence, exemplified in science, supreme in education. There is nothing in the inherent nature of habit that prevents intelligent method from becoming itself habitual; and there is nothing in the nature of emotion to prevent the development of intense emotional allegiance to the method.

The case of science is here employed as an illustration of progressive selection of subject-matter resident in present experience towards organization: an organization which is free, not externally imposed, because it is in accord with the growth of experience itself. The utilization of subject-matter found in the present life-experience of the learner towards science is perhaps the best illustration that can be found of the basic principle of using existing experience as the means of carrying learners on to a wider, more refined, and better organized environing world, physical and human, than is found in the experiences from which educative growth sets out. Hogben's recent work, *Mathematics for the Million,* shows how mathematics, if it is treated as a mirror of civilization and as a main agency in its progress, can contribute to the desired goal as surely as can the physical sciences. The underlying ideal in any case is that of progressive organization of knowledge. It is with reference to organization of knowledge that we are likely to find *Either-Or* philosophies most acutely active. In practice, if not in so many words, it is often held that since traditional education rested upon a conception of organization of knowledge that was almost completely contemptuous of living present experience, therefore education based upon living experience should be contemptuous of the organization of facts and ideas.

When a moment ago I called this organization an *ideal,* I meant, on the negative side, that the educator cannot start with knowledge already organized and proceed to ladle it out in doses. But as an ideal the active process of organizing facts and ideas is an ever-present educational process. No experience is educative that does not tend both to knowledge of more facts and entertaining of more ideas and to a better, a more orderly, arrangement of them. It is not true that organization is a principle foreign to experience. Otherwise experience would be so dispersive as to be chaotic. The experience of young children centers about persons and the home. Disturbance of the normal order of relationships in the family is now known by psychiatrists to be a fertile source of later mental and emotional troubles—a fact which testifies to the reality of this kind of organization. One of the great advances in early school education, in the kindergarten and early grades, is that it preserves the social and human center of the organization of experience, instead of the older violent shift of the center of gravity. But one of the outstanding problems of education, as of music, is modulation. In the case of education, modulation means movement from a social and human center toward a more objective intellectual scheme of organization, always bearing in mind, however, that intellectual organization is not an end in itself but is the means by which social relations, distinctively human ties and bonds, may be understood and more intelligently ordered.

When education is based in theory and practice upon experience, it goes without saying that the organized subject-matter of the adult and the specialist cannot provide the starting point. Nevertheless, it represents the goal toward which education should continuously move. It is hardly necessary to say that one of the most fundamental principles of the scientific organization of knowledge is the principle of cause-and-effect. The way in which this principle is grasped and formulated by the scientific specialist is certainly very different from the way in which it can be approached in the experience of the young. But neither the relation nor grasp of its meaning is foreign to the experience of even the young child. When a child two or three years of age learns not to approach a flame too closely and yet to draw near enough a stove to get its warmth he is grasping and using the causal relation. There is no intelligent activity that does not conform to the requirements of the relation, and it is intelligent in the degree in which it is not only conformed to but consciously borne in mind.

In the earlier forms of experience the causal relation

does not offer itself in the abstract but in the form of the relation of means employed to ends attained; of the relation of means and consequences. Growth in judgment and understanding is essentially growth in ability to form purposes and to select and arrange means for their realization. The most elementary experiences of the young are filled with cases of the means-consequence relation. There is not a meal cooked nor a source of illumination employed that does not exemplify this relation. The trouble with education is not the absence of situations in which the causal relation is exemplified in the relation of means and consequences. Failure to utilize the situations so as to lead the learner on to grasp the relation in the given cases of experience is, however, only too common. The logician gives the names "analysis and synthesis" to the operations by which means are selected and organized in relation to a purpose.

This principle determines the ultimate foundation for the utilization of *activities* in school. Nothing can be more absurd educationally than to make a plea for a variety of active occupations in the school while decrying the need for progressive organization of information and ideas. Intelligent activity is distinguished from aimless activity by the fact that it involves selection of means—analysis—out of the variety of conditions that are present, and their arrangement—synthesis—to reach an intended aim or purpose. That the more immature the learner is, the simpler must be the ends held in view and the more rudimentary the means employed, is obvious. But the principle of organization of activity in terms of some perception of the relation of consequences to means applies even with the very young. Otherwise an activity ceases to be educative because it is blind. With increased maturity, the problem of interrelation of means becomes more urgent. In the degree in which intelligent observation is transferred from the relation of means to ends to the more complex question of the relation of means to one another, the idea of cause and effect becomes prominent and explicit. The final justification of shops, kitchens, and so on in the school is not just that they afford opportunity for activity, but that they provide opportunity for the *kind* of activity or for the acquisition of mechanical skills which leads students to attend to the relation of means and ends, and then to consideration of the way things interact with one another to produce definite effects. It is the same in principle as the ground for laboratories in scientific research.

Unless the problem of intellectual organization can be worked out on the ground of experience, reaction is sure to occur toward externally imposed methods of organization. There are signs of this reaction already in evidence. We are told that our schools, old and new, are failing in the main task. They do not develop, it is said, the capacity for critical discrimination and the ability to reason. The ability to think is smothered, we are told, by accumulation of miscellaneous ill-digested information, and by the attempt to acquire forms of skill which will be immediately useful in the business and commercial world. We are told that these evils spring from the influence of science and from the magnification of present requirements at the expense of the tested cultural heritage from the past. It is argued that science and its method must be subordinated; that we must return to the logic of ultimate first principles expressed in the logic of Aristotle and St. Thomas, in order that the young may have sure anchorage in their intellectual and moral life, and not be at the mercy of every passing breeze that blows.

If the method of science had ever been consistently and continuously applied throughout the day-by-day work of the school in all subjects, I should be more impressed by this emotional appeal than I am. I see at bottom but two alternatives between which education must choose if it is not to drift aimlessly. One of them is expressed by the attempt to induce educators to return to the intellectual methods and ideals that arose centuries before scientific method was developed. The appeal may be temporarily successful in a period when general insecurity, emotional and intellectual as well as economic, is rife. For under these conditions the desire to lean on fixed authority is active. Nevertheless, it is so out of touch with all the conditions of modern life that I believe it is folly to seek salvation in this direction. The other alternative is systematic utilization of scientific method as the pattern and ideal of intelligent exploration and exploitation of the potentialities inherent in experience.

The problem involved comes home with peculiar force to progressive schools. Failure to give constant attention to development of the intellectual content of experiences and to obtain ever-increasing organization of facts and ideas may in the end merely strengthen the tendency toward a reactionary return to intellectual and moral authoritarianism. The present is not the time nor place for a disquisition upon scientific method. But certain features of it are so closely connected with any educational scheme based upon experience that they should be noted.

In the first place, the experimental method of science attaches more importance, not less, to ideas as ideas than do other methods. There is no such thing as experiment in the scientific sense unless action is directed by some leading idea. The fact that the ideas employed are hypotheses, not final truths, is the reason why ideas are more jealously guarded and tested in science than anywhere else. The moment they are taken to be first truths in themselves there ceases to be any reason for scrupulous examination of them. As fixed truths they must be accepted and that is the end of the matter. But as hypotheses, they must be continuously tested and revised, a requirement that demands they be accurately formulated.

In the second place, ideas or hypotheses are tested by the consequences which they produce when they are acted upon. This fact means that the consequences of action must be carefully and discriminatingly observed. Activity that is not checked by observation of what follows from it may be temporarily enjoyed. But intellectually it leads nowhere. It does not provide knowledge about the situations in which action occurs nor does it lead to clarification and expansion of ideas.

In the third place, the method of intelligence manifested in the experimental method demands keeping track of ideas, activities, and observed consequences. Keeping track is a matter of reflective review and summarizing, in which there is both discrimination and record of the significant features of a developing experience. To reflect is to look back over what has been done so as to extract the net meanings which are the capital stock for intelligent dealing with further experiences. It is the heart of intellectual organization and of the disciplined mind.

I have been forced to speak in general and often abstract language. But what has been said is organically connected with the requirement that experiences in order to be educative must lead out into an expanding world of subject-matter, a subject-matter of facts or information and of ideas. This condition is satisfied only as the educator views teaching and learning as a continuous process of reconstruction of experience. This condition in turn can be satisfied only as the educator has a long look ahead, and views every present experience as a moving force in influencing what future experiences will be. I am aware that the emphasis I have placed upon scientific method may be misleading, for it may result only in calling up the special technique of laboratory research as that is conducted by specialists. But the meaning of the emphasis placed upon scientific method has little to do with specialized techniques. It means that scientific method is the only authentic means at our command for getting at the significance of our everyday experiences of the world in which we live. It means that scientific method provides a working pattern of the way in which and the conditions under which experiences are used to lead ever onward and outward. Adaptation of the method to individuals of various degrees of maturity is a problem for the educator, and the constant factors in the problem are the formation of ideas, acting upon ideas, observation of the conditions which result, and organization of facts and ideas for future use. Neither the ideas, nor the activities, nor the observations, nor the organization are the same for a person six years old as they are for one twelve or eighteen years old, to say nothing of the adult scientist. But at every level there is an expanding development of experience if experience is educative in effect. Consequently, whatever the level of experience, we have no choice but either to operate in accord with the pattern it provides or else to neglect the place of intelligence in the development and control of a living and moving experience.

Chapter 8

Experience—The Means and Goal of Education

IN WHAT I HAVE SAID I have taken for granted the soundness of the principle that education in order to accomplish its ends both for the individual learner and for society must be based upon experience—which is always the actual life-experience of some individual. I have not argued for the acceptance of this principle nor attempted to justify it. Conservatives as well as radicals in education are profoundly discontented with the present educational situation taken as a whole. There is at least this much agreement among intelligent persons of both schools of educational thought. The educational system must move one way or another, either backward to the intellectual and moral standards of a pre-scientific age or forward to ever greater utilization of scientific method in the development of the possibilities of growing, expanding experience. I have but endeavored to point out some of the conditions which must be satisfactorily fulfilled if education takes the latter course.

For I am so confident of the potentialities of education when it is treated as intelligently directed development of the possibilities inherent in ordinary experience that I do not feel it necessary to criticize here the other route nor to advance arguments in favor of taking the route of experience. The only ground for anticipating failure in taking this path resides to my mind in the danger that experience and the experimental method will not be adequately conceived. There is no discipline in the world so severe as the discipline of experience subjected to the tests of intelligent development and direction. Hence the only ground I can see for even a temporary reaction against the standards, aims, and methods of the newer education is the failure of educators who professedly adopt them to be faithful to them in practice. As I have emphasized more than once, the road of the new education is not an easier one to follow than the old road but a more strenuous and difficult one. It will remain so until it has attained its majority and that attainment will require many years of serious co-operative work on the part of its adherents. The greatest danger that attends its future is, I believe, the idea that it is an easy way to follow, so easy that its course may be improvised, if not in an impromptu fashion, at least almost from day to day or from week to week. It is for this reason that instead of extolling its principles, I have confined myself to showing certain conditions which must be fulfilled if it is to have the successful career which by right belongs to it.

I have used frequently in what precedes the words "progressive" and "new" education. I do not wish to close, however, without recording my firm belief that the fundamental issue is not of new versus old education nor of progressive against traditional education but a question of what anything whatever must be to be worthy of the name *education*. I am not, I hope and believe, in favor of any ends or any methods simply because the name progressive may be applied to them. The basic question concerns the nature of education with no qualifying adjectives prefixed. What we want and need is education pure and simple, and we shall make surer and faster progress when we devote ourselves to finding out just what education is and what conditions have to be satisfied in order that education may be a reality and not a name or a slogan. It is for this reason alone that I have emphasized the need for a sound philosophy of experience.

John Ruskin,   SESAME: OF KINGS' TREASURIES

1. What are Ruskin's main criticisms of education in 19th century England?

2. What does Ruskin see as the strongest motivations for education?

3. Compare the attitude of Ruskin with that of Rousseau on the reading of books.

4. How should one approach the reading of books, according to Ruskin?

5. What would Ruskin's reaction be to "speed reading"?

6. To what extent do you agree or disagree with Ruskin on the importance of diction?

7. Summarize Ruskin's advice on how to read books.

8. What does Ruskin mean by one statement, "It is simply and sternly impossible for the English public, at this moment, to understand any thoughtful writing"?

9. What is your reaction to Ruskin's charge that the people have "despised literature," "despised science," "despised art," "despised nature," "despised compassion"?

10. How does Ruskin relate the intellectual climate to the economic situation?

Born in London and educated at Oxford, John Ruskin (1819-1900) became an accomplished painter as well as an outstanding critic of the arts. He has been called "the greatest master of ornate prose in the English language." This selection was first presented as a public lecture in Manchester in 1864.

LECTURE I.—SESAME: OF KINGS' TREASURIES[1]

"You shall each have a cake of sesame,—and ten pound."
LUCIAN: *The Fisherman.*

MY first duty this evening is to ask your pardon for the ambiguity of title under which the subject of lecture has been announced: for indeed I am not going to talk of kings, known as regnant, nor of treasuries, understood to contain wealth; but of quite another order of royalty, and another material of riches, than those usually acknowledged. I had even intended to ask your attention for a little while on trust, and (as sometimes one contrives, in taking a friend to see a favorite piece of scenery) to hide what I wanted most to show, with such imperfect cunning as I might, until we unexpectedly reached the best point of view by winding paths. But—and as also I have heard it said, by men practised in public address, that hearers are never so much fatigued as by the endeavor to follow a speaker who gives them no clue to his purposes,—I will take the slight mask off at once, and tell you plainly that I want to speak to you about the treasures hidden in books; and about the way we find them, and the way we lose them. A grave subject, you will say; and a wide one! Yes; so wide that I shall make no effort to touch the compass of it. I will try only to bring before you a few simple thoughts about reading, which press themselves upon me every day more deeply, as I watch the course of the public mind with respect to our daily enlarging means of education; and the answeringly wider spreading on the levels, of the irrigation of literature.

2. It happens that I have practically some connection with schools for different classes of youth; and I receive many letters from parents

---

[1] This lecture was given December 6, 1864, at Rusholme Town Hall, Manchester, in aid of a library fund for the Rusholme Institute.

respecting the education of their children. In the mass of these letters I am always struck by the precedence which the idea of a "position in life" takes above all other thoughts in the parents'—more especially in the mothers'—minds. "The education befitting such and such a *station in life*"—this is the phrase, this the object, always. They never seek, as far as I can make out, an education good in itself; even the conception of abstract rightness in training rarely seems reached by the writers. But an education "which shall keep a good coat on my son's back;—which shall enable him to ring with confidence the visitors' bell at double-belled doors; which shall result ultimately in establishment of a double-belled door to his own house;—in a word, which shall lead to 'advancement in life';—*this* we pray for on bent knees—and this is *all* we pray for." It never seems to occur to the parents that there may be an education which, in itself, *is* advancement in Life;—that any other than that may perhaps be advancement in Death; and that this essential education might be more easily got, or given, than they fancy, if they set about it in the right way; while it is for no price, and by no favor, to be got, if they set about it in the wrong.

3. Indeed, among the ideas most prevalent and effective in the mind of this busiest of countries, I suppose the first—at least that which is confessed with the greatest frankness, and put forward as the fittest stimulus to youthful exertion—is this of "Advancement in Life." May I ask you to consider with me what this idea practically includes, and what it should include?

Practically, then, at present, "advancement in life" means, becoming conspicuous in life;—obtaining a position which shall be acknowledged by others to be respectable or honorable. We do not understand by this advancement in general, the mere making of money, but the being known to have made it; not the accomplishment of any great aim, but the being seen to have accomplished it. In a word, we mean the gratification of our thirst for applause. That thirst, if the last infirmity of noble minds, is also the first infirmity of weak ones; and, on the whole, the strongest impulsive influence of average humanity: the greatest efforts of the race have always been traceable to the love of praise, as its greatest catastrophes to the love of pleasure.

4. I am not about to attack or defend this impulse. I want you only to feel how it lies at the root of effort; especially of all modern effort. It is the gratification of vanity which is, with us, the stimulus of toil, and balm of repose; so closely does it touch the very springs of life that the wounding of our vanity is always spoken of (and truly) as in its measure *mortal;* we call it "mortification," using the same expression which we should apply to a gangrenous and incurable bodily hurt. And although few of us may be physicians enough to recognize the various effect of this passion upon health and energy, I believe most honest men know, and would at once acknowledge, its leading power with them as a motive. The seaman does not commonly desire to be made captain only because he knows he can manage the ship better than any other sailor on board. He wants to be made captain that he may be *called* captain. The clergyman does not usually want to be made a bishop only because he believes no other hand can, as firmly as his, direct the diocese through its difficulties. He wants to be made bishop primarily that he may be called "My Lord." And a prince does not usually desire to enlarge, or a subject to gain, a kingdom, because he believes that no one else can as well serve the State, upon its throne; but, briefly, because he wishes to be addressed as "Your Majesty," by as many lips as may be brought to such utterance.

5. This, then, being the main idea of "advancement in life," the force of it applies, for all of us, according to our station, particularly to that secondary result of such advancement which we call "getting into good society." We want to get into good society, not that we may have it, but that we may be seen in it; and our notion of its goodness depends primarily on its conspicuousness.

Will you pardon me if I pause for a moment to put what I fear you may think an impertinent question? I never can go on with an address unless I feel, or know, that my audience are either with me or against me: I do not much care which, in beginning; but I must know where they are; and I would fain find out, at this instant, whether you think I am putting the motives of popular action too low. I am resolved, to-night, to state them low enough to be admitted as probable; for whenever, in my writings on Political Economy, I assume that a little honesty, or generosity—or what used to be called "virtue"—may be calculated upon as a human motive of action, people always answer me, saying, "You must not calculate on that: that is not in human nature: you must not assume anything to be common to men but acquisitiveness and jealousy; no other feeling ever has influence on them, except accidentally, and in matters out of the way of business." I begin, accordingly, to-night low in the scale of motives; but I must know if you think me right in doing so. Therefore, let me ask those who admit the love of praise to be usually the strongest motive in men's minds in seeking advancement, and the honest desire of doing any kind of duty to be an entirely secondary one, to hold up their hands. (*About a dozen hands held up—the audience, partly not being sure the lecturer is serious, and, partly, shy of expressing opinion.*) I am quite serious—I really do want to know what you think; however, I can judge by putting the reverse question. Will those who think that duty is generally the first, and love of praise the second, motive, hold up their hands? (*One hand reported to have been held up, behind the lecturer.*) Very good; I see you are with me, and that you think I have not begun too near the ground. Now, without teasing you by putting farther question, I venture to assume that you will admit duty as at least a secondary or tertiary motive. You think that the desire of doing something useful, or obtaining some real good, is indeed an existent collateral idea, though a secondary one, in most men's desire of advancement. You will grant that moderately honest men desire place and office, at least in some measure, for the sake of beneficent power; and would wish to associate rather with sensible and well-informed persons than with fools and ignorant persons, whether they are seen in the company of the sensible ones or not. And finally, without being troubled by repetition of any common truisms about the preciousness of friends, and the influence of companions, you will admit, doubtless, that according to the sincerity of our desire that our friends may be true, and our companions wise,—and in proportion to the earnestness and discretion with which we choose both, will be the general chances of our happiness and usefulness.

6. But, granting that we had both the will and the sense to choose our friends well, how few of us have the power! or, at least, how

limited, for most, is the sphere of choice! Nearly all our associations are determined by chance, or necessity; and restricted within a narrow circle. We cannot know whom we would; and those whom we know, we cannot have at our side when we most need them. All the higher circles of human intelligence are, to those beneath, only momentarily and partially open. We may, by good fortune, obtain a glimpse of a great poet, and hear the sound of his voice; or put a question to a man of science, and be answered good-humoredly. We may intrude ten minutes' talk on a cabinet minister, answered probably with words worse than silence, being deceptive; or snatch, once or twice in our lives, the privilege of throwing a bouquet in the path of a Princess, or arresting the kind glance of a Queen. And yet these momentary chances we covet; and spend our years, and passions, and powers in pursuit of little more than these; while, meantime, there is a society continually open to us, of people who will talk to us as long as we like, whatever our rank or occupation;—talk to us in the best words they can choose, and of the things nearest their hearts. And this society, because it is so numerous and so gentle, and can be kept waiting round us all day long,—kings and statesmen lingering patiently, not to grant audience, but to gain it!—in those plainly furnished and narrow anterooms, our bookcase shelves,—we make no account of that company,—perhaps never listen to a word they would say, all day long!

7. You may tell me, perhaps, or think within yourselves, that the apathy with which we regard this company of the noble, who are praying us to listen to them; and the passion with which we pursue the company, probably of the ignoble who despise us, or who have nothing to teach us, are grounded in this,—that we can see the faces of the living men, and it is themselves, and not their sayings, with which we desire to become familiar. But it is not so. Suppose you never were to see their faces;—suppose you could be put behind a screen in the statesman's cabinet, or the prince's chamber, would you not be glad to listen to their words, though you were forbidden to advance beyond the screen? And when the screen is only a little less, folded in two instead of four, and you can be hidden behind the cover of the two boards that bind a book, and listen all day long, not to the casual talk, but to the studied, determined, chosen addresses

of the wisest of men;—this station of audience, and honorable privy council, you despise!

8. But perhaps you will say that it is because the living people talk of things that are passing, and are of immediate interest to you, that you desire to hear them. Nay; that cannot be so, for the living people will themselves tell you about passing matters much better in their writings than in their careless talk. But I admit that this motive does influence you, so far as you prefer those rapid and ephemeral writings to slow and enduring writings,—books, properly so called. For all books are divisible into two classes, the books of the hour, and the books of all time. Mark this distinction—it is not one of quality only. It is not merely the bad book that does not last, and the good one that does. It is a distinction of species. There are good books for the hour, and good ones for all time; bad books for the hour, and bad ones for all time. I must define the two kinds before I go farther.

9. The good book of the hour, then,—I do not speak of the bad ones,—is simply the useful or pleasant talk of some person whom you cannot otherwise converse with, printed for you. Very useful often, telling you what you need to know; very pleasant often, as a sensible friend's present talk would be. These bright accounts of travels; good-humored and witty discussions of question; lively or pathetic story-telling in the form of novel; firm fact-telling, by the real agents concerned in the events of passing history;—all these books of the hour, multiplying among us as education becomes more general, are a peculiar possession of the present age; we ought to be entirely thankful for them, and entirely ashamed of ourselves if we make no good use of them. But we make the worst possible use if we allow them to usurp the place of true books: for strictly speaking, they are not books at all, but merely letters or newspapers in good print. Our friend's letter may be delightful, or necessary, to-day: whether worth keeping or not, is to be considered. The newspaper may be entirely proper at breakfast time, but assuredly it is not reading for all day. So, though bound up in a volume, the long letter which gives you so pleasant an account of the inns, and roads, and weather last year at such a place, or which tells you that amusing story, or gives you the real circumstances of such and such events,

however valuable for occasional reference, may not be, in the real sense of the word, a "book" at all, nor in the real sense, to be "read." A book is essentially not a talked thing, but a written thing; and written, not with the view of mere communication, but of permanence. The book of talk is printed only because its author cannot speak to thousands of people at once; if he could, he would—the volume is mere *multiplication* of his voice. You cannot talk to your friend in India; if you could, you would; you write instead: that is mere *conveyance* of voice. But a book is written, not to multiply the voice merely, not to carry it merely, but to perpetuate it. The author has something to say which he perceives to be true and useful, or helpfully beautiful. So far as he knows, no one has yet said it; so far as he knows, no one else can say it. He is bound to say it, clearly and melodiously if he may; clearly, at all events. In the sum of his life he finds this to be the thing, or group of things, manifest to him; —this, the piece of true knowledge, or sight, which his share of sunshine and earth has permitted him to seize. He would fain set it down forever; engrave it on rock, if he could; saying, "This is the best of me; for the rest, I ate, and drank, and slept, loved, and hated, like another; my life was as the vapor and is not; but this I saw and knew: this, if anything of mine, is worth your memory." That is his "writing"; it is, in his small human way, and with whatever degree of true inspiration is in him, his inscription, or scripture. That is a "Book."

10. Perhaps you think no books were ever so written.

But, again, I ask you, do you at all believe in honesty, or at all in kindness? or do you think there is never any honesty or benevolence in wise people? None of us, I hope, are so unhappy as to think that. Well, whatever bit of a wise man's work is honestly and benevolently done, that bit is his book, or his piece of art.[2] It is mixed always with evil fragments—ill-done, redundant, affected work. But if you read rightly, you will easily discover the true bits, and those *are* the book.

11. Now books of this kind have been written in all ages by their greatest men:—by great readers, great statesmen, and great thinkers. These are all at your choice; and Life is short. You have heard as much before;—yet have you measured and mapped out this short

[2] Note this sentence carefully, and compare the "Queen of the Air," § 106.

life and its possibilities? Do you know, if you read this, that you cannot read that—that what you lose to-day you cannot gain to-morrow? Will you go and gossip with your housemaid, or your stableboy, when you may talk with queens and kings; or flatter yourselves that it is with any worthy consciousness of your own claims to respect that you jostle with the hungry and common crowd for *entrée* here, and audience there, when all the while this eternal court is open to you, with its society, wide as the world, multitudinous as its days, the chosen, and the mighty, of every place and time? Into that you may enter always; in that you may take fellowship and rank according to your wish; from that, once entered into it, you can never be outcast but by your own fault; by your aristocracy of companionship there, your own inherent aristocracy will be assuredly tested, and the motives with which you strive to take high place in the society of the living, measured, as to all the truth and sincerity that are in them, by the place you desire to take in this company of the Dead.

12. "The place you desire," and the place you *fit yourself for,* I must also say; because, observe, this court of the past differs from all living aristocracy in this:—it is open to labor and to merit, but to nothing else. No wealth will bribe, no name overawe, no artifice deceive, the guardian of those Elysian gates. In the deep sense, no vile or vulgar person ever enters there. At the portières of that silent Faubourg St. Germain, there is but brief question:—"Do you deserve to enter? Pass. Do you ask to be the companion of nobles? Make yourself noble, and you shall be. Do you long for the conversation of the wise? Learn to understand it, and you shall hear it. But on other terms?—no. If you will not rise to us, we cannot stoop to you. The living lord may assume courtesy, the living philosopher explain his thought to you with considerate pain; but here we neither feign nor interpret; you must rise to the level of our thoughts if you would be gladdened by them, and share our feelings, if you would recognize our presence."

13. This, then, is what you have to do, and I admit that it is much. You must, in a word, love these people, if you are to be among them. No ambition is of any use. They scorn your ambition. You must love them, and show your love in these two following ways:

I.—First, by a true desire to be taught by them, and to enter into their thoughts. To enter into theirs, observe; not to find your own expressed by them. If the person who wrote the book is not wiser than you, you need not read it; if he be, he will think differently from you in many respects.

Very ready we are to say of a book, "How good this is—that's exactly what I think!" But the right feeling is, "How strange that is! I never thought of that before, and yet I see it is true; or if I do not now, I hope I shall, some day." But whether thus submissively or not, at least be sure that you go to the author to get at *his* meaning, not to find yours. Judge it afterwards, if you think yourself qualified to do so; but ascertain it first. And be sure also, if the author is worth anything, that you will not get at his meaning all at once;—nay, that at his whole meaning you will not for a long time arrive in any wise. Not that he does not say what he means, and in strong words too; but he cannot say it all; and what is more strange, *will* not, but in a hidden way and in parables, in order that he may be sure you want it. I cannot quite see the reason of this, nor analyze that cruel reticence in the breasts of wise men which makes them always hide their deeper thought. They do not give it to you by way of help, but of reward; and will make themselves sure that you deserve it before they allow you to reach it. But it is the same with the physical type of wisdom, gold. There seems, to you and me, no reason why the electric forces of the earth should not carry whatever there is of gold within it at once to the mountain tops, so that kings and people might know that all the gold they could get was there; and without any trouble of digging, or anxiety, or chance, or waste of time, cut it away, and coin as much as they needed. But Nature does not manage it so. She puts it in little fissures in the earth, nobody knows where: you may dig long and find none; you must dig painfully to find any.

14. And it is just the same with men's best wisdom. When you come to a good book, you must ask yourself, "Am I inclined to work as an Australian miner would? Are my pickaxes and shovels in good order, and am I in good trim myself, my sleeves well up to the elbow, and my breath good, and my temper?" And, keeping the figure a little longer, even at the cost of tiresomeness, for it is a thor-

oughly useful one, the metal you are in search of being the author's mind or meaning, his words are as the rock which you have to crush and smelt in order to get at it. And your pickaxes are your own care, wit, and learning; your smelting-furnace is your own thoughtful soul. Do not hope to get at any good author's meaning without those tools and that fire; often you will need sharpest, finest chiseling, and patientest fusing, before you can gather one grain of the metal.

15. And therefore, first of all, I tell you, earnestly and authoritatively (I *know* I am right in this), you must get into the habit of looking intensely at words, and assuring yourself of their meaning, syllable by syllable—nay, letter by letter. For though it is only by reason of the opposition of letters in the function of signs, to sounds in the function of signs, that the study of books is called "literature," and that a man versed in it is called, by the consent of nations, a man of letters instead of a man of books, or of words, you may yet connect with that accidental nomenclature this real fact:—that you might read all the books in the British Museum (if you could live long enough) and remain an utterly "illiterate," uneducated person; but that if you read ten pages of a good book, letter by letter,—that is to say, with real accuracy,—you are forevermore in some measure an educated person. The entire difference between education and non-education (as regards the merely intellectual part of it) consists in this accuracy. A well-educated gentleman may not know many languages,—may not be able to speak any but his own,—may have read very few books. But whatever language he knows, he knows precisely; whatever word he pronounces, he pronounces rightly; above all, he is learned in the *peerage* of words; knows the words of true descent and ancient blood at a glance, from words of modern canaille; remembers all their ancestry, their inter-marriages, distant relationships, and the extent to which they were admitted, and offices they held, among the national noblesse of words at any time, and in any country. But an uneducated person may know, by memory, many languages, and talk them all, and yet truly know not a word of any,—not a word even of his own. An ordinarily clever and sensible seaman will be able to make his way ashore at most ports; yet he has only to speak a sentence of any language to

be known for an illiterate person: so also the accent, or turn of expression of a single sentence, will at once mark a scholar. And this is so strongly felt, so conclusively admitted by educated persons, that a false accent or a mistaken syllable is enough, in the parliament of any civilized nation, to assign to a man a certain degree of inferior standing forever.

16. And this is right; but it is a pity that the accuracy insisted on is not greater, and required to a serious purpose. It is right that a false Latin quantity should excite a smile in the House of Commons; but it is wrong that a false English *meaning* should *not* excite a frown there. Let the accent of words be watched; and closely: let their meaning be watched more closely still, and fewer will do the work. A few words well chosen and distinguished, will do work that a thousand cannot, when every one is acting, equivocally, in the function of another. Yes; and words, if they are not watched, will do deadly work sometimes. There are masked words droning and skulking about us in Europe just now,—(there never were so many, owing to the spread of a shallow, blotching, blundering, infectious "information," or rather deformation, everywhere, and to the teaching of catechisms and phrases at schools instead of human meanings)—there are masked words abroad, I say, which nobody understands, but which everybody uses, and most people will also fight for, live for, or even die for, fancying they mean this or that, or the other, of things dear to them: for such words wear chameleon cloaks— "ground-lion" cloaks, of the color of the ground of any man's fancy: on that ground they lie in wait, and rend him with a spring from it. There never were creatures of prey so mischievous, never diplomatists so cunning, never poisoners so deadly, as these masked words; they are the unjust stewards of all men's ideas: whatever fancy or favorite instinct a man most cherishes, he gives to his favorite masked word to take care of for him; the word at last comes to have an infinite power over him,—you cannot get at him but by its ministry.

17. And in languages so mongrel in breed as the English, there is a fatal power of equivocation put into men's hands, almost whether they will or no, in being able to use Greek or Latin words for an idea when they want it to be awful; and Saxon or otherwise common words when they want it to be vulgar. What a singular and

salutary effect, for instance, would be produced on the minds of people who are in the habit of taking the Form of the "Word" they live by, for the Power of which that Word tells them, if we always either retained, or refused, the Greek form "biblos," or "biblion," as the right expression for "book"—instead of employing it only in the one instance in which we wish to give dignity to the idea, and translating it into English everywhere else. How wholesome it would be for many simple persons, if, in such places (for instance) as Acts xix. 19, we retained the Greek expression, instead of translating it, and they had to read—"Many of them also which used curious arts, brought their bibles together, and burnt them before all men; and they counted the price of them, and found it fifty thousand pieces of silver"! Or if, on the other hand, we translated where we retain it, and always spoke of "The Holy Book," instead of "Holy Bible," it might come into more heads than it does at present, that the Word of God, by which the heavens were, of old, and by which they are now kept in store,[3] cannot be made a present of to anybody in morocco binding; nor sown on any wayside by help either of steam plough or steam press; but is nevertheless being offered to us daily, and by us with contumely refused; and sown in us daily, and by us, as instantly as may be, choked.

18. So, again, consider what effect has been produced on the English vulgar mind by the use of the sonorous Latin form "damno," in translating the Greek κατακρίνω, when people charitably wish to make it forcible; and the substitution of the temperate "condemn" for it, when they choose to keep it gentle; and what notable sermons have been preached by illiterate clergymen on—"He that believeth not shall be damned"; though they would shrink with horror from translating Heb. xi. 7, "The saving of his house, by which he damned the world"; or John viii. 10, 11, "Woman, hath no man damned thee? She saith, No man, Lord. Jesus answered her, Neither do I damn thee; go and sin no more." And divisions in the mind of Europe, which have cost seas of blood and in the defense of which the noblest souls of men have been cast away in frantic desolation, countless as forest leaves—though, in the heart of them, founded on deeper

[3] 2 Peter iii. 5–7.

causes—have nevertheless been rendered practicably possible, namely, by the European adoption of the Greek word for a public meeting, "ecclesia," to give peculiar respectability to such meetings, when held for religious purposes; and other collateral equivocations, such as the vulgar English one of using the word "priest" as a contraction for "presbyter."

19. Now, in order to deal with words rightly, this is the habit you must form. Nearly every word in your language has been first a word of some other language—of Saxon, German, French, Latin, or Greek (not to speak of eastern and primitive dialects). And many words have been all these;—that is to say, have been Greek first, Latin next, French and German next, and English last: undergoing a certain change of sense and use on the lips of each nation; but retaining a deep vital meaning, which all good scholars feel in employing them, even at this day. If you do not know the Greek alphabet, learn it; young or old—girl or boy—whoever you may be, if you think of reading seriously (which, of course, implies that you have some leisure at command), learn your Greek alphabet; then get good dictionaries of all these languages, and whenever you are in doubt about a word, hunt it down patiently. Read Max Müller's lectures thoroughly, to begin with; and, after that, never let a word escape you that looks suspicious. It is severe work; but you will find it, even at first, interesting, and at last, endlessly amusing. And the general gain to your character, in power and precision, will be quite incalculable.

Mind, this does not imply knowing, or trying to know, Greek or Latin, or French. It takes a whole life to learn any language perfectly. But you can easily ascertain the meanings through which the English word has passed; and those which in a good writer's work it must still bear.

20. And now, merely for example's sake, I will, with your permission, read a few lines of a true book with you, carefully; and see what will come out of them. I will take a book perfectly known to you all. No English words are more familiar to us, yet few perhaps have been read with less sincerity. I will take these few following lines of "Lycidas":

"Last came, and last did go,
　The pilot of the Galilean lake;
　Two massy keys he bore of metals twain
　(The golden opes, the iron shuts amain),
　He shook his mitred locks, and stern bespake,
　'How well could I have spar'd for thee, young swain,
　Enow of such as for their bellies' sake
　Creep, and intrude, and climb into the fold!
　Of other care they little reckoning make,
　Than how to scramble at the shearers' feast,
　And shove away the worthy bidden guest;
　Blind mouths! that scarce themselves know how to hold
　A sheep-hook, or have learn'd aught else, the least
　That to the faithful herdsman's art belongs!
　What recks it them? What need they? They are sped;
　And when they list, their lean and flashy songs
　Grate on their scrannel pipes of wretched straw;
　The hungry sheep look up, and are not fed,
　But, swoln with wind, and the rank mist they draw,
　Rot inwardly, and foul contagion spread;
　Besides what the grim wolf with privy paw
　Daily devours apace, and nothing said.' "

Let us think over this passage, and examine its words.

First, is it not singular to find Milton assigning to St. Peter, not only his full episcopal function, but the very types of it which Protestants usually refuse most passionately? His "mitred" locks! Milton was no Bishop-lover; how comes St. Peter to be "mitred"? "Two massy keys he bore." Is this, then, the power of the keys claimed by the Bishops of Rome, and is it acknowledged here by Milton only in a poetical license, for the sake of its picturesqueness, that he may get the gleam of the golden keys to help his effect? Do not think it. Great men do not play stage tricks with doctrines of life and death: only little men do that. Milton means what he says; and means it with his might too—is going to put the whole strength of his spirit presently into the saying of it. For though not a lover of false bishops, he *was* a lover of true ones; and the Lake-pilot is here, in his thoughts, the type and head of true episcopal power. For Milton reads that text, "I will give unto thee the keys of the kingdom of heaven" quite honestly. Puritan though he be, he would not blot it out of the book because there have been bad bishops; nay, in order to understand *him,* we must understand that verse first; it will not do to eye it askance, or whisper it under our breath, as if it were a weapon of an adverse sect. It is a solemn, universal assertion, deeply to be kept in mind by all sects. But perhaps we shall be better able to reason on it if we go on a little farther, and come back to it. For clearly this marked insistence on the power of the true episcopate is to make us feel more weightily what is to be charged against the false claimants of episcopate; or generally, against false claimants of power and rank in the body of the clergy; they who, "for their bellies' sake, creep, and intrude, and climb into the fold."

21. Never think Milton uses those three words to fill up his verse, as a loose writer would. He needs all the three; especially those three, and no more than those—"creep," and "intrude," and "climb"; no other words would or could serve the turn, and no more could be added. For they exhaustively comprehend the three classes, correspondent to the three characters, of men who dishonestly seek ecclesiastical power. First, those who *"creep"* into the fold; who do not care for office, nor name, but for secret influence, and do all things occultly and cunningly, consenting to any servility of office or conduct, so only that they may intimately discern, and unawares direct, the minds of men. Then those who "intrude" (thrust, that is) themselves into the fold, who by natural insolence of heart, and stout eloquence of tongue, and fearlessly perseverant self-assertion, obtain hearing and authority with the common crowd. Lastly, those who "climb," who by labor and learning, both stout and sound, but selfishly exerted in the cause of their own ambition, gain high dignities and authorities, and become "lords over the heritage," though not "ensamples to the flock."

22. Now go on:—

> "Of other care they little reckoning make,
>   Than how to scramble at the shearers' feast.
>   *Blind mouths—*"

I pause again, for this is a strange expression; a broken metaphor, one might think, careless and unscholarly.

Not so: its very audacity and pithiness are intended to make us look close at the phrase and remember it. Those two monosyllables express the precisely accurate contraries of right character, in the two great offices of the Church—those of bishop and pastor.

A "Bishop" means a "person who sees."

A "Pastor" means a "person who feeds."

The most unbishoply character a man can have is therefore to be Blind.

The most unpastoral is, instead of feeding, to want to be fed,—to be a Mouth.

Take the two reverses together, and you have "blind mouths." We may advisably follow out this idea a little. Nearly all the evils in the Church have arisen from bishops desiring *power* more than *light*. They want authority, not outlook. Whereas their real office is not to rule; though it may be vigorously to exhort and rebuke; it is the king's office to rule; the bishop's office is to *oversee* the flock; to number it, sheep by sheep; to be ready always to give full account of it. Now it is clear he cannot give account of the souls, if he has not so much as numbered the bodies of his flock. The first thing, therefore, that a bishop has to do is at least to put himself in a position in which, at any moment, he can obtain the history, from childhood, of every living soul in his diocese, and of its present state. Down in that back street, Bill and Nancy, knocking each other's teeth out!—Does the bishop know all about it? Has he his eye upon them? Has he *had* his eye upon them? Can he circumstantially explain to us how Bill got into the habit of beating Nancy about the head? If he cannot, he is no bishop, though he had a mitre as high as Salisbury steeple; he is no bishop,—he has sought to be at the helm instead of the masthead; he has no sight of things. "Nay," you say, "it is not his duty to look after Bill in the back street." What! the fat sheep that have full fleeces—you think it is only those he should look after, while (go back to your Milton) "the hungry sheep look up, and are not fed, besides what the grim wolf with privy paw" (bishops knowing nothing about it) "daily devours apace, and nothing said"?

"But that's not our idea of a bishop." [4] Perhaps not; but it was St. Paul's; and it was Milton's. They may be right, or we may be;

[4] Compare the 13th Letter in "Time and Tide."

but we must not think we are reading either one or the other by putting our meaning into their words.

23. I go on.

"But, swoln with wind, and the rank mist they draw."

This is to meet the vulgar answer that "if the poor are not looked after in their bodies, they are in their souls; they have spiritual food."

And Milton says, "They have no such thing as spiritual food; they are only swollen with wind." At first you may think that is a coarse type, and an obscure one. But again, it is a quite literally accurate one. Take up your Latin and Greek dictionaries, and find out the meaning of "Spirit." It is only a contraction of the Latin word "breath," and an indistinct translation of the Greek word for "wind." The same word is used in writing, "The wind bloweth where it listeth"; and in writing, "So is every one that is born of the Spirit"; born of the *breath,* that is; for it means the breath of God, in soul and body. We have the true sense of it in our words "inspiration" and "expire." Now, there are two kinds of breath with which the flock may be filled; God's breath, and man's. The breath of God is health, and life, and peace to them, as the air of heaven is to the flocks on the hills; but man's breath—the word which *he* calls spiritual,—is disease and contagion to them, as the fog of the fen. They rot inwardly with it; they are puffed up by it, as a dead body by the vapors of its own decomposition. This is literally true of all false religious teaching; the first and last, and fatalest sign of it is that "puffing up." Your converted children, who teach their parents; your converted convicts, who teach honest men; your converted dunces, who, having lived in cretinous stupefaction half their lives, suddenly awakening to the fact of there being a God, fancy themselves therefore His peculiar people and messengers; your sectarians of every species, small and great, Catholic or Protestant, of high church or low, in so far as they think themselves exclusively in the right and others wrong; and preëminently, in every sect, those who hold that men can be saved by thinking rightly instead of doing rightly, by word instead of act, and wish instead of work:—these are the true fog children—clouds, these, without water; bodies, these, of putrescent vapor and skin, without blood or flesh: blown bag-pipes for the fiends to pipe with—corrupt, and corrupting,—"Swollen with wind, and the rank mist they draw."

24. Lastly, let us return to the lines respecting the power of the keys, for now we can understand them. Note the difference between Milton and Dante in their interpretation of this power: for once, the latter is weaker in thought; he supposes *both* the keys to be of the gate of heaven; one is of gold, the other of silver: they are given by St. Peter to the sentinel angel; and it is not easy to determine the meaning either of the substances of the three steps of the gate, or of the two keys. But Milton makes one, of gold, the key of heaven; the other, of iron, the key of the prison in which the wicked teachers are to be bound who "have taken away the key of knowledge, yet entered not in themselves."

We have seen that the duties of bishop and pastor are to see and feed; and of all who do so it is said, "He that watereth, shall be watered also himself." But the reverse is truth also. He that watereth not, shall be *withered* himself, and he that seeth not, shall himself be shut out of sight—shut into the perpetual prison-house. And that prison opens here, as well as hereafter: he who is to be bound in heaven must first be bound on earth. That command to the strong angels, of which the rock-apostle is the image, "Take him, and bind him hand and foot, and cast him out," issues, in its measure, against the teacher, for every help withheld, and for every truth refused, and for every falsehood enforced; so that he is more strictly fettered the more he fetters, and farther outcast, as he more and more misleads, till at last the bars of the iron cage close upon him, and as "the golden opes, the iron shuts amain."

25. We have got something out of the lines, I think, and much more is yet to be found in them; but we have done enough by way of example of the kind of word-by-word examination of your author which is rightly called "reading"; watching every accent and expression, and putting ourselves always in the author's place, annihilating our own personality, and seeking to enter into his, so as to be able assuredly to say, "Thus Milton thought," not "Thus *I* thought, in mis-reading Milton." And by this process you will gradually come to attach less weight to your own "Thus I thought" at other times.

You will begin to perceive that what *you* thought was a matter of no serious importance;—that your thoughts on any subject are not perhaps the clearest and wisest that could be arrived at thereupon:—in fact, that unless you are a very singular person, you cannot be said to have any "thoughts" at all; that you have no materials for them, in any serious matters;[5]—no right to "think," but only to try to learn more of the facts. Nay, most probably all your life (unless, as I said, you are a singular person) you will have no legitimate right to an "opinion" on any business, except that instantly under your hand. What must of necessity be done, you can always find out, beyond question, how to do. Have you a house to keep in order, a commodity to sell, a field to plough, a ditch to cleanse? There need be no two opinions about these proceedings; it is at your peril if you have not much more than an "opinion" on the way to manage such matters. And also, outside of your own business, there are one or two subjects on which you are bound to have but one opinion. That roguery and lying are objectionable, and are instantly to be flogged out of the way whenever discovered;—that covetousness and love of quarreling are dangerous dispositions even in children, and deadly dispositions in men and nations;—that in the end, the God of heaven and earth loves active, modest, and kind people, and hates idle, proud, greedy, and cruel ones;—on these general facts you are bound to have but one, and that a very strong, opinion. For the rest, respecting religions, governments, sciences, arts, you will find that, on the whole, you can know NOTHING,—judge nothing; that the best you can do, even though you may be a well-educated person, is to be silent, and strive to be wiser every day, and to understand a little more of the thoughts of others, which so soon as you try to do honestly, you will discover that the thoughts even of the wisest are very little more than pertinent questions. To put the difficulty into a clear shape, and exhibit to you the grounds for *in*decision, that is all they can generally do for you!—and well for them and for us, if indeed they are able "to mix the music with our thoughts, and sadden us with heavenly doubts." This writer, from whom I have been reading to you, is not among the first or wisest: he sees shrewdly as

---

[5] Modern "education" for the most part signifies giving people the faculty of thinking wrong on every conceivable subject of importance to them.

far as he sees, and therefore it is easy to find out his full meaning;
but with the greater men, you cannot fathom their meaning; they
do not even wholly measure it themselves,—it is so wide. Suppose
I had asked you, for instance, to seek for Shakespeare's opinion,
instead of Milton's, on this matter of Church authority?—or for
Dante's? Have any of you, at this instant, the least idea what either
thought about it? Have you ever balanced the scene with the bishops
in "Richard III." against the character of Cranmer? the description
of St. Francis and St. Dominic against that of him who made Virgil
wonder to gaze upon him,—"disteso, tanto vilmente, nell' eterno
esilio"; or of him whom Dante stood beside, "come 'l frate che con-
fessa lo perfido assassin?" [6] Shakespeare and Alighieri knew men
better than most of us, I presume! They were both in the midst of
the main struggle between the temporal and spiritual powers. They
had an opinion, we may guess. But where is it? Bring it into court!
Put Shakespeare's or Dante's creed into articles, and send *it* up for
trial by the Ecclesiastical Courts!

26. You will not be able, I tell you again, for many and many a
day, to come at the real purposes and teaching of these great men;
but a very little honest study of them will enable you to perceive that
what you took for your own "judgment" was mere chance prejudice,
and drifted, helpless, entangled weed of castaway thought: nay, you
will see that most men's minds are indeed little better than rough
heath wilderness, neglected and stubborn, partly barren, partly over-
grown with pestilent brakes, and venomous, wind-sown herbage of
evil surmise; that the first thing you have to do for them, and yourself, is eagerly and scornfully to set fire to *this;* burn all the jungle
into wholesome ash heaps, and then plough and sow. All the true
literary work before you, for life, must begin with obedience to that
order, "Break up your fallow ground, and *sow not among thorns.*"

27. II.[7]—Having then faithfully listened to the great teachers, that
you may enter into their Thoughts, you have yet this higher advance
to make;—you have to enter into their Hearts. As you go to them
first for clear sight, so you must stay with them, that you may share
at last their just and mighty Passion. Passion, or "sensation." I am

---

[6] "Inferno," xxiii. 125, 126; xix. 49, 50.
[7] Compare § 13 above.

not afraid of the word; still less of the thing. You have heard many outcries against sensation lately; but, I can tell you, it is not less sensation we want, but more. The ennobling difference between one man and another,—between one animal and another,—is precisely in this, that one feels more than another. If we were sponges, perhaps sensation might not be easily got for us; if we were earthworms, liable at every instant to be cut in two by the spade, perhaps too much sensation might not be good for us. But, being human creatures, *it is* good for us; nay, we are only human in so far as we are sensitive, and our honor is precisely in proportion to our passion.

28. You know I said of that great and pure society of the dead, that it would allow "no vain or vulgar person to enter there." What do you think I meant by a "vulgar" person? What do you yourselves mean by "vulgarity"? You will find it a fruitful subject of thought; but, briefly, the essence of all vulgarity lies in want of sensation. Simple and innocent vulgarity is merely an untrained and undeveloped bluntness of body and mind; but in true inbred vulgarity, there is a deathful callousness, which, in extremity, becomes capable of every sort of bestial habit and crime, without fear, without pleasure, without horror, and without pity. It is in the blunt hand and the dead heart, in the diseased habit, in the hardened conscience, that men become vulgar; they are forever vulgar, precisely in proportion as they are incapable of sympathy,—of quick understanding,—of all that, in deep insistence on the common, but most accurate term, may be called the "tact" or "touch-faculty" of body and soul; that tact which the Mimosa has in trees, which the pure woman has above all creatures;—fineness and fullness of sensation beyond reason;—the guide and sanctifier of reason itself. Reason can but determine what is true:—it is the God-given passion of humanity which alone can recognize what God has made good.

29. We come then to the great concourse of the Dead, not merely to know from them what is True, but chiefly to feel with them what is just. Now, to feel with them, we must be like them; and none of us can become that without pains. As the true knowledge is disciplined and tested knowledge,—not the first thought that comes,—so the true passion is disciplined and tested passion,—not the first passion that comes. The first that come are the vain, the false, the

treacherous; if you yield to them they will lead you wildly and far
in vain pursuit, in hollow enthusiasm, till you have no true purpose
and no true passion left. Not that any feeling possible to humanity
is in itself wrong, but only wrong when undisciplined. Its nobility
is in its force and justice; it is wrong when it is weak, and felt for
paltry cause. There is a mean wonder, as of a child who sees a jug-
gler tossing golden balls, and this is base, if you will. But do you
think that the wonder is ignoble, or the sensation less, with which
every human soul is called to watch the golden balls of heaven tossed
through the night by the Hand that made them? There is a mean
curiosity, as of a child opening a forbidden door, or a servant prying
into her master's business;—and a noble curiosity, questioning, in
the front of danger, the source of the great river beyond the sand,—
the place of the great continents beyond the sea;—a nobler curiosity
still, which questions of the source of the River of Life, and of the
space of the Continent of Heaven,—things which "the angels desire
to look into." So the anxiety is ignoble, with which you linger over
the course and catastrophe of an idle tale; but do you think the
anxiety is less, or greater, with which you watch, or *ought* to watch,
the dealings of fate and destiny with the life of an agonized nation?
Alas! it is the narrowness, selfishness, minuteness, of your sensation
that you have to deplore in England at this day;—sensation which
spends itself in bouquets and speeches; in revelings and junketings;
in sham fights and gay puppet shows, while you can look on and
see noble nations murdered, man by man, without an effort or a tear.

30. I said "minuteness" and "selfishness" of sensation, but in a
word, I ought to have said "injustice" or "unrighteousness" of sensation. For as in nothing is a gentleman better to be discerned from
a vulgar person, so in nothing is a gentle nation (such nations have
been) better to be discerned from a mob, than in this,—that their
feelings are constant and just, results of due contemplation, and of
equal thought. You can talk a mob into anything; its feelings may
be—usually are—on the whole, generous and right; but it has no
foundation for them, no hold of them; you may tease or tickle it
into any, at your pleasure; it thinks by infection, for the most part,
catching an opinion like a cold, and there is nothing so little that it
will not roar itself wild about, when the fit is on;—nothing so great

but it will forget in an hour, when the fit is past. But a gentleman's, or a gentle nation's, passions are just, measured, and continuous. A great nation, for instance, does not spend its entire national wits for a couple of months in weighing evidence of a single ruffian's having done a single murder; and for a couple of years see its own children murder each other by their thousands or tens of thousands a day, considering only what the effect is likely to be on the price of cotton, and caring nowise to determine which side of battle is in the wrong. Neither does a great nation send its poor little boys to jail for stealing six walnuts; and allow its bankrupts to steal their hundreds or thousands with a bow, and its bankers, rich with poor men's savings, to close their doors "under circumstances over which they have no control," with a "by your leave"; and large landed estates to be bought by men who have made their money by going with armed steamers up and down the China Seas, selling opium at the cannon's mouth, and altering, for the benefit of the foreign nation, the common highwayman's demand of "your money *or* your life," into that of "your money *and* your life." Neither does a great nation allow the lives of its innocent poor to be parched out of them by fog fever, and rotted out of them by dunghill plague, for the sake of sixpence a life extra per week to its landlords;[8] and then debate, with driveling tears, and diabolical sympathies, whether it ought not piously to save, and nursingly cherish, the lives of its murderers. Also, a great nation, having made up its mind that hanging is quite the wholesomest process for its homicides in general, can yet with mercy distinguish between the degrees of guilt in homicides; and does not yelp like a pack of frost-pinched wolf-cubs on the blood-track of an unhappy crazed boy, or gray-haired clodpate Othello, "perplexed i' the extreme," at the very moment that it is sending a Minister of the Crown to make polite speeches to a man who is bayoneting young girls in their father's sight, and killing noble youths in cool blood, faster than a country butcher kills lambs in spring. And, lastly, a great nation does not mock Heaven and its Powers, by pretending belief in a revelation which asserts the love of money to be the root of *all* evil, and declaring, at the same time, that it is actuated, and

---

[8] See note at end of lecture. I have put it in large type, because the course of matters since it was written has made it perhaps better worth attention.

intends to be actuated, in all chief national deeds and measures, by no other love.

31. My friends, I do not know why any of us should talk about reading. We want some sharper discipline than that of reading; but, at all events, be assured, we cannot read. No reading is possible for a people with its mind in this state. No sentence of any great writer is intelligible to them. It is simply and sternly impossible for the English public, at this moment, to understand any thoughtful writing,—so incapable of thought has it become in its insanity of avarice. Happily, our disease is, as yet, little worse than this incapacity of thought; it is not corruption of the inner nature; we ring true still, when anything strikes home to us; and though the idea that everything should "pay" has infected our every purpose so deeply, that even when we would play the good Samaritan, we never take out our twopence and give them to the host without saying, "When I come again, thou shalt give me fourpence," there is a capacity of noble passion left in our hearts' core. We show it in our work,—in our war,—even in those unjust domestic affections which make us furious at a small private wrong, while we are polite to a boundless public one: we are still industrious to the last hour of the day, though we add the gambler's fury to the laborer's patience; we are still brave to the death, though incapable of discerning true cause for battle; and are still true in affection to our own flesh, to the death, as the sea-monsters are, and the rock-eagles. And there is hope for a nation while this can be still said of it. As long as it holds its life in its hand, ready to give it for its honor (though a foolish honor), for its love (though a selfish love), and for its business (though a base business), there is hope for it. But hope only; for this instinctive, reckless virtue cannot last. No nation can last, which has made a mob of itself, however generous at heart. It must discipline its passions, and direct them, or they will discipline *it,* one day, with scorpion whips. Above all a nation cannot last as a money-making mob: it cannot with impunity,—it cannot with existence,—go on despising literature, despising science, despising art, despising nature, despising compassion, and concentrating its soul on Pence. Do you think these are harsh or wild words? Have patience with

me but a little longer. I will prove their truth to you, clause by clause.

32. I.—I say first we have despised literature. What do we, as a nation, care about books? How much do you think we spend altogether on our libraries, public or private, as compared with what we spend on our horses? If a man spends lavishly on his library you call him mad—a bibliomaniac. But you never call any one a horsemaniac, though men ruin themselves every day by their horses, and you do not hear of people ruining themselves by their books. Or, to go lower still, how much do you think the contents of the book-shelves of the United Kingdom, public and private, would fetch, as compared with the contents of its wine-cellars? What position would its expenditure on literature take, as compared with its expenditure on luxurious eating? We talk of food for the mind, as of food for the body; now a good book contains such food inexhaustibly; it is a provision for life, and for the best part of us; yet how long most people would look at the best book before they would give the price of a large turbot for it! though there have been men who have pinched their stomachs and bared their backs to buy a book, whose libraries were cheaper to them, I think, in the end, than most men's dinners are. We are few of us put to such trial, and more the pity; for, indeed, a precious thing is all the more precious to us if it has been won by work or economy; and if public libraries were half as costly as public dinners, or books cost the tenth part of what bracelets do, even foolish men and women might sometimes suspect there was good in reading, as well as in munching and sparkling; whereas the very cheapness of literature is making even wise people forget that if a book is worth reading, it is worth buying. No book is worth anything which is not worth *much;* nor is it serviceable, until it has been read, and reread, and loved, and loved again; and marked, so that you can refer to the passages you want in it as a soldier can seize the weapon he needs in an armory, or a housewife bring the spice she needs from her store. Bread of flour is good: but there is bread, sweet as honey, if we would eat it, in a good book; and the family must be poor indeed which, once in their lives, cannot, for such multipliable barley-loaves, pay their baker's bill. We

call ourselves a rich nation, and we are filthy and foolish enough to thumb each other's books out of circulating libraries!

33. II.—I say we have despised science. "What!" you exclaim, "are we not foremost in all discovery,[9] and is not the whole world giddy by reason, or unreason, of our inventions?" Yes; but do you suppose that is national work? That work is all done *in spite of* the nation; by private people's zeal and money. We are glad enough, indeed, to make our profit of science; we snap up anything in the way of a scientific bone that has meat on it, eagerly enough; but if the scientific man comes for a bone or a crust to *us,* that is another story. What have we publicly done for science? We are obliged to know what o'clock it is, for the safety of our ships, and therefore we pay for an observatory; and we allow ourselves, in the person of our Parliament, to be annually tormented into doing something, in a slovenly way, for the British Museum; sullenly apprehending that to be a place for keeping stuffed birds in, to amuse our children. If anybody will pay for his own telescope, and resolve another nebula, we cackle over the discernment as if it were our own; if one in ten thousand of our hunting squires suddenly perceives that the earth was indeed made to be something else than a portion for foxes, and burrows in it himself, and tells us where the gold is, and where the coals, we understand that there is some use in that; and very properly knight him; but is the accident of his having found out how to employ himself usefully any credit to *us?* (The negation of such discovery among his brother squires may perhaps be some *dis*credit to us, if we would consider of it.) But if you doubt these generalities, here is one fact for us all to meditate upon, illustrative of our love of science. Two years ago there was a collection of the fossils of Solenhofen to be sold in Bavaria; the best in existence, containing many specimens unique for perfectness, and one unique as an example of a species (a whole kingdom of unknown living creatures being announced by that fossil). This collection, of which the mere market worth, among private buyers, would probably have been some thousand or twelve hundred pounds, was offered to the English nation for seven hundred; but we would not give seven hundred,

[9] Since this was written, the answer has become definitely—No; we have surrendered the field of Arctic discovery to the Continental nations, as being ourselves too poor to pay for ships.

and the whole series would have been in the Munich Museum at this moment, if Professor Owen[10] had not with loss of his own time, and patient tormenting of the British public in person of its representatives, got leave to give four hundred pounds at once, and himself become answerable for the other three! which the said public will doubtless pay him eventually, but sulkily, and caring nothing about the matter all the while; only always ready to cackle if any credit comes of it. Consider, I beg of you, arithmetically, what this fact means. Your annual expenditure for public purposes (a third of it for military apparatus) is at least fifty millions. Now 700*l.* is to 50,000,000*l.*, roughly, as seven pence to two thousand pounds. Suppose, then, a gentleman of unknown income, but whose wealth was to be conjectured from the fact that he spent two thousand a year on his park-walls and footmen only, professes himself fond of science; and that one of his servants comes eagerly to tell him that an unique collection of fossils, giving clue to a new era of creation, is to be had for the sum of seven pence sterling; and that the gentleman, who is fond of science, and spends two thousand a year on his park, answers, after keeping his servant waiting several months, "Well! I'll give you four pence for them, if you will be answerable for the extra three pence yourself, till next year!"

34. III.—I say you have despised Art! "What!" you again answer, "have we not Art exhibitions, miles long? and do we not pay thousands of pounds for single pictures? and have we not Art schools and institutions, more than ever nation had before?" Yes, truly, but all that is for the sake of the shop. You would fain sell canvas as well as coals, and crockery as well as iron; you would take every other nation's bread out of its mouth if you could;[11] not being able to do that, your ideal of life is to stand in the thoroughfares of the world, like Ludgate apprentices, screaming to every passer-by, "What d'ye lack?" You know nothing of your own faculties or circumstances; you fancy that, among your damp, flat fields of clay, you can have as quick art-fancy as the Frenchman among his bronzed

---

[10] I state this fact without Professor Owen's permission: which of course he could not with propriety have granted, had I asked it; but I consider it so important that the public should be aware of the fact that I do what seems to be right, though rude.

[11] That was our real idea of "Free Trade"—"All the trade to myself." You find now that by "competition" other people can manage to sell something as well as you—and now we call for Protection again. Wretches!

vines, or the Italian under his volcanic cliffs;—that Art may be learned as bookkeeping is, and when learned, will give you more books to keep. You care for pictures, absolutely, no more than you do for the bills pasted on your dead walls. There is always room on the walls for the bills to be read,—never for the pictures to be seen. You do not know what pictures you have (by repute) in the country, nor whether they are false or true, nor whether they are taken care of or not; in foreign countries, you calmly see the noblest existing pictures in the world rotting in abandoned wreck—(in Venice you saw the Austrian guns deliberately pointed at the palaces containing them), and if you heard that all the fine pictures in Europe were made into sand-bags to-morrow on the Austrian forts, it would not trouble you so much as the chance of a brace or two of game less in your own bags, in a day's shooting. That is your national love of Art.

35. IV.—You have despised Nature; that is to say, all the deep and sacred sensations of natural scenery. The French revolutionists made stables of the cathedrals of France; you have made race-courses of the cathedrals of the earth. Your *one* conception of pleasure is to drive in railroad carriages round their aisles, and eat off their altars.[12] You have put a railroad bridge over the fall of Schaffhausen. You have tunneled the cliffs of Lucerne by Tell's chapel; you have destroyed the Clarens shore of the Lake of Geneva; there is not a quiet valley in England that you have not filled with bellowing fire; there is no particle left of English land which you have not trampled coal ashes into[13]—nor any foreign city in which the spread of your presence is not marked among its fair old streets and happy gardens by a consuming white leprosy of new hotels and perfumers' shops: the Alps themselves, which your own poets used to love so reverently, you look upon as soaped poles in a bear-garden, which you set yourselves to climb, and slide down again with "shrieks of delight." When you are past shrieking, having no human articulate voice to

[12] I meant that the beautiful places of the world—Switzerland, Italy, South Germany, and so on—are, indeed, the truest cathedrals—places to be reverent in, and to worship in; and that we only care to drive through them, and to eat and drink at their most sacred places.

[13] I was singularly struck, some years ago, by finding all the river shore at Richmond, in Yorkshire, black in its earth, from the mere drift of soot-laden air from places many miles away.

say you are glad with, you fill the quietude of their valleys with gunpowder blasts, and rush home, red with cutaneous eruption of conceit, and voluble with convulsive hiccough of self-satisfaction. I think nearly the two sorrowfullest spectacles I have ever seen in humanity, taking the deep inner significance of them, are the English mobs in the valley of Chamouni, amusing themselves with firing rusty howitzers; and the Swiss vintagers of Zurich expressing their Christian thanks for the gift of the vine, by assembling in knots in the "towers of the vineyards," and slowly loading and firing horse-pistols from morning till evening. It is pitiful to have dim conceptions of duty; more pitiful, it seems to me, to have conceptions like these, of mirth.

36. Lastly. You despise compassion. There is no need of words of mine for proof of this. I will merely print one of the newspaper paragraphs which I am in the habit of cutting out and throwing into my store-drawer; here is one from a *Daily Telegraph* of an early date this year (1867) (date which, though by me carelessly left unmarked, is easily discoverable; for on the back of the slip, there is the announcement that "yesterday the seventh of the special services of this year was performed by the Bishop of Ripon in St. Paul's"); it relates only one of such facts as happen now daily; this, by chance, having taken a form in which it came before the coroner. . . .

"An inquiry was held on Friday by Mr. Richards, deputy coroner, at the White Horse Tavern, Christ Church, Spitalfields, respecting the death of Michael Collins, aged 58 years. Mary Collins, a miserable-looking woman, said that she lived with the deceased and his son in a room at 2, Cobb's Court, Christ Church. Deceased was a 'translator' of boots. Witness went out and bought old boots; deceased and his son made them into good ones, and then witness sold them for what she could get at the shops, which was very little indeed. Deceased and his son used to work night and day to try and get a little bread and tea, and pay for the room (2s. a week), so as to keep the home together. On Friday night week, deceased got up from his bench and began to shiver. He threw down the boots, saying, 'Somebody else must finish them when I am gone, for I can do no more.' There was no fire, and he said, 'I would be better if I was warm.' Witness therefore took two pairs of translated boots[14] to sell at the shop, but she could only get 14*d*. for the two pairs, for the people at the shop said, 'We must have our profit.' Witness got 14 lbs. of coal and a little tea and bread. Her son sat up the whole night to make the 'translations,' to get money, but deceased died on Saturday morning. The family never had enough to eat.—Coroner: 'It seems to me deplorable that you did not go into the workhouse.' Witness: 'We wanted the comforts of our little home.' A juror asked what the comforts were, for he only saw a little straw in the corner of the room, the windows of which were broken. The witness began to cry, and said that they had a quilt and other little things. The deceased said he never would go into the workhouse. In summer, when the season was good, they sometimes made as much as 10*s*. profit in a week. They then always saved towards the next week, which was generally a bad one. In winter they made not half so much. For three years they had been getting from bad to worse.—Cornelius Collins said that he had assisted his father since 1847. They used to work so far into the night that both nearly lost their eyesight. Witness now had a film over his eyes. Five years ago deceased applied to the parish for aid. The relieving officer gave him a 4-lb. loaf, and told him if he came again he should 'get the stones.' [15]

[14] One of the things which we must very resolutely enforce, for the good of all classes, in our future arrangements, must be that they wear no "translated" articles of dress.

[15] This abbreviation of the penalty of useless labor is curiously coincident in verbal form with a certain passage which some of us may remember. It may, perhaps, be well to preserve beside this paragraph another cutting out of my store-drawer, from the *Morning Post*, of about a parallel date, Friday, March 10th, 1865:— "The *salons* of Mme. C——, who did the honors with clever imitative grace and elegance, were crowded with princes, dukes, marquises, and counts—in fact, with the same *male* company as one meets at the parties of the Princess Metternich and Madame Drouyn de Lhuys. Some English peers and members of Parliament were present, and appeared to enjoy the animated and dazzlingly improper scene. On the second floor the supper-tables were loaded with every delicacy of the season. That your readers may form some idea of the dainty fare of the Parisian demi-monde, I copy the menu of the supper, which was served to all the guests (about 200) seated at four o'clock. Choice Yquem, Johannisberg, Lafitte, Tokay, and champagne of the finest vintages were served most lavishly throughout the morning. After supper dancing was resumed with increased animation, and the ball terminated with a *chaîne diabolique* and a *cancan d'enfer* at seven in the morning. (Morning-service—'Ere the fresh lawns appeared, under the opening eyelids of the Morn.—') Here is the menu:—'Consommé de volaille à la Bagration; 16 hors-d'œuvres variés. Bouchées à la Talleyrand. Saumons froids, sauce Ravigote. Filets de bœuf en Bellevue, timbales milanaises chaudfroid de gibier. Dindes truffées. Pâtés de foies gras, buissons d'écrevisses, salades vénétiennes, gelées blanches aux fruits, gâteaux mancini, parisiens et parisiennes. Fromages glacés. Ananas. Dessert.' "

That disgusted deceased, and he would have nothing to do with them since. They got worse and worse until last Friday week, when they had not even a halfpenny to buy a candle. Deceased then lay down on the straw, and said he could not live till morning.—A juror: 'You are dying of starvation yourself, and you ought to go into the house until the summer.' Witness: 'If we went in we should die. When we come out in the summer we should be like people dropped from the sky. No one would know us, and we would not have even a room. I could work now if I had food, for my sight would get better.' Dr. G. P. Walker said deceased died from syncope, from exhaustion, from want of food. The deceased had had no bedclothes. For four months he had had nothing but bread to eat. There was not a particle of fat in the body. There was no disease, but if there had been medical attendance, he might have survived the syncope or fainting. The coroner having remarked upon the painful nature of the case, the jury returned the following verdict: 'That deceased died from exhaustion, from want of food and the common necessaries of life; also through want of medical aid.' "

37. "Why would witness not go into the workhouse?" you ask. Well, the poor seem to have a prejudice against the workhouse which the rich have not; for, of course, every one who takes a pension from Government goes into the workhouse on a grand scale;[16] only the workhouses for the rich do not involve the idea of work, and should be called play-houses. But the poor like to die independently, it appears; perhaps if we made the play-houses for them pretty and pleasant enough, or gave them their pensions at home, and allowed them a little introductory peculation with the public money, their minds might be reconciled to the conditions. Meantime, here are the facts: we make our relief either so insulting to them, or so painful, that they rather die than take it at our hands; or, for third alternative, we leave them so untaught and foolish that they starve like brute creatures, wild and dumb, not knowing what to do, or what to ask. I say, you despise compassion; if you did not, such a newspaper paragraph would be as impossible in a Christian country as a

---

[16] Please observe this statement, and think of it, and consider how it happens that a poor old woman will be ashamed to take a shilling a week from the country—but no one is ashamed to take a pension of a thousand a year.

deliberate assassination permitted in its public streets.[17] "Christian," did I say? Alas, if we were but wholesomely *un*-Christian, it would be impossible; it is our imaginary Christianity that helps us to commit these crimes, for we revel and luxuriate in our faith, for the lewd sensation of it; dressing *it* up, like everything else, in fiction. The dramatic Christianity of the organ and aisle, of dawn-service and twilight-revival—the Christianity which we do not fear to mix the mockery of, pictorially, with our play about the devil, in our Satanellas,—Roberts,—Fausts; chanting hymns through traceried windows for background effect, and artistically modulating the "Dio" through variation on variation of mimicked prayer (while we distribute tracts, next day, for the benefit of uncultivated swearers, upon what we suppose to be the signification of the Third Commandment);—this gas-lighted, and gas-inspired, Christianity, we are triumphant in, and draw back the hem of our robes from the touch of the heretics who dispute it. But to do a piece of common Christian righteousness in a plain English word or deed; to

[17] I am heartily glad to see such a paper as the *Pall Mall Gazette* established; for the power of the press in the hands of highly educated men, in independent position, and of honest purpose, may, indeed, become all that it has been hitherto vainly vaunted to be. Its editor will, therefore, I doubt not, pardon me, in that, by very reason of my respect for the journal, I do not let pass unnoticed an article in its third number, page 5, which was wrong in every word of it, with the intense wrongness which only an honest man can achieve who has taken a false turn of thought in the outset, and is following it, regardless of consequences. It contained at the end this notable passage:—

"The bread of affliction, and the water of affliction—aye, and the bedsteads and blankets of affliction, are the very utmost that the law ought to give to *outcasts merely as outcasts*." I merely put beside this expression of the gentlemanly mind of England in 1865, a part of the message which Isaiah was ordered to "lift up his voice like a trumpet" in declaring to the gentlemen of his day: "Ye fast for strife, and to smite with the fist of wickedness. Is not this the fast that I have chosen, to deal thy bread to the hungry, and that thou bring the poor *that are cast out* (margin, 'afflicted') to *thy* house?" The falsehood on which the writer had mentally founded himself, as previously stated by him, was this: "To confound the functions of the dispensers of the poor-rates which those of the dispensers of a charitable institution is a great and pernicious error." This sentence is so accurately and exquisitely wrong, that its substance must be thus reversed in our minds before we can deal with any existing problem of national distress. "To understand that the dispensers of the poor-rates are the almoners of the nation, and should distribute its alms with a gentleness and freedom of hand as much greater and franker than that possible to individual charity, as the collective national wisdom and power may be supposed greater than those of any single person, is the foundation of all law respecting pauperism." (Since this was written the *Pall Mall Gazette* has become a mere party paper—like the rest; but it writes well, and does more good than mischief on the whole.)

make Christian law any rule of life, and found one National act or hope thereon,—we know too well what our faith comes to for that! You might sooner get lightning out of incense smoke than true action or passion out of your modern English religion. You had better get rid of the smoke, and the organ-pipes, both; leave them, and the Gothic windows, and the painted glass, to the property-man; give up your carburetted hydrogen ghost in one healthy expiration, and look after Lazarus at the doorstep. For there is a true Church wherever one hand meets another helpfully, and that is the only holy or Mother Church which ever was, or ever shall be.

38. All these pleasures, then, and all these virtues, I repeat, you nationally despise. You have, indeed, men among you who do not; by whose work, by whose strength, by whose life, by whose death, you live, and never thank them. Your wealth, your amusement, your pride, would all be alike impossible, but for those whom you scorn or forget. The policeman, who is walking up and down the black lane all night to watch the guilt you have created there, and may have his brains beaten out, and be maimed for life, at any moment, and never be thanked; the sailor wrestling with the sea's rage; the quiet student poring over his book or his vial; the common worker, without praise, and nearly without bread, fulfilling his task as your horses drag your carts, hopeless, and spurned of all: these are the men by whom England lives; but they are not the nation; they are only the body and nervous force of it, acting still from old habit in a convulsive perseverance, while the mind is gone. Our National wish and purpose are to be amused; our National religion is the performance of church ceremonies, and preaching of soporific truths (or untruths) to keep the mob quietly at work, while we amuse ourselves; and the necessity for this amusement is fastening on us as a feverous disease of parched throat and wandering eyes— senseless, dissolute, merciless. How literally that word *Dis*-Ease, the Negation and impossibility of Ease, expresses the entire moral state of our English Industry and its Amusements!

39. When men are rightly occupied, their amusement grows out of their work, as the color-petals out of a fruitful flower;—when they are faithfully helpful and compassionate, all their emotions become steady, deep, perpetual, and vivifying to the soul as the natural pulse

of the body. But now, having no true business, we pour our whole masculine energy into the false business of money-making; and having no true emotion, we must have false emotions dressed up for us to play with, not innocently, as children with dolls, but guiltily and darkly, as the idolatrous Jews with their pictures on cavern walls, which men had to dig to detect. The justice we do not execute, we mimic in the novel and on the stage; for the beauty we destroy in nature, we substitute the metamorphosis of the pantomime, and (the human nature of us imperatively requiring awe and sorrow of *some* kind) for the noble grief we should have borne with our fellows, and the pure tears we should have wept with them, we gloat over the pathos of the police court, and gather the night-dew of the grave.

40. It is difficult to estimate the true significance of these things; the facts are frightful enough;—the measure of national fault involved in them is, perhaps, not as great as it would at first seem. We permit, or cause, thousands of deaths daily, but we mean no harm; we set fire to houses, and ravage peasants' fields; yet we should be sorry to find we had injured anybody. We are still kind at heart; still capable of virtue, but only as children are. Chalmers, at the end of his long life, having had much power with the public, being plagued in some serious matter by a reference to "public opinion," uttered the impatient exclamation, "The public is just a great baby!" And the reason that I have allowed all these graver subjects of thought to mix themselves up with an inquiry into methods of reading, is that, the more I see of our national faults and miseries, the more they resolve themselves into conditions of childish illiterateness, and want of education in the most ordinary habits of thought. It is, I repeat, not vice, not selfishness, not dullness of brain, which we have to lament; but an unreachable schoolboy's recklessness, only differing from the true schoolboy's in its incapacity of being helped, because it acknowledges no master.

41. There is a curious type of us given in one of the lovely, neglected works of the last of our great painters. It is a drawing of Kirkby Lonsdale churchyard, and of its brook, and valley, and hills, and folded morning sky beyond. And unmindful alike of these, and of the dead who have left these for other valleys and for other skies,

a group of schoolboys have piled their little books upon a grave, to strike them off with stones. So, also, we play with the words of the dead that would teach us, and strike them far from us with our bitter, reckless will; little thinking that those leaves which the wind scatters had been piled, not only upon a gravestone, but upon the seal of an enchanted vault—nay, the gate of a great city of sleeping kings, who would awake for us, and walk with us, if we knew but how to call them by their names. How often, even if we lift the marble entrance gate, do we but wander among those old kings in their repose, and finger the robes they lie in, and stir the crowns on their foreheads; and still they are silent to us, and seem but a dusty imagery; because we know not the incantation of the heart that would wake them;—which, if they once heard, they would start up to meet us in their power of long ago, narrowly to look upon us, and consider us; and, as the fallen kings of Hades meet the newly fallen, saying, "Art thou also become weak as we—art thou also become one of us?" so would these kings, with their undimmed, unshaken diadems, meet us, saying, "Art thou also become pure and mighty of heart as we—art thou also become one of us?"

42. Mighty of heart, mighty of mind—"magnanimous"—to be this, is, indeed, to be great in life; to become this increasingly, is, indeed, to "advance in life,"—in life itself—not in the trappings of it. My friends, do you remember that old Scythian custom, when the head of a house died? How he was dressed in his finest dress, and set in his chariot, and carried about to his friends' houses; and each of them placed him at his table's head, and all feasted in his presence? Suppose it were offered to you, in plain words, as it *is* offered to you in dire facts, that you should gain this Scythian honor, gradually, while you yet thought yourself alive. Suppose the offer were this: You shall die slowly; your blood shall daily grow cold, your flesh petrify, your heart beat at last only as a rusted group of iron valves. Your life shall fade from you, and sink through the earth into the ice of Caina; but, day by day, your body shall be dressed more gaily, and set in higher chariots, and have more orders on its breast—crowns on its head, if you will. Men shall bow before it, stare and shout round it, crowd after it up and down the streets; build palaces for it, feast with it at their tables' heads all the night

long; your soul shall stay enough within it to know what they do, and feel the weight of the golden dress on its shoulders, and the furrow of the crown-edge on the skull;—no more. Would you take the offer, verbally made by the death-angel? Would the meanest among us take it, think you? Yet practically and verily we grasp at it, every one of us, in a measure; many of us grasp at it in its fullness of horror. Every man accepts it, who desires to advance in life without knowing what life is; who means only that he is to get more horses, and more footmen, and more fortune, and more public honor, and—*not* more personal soul. He only is advancing in life, whose heart is getting softer, whose blood warmer, whose brain quicker, whose spirit is entering into Living peace. And the men who have this life in them are the true lords or kings of the earth—they, and they only. All other kingships, so far as they are true, are only the practical issue and expression of theirs; if less than this, they are either dramatic royalties,—costly shows, set off, indeed, with real jewels instead of tinsel,—but still only the toys of nations; or else they are no royalties at all, but tyrannies, or the mere active and practical issue of national folly; for which reason I have said of them elsewhere, "Visible governments are the toys of some nations, the diseases of others, the harness of some, the burdens of more."

43. But I have no words for the wonder with which I hear Kinghood still spoken of, even among thoughtful men, as if governed nations were a personal property, and might be bought and sold, or otherwise acquired, as sheep, of whose flesh their king was to feed, and whose fleece he was to gather; as if Achilles' indignant epithet of base kings, "people-eating," were the constant and proper title of all monarchs; and enlargement of a king's dominion meant the same thing as the increase of a private man's estate! Kings who think so, however powerful, can no more be the true kings of the nation than gadflies are the kings of a horse; they suck it, and may drive it wild, but do not guide it. They, and their courts, and their armies are, if one could see clearly, only a large species of marsh mosquito, with bayonet proboscis and melodious, band-mastered trumpeting in the summer air; the twilight being, perhaps, sometimes fairer, but hardly more wholesome, for its glittering mists of midge companies. The true kings, meanwhile, rule quietly, if at

all, and hate ruling; too many of them make "il gran rifiúto";[18] and
if they do not, the mob, as soon as they are likely to become useful
to it, is pretty sure to make *its* "gran rifiúto" of *them*.

44. Yet the visible king may also be a true one, some day, if ever
day comes when he will estimate his dominion by the *force* of it,—
not the geographical boundaries. It matters very little whether Trent
cuts you a cantel out here, or Rhine rounds you a castle less there.
But it does matter to you, king of men, whether you can verily say
to this man, "Go," and he goeth; and to another, "Come," and he
cometh. Whether you can turn your people, as you can Trent—and
where it is that you bid them come, and where go. It matters to
you, king of men, whether your people hate you, and die by you, or
love you, and live by you. You may measure your dominion by
multitudes better than by miles; and count degrees of love latitude,
not from, but to, a wonderfully warm and indefinite equator.

45. Measure! nay, you cannot measure. Who shall measure the
difference between the power of those who "do and teach," and who
are greatest in the kingdoms of earth, as of heaven—and the power
of those who undo, and consume—whose power, at the fullest, is
only the power of the moth and the rust? Strange! to think how
the Moth-kings lay up treasures for the moth; and the Rust-kings,
who are to their peoples' strength as rust to armor, lay up treasures
for the rust; and the Robber-kings, treasures for the robber; but how
few kings have ever laid up treasures that needed no guarding—
treasures of which, the more thieves there were, the better! Broidered
robe, only to be rent; helm and sword, only to be dimmed; jewel and
gold, only to be scattered;—there have been three kinds of kings who
have gathered these. Suppose there ever should arise a Fourth order
of kings, who had read, in some obscure writing of long ago, that
there was a Fourth kind of treasure, which the jewel and gold could
not equal, neither should it be valued with pure gold. A web made
fair in the weaving, by Athena's shuttle; an armor, forged in divine
fire by Vulcanian force—a gold to be mined in the sun's red heart,
where he sets over the Delphian cliffs;—deep-pictured tissue,
impenetrable armor, potable gold!—the three great Angels of Conduct, Toil, and Thought, still calling to us, and waiting at the posts

[18] The great renunciation.

of our doors, to lead us, with their winged power, and guide us, with their unerring eyes, by the path which no fowl knoweth, and which the vulture's eye has not seen! Suppose kings should ever arise, who heard and believed this word, and at last gathered and brought forth treasures of—Wisdom—for their people?

46. Think what an amazing business *that* would be! How inconceivable, in the state of our present national wisdom! That we should bring up our peasants to a book exercise instead of a bayonet exercise!—organize, drill, maintain with pay, and good generalship, armies of thinkers, instead of armies of stabbers!—find national amusement in reading-rooms as well as rifle-grounds; give prizes for a fair shot at a fact, as well as for a leaden splash on a target. What an absurd idea it seems, put fairly in words, that the wealth of the capitalists of civilized nations should ever come to support literature instead of war!

47. Have yet patience with me, while I read you a single sentence out of the only book, properly to be called a book, that I have yet written myself, the one that will stand (if anything stand) surest and longest of all work of mine.

"It is one very awful form of the operation of wealth in Europe that it is entirely capitalists' wealth that supports unjust wars. Just wars do not need so much money to support them; for most of the men who wage such, wage them gratis; but for an unjust war, men's bodies and souls have both to be bought; and the best tools of war for them besides, which make such war costly to the maximum; not to speak of the cost of base fear, and angry suspicion, between nations which have not grace nor honesty enough in all their multitudes to buy an hour's peace of mind with; as, at present, France and England, purchasing of each other ten millions' sterling worth of consternation, annually (a remarkably light crop, half thorns and half aspen leaves, sown, reaped, and granaried by the 'science' of the modern political economist, teaching covetousness instead of truth). And, all unjust war being supportable, if not by pillage of the enemy, only by loans from capitalists, these loans are repaid by subsequent taxation of the people, who appear to have no will in the matter, the capitalists' will being the primary root of the war; but its real root is the covetousness of the whole nation, rendering it incapable of faith, frankness, or justice, and bringing about, therefore, in due time, his own separate loss and punishment to each person."

48. France and England literally, observe, buy *panic* of each other; they pay, each of them, for ten thousand thousand pounds' worth of terror, a year. Now suppose, instead of buying these ten millions' worth of panic annually, they made up their minds to be at peace with each other, and buy ten millions' worth of knowledge annually; and that each nation spent its ten thousand thousand pounds a year in founding royal libraries, royal art galleries, royal museums, royal gardens, and places of rest. Might it not be better somewhat for both French and English?

49. It will be long, yet, before that comes to pass. Nevertheless, I hope it will not be long before royal or national libraries will be founded in every considerable city, with a royal series of books in them; the same series in every one of them, chosen books, the best in every kind, prepared for that national series in the most perfect way possible; their text printed all on leaves of equal size, broad of margin, and divided into pleasant volumes, light in the hand, beautiful, and strong, and thorough as examples of binders' work; and that these great libraries will be accessible to all clean and orderly persons at all times of the day and evening; strict law being enforced for this cleanliness and quietness.

50. I could shape for you other plans for art galleries, and for natural history galleries, and for many precious—many, it seems to me, needful—things; but this book plan is the easiest and needfullest, and would prove a considerable tonic to what we call our British constitution, which has fallen dropsical of late, and has an evil thirst, and evil hunger, and wants healthier feeding. You have got its corn laws repealed for it; try if you cannot get corn laws established for it dealing in a better bread;—bread made of that old enchanted Arabian grain, the Sesame, which opens doors;—doors not of robbers', but of Kings' Treasuries.

NOTE TO §30

Respecting the increase of rent by the deaths of the poor, for evidence of which see the preface to the Medical officers' report to the Privy Council, just published, there are suggestions in its preface which will make some stir among us, I fancy, respecting which let me note these points following:—

There are two theories on the subject of land now abroad, and in contention; both false.

The first is that, by Heavenly law, there have always existed, and must continue to exist, a certain number of hereditarily sacred persons to whom the earth, air, and water of the world belong, as personal property; of which earth, air, and water, these persons may, at their pleasure, permit, or forbid, the rest of the human race to eat, breathe, or to drink. This theory is not for many years longer tenable. The adverse theory is that a division of the land of the world among the mob of the world would immediately elevate the said mob into sacred personages; that houses would then build themselves, and corn grow of itself; and that everybody would be able to live, without doing any work for his living. This theory would also be found highly untenable in practice.

It will, however, require some rough experiments, and rougher catastrophes, before the generality of persons will be convinced that no law concerning anything—least of all concerning land, for either holding or dividing it, or renting it high, or renting it low—would be of the smallest ultimate use to the people, so long as the general contest for life, and for the means of life, remains one of mere brutal competition. That contest, in an unprincipled nation, will take one deadly form or another, whatever laws you make against it. For instance, it would be an entirely wholesome law for England, if it could be carried, that maximum limits should be assigned to incomes according to classes; and that every nobleman's income should be paid to him as a fixed salary or pension by the nation; and not squeezed by him in variable sums, at discretion, out of the tenants of his land. But if you could get such a law passed to-morrow, and if, which would be farther necessary, you could fix the value of the assigned incomes by making a given weight of pure bread for a given sum, a twelvemonth would not pass before another currency would have been tacitly established, and the power of accumulative wealth would have reasserted itself in some other article, or some other imaginary sign. There is only one cure for public distress—and that is public education, directed to make men thoughtful, merciful, and just. There are, indeed, many laws conceivable which would gradually better and strengthen the national temper; but, for the most part, they are such as the national temper must be much bettered before it would bear. A nation in its youth may be helped by laws, as a weak child by backboards, but when it is old it cannot that way straighten its crooked spine.

And besides, the problem of land, at its worst, is a bye one; distribute the earth as you will, the principal question remains inexorable,—Who is to dig it? Which of us, in brief words, is to do the hard and dirty work for the rest—and for what pay? Who is to do the pleasant and clean work, and for what pay? Who is to do no work, and for what pay? And there are curious moral and religious questions connected with these. How far is it lawful to suck a portion of the soul out of a great many persons, in order to put the abstracted psychical quantities together and make one very beautiful or ideal soul? If we had to deal with mere blood, instead of spirit (and the thing might literally be done—as it has been done with infants before now)—so that it were possible by taking a certain quantity of blood from the arms of a given number of the mob, and putting it all into one person, to make a more azure-blooded gentleman of him, the thing would of course be managed; but secretly, I should conceive. But now, because it is brain and soul that we abstract, not visible blood, it can be done quite openly, and we live, we gentlemen, on delicatest prey, after the manner of weasels; that is to say, we keep a certain number of clowns digging and ditching, and generally stupefied, in order that we, being fed gratis, may have all the thinking and feeling to ourselves. Yet there is a great deal to be said for this. A highly-bred and trained English, French, Austrian, or Italian gentleman (much more a lady) is a great production,—a better production than most statues; being beautifully colored as well as shaped, and plus all the brains; a glorious thing to look at, a wonderful thing to talk to; and you cannot have it, any more than a pyramid or a church, but by sacrifice of much contributed life. And it is, perhaps, better to build a beautiful human creature than a beautiful dome or steeple—and more delightful to look up reverently to a creature far above us, than to a wall; only the beautiful human creature will have some duties to do in return—duties of living belfry and rampart—of which presently.